CALL Design: Principles and Practice

Proceedings of the 2014 EUROCALL Conference, Groningen, The Netherlands

Edited by Sake Jager, Linda Bradley, Estelle J. Meima, and Sylvie Thouësny

Published by Research-publishing.net, not-for-profit association
Dublin, Ireland; Voillans, France, info@research-publishing.net

© 2014 by Research-publishing.net
Each author retains their own copyright

CALL Design: Principles and Practice
Proceedings of the 2014 EUROCALL Conference, Groningen, The Netherlands
Edited by Sake Jager, Linda Bradley, Estelle J. Meima, and Sylvie Thouësny

Rights: All articles in this collection are published under the Attribution-NonCommercial -NoDerivatives 4.0 International (CC BY-NC-ND 4.0) licence. Under this licence, the contents are freely available online (as PDF files) for anybody to read, download, copy, and redistribute provided that the author(s), editorial team, and publisher are properly cited. Commercial use and derivative works are, however, not permitted.

Disclaimer: Research-publishing.net does not take any responsibility for the content of the pages written by the authors of this book. The authors have recognised that the work described was not published before, or that it is not under consideration for publication elsewhere. While the information in this book are believed to be true and accurate on the date of its going to press, neither the editorial team, nor the publisher can accept any legal responsibility for any errors or omissions that may be made. The publisher makes no warranty, expressed or implied, with respect to the material contained herein. While Research-publishing.net is committed to publishing works of integrity, the words are the authors' alone.

Trademark notice: product or corporate names may be trademarks or registered trademarks, and are used only for identification and explanation without intent to infringe.

Copyrighted material: every effort has been made by the editorial team to trace copyright holders and to obtain their permission for the use of copyrighted material in this book. In the event of errors or omissions, please notify the publisher of any corrections that will need to be incorporated in future editions of this book.

Typeset by Research-publishing.net
Cover design: © Raphaël Savina (raphael@savina.net)
Fonts used are licensed under a SIL Open Font License

ISBN13: 978-1-908416-19-3 (Paperback - Print on demand, black and white)
Print on demand technology is a high-quality, innovative and ecological printing method; with which the book is never 'out of stock' or 'out of print'.

ISBN13: 978-1-908416-20-9 (Ebook, PDF, colour)
ISBN13: 978-1-908416-21-6 (Ebook, EPUB, colour)

Legal deposit, Ireland: The National Library of Ireland, The Library of Trinity College, The Library of the University of Limerick, The Library of Dublin City University, The Library of NUI Cork, The Library of NUI Maynooth, The Library of University College Dublin, The Library of NUI Galway.

Legal deposit, United Kingdom: The British Library.
British Library Cataloguing-in-Publication Data.
A cataloguing record for this book is available from the British Library.

Legal deposit, France: Bibliothèque Nationale de France - Dépôt légal: décembre 2014.

Table of Contents

x	Foreword
xii	Conference Committees
1	Wiki-based collaborative writing activities in EFL classrooms: Exploring teachers' intervention in the collaborative process *Maha Alghasab*
6	Diagnostic CALL tool for Arabic learners *Majed Alsabaan and Allan Ramsay*
12	SpeakApps 2: Speaking practice in a foreign language through ICT tools *Christine Appel, Mairéad Nic Giolla Mhichíl, Sake Jager, and Adriana Prizel-Kania*
18	The use of a wiki at a college in Hungary as a tool to enhance personal learning *Réka Asztalos*
23	Is ICT really essential for learning? Perceptions and uses of ICTs for language acquisition in secondary level environments *Silvia Benini*
29	The effects and functions of speaker status in CALL-oriented communities *Judith Buendgens-Kosten*
35	SNS for learners at beginner level: An alternative use of FB *Tiziana Carpi*
40	Preliminary conclusions after the design and implementation of mobile learning apps for professionals *María Dolores Castrillo, Elena Bárcena, and Antonio Pareja-Lora*
47	A case study on English language learners' task-based interaction and avatar identities in Second Life: A mixed-methods design *Julian ChengChiang Chen*
52	Fostering collaboration in CALL: Benefits and challenges of using virtual language resource centres *Liliana Cuesta Medina and Claudia Patricia Alvarez*

59	Tableaux vivants as vehicles for cultural exchange *Joseph V. Dias*
65	Designing a task based curriculum for intensive language training *Joost Elshoff*
72	Integrating CALL in ESOL classrooms: Understanding teachers' perspectives and meeting students' needs *Sara Farshad Nia and Ronnie Davey*
77	Digital literacy and netiquette: Awareness and perception in EFL learning context *Sara Farshad Nia and Susan Marandi*
83	A context-aware solution in mobile language learning *Majid Fatahipour and Mahnaz Ghaseminajm*
88	Investigating an open methodology for designing domain-specific language collections *Alannah Fitzgerald, Shaoqun Wu, and Martin Barge*
96	Effects of online translation on morphosyntactic and lexical-pragmatic accuracy in essay writing in Spanish as a foreign language *Kent Fredholm*
102	Encouraging self-directed group learning through an e-portfolio system *Eri Fukuda, Mitsuko Suzuki, Shinichi Hashimoto, and Hironobu Okazaki*
107	Supporting content and language integrated learning through technology *Ana Gimeno-Sanz, Caoimhín Ó Dónaill, and Kent Andersen*
113	Learning strategies and motivation among procrastinators of various English proficiency levels *Yoshiko Goda, Masanori Yamada, Takeshi Matsuda, Hiroshi Kato, Yutaka Saito, and Hiroyuki Miyagawa*
119	Evaluation of a web conferencing tool and collaborative tasks in an online Chinese course *Sijia Guo*

127	A follow-up study of the Facebook project for Japanese university students: Has it been enhancing student interaction, learner autonomy, and English learning? *Mayumi Hamada*
134	Linking CALL and SLA: Using the IRIS database to locate research instruments *Zöe Handley and Emma Marsden*
140	Underspecification-based grammatical feedback generation tailored to the learner's current acquisition level in an e-learning system for German as second language *Karin Harbusch, Christel-Joy Cameran, and Johannes Härtel*
146	Task design for intercultural telecollaboration in secondary schools: Insights from the EU project TILA *Petra Hoffstaedter and Kurt Kohn*
151	Challenges and opportunities for business communication: A Facebook approach conundrum *Chung-Kai Huang, Chun-Yu Lin, and Daniel Steve Villarreal*
158	Contextual language learning: Educational potential and use of social networking technology in higher education *Chung-Kai Huang, Chun-Yu Lin, and Daniel Steve Villarreal*
165	EFL learners' perceived use of conversation maintenance strategies during synchronous computer-mediated communication with native English speakers *Atsushi Ino*
172	Medical students' perceptions of using mobile phones for their English study *Jun Iwata, Yuko Tamaki, Wang Shudong, John Telloyan, Yuri Ajiki, and John Clayton*
179	An intelligent tutoring system for learning Chinese with a cognitive model of the learner *Michał Kosek and Pierre Lison*
185	Language learning 2.0 – international collaboration made easy *Tuula-Harriet Kotikoski and Natasha Doshi*

191   Guiding learners to near native fluency in English through an adaptive programme of activities which includes phoneme and prosody analysis
Alistair Lawson, Ann Attridge, and Paul Lapok

196   Corpus-based learning of Cantonese for Mandarin speakers
John Lee and Tak-Sum Wong

202   Collaborative enquiry through the tabletop for second/foreign language learners
Mei Lin, Anne Preston, Ahmed Kharrufa, and Zhuoran Kong

209   PETALL: A European project on technology-mediated TBLT
António Lopes

214   Effects of summary writing on oral proficiency performance within a computer-based test for integrated listening-speaking tasks
Zhihong Lu and Yanfei Wang

220   Telecollaborative desktop-videoconferencing exchange: The case of Mark
Véronique Martin

225   Seamless integration of desktop and mobile learning experience through an ontology-based adaptation engine: Report of a pilot-project
Marco Mercurio, Ilaria Torre, and Simone Torsani

230   Partial and synchronized captioning: A new tool for second language listening development
Maryam Sadat Mirzaei, Yuya Akita, and Tatsuya Kawahara

237   Modelling typical online language learning activity
Carlos Montoro, Regine Hampel, and Ursula Stickler

241   The Euroversity Good Practice Framework (EGPF) and its application to minority languages and elder learners
Gary Motteram, Ton Koenraad, Hanna Outakoski, Kristi Jauregi, Judith Molka-Danielsen, and Christel Schneider

248   Authentic oral language production and interaction in CALL: An evolving conceptual framework for the use of learning analytics within the SpeakApps project
Mairéad Nic Giolla Mhichíl, Jeroen van Engen, Colm Ó Ciardúbháin, Gearóid Ó Cléircín, and Christine Appel

255	Language learning in virtual worlds: Designing for languaging, the role of affordances *Susanna Nocchi*
261	Creating tasks in a less-commonly taught language for an open educational resource: Why the CEFR is important for Irish *Colm Ó Ciardúbháin and Mairéad Nic Giolla Mhichíl*
267	Impact of a blended environment with m-learning on EFL skills *Hiroyuki Obari and Stephen Lambacher*
273	The LMS development for a blended EFL e-learning *Takeshi Okada, Yasunobu Sakamoto, and Kensuke Sugiura*
278	Development of an automatic judging system for determining the difficulty levels of English audio materials *Hironobu Okazaki, Kanji Watanabe, Shinichi Hashimoto, Mitsuko Suzuki, Eri Fukuda, and Kazuhiko Kido*
284	Patterns and effectiveness of mobile device usage by Japanese undergraduates for L2 acquisition purposes *James W. Pagel and Stephen G. Lambacher*
290	L2 immersion in 3D Virtual Worlds: The next thing to being there? *Edith Paillat*
296	ICT in EFL: The global effect of new technologies in the language classroom *Salomi Papadima-Sophocleous, Christina Nicole Giannikas, and Elis Kakoulli-Constantinou*
301	Are we there yet? Normalising CALL in the context of primary languages in England *Monika Pazio*
307	Peer assessment in the classroom using mobile devices *William Pellowe, Trevor Holster, and J. Lake*
312	Innovative training of oral communication: Berlin Kompass *Laura Pihkala-Posti*

- 318   Getting off the straight and narrow: Exploiting non-linear, interactive narrative structures in digital stories for language teaching
  Andrew Prosser

- 324   The *7 Keys of the Dragon*: An e-learning game-like environment for Albanian and Russian
  Anthi Revithiadou, Vasilia Kourtis-Kazoullis, Maria Soukalopoulou, Konstantinos Konstantoudakis, Christos Zarras, and Nestoras Pelesoglou

- 329   Mobile purposive-extensive-podcast-listening versus mobile self-regulated-podcast-development: A critical framework for designing foreign language listening
  Serkan Şendağ, Mustafa Caner, and Hüseyin Kafes

- 334   Learning by doing: A city trip combining TBLLT, blended learning and social media
  Leen Stevens and Viviane Grisez

- 340   Student engagement in learning vocabulary with CALL
  Robert Stroud

- 345   A quantitative and qualitative evaluation of student participants' contribution to carrying out an online international collaborative project on education
  Chizuko Suzuki, Kenichi Ishida, Shota Yoshihara, Klaudia Schultheis, and Barbara Riedhammer

- 352   Bring your own device to language class – applying handheld devices in classroom learning
  Tord Talmo, Even Einum, and Robin Støckert

- 358   Online Estonian language learning
  Maarika Teral and Sirje Rammo

- 363   Discovering English with the Sketch Engine
  James Thomas

- 368   Applying dynamic assessment principles to online peer revisions in written English for specific purposes
  Sylvie Thouësny and Linda Bradley

374	Mobile voting tools for creating collaboration environment and a new educational design of the university lecture *Svetlana Titova*
379	Investigating EFL teachers' technological pedagogical content knowledge: Students' perceptions *Jun-Jie Tseng*
385	Using iPads to help teens design their own activities *Joshua Underwood*
391	MALL in the wild: Learners' designs for scaffolding vocabulary learning trajectories *Joshua Underwood, Rosemary Luckin, and Niall Winters*
398	Social networking: Developing intercultural competence and fostering autonomous learning *Ruby Vurdien*
403	Context-aware writing support for SNS: Connecting formal and informal learning *Ikumi Waragai, Shuichi Kurabayashi, Tatsuya Ohta, Marco Raindl, Yasushi Kiyoki, and Hideyuki Tokuda*
408	'Sizing up' the online course: Adapting learning designs to meet growing participant numbers *Julie Watson*
413	Instructional interaction development and its effects in online foreign language learning *Rong Zhao*
422	Author Index

Foreword

The annual conference of the European Association for Computer-Assisted Language Learning (EUROCALL) was held from the 20th to the 23rd of August 2014 at the University of Groningen, the Netherlands. In 2014, this second oldest university of the Netherlands celebrated its 400th anniversary, using the motto "For Infinity – 4∞" to underline its ambitions to work for and on the future of education, research and society in the Netherlands and beyond. The EUROCALL2014 conference was a good occasion for sharing these ambitions with colleagues from all over the world.

The theme of EUROCALL2014 was "CALL Design: Principles and Practice", which attracted approximately 280 practitioners, researchers and students from CALL and related disciplines of more than 40 different nationalities. Over 170 presentations were delivered on topics related to this overarching theme. The topics included:

- Applying principles from SLA and TBLT in CALL
- Applying specific instructional models in CALL
- Preparing and delivering open educational resources, open courseware and open online courses for language learning
- Designing for open and independent online language learning
- Using competence or outcome-based frameworks (CEFR, IATFL, etc.) in CALL design
- Designing, applying and evaluating computer-based language tests
- Applying corpus-based designs and technologies
- Learning analytics and CALL design
- Synchronous and asynchronous CMC
- Gaming and virtual worlds
- Mobile apps for CALL
- Telecollaboration and Online Intercultural Exchanges
- Using NLP and AI-based designs and technologies
- Using specific design tools for CALL
- CALL for specific contexts and purposes (institutional setting, independent use)
- CALL for specific skills
- Successful CALL project designs
- Developing strategies for teacher education and professional development

The conference programme consisted of workshops, symposia, and presentations and poster sessions on research, research and development, reflective practice and European projects relating to these areas. Besides colleagues working in CALL, several specialists and practitioners from outside the field of CALL –many of them first-time visitors to EUROCALL– contributed to the programme. These contributions helped to broaden the scope of CALL and it is hoped that the interdisciplinary content and contacts will suggest new ways forward for our field in the coming years.

The keynote presentations also shed light from different perspectives on developments in CALL. In an inspiring Graham Davies keynote address, Carol Chapelle (Iowa State University) presented five lines of argument for evaluating the use of technology in language learning and teaching. Bart Rienties (The Open University UK), in an entertaining keynote drawing on recent Dutch success (or failure) in the FIFA World Cup, discussed critical aspects of bringing learning analytics to the arena of formal education. And finally, in a very instructive session, John H.A.L. de Jong (VU University Amsterdam/Pearson Education) took the audience to the world of computer-based testing and recent advances in automatic scoring of student essays.

Recordings of these keynote addresses, as well as the full programme and session abstracts may be found at the conference website http://www.eurocall2014.nl, which will be kept online for the next few years.

We are also very pleased to include a total of 71 extended versions of papers presented at the conference in these proceedings. These were submitted by the authors just before the conference and edited and revised in the months following the conference. The papers are representative of the great variety of subjects presented at EUROCALL2014. In the conference evaluation survey, delegates indicated that they were very satisfied with the overall quality of the academic programme, and we hope readers will find this quality reflected in these proceedings.

There is one colleague whose contributions at EUROCALL conferences will be sadly missed. Our dear colleague, Dr Kenji Kitao, a full professor at Doshisha University, Kyoto, Japan, passed away suddenly while attending EUROCALL2014. Kenji Kitao and his wife Kathleen Kitao were going to present two papers together at EUROCALL2014. Kenji Kitao will always be remembered for his remarkable personality and his dedicated membership of EUROCALL. We wish Kathleen, her family and friends great strength in bearing this sad loss.

Sake Jager, Estelle Meima, and Marjolijn Verspoor
Local organising team of EUROCALL2014

Conference Committees

The 2014 EUROCALL Conference on *CALL Design: Principles and Practice* was organised by the University of Groningen, the Netherlands.

Programme Committee

Programme chairs
- Peppi Taalas (chair), *University of Jyvaskylä, Finland*
- John Gillespie (co-chair), *University of Ulster, United Kingdom*

Committee members
- David Barr, *University of Ulster, UK*
- Becky Bergman, *Chalmers University of Technology, Sweden*
- Alex Boulton, *Université 2, Nancy, France*
- Angela Chambers, *University of Limerick, Ireland*
- Thierry Chanier, *Université Blaise Pascal, France*
- Jozef Colpaert, *University of Antwerp, Belgium*
- Muriel Grosbois, *Université de Paris 4, France*
- Nicolas Guichon, *Université de Lyon 2, France*
- Regine Hampel, *The Open University, UK*
- Mirjam Hauck, *The Open University, UK*
- Trude Heift, *Simon Fraser University, Canada*
- Francesca Helm, *Università degli studi di Padova, Italy*
- Phil Hubbard, *Stanford University, USA*
- Juha Jalkanen, *University of Jyväskylä, Finland*
- Leena Kuure, *University of Oulu, Finland*
- Dominique Macaire, *Université de Lorraine, France*
- Liam Murray, *University of Limerick, Ireland*
- John Nerbonne, *University of Groningen, the Netherlands*
- Robert O'Dowd, *Universidad de León, Spain*
- Sue K. Otto, *University of Iowa, USA*
- Vera Paiva, *UFMG, Brazil*
- Salomi Papadima-Sophocleous, *Cyprus University of Technology, Cyprus*
- Hans Paulussen, *University of Leuven, Belgium*
- Pascual Pérez-Paredes, *Universidad de Murcia, Spain*
- Mathias Schulze, *University of Waterloo, Canada*
- Lesley Shield, *Freelance CALL Consultant, UK*
- Claire Siskin, *Regional Institute of English, Chandigarh, India*

- Oranna Speicher, *University of Nottingham, UK*
- Glenn Stockwell, *Waseda University, Japan*
- Maija Tammelin, *Independent Consultant, Finland*
- June Thompson, *ReCALL, United Kingdom*
- Sylvie Thouësny, *Research-publishing.net, Ireland*
- Cornelia Tschichold, *Swansea University, UK*
- Sylvi Vigmo, *University of Gothenburg, Sweden*
- Sabine Ylönen, *University of Jyväskylä, Finland*

Local Organising Committee

- Sake Jager (Chair), Head/Project manager ICT in Education, Lecturer in Applied Linguistics
- Estelle Meima, Lecturer in English, Coordinator Language Centre Testing Unit
- Mariska Pater, Director Groningen Congres Bureau
- Marjolijn Verspoor, Associate Professor in Applied Linguistics

EUROCALL Executive Committee 2013/2014

President and vice-president
- Françoise Blin, Presisent, *Dublin City University, Ireland*
- Peppi Taalas, Vice-President, *University of Jyväskylä, Finland*

Members, elected and co-opted officers
- Kent Andersen, *Syddansk Erhvervsskole, Denmark*
- Alex Boulton, *University of Lorraine, France*
- Mirjam Hauck, *Open University, UK*
- Francesca Helm, *University of Padova, Italy*
- Sake Jager, *University of Groningen, the Netherlands*
- Maria João Marçalo, *University of Évora, Portugal*
- Oranna Speicher, *University of Nottingham, UK*
- Sake Jager, *University of Groningen, the Netherlands*

Appointed officers
- John Gillespie, Treasurer, *University of Ulster, Coleraine, Northern Ireland*
- Toni Patton, Secretary, *University of Ulster, Coleraine, Northern Ireland*

university of groningen

Wiki-based collaborative writing activities in EFL classrooms: Exploring teachers' intervention in the collaborative process

Maha Alghasab[1]

Abstract. This pilot study was designed to explore EFL teachers' and students' online interaction during wiki based collaborative writing activities. It aims to explore the collaborative behaviours that students engaged in and to what extent the teachers' intervention can promote students' collaboration. The study has a multiple qualitative case study design. Two EFL teachers and 18 of their secondary school students (aged 17-18 years) from a summer camp in Kuwait participated in a five-week-study. Data was collected from multiple resources, such as the wiki discussion page and history logs, and then triangulated with the teachers' and students' interviews. Variations were observed between the two teachers in terms of how they intervened in the students' online interactions at the organisational, socio-cognitive and socio-affective levels. At the wider levels, it appeared that the traditional classroom teaching and learning practices shaped the way in which the teachers interacted in the wiki. These practices seemed to influence the way in which the students collaborated together via the threaded mode and text mode. Some teachers' practices seemed to promote students' collaboration while others hindered it in various ways. It can be concluded that the mere presence of teachers can promote students' participation but does not necessarily assist collaboration.

Keywords: wikis, collaborative writing, computer mediated collaborative language learning, teacher role.

---

1. University of York, UK; ma716@york.ac.uk.

How to cite this article: Alghasab, M. (2014). Wiki-based collaborative writing activities in EFL classrooms: Exploring teachers' intervention in the collaborative process. In S. Jager, L. Bradley, E. J. Meima, & S. Thouësny (Eds), *CALL Design: Principles and Practice*; Proceedings of the 2014 EUROCALL Conference, Groningen, The Netherlands (pp. 1-5). Dublin: Research-publishing.net. doi:10.14705/rpnet.2014.000185

1. Introduction

In a language learning context, collaborative writing is defined as "the joint production or the co-authoring of a text by two or more writers" (Storch, 2011, p. 275). For interaction to be called collaboration, it should involve a high degree of equality and mutuality in which dialogue is used to construct knowledge (Tan, Wigglesworth, & Storch, 2010). That is, students need to be equal contributors to the task and mutually discuss their ideas in order to construct knowledge.

Wikis are examples of second-generation web tools that facilitate collaborative writing activities. CALL researchers who are interested in the application of wikis have reported on the tool's potential benefits for developing writing and revision skills (Mak & Coniam, 2008) and generating collaborative behaviours in the process of constructing a text (Li & Zhu, 2011; Lund, 2008). However, further investigation into the effectiveness of the use of wikis in a language learning context is required to address the following gaps. First, the majority of studies have focused on adult language students at university levels, with only a limited amount of research being conducted in the school contexts (Lund, 2008; Mak & Coniam, 2008). Second, as far as the collaborative writing process is concerned, the majority of studies have examined student-student interaction, marginalising the role of teachers' participation in regulating students' collaboration. The effectiveness of the teachers' roles in regulating students' collaboration has been reported in Face-to-Face (FTF) and other online contexts (Mangenot & Nissen, 2006; Yoon & Kim, 2012). Third, to date, the majority of research has limited their analysis to either the wiki forum (threaded mode) or the wiki page (text mode). That is, researchers interested in analysing collaboration in the wiki have tended to analyse the discussions that occur between students without considering alterations to the text as additional indicators of collaboration. Therefore, this exploratory study aims to fill these gaps by addressing the following research questions:

- How do EFL teachers and students interact in online wiki based collaborative writing activities?
- What collaborative behaviours do students engage in while constructing their wiki text?
- How can teachers intervene in students' online wiki collaborative writing activities?

2. Method

A convenience sample, comprising of two 12-grade secondary school teachers and 18 of their Kuwaiti EFL students, studying at a summer camp in Kuwait, was used in this study. The study duration was five weeks. Teachers and students in both classes were trained to use the wiki in a computer laboratory during the first week. They were then asked to engage in out-of-class wiki collaborative writing activities, and more specifically to design a poster about Kuwait. The collaborative writing activity was adapted from the students' textbook. The teachers were asked to engage with the students during this activity. Each class has its own private PB wiki space. Data was collected primarily from the wiki platform (i.e. discussion and history pages), and triangulated with two teachers' stimulated recall interviews and semi-structured interviews with the students.

To analyse the collaborative process and teachers' intervention, several frameworks were employed for the threaded mode and text mode. Mangenot and Nissen's (2006), Nguyen's (2011), and Curtis and Lawson's (2001) frameworks were used to analyse the online discussion. The frameworks classify collaboration and teachers' intervention into three categories: interaction at the organisational, socio-cognitive and socio-affective levels. To understand the interaction, principles of Computer Mediated Discourse Analysis (CMDA) (Herring, 2004) were considered for the online discussion. Furthermore, based on the timestamps of the discussion posts, the teachers' and students' writing behaviour were also considered from the page history. Where appropriate, the editing behaviour was matched with the discussion that took place. To classify editing behaviour, an adapted framework from Mak and Coniam's (2008) study was used.

3. Results and discussion

In both classes, the students appeared to be engaging in different collaborative behaviour at three collaborative levels and the teachers were intervening in the students' interactions at the three levels in different ways. The broader traditional FTF classroom practices seem to influence the way in which the teachers and students interacted in the wiki. The degree of students' participation was reasonable; however, the students directed most of their questions to the teachers. Furthermore, on occasion, the teachers themselves adopted a more authoritative role by posting instructions for the students and editing their texts rather than promoting collaborative behaviour among the students.

At the organisational level, teacher A had structured the activity from the outset and adopted a more directorial role, which appeared to help the students to comprehend how the wiki works. This approach seemed to enable them to collaborate effectively over planning their activity and managing their work autonomously. While the students were interacting online, the teacher monitored their processes, notified inactive students of the need to contribute and encouraged the students to plan the work together. In contrast, teacher B left the wiki activity to the students and stepped back, without making any effort to organise the students' work. She was focusing on the final accomplishment, that is, the product rather than the process. On occasion, the online discussion data suggests that she was interrupting the students' planning and asking them to start writing directly.

At the socio-cognitive level, teacher A exhibited different online behaviours, apparently to promote student-student collaboration (S/S). She encouraged her students to collaborate not only using the text mode by editing each other's errors and modelling this behaviour, but also using the threaded mode by promoting students' discussion. She asked the students open questions about language and delayed giving her responses to the students' questions in order to stimulate their discussion. However, teacher B adopted a more authoritative role, which was limited to answering the students' questions, posting instructions and editing texts. The interaction in her embedded case exhibited a very structured pattern which was teacher initiation/student response or student initiation/teacher response. This limited the S/S collaboration as the students were reliant on the teacher rather than on each other.

At the socio-affective level, teacher A actively engaged in promoting and encouraging students to work together as well as appreciating their work as a group. Likewise, teacher B also posted socio-affective comments for the students; however, she appeared to encourage individuals rather than the group as a whole. In relation to this category, the students' interaction in both classes was rather limited, and they rarely showed a marked effort to engage in social talk or praise each other's work.

4. Conclusion

Although CALL researchers have called for teachers' intervention in the wiki environment to promote collaboration (Kessler, 2009), this study found that while the mere presence of the teacher could indeed promote participation, it does not necessarily enhance collaboration. Students may be more willing to participate because a teacher is present, but this does not mean that they will be mutually engaged with others. Furthermore, the teachers themselves may impede the collaborative process by transferring FTF traditional classroom practices to the wiki, which may consequently increase the teacher dependency among the students, such that the majority of the interaction becomes student/teacher rather than student/student.

The implications of this study affirm the role that teachers play in regulating students' online wiki collaboration. However, the study also highlights that teachers must not only be present in the wiki, but actively encourage dialogic interaction between the students themselves and try to align their practices regarding the wiki. From the sociocultural perspective, teachers should be aware of the degree of assistance needed by learners and to use language in a way that will encourage learners to move towards assuming greater responsibility for their online wiki learning.

Acknowledgments. I am grateful to my supervisor Dr Zöe Handley for her great support and constructive feedback. In addition, my gratitude goes to the teachers and students who participated in my study.

References

Curtis, D., & Lawson, M. (2001). Exploring collaborative online learning. *Journal of Asynchronous Learning Networks, 5*(1), 21-34.

Herring, S. C. (2004). Computer mediated discourse analysis: An approach to researching online behavior. In S. Barab, R. Kling, & J. Gray (Eds), *Designing for Virtual communities in the service of learning* (pp. 338-376). New York: Cambridge University Press. doi:10.1017/CBO9780511805080.016

Kessler, G. (2009). Student-initiated attention to form in wiki-based collaborative writing. *Language learning and Technology, 13*(1), 79-95.

Li, M., & Zhu, W. (2011). Patterns of computer mediated interaction in small writing groups using wiki. *Computer assisted language learning, 26*(1), 61-82. doi:10.1080/09588221.2011.631142

Lund, A. (2008). Wikis: A collective approach to language production. *ReCALL, 20*(1), 35-54. doi:10.1017/S0958344008000414

Mak, B., & Coniam, D. (2008). Using wikis to enhance and develop writing skills among secondary school students in Hong Kong. *System, 38*(3), 437-455. doi:10.1016/j.system.2008.02.004

Mangenot, F., & Nissen, E. (2006). Collective activity and tutor involvement in e-learning environment for language teachers and learners. *CALICO Journal, 23*(3), 601-621.

Nguyen, L. (2011). *Computer mediated collaborative learning in a Vietnamese tertiary EFL context: process, product, and learners' perceptions*. Published PhD thesis, Massey University.

Storch, N. (2011). Collaborative writing in L2 contexts: Processes, outcomes, and future directions. *Annual review of applied linguistics, 31*, 275-288. doi:10.1017/S0267190511000079

Tan, L., Wigglesworth, G., & Storch, N. (2010). Pair interaction and mode of communication: comparing face to face and computer mediated communication. *Australian Review of Applied Linguitics, 33*(3), 1-27.

Yoon, B., & Kim, H. (Eds). (2012). *Teachers' roles in second language learning: classroom applications of sociocultural theory*. USA: Information Age Publishing.

Diagnostic CALL tool for Arabic learners

Majed Alsabaan[1] and Allan Ramsay[2]

Abstract. Our proposed work is aimed at teaching non-native Arabic speakers how to improve their pronunciation. This paper reports on a diagnostic tool for helping non-native speakers of Arabic improve their pronunciation, particularly of words involving sounds that are not distinguished in their native languages. The tool involves the implementation of several substantial pieces of software. The first task is to ensure the system we are building can distinguish between the more challenging sounds when they are produced by a native speaker, since without that, it will not be possible to classify learners' attempts at these sounds. To this end, we carried out a number of experiments with the well-known speech recognition Hidden Markov Model Toolkit (HTK), in order to ensure that it can distinguish between confusable sounds, such as the ones that people have difficulty with. Our diagnostic tool provides feedback in three different forms: as an animation of the vocal tract, as a synthesised version of the target utterance, and as a set of written instructions. We have evaluated the tool by placing it in a classroom setting, asking 40 Arabic students to use the different versions of the tool. Each student had a thirty minute session with the tool, working their way through a set of pronunciation exercises at their own pace. Preliminary results from this pilot group show that their pronunciation does improve over the course of the session.

Keywords: language learning, pronunciation support, articulation, non-native speaker, Arabic, speech recogniser, animated head, synthesised speech.

---

1. malsabaan@cs.man.ac.uk.
2. allan.ramsay@cs.man.ac.uk.

How to cite this article: Alsabaan, M., & Ramsay, A. (2014). Diagnostic CALL tool for Arabic learners. In S. Jager, L. Bradley, E. J. Meima, & S. Thouësny (Eds), *CALL Design: Principles and Practice*; *Proceedings of the 2014 EUROCALL Conference, Groningen, The Netherlands* (pp. 6-11). Dublin: Research-publishing.net. doi:10.14705/rpnet.2014.000186

1. Introduction

Nowadays, learning a foreign language is an essential activity for many people. Proficiency in a foreign language is based on four different skills; reading, listening, writing, and pronunciation or speaking skills. We are particularly interested in pronunciation skills, and this paper aims to describe an attempt to give non-native Arabic speakers pronunciation support on how to make the different sounds that make up Arabic (i.e. help them sound more like native speakers) by giving them three forms of feedback: (1) an animation of the vocal tract corresponding to both the sounds learners have made and the sounds they should have made (i.e. the correct sounds), (2) a synthesised version of both what they said and what they should have said, and (3) an explanatory text of how they can pronounce the target sample correctly.

This project uses a speech recogniser called the HTK (Young et al, 2006) to identify the properties of speech signals for both native and non-native speakers. We trained the HTK to recognise phonemes of the input speech in order to obtain a phonetic analysis which has been used to give feedback to the learner. The HTK analyses the differences between the user's pronunciation and that of a native speaker by using *minimal pairs*, where each utterance is treated as coming from a family of similar words (i.e. two words with different meanings when only one sound is changed). This enables us to categorise learners' errors; for example, if someone is trying to say *cat* and the recogniser determines they have said cad, then it is likely that they are voicing the final consonant when it should be unvoiced.

Extensive testing shows that the system can reliably distinguish such minimal pairs when they are produced by a native speaker, and that this approach does provide effective diagnostic information about errors. In this way, we can provide feedback on acoustic data which we hope will enable learners to adjust their pronunciation.

The novel aspect about the current work is that (1) we will be applying these notions to Arabic, for which speech recognition is inherently harder than for English, (2) we will be giving multiple kinds of feedback to the learners and allowing them to choose between them, and (3) since we are providing multiple forms of feedback, we can evaluate the comparative effectiveness of each of them.

The evaluation has been done from three points of view: quantitative analysis, qualitative analysis, and questionnaire. Firstly, the quantitative analysis provides raw numbers indicating whether a learner is improving his/her pronunciation or not. Secondly, the qualitative analysis shows a behaviour pattern of what a learner did and how he/she used the tool. Thirdly, the questionnaire gives us a feedback from a learner and his/her comments about the tool.

2. Method

2.1. HTK experiments

The HTK experiments are a major stage to help determine what will be needed in order to animate the vocal tract and synthesise the phoneme sequence as feedback to learners. In our experiments, we used isolated words for the training samples. These samples were chosen by using the minimal pair technique. This technique helped learners distinguish between similar and problematic sounds in the target language (i.e. Arabic) through listening discrimination and spoken practice.

We investigated many factors (gender, words as terminal symbols, phonemes as terminal symbols) in order to improve the recognition accuracy as we reached an accuracy of 77%. Using these experiments, the HTK, with this acceptable recognition accuracy, was embedded into our Computer Assisted Language Learning (CALL) tool, giving us what a learner said while he/she was using our CALL tool.

2.2. The morphing

Prior to morphing, we had to draw the vocal tract for each phoneme. This drawing was done by tracing a set of pictures of Arabic phonemes and getting their coordinates. After that, we morphed from one drawing to another, in which we assigned phonetic units to individual snapshots. In more detail, we generated a set of morphs from a set of drawings using a hash table written in Java. This table, containing all the geometries that made up the animation we were trying to obtain, was generated using Dynamic Time Warping (DTW), which matched points in the two images to be morphed. This alignment must be done because the morphing cannot be carried out unless all morphed pictures have the same length sequences (i.e. same number of points). The animation of these pictures was done using Java3D.

Other researchers have done similar work using an animated head for this kind of task, but the underlying technology that they use is different (Liu, Massaro, Chen, Chan, & Perfetti, 2007; Massaro, 2004; Massaro & Cohen, 1995; Massaro & Light, 2003, 2004; Ouni, Cohen, & Massaro, 2005).

2.3. Speech synthesis

We used synthetic speech as one source of feedback to learners. To generate synthetic speech from a set of phonetic transcriptions, we used a tool called MBROLA. This tool is a text-to-speech system for most languages including Arabic. We supplied MBROLA with the phonemes of each word used in the training samples. MBROLA converted the script of word phonemes into speech. However, this speech sounds robotic and flat because we have a fixed length for each phoneme and a fixed pitch. To accurately estimate the length for a phoneme, we used both the alignment with real speech and a tool called Praat in order to get the phone length right. To improve pitch variations, we used a stress assignment program (Ramsay, Alsharhan, & Ahmed, 2014) which helped to find the stress of a given word and add the right pitch values. By having appropriate values of both phone length and pitch, the generated speech from MBROLA became more realistic, helping learners to listen to the correct pronunciation clearly.

2.4. The integration

The integration step is the last step for getting our diagnostic tool. In this step, we carried out a major piece of implementation which was done by integrating the two existing pieces of software. The first piece of software was for identifying mispronunciation by driving the speech recogniser (i.e. the HTK) in which we used phonemes as terminal symbols instead of words. The second piece of software was for animating a sequence of images of articulatory positions and performing a speech synthesis.

3. Discussion

In general, CALL tools are very difficult to evaluate because learning a language is a long, slow process and measuring the effect of a tool requires carrying out a large scale longitudinal study. The designers of Baldi (Massaro & Cohen, 1995) suggest that people's pronunciation does, in fact, improve quickly if they are given a tool like this. Therefore, we have talked to people in some schools where they teach Arabic and allowed them to use our tool with each student for a period of half an hour. We had 40 Arabic students in total who use five different versions of our CALL tool. These versions are the full version (i.e. includes all facilities), animation version, synthesised version, instruction version, and null feedback version. We have divided the students into five equal groups, which means that eight students would use one type of the previous five versions. Each student had a thirty-minute session with the tool, working their way through a set of pronunciation exercises at their own pace. The exercises concentrated on sounds, which prior experience has shown, learners have difficulty with, in particular on sounds that are not differentiated in English.

The results show that the pronunciation of the students has improved using all different versions of our tool. The students have improved their pronunciation by 27% with the synthesised version, by 17% with the full version, and by 14% with the animation version. These are the highest percentages of pronunciation improvement which gives an indication that these versions (i.e. synthesised, full, animation) are the most useful ones for learners. The lowest percentage of improvement is 4% with null version. This version does not provide the student with feedback on his/her pronunciation, whether it is correct or incorrect, while other versions do. The fact that this version does not offer the user any results could be interpreted as the reason of low percentage of improvement when using the null version.

4. Conclusions

We aimed to teach non-native Arabic speakers how to sound like native speakers. Therefore, we have done a considerable amount of work to achieve our aim. Briefly, this work consists of the following; a) conducting HTK experiments on confusable sounds, b) devising a new way of carrying out an animation of the vocal tract which is done in a less computationally expensive way than similar tools such as Baldi, but it produces realistic effects, and c) performing some experiments for improving the naturalness of synthesised speech. We have integrated all this work together resulting in a CALL tool that helps learners to improve their pronunciation.

Acknowledgements. Majed Alsabaan owes his deepest gratitude to Saudi Ministry of Higher Education and Cultural Bureau in London for financial support in his PhD study. Allan Ramsay's contribution to this work was partially supported by the Qatar National Research Fund (grant NPRP 09 - 046 - 6 - 001).

References

Liu, Y., Massaro, D. W., Chen, T. H., Chan, D., & Perfetti, C. (2007). *Using visual speech for training Chinese pronunciation: An in-vivo experiment* (pp. 29-32). InSLaTE. Retrieved from http://mambo.ucsc.edu/pdf/UsingVisualSpeechforTrainingChinesePronounciation.pdf

Massaro, D. W. (2004). Symbiotic value of an embodied agent in language learning. *In System Sciences, 2004. Proceedings of the 37th Annual Hawaii International Conference* (pp. 10-pp), IEEE.

Massaro, D. W., & Cohen, M. M. (1995). Perceiving talking faces. *Current Directions in Psychological Science, 4*(4), 104-109. doi:10.1111/1467-8721.ep10772401

Massaro, D. W., & Light, J. (2003). Read my tongue movements: bimodal learning to perceive and produce non-native speech/r/and/l/. *InINTERSPEECH*.

Massaro, D. W., & Light, J. (2004). Using visible speech to train perception and production of speech for individuals with hearing loss. *Journal of Speech, Language, and Hearing Research, 47*(2), 304-320. doi:10.1044/1092-4388(2004/025)

Ouni, S., Cohen, M. M., & Massaro, D. W. (2005). Training Baldi to be multilingual: A case study for an Arabic Badr. *Speech Communication, 45*(2), 115-137. doi:10.1016/j.specom.2004.11.008

Ramsay, A., Alsharhan, I., & Ahmed, H. (2014). Generation of a phonetic transcription for modern standard Arabic: A knowledge-based model. *Computer Speech & Language, 28*(4), 959-978. doi:10.1016/j.csl.2014.02.005

Young, S., Evermann, G., Gales, M., Hain, T., Kershaw, D., Liu, X., Moore, G., Odell, J., Povey, D., Valtchev, V., & Woodland, P. (2006). *The HTK book (for HTK version 3.4)*. Cambridge university engineering department. Retrieved from http://speech.ee.ntu.edu.tw/homework/DSP_HW2-1/htkbook.pdf

SpeakApps 2: Speaking practice in a foreign language through ICT tools

Christine Appel[1], Mairéad Nic Giolla Mhichíl[2], Sake Jager[3], and Adriana Prizel-Kania[4]

Abstract. SpeakApps 2 is a project with support of the Lifelong Learning Programme, Accompanying Measures. It follows up on the work and results reached during the KA2 project "*SpeakApps: Oral production and interaction in a foreign language through ICT tools*". The overarching aim of SpeakApps 2 is to further enhance Europeans' language learning skills through both self-directed learning and purposeful, teacher-designed materials that can leverage an ever-growing body of Open Educational Resources (OER). SpeakApps 2 targets not only HE educators and teacher trainers, but also those in VET and Secondary Education, and aims to widen the pool of resources for building language teaching skills via scalable trans-European collaborations and innovation using ICT and mobile technologies. SpeakApps 2 now takes further steps to diffuse the results in new countries and to synchronize efforts in European language teaching, in particular using OER. To achieve this, SpeakApps 2 has the objectives of a) integrating five new languages and including new education sectors, and b) developing a scalable digital framework able to bring in more languages, while spreading SpeakApps 2's methodologies and mobile solutions through a series of workshops, targeting the interests of open source communities and other projects for the sharing of resources and future innovations.

Keywords: speaking skills, OERs, tandem, teacher training, KA2 languages.

---

1. Universitat Oberta de Catalunya, Barcelona, Spain; mappel@uoc.edu.
2. Dublin City University, Dublin, Ireland; mairead.nicgiollamhichil@dcu.ie.
3. Rijksuniversiteit Groningen, Groningen, Netherlands; s.jager@rug.nl.
4. Uniwersytet Jagielloński w Krakowie, Krakow, Poland; prizelkania@gmail.com.

How to cite this article: Appel, C., Nic Giolla Mhichíl, M., Jager, S., & Prizel-Kania, A. (2014). SpeakApps 2: Speaking practice in a foreign language through ICT tools. In S. Jager, L. Bradley, E. J. Meima, & S. Thouësny (Eds), *CALL Design: Principles and Practice*; Proceedings of the 2014 EUROCALL Conference, Groningen, The Netherlands (pp. 12-17). Dublin: Research-publishing.net. doi:10.14705/rpnet.2014.000187

1. Introduction

A needs-analysis study conducted at the beginning of the project in 2011 (available from the project website http://www.speakapps.eu) confirmed that the teaching and learning of oral skills is one of the greatest challenges faced by language learners and teachers, especially in foreign language classrooms. With the internet, access to authentic oral texts in the L2 is becoming less problematic, but for learners, opportunities for guided production and interaction in the L2 are still difficult to come by. There is too little time in the traditional or blended classroom, particularly if the class size is large.

In addition, even when learners manage to speak, given the ephemeral nature of speech, it is difficult for teachers to give learners adequate feedback. If all of the students speak in small groups, the teacher cannot possibly listen to all of them, much less provide feedback, and students are more likely to lapse into their native languages or wander from the task. If only a few students speak, the rest of the class is silent and wastes the precious little time they have to speak; although the teacher can listen and provide oral feedback on the spot in such a situation, learners often do not benefit from this feedback unless they have an opportunity to interact and to produce an output (Gass, Mackey, & Ross-Feldman, 2005). A recording provides an opportunity for those students who have interacted with the teacher to review feedback and indeed if appropriate to produce further oral output.

In distance learning, there are acknowledged barriers for learners to communicate with one another (Berge, 2013). Although they can speak with one another synchronously via applications such as Skype and even record themselves if they purchase appropriate software, recordings must often be delivered to the teacher separately and it is difficult for the teacher to monitor what the students have actually done. In this context opportunities for peer-feedback are also missed.

2. Method

2.1. SpeakApps tools

The SpeakApps project began at the Universitat Oberta de Catalunya (Open University of Catalonia, hereafter "UOC") to address the need for a means by which learners could engage in L2 production and interaction in a completely online environment. The priority was to develop open-source tools complying with Learning Tools Interoperability (LTI) (http://www.imsglobal.org/tools interoperability2.cfm) standards in order to make the integration of the tools into different learning management systems (LMS) or other virtual spaces easy and transparent to the users.

Several tools were developed to meet these needs, and over the years through collaboration with SpeakApps partners and piloting in different institutions and contexts, the following four tools are the result.

2.1.1. Langblog

Langblog provides a blog in which teachers and learners can make audio and video contributions from a web browser without the need to install any additional programmes. It was designed with asynchronous oral production in mind, and facilitating peer-feedback was a priority in its design. It has the additional advantage of being secure, such as being open only to participants in a course, thanks to its LTI specifications which allow the tools to inherit the existing user permissions information in the virtual classroom. This is an important feature for primary and secondary educational sectors, but also for language teachers and students in general.

2.1.2. Tandem

Essentially an activity manager, Tandem delivers materials to pairs of learners in real time and shows teachers' temporal statistics. It is designed to be used with Videochat but can be used with any synchronous communication application (e.g. Skype). The Tandem tool allows students to engage in information-gap activities and role-plays outside the classroom and without the intervention of the teacher, who can then access the recording of the conversation at a later stage in order to give feedback to the students. Teachers and instructional designers have access to activity logs providing information on how students proceeded from one activity to the other, which has allowed for continuous improvement of the activities.

2.1.3. Videochat

Videochat provides up to six participants with an online application for videoconferencing and recording. There is no need to download anything for it to work or to export or send recordings –all features are integrated in the tool itself. In this way, learners can work independently, setting up sessions, recording conversations and archiving them in the virtual classroom without the need for teacher intervention.

2.1.4. The SpeakApps OER

The SpeakApps Open Educational Resources is an x-wiki-based repository for oral activities that is open to the global community. In addition to acting as a library for oral activities, it also serves as an authoring tool for the creation of Tandem tasks. The OER is searchable by language, CEFR level, resource type, as well as task type, and users are invited to tag activities as well as leave comments on those created by others. Tasks can also be downloaded in pdf format.

2.2. Use of the tools

At the Universitat Oberta de Catalunya (Barcelona), Langblog has been used in foreign language classrooms for the past five years, and Tandem for the past three, by approximately 8,000 learners per semester. The tools have also been used extensively at the University of Groningen (The Netherlands), Dublin City University (Ireland), Jagiellonian University (Krakow, Poland), and the University of Jyväskylä (Finland), all members of the SpeakApps project, as well as dozens of other institutions in more than 100 pilots around the world.

In line with the exploitation and sustainability plan laid out in the first phase of the project (2011-2012), the SpeakApps tools are now entering the post-development phase, in which SpeakApps offers paid service packages for installation and maintenance of the tools. The tools themselves are open source, and therefore can be downloaded from Sourceforge (http://sourceforge.net/) and used by anyone for free. The service is offered for those who lack the necessary technological infrastructure or who prefer to contract such a service.

There are essentially three modes of use available:

- Institutions install the open-source SpeakApps tools in their own ICT infrastructure, which requires video-conferencing licenses and an LMS. Such institutions can enter into development collaboration with the project.

- Institutions contract the UOC to provide a full Moodle platform with the SpeakApps tools installed. The UOC hosts these services in the cloud.

- Institutions contract the UOC to integrate the tools into their own LMS. The integration is transparent and is maintained in the SpeakApps cloud service.

3. Discussion

The project is continuing to grow and develop mainly in four areas: target languages, teacher training, activities in the OER and developments of apps for the use of the tools from mobile devices.

In the first phase of the SpeakApps project (2011-2012), the principal languages were English plus those of the research partners: Catalan, Irish, Polish, Dutch and Swedish. The second phase of the project (2013-2014) has seen the expansion of this set of languages to include Spanish, French, Croatian, and Italian. Each of the tools has an interface in each of these languages, as well as a category for content in that language in the OER. The tools' user information manuals (http://langblog.speakapps.org/speakappsinfo/) have also been translated into many of these languages. The interfaces of the tools in particular were designed to make crowd translation possible, and currently we are in discussion with users of the tools in Basque language education. Offers to translate the tool interfaces, manuals and pedagogical content into other languages are more than welcome from anyone interested in collaborating.

Thirty-six teacher training courses have been run in most of the project's languages, and free online training courses are regularly offered on the project's website (http://www.speakapps.eu/). These courses introduce teachers to teaching languages online, the use of the tools in such teaching, and about other matters such as feedback, grading, and task design and delivery. Several of the courses have been organized and run by teachers who have come to use the tools at their institutions, and the project is happy to provide support for such courses.

The SpeakApps OER has seen significant growth over the second phase of the project and shows every sign of continuing to do so in line with the growing body of SpeakApps users. In response to the project's own iterative approach to development and the contributions of users in this respect, new features, such as more robust search functionalities, have been introduced. Other new features such as rating systems and other means of quality assurance are in the planning stages and will be introduced as they are developed.

Mobile versions of Langblog and Videochat and a mobile-specific version of Tandem (which already works on many devices) are in production in response to multiple institutions' and users' demands. The project has reports of Tandem already in use in pair work in classrooms –learners view oral tasks on tablets in an effort to streamline logistics, to increase student motivation, not to mention save paper.

4. Conclusions

The SpeakApps project has developed since its start in 2011 in line with technological and pedagogical innovations in the area of education and ICT. The need for more practice time in order to become fluent in a second/foreign language is going to continue to be key for language learners and the project aims to outlast the current solutions and be ready for flexible adaptation as new solutions become possible.

New lines of activity in the future include a MOOC which will be run on the SpeakApps platform in the fall of 2014 for Spanish native speakers learning English and English native speakers learning Spanish. This MOOC aims at equipping students with strategies to benefit from opportunities to converse online with native speakers of their target language. Although numerous such opportunities already exist in social networks devoted to language learning, findings in studies of these networks show that the sustainability of such activity is low in that participants do not stay long in these networks or report poor results in terms of language learning. In equipping students with strategies to maximize their learning, students will be able to take full advantage of their participation in oral tasks with native speakers, as well as prepare for B2 official examinations.

The project partners are currently looking to contact new partners for continuing work mainly in two directions: a) research on different aspects of the acquisition of oral skills in a foreign language online, in particular task design and e-feedback, and b) future development of the tools and platform to add features that will enhance and facilitate evaluation and feedback.

Acknowledgements. This project has been funded with support from the Lifelong Learning Programme of the European Commission. This paper reflects only the views of the authors, and the European Commission cannot be held responsible for any use which may be made of the information contained herein.

References

Berge, Z. L. (2013). Barriers to communication in distance education. *Turkish Online Journal of Distance Education, 14*(1), 374-388. Retrieved from http://tojde.anadolu.edu.tr/tojde50/pdf/article_31.pdf

Gass, S. M., Mackey, A., & Ross-Feldman, L. (2005). Task-based interactions in classroom and laboratory settings. *Language and Learning, 55*(4), 575-61. doi:10.1111/j.0023-8333.2005.00318.x

The use of a wiki at a college in Hungary as a tool to enhance personal learning

Réka Asztalos[1]

Abstract. Wikis have been extensively used in language teaching for collaborative writing. However, there are very few studies about wikis as holistic learning environments. To fill this niche, the present research project aimed to explore the potential of the wiki as a platform for knowledge building and personalized learning that may enhance lifelong learning and students' self-regulation. Individual learning paths were encouraged by the introduction of a personalized evaluation system, in which points were given for any task the students had completed. A further aim was to find out about students' perceived language development, their disposition towards the wiki and the evaluation system with the help of mid-course and end-of-course questionnaires. The participants of the study were 26 tourism BA students at a university in Budapest who used the wiki for all the three terms of their language course. Results show that the integration of a wiki in a professional English course in higher education is received positively by the students.

Keywords: wiki, personal learning, knowledge sharing, case study.

1. Introduction

As websites that can be freely edited by their users, wikis can further collaboration and knowledge sharing, as well as student-centred, self-directed and personalized learning. However, little research has been conducted on the use of wikis as holistic language learning environments serving multiple purposes. Most case studies have focused on wikis as platforms for collaborative writing investigating the writing process, the writing product, students' and teachers' perceptions of collaborative writing or the effect of tasks (e.g. Li, 2012).

---

1. Budapest Business School, College of Commerce, Language Department; Asztalos.Reka@kvifk.bgf.hu.

How to cite this article: Asztalos, R. (2014). The use of a wiki at a college in Hungary as a tool to enhance personal learning. In S. Jager, L. Bradley, E. J. Meima, & S. Thouësny (Eds), *CALL Design: Principles and Practice*; Proceedings of the 2014 EUROCALL Conference, Groningen, The Netherlands (pp. 18-22). Dublin: Research-publishing.net. doi:10.14705/rpnet.2014.000188

The use of wikis was evaluated positively by the students in studies that were conducted in English for specific purposes (ESP) courses in tertiary education. For example, Kovacic, Bubas, and Zlatovic (2008) used various online learning activities (e-tivities) in a university business English course, which were perceived to be efficient and useful by the students. Similarly, positive results were found by Papadima-Sophocleous and Yerou (2013), who investigated the perceived effect of using wikis in a course for English for Commerce, Finance and Shipping. They used the wiki for various purposes: students created and edited glossaries, gathered and organized homework, shared material, and created links and an electronic portfolio. Participants regarded the wiki as useful and promoting their learning in several areas. Furthermore, sociology students' perceptions of collaboration in the wiki in an ESP course were examined by Zorko (2009) in a problem-based blended learning environment. She found that the wiki enhanced certain types of collaboration, such as learning from each other and communicating with the teacher, but communicating with peers and co-constructing products were less successfully promoted.

This paper describes a reflective practice project which is part of this researcher's on-going PhD research project and explores the possibility of integrating a wiki into teaching professional English at a higher education institution in Hungary. The main purpose of using the wiki in this project was to motivate students, most of whom had been learning English for eight or more years and perceived their knowledge as sufficient for communication and felt tired of learning the same topics and structures again and again. The wiki was also intended to help them prepare for lifelong learning and experience knowledge sharing. A further aim was to provide tools for self-study and enhance self-regulated learning to compensate for the limited number of classes and the mixed levels of students (B1-C1).

2. Method

2.1. The project

In order to gain in-depth experience about the use of the wiki, a longitudinal case study was designed for three terms. To achieve the goals outlined in the introduction, a wiki was created on Wikispaces for two groups of tourism BA students ($N=26$) in 2012 to support and supplement the two 90-minute face-to-face classes per week for three academic terms. The wiki was first used in class in a computer room, where students were trained on how to use it. After that, students used it at home for assignments, supplementary tasks and individual study. To encourage lifelong learning, links to useful websites were collected that could be used for studying

English at any time in the future. These websites included online dictionaries, pages for practicing grammar, learning vocabulary and other resources. Knowledge sharing was realized within the group by uploading students' work on the wiki, where each group member could read them, comment on them and use them for studying. In order to enhance self-study and personalized learning, students were encouraged to use the wiki at home to meet their own needs and goals.

2.2. The evaluation system

To promote individual learning, a personalized evaluation system was introduced in both groups in the second term. It was based on Prievara's (2013) model, designed for secondary school students in Budapest. At the beginning of the term, students had to assess their skills and decide which skills they would like to improve as well as lay down their immediate and long-term aims. They were encouraged to first select tasks freely for themselves from given sources, then from any source, which allowed them to tailor the tasks to their individual needs and learning styles. Each student had a page on the wiki which functioned as a portfolio where they could upload all the tasks they had carried out. Assessment was based on points students earned for any task they had completed depending on the length and difficulty, which were calculated into grades at the end of the term. Although this system was employed as a supplement to in-class work, where compulsory material was covered, points earned on the wiki could compensate for lower performance in class. The use of the wiki and the assessment system was evaluated quantitatively by pre- and post-questionnaires. Three areas were investigated: students' perceived language development, their disposition towards using the wiki in the project and in the future, and the evaluation of the personal assessment system.

3. Discussion

Results of the questionnaires administered in the second term and at the end of the three terms were compared to establish any differences between students' perceptions in the middle of and after the wiki project (Survey 1 and 2).

3.1. Students' perceived language development

Students had to indicate how much their English knowledge had improved during the second and the third term on a five-point scale. While in the first survey (S1) 35% of the students chose 4 or 5, indicating their perceived language development was *quite a lot* or *a lot* ($M=3.35$), in the second one (S2) it was higher, at 54% ($M=3.57$). The results were very similar for all the subskills and areas, apart from the perceived development of their professional vocabulary, where the mean score was 4.3 in both terms. This could be caused by the fact that they had never studied that area before, and consequently progress could be perceived more easily.

3.2. Students' disposition towards the wiki

Similarly to previous research findings, most of the students had positive feelings towards the wiki. The results of the questionnaires show that 81% of the students found the wiki useful in both surveys, while in S1 35% thought it was interesting, in S2 the number increased to 42%. The number of students who thought using the wiki was easy almost doubled from 15% to 27% in the second survey. This relatively low number shows that even today's students who are considered digitally literate need training when a new tool is introduced to them for educational purposes. At the same time, the perceived difficulty in using the wiki did not prevent them from acknowledging its usefulness. The fact that the majority of the students think they will use the wiki in the future after completing the English course (77% yes, 19% maybe) shows that the use of the wiki has the potential to encourage the idea of lifelong learning. The areas where they plan to use it include exam preparation (88%), writing letters (85%), preparing for a job interview and writing a CV (38%), practising grammar (32%) and using online dictionaries (15%).

3.3. Students' disposition towards the evaluation system

When the evaluation system based on individually selected tasks was introduced in the second term, students found it very difficult to understand it and adapt to it. The freedom of choice made them incapable of making decisions. Thus, several sources were presented to them where they could find tasks for practice and it was suggested that they should choose exercises which could improve their weaknesses. However, in the first survey only 19% of the students claimed they had chosen *tasks to improve their weaknesses*, while 65% selected *interesting* and 42% *useful tasks*. In the second survey the proportions changed significantly; only 46% of students chose *interesting tasks*, whereas 35% preferred *tasks to improve their weaknesses*. The usefulness of tasks still seemed to be important (46%) and a new category emerged; *tasks for exam preparation* (27%), which can probably be explained by the fact that the students had to take a B2 level professional language exam after the third term. Regarding the assessment system, the majority of students considered it useful in both surveys (65% and 69%) and would recommend it for other groups (69% and 73%). While in the first survey 58% thought it was fair, in the second one it rose to 73%. At the same time, the percentage of students who found the system complicated decreased from 19% to 4%.

4. Conclusions

Concerning pedagogical implications, the findings suggest that the integration of a wiki in a professional English course in higher education can motivate students and enhance personal learning, which can lead to more intensive language development. The finding that students' perceived language development increased, while their disposition towards the wiki and the personalized evaluation system became more positive by the end of the project suggests that the successful implementation of a new tool not only needs utmost care and planning but also a considerable amount of time. Further research with a modified course design based on the results of the study should be carried out in the future to explore the adaptability of this methodology for other groups at the college.

References

Kovacic, A., Bubas, G., & Zlatovic, M. (2008). E-tivities with a wiki: Innovative teaching of English as a foreign language. *Paper presented at the 14th congress of the European University Information Systems Organisation (EUNIS), Aarhus, Denmark.*

Li, M. (2012). Use of wikis in second/foreign language classes: A literature review. *CALL-EJ Online, 13*(1), 17-35.

Papadima-Sophocleous, S., & Yerou, C. (2013). Using wikis in an English for specific academic purposes (ESAP) context: university students' perceptions and reflections. *Teaching English with Technology, 13*(2), 23-54.

Prievara, T. (2013). 21. századi pedagógia a gyakorlatban [21st century pedagogy in practice]. In D. Lévai & J. Szekszárdi (Eds), *Digitális pedagógus konferencia konferenciakötet* (pp. 17-22). Budapest: ELTE PPK.

Zorko, V. (2009). Factors affecting the way students collaborate in a wiki for English language learning. *Australasian Journal of Educational Technology, 25*(5), 645-665.

Is ICT really essential for learning?
Perceptions and uses of ICTs for language acquisition in secondary level environments

Silvia Benini[1]

Abstract. Information and communications technology (ICT) has become an acknowledged and integral part of everyday life for many people. As research shows, the use of ICT in appropriate contexts in education can add value to teaching and learning by enhancing the effectiveness of learning itself and being a significant motivational factor in the students' acquisition process by supporting student's engagement with collaborative learning, and by promoting deep active lifelong learning (Barak, 2006; Lau & Sim, 2008). Despite all these significant benefits, it seems that ICT is not widely and successfully integrated into the educational system and consequently, its learning potential is not fully exploited. The purpose of this paper is to reflect and understand the current uses and expectations of ICT for learning in general and language learning in particular presenting some of the findings of a major case study. The results of this study are pertinent to future developments in school practice and national policies.

Keywords: ICT, education, language learning, post-primary education environments.

1. Introduction

ICT has become an essential part of most organizations and businesses these days and it has also gained a strong position in the educational field. The integration of ICT into the educational practice has had a rapid development in the past 20 years, obliging the schools to "re-think" and renovate their pedagogical approaches and to avail and exploit new technological resources. There are high expectations on

---

1. University of Limerick, Ireland; silvia.benini@ul.ie.

How to cite this article: Benini, S. (2014). Is ICT really essential for learning? Perceptions and uses of ICTs for language acquisition in secondary level environments. In S. Jager, L. Bradley, E. J. Meima, & S. Thouësny (Eds), *CALL Design: Principles and Practice*; Proceedings of the 2014 EUROCALL Conference, Groningen, The Netherlands (pp. 23-28). Dublin: Research-publishing.net. doi:10.14705/rpnet.2014.000189

ICT as, from a policy perspective, it holds the potential to sustain and promote competitiveness in the global market and, from an institutional one, it endorses a profound transformation in education (McGarr, 2009; Ottesen, 2006). As a consequence, a large number of education initiatives and research have been directed towards ICT integration in schools. One example is in Ireland, where the integration of ICT in post-primary schools was marked by the launch of the Schools IT2000 initiative. According to policy makers, the use of ICT in schools would offer important educational and pedagogical outcomes, beneficial for both teachers and students (OFSTED, 2002, 2004). Research indicates that the use of ICT in education can increase student's motivation, promote deep and collaborative understanding, facilitate lifelong learning, offer easy access to information and shared resources, and help students to think and communicate creatively (Jimoyiannis & Komis, 2007; Jonassen, 2000; Webb, 2005). Furthermore, students in technology-rich environments seem to perform better in the different subjects and ICT inclusion would encourage deep and interactive learning in a context where schools are more capable to respond effectively to the changing needs of todays' students (Barak, 2006; Lau & Sim, 2008).

Overall, ICT seems to support the modern principles of learning and, in our case, of language acquisition. Specifically, interaction, individualization, students' motivation and autonomy, often considered paramount in modern education theories, seem to perfectly mirror the ICT principles and processes. Despite all these significant benefits, it has been shown that ICT is often not widely and successfully integrated and where it is in place and available, there is no evidence that it has influenced teaching approaches (Levin & Wadmany, 2005). Many reasons have been given for the low level of ICT impact in the classroom. Among these are inadequate infrastructure, limited access to technology, lack of training and personal expertise, weak technical support, poor planning and teacher beliefs (Baek, Jung, & Kim, 2008; Ringstaff & Kelley, 2002). These barriers, together with the tools and benefits offered by new technologies, are some of the major aspects characterizing this research.

2. Method

2.1. Background information: settings and participants

The research reported here is part of a PhD project. This study employed a mixed-methods approach conducting semi-structured interviews together with surveys and classroom observations. The case study was conducted in two secondary schools, both located in the Munster region, Republic of Ireland. The first (School A) is a mixed community school that offers progressive educational programs focusing particularly on science, languages, Information and Communication Technology and an overall commitment to innovation and heavy use of ICT in their pedagogies. Here, the majority of students are equipped with notebooks or tablet computers as are all of their teachers. The second school (School B) is a Catholic female school. In School B, the environment and the teaching reveal a more traditional book-based approach with small class sizes, a close teacher-students relationship, and limited access to one computer lab for all classes. The participants of the study were 2nd, 3rd, and 5th year students and their Italian and Irish language teachers.

2.2. Data collection

The data elicitation phase lasted 18 weeks and started by asking the participants to complete a pre-interview survey to discover their perceptions and uses of ICT inside and outside the classroom. From the 12th to the 15th week, semi-structured and focus group interviews were held to investigate the students' and teachers' access and use of ICT focusing particularly on Irish and Italian learning and teaching. In this paper, I will introduce the data from the surveys and the related analysis in order to address some of the research concerns and consequently, offer future recommendations for teachers, learners, and second level institutions.

3. Discussion and conclusions

In the surveys provided, students of both secondary schools were asked to indicate how important the use of ICT in their institutions was.

Figure 1. Students' perceived importance of ICT

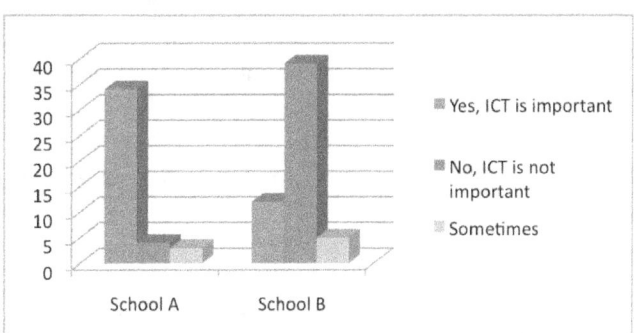

As shown in Figure 1, comparing the results of School A with School B, we have interestingly different perspectives. On one hand, the majority of School A respondents (83%) openly addressed the importance of ICT in their institution as something being strongly emphasized and widely used for different subjects. Ten percent of the students reported that ICT was not as important as the school itself was stating but some teachers relied on it for teaching methods. The rest of the students (7%) argued that ICT was not essential in their learning process but it would definitely help in some cases and specific subjects.

On the other hand, the majority of School B respondents (70%) strongly stated that ICT was not important in their school primarily because the lack of resources and facilities available. Furthermore, students reported that books and traditional tools were regularly used for their learning. However, they felt that ICT should be promoted and used in their learning experience. Twenty-one percent of the respondents reported that ICT was important in their school especially for specific subjects; younger teachers used it for basic presentations or showing videos. Finally, 9% of the students stated that ICT was not important in their learning environment except in certain cases and specific subjects.

Students and teachers were then interviewed on the importance of ICT for Language Learning. In School A, more than half of students stated that ICT was important for their language learning process because it helped to investigate different methods of study by broadening the learning and making it easier. According to them, new technologies were important as a great source of information and an important support to rely on.

> "Yes, it is important; not all the information are in the book and it is very helpful to have technology to fall back on" (Male 5th year students).

Teachers confirmed the importance of ICT in their teaching recognizing, and at the same time, its limitations due to the extra time involved for training and preparing integrated technology lessons together with potential technical problems often encountered.

> "Very important. It is the conduit through which I can reach the students" (Male Irish Language Teacher).

In School B, ICT was not perceived as essential for language acquisition. During the Irish and Italian language classes, digital technologies were not used as students keenly relied on teachers and books for their learning. At home, some tools (mainly online dictionaries and translators) may be used independently by students as an extra support for their language activities.

"In school we don't really use ICT resources during language classes. For me, at home, I do use the Internet to help me with languages" (Female 5th year student).

"ICT is important however students do not always enjoy the use of ICT. Some students dislike Powerpoints and prefer if you do not use ICT" (Female, Irish Language Teacher).

The results of this study show that in both schools there was a general positive attitude but also the same concerns (i.e. accessibility and availability of resources) towards ICT inclusion even though the *technological orientation* was very different. Teachers favourably viewed ICT as a pedagogical device. However, many of them, especially in school B, are still not fully trained in the use of ICT. Consequently, they are reluctant to integrate it in their teaching. Finally, a strong sentiment echoed in both institutions revealing technology as an important and effective tool, but it was still not considered essential and central to the teaching and learning process. ICT seems to be often used as a backup for consolidating student learning and not as a way of preparing students for new knowledge acquisition.

Acknowledgements. Strong support for this project has been provided by the School of Languages, Literature, Culture and Communications, University of Limerick. The author would like acknowledge the support, availability and collaboration of the staff members of the two targeted schools and all their students.

References

Baek, Y., Jung, J., & Kim, B. (2008). What makes teachers use technology in the classroom? Exploring the factors affecting facilitation of technology with a Korean sample. *Computers & Education, 50*(1), 224-234. doi:10.1016/j.compedu.2006.05.002

Barak, M. (2006). Instructional principles for fostering learning with ICT: Teachers' perspectives as learners and instructors. *Education and information technologies, 11*(2), 121-135. doi:10.1007/s11134-006-7362-9

Jimoyiannis, A., & Komis, V. (2007). Examining teachers' beliefs about ICT in education: Implications of a teacher preparation programme. *Teacher Development, 11*(2), 149-173. doi:10.1080/13664530701414779

Jonassen, D. H. (2000). *Computers as mindtools for schools: Engaging critical thinking.* Michigan: Merrill.

Lau, B., & Sim, C. (2008). Exploring the extent of ICT adoption among secondary school teachers in Malaysia. *International Journal of Computing and ICT Research, 2*(2), 19-36.

Levin, T., & Wadmany, R. (2005). Changes in educational beliefs and classroom practices of teachers and students in rich technology-based classrooms [1]. *Technology, Pedagogy and Education, 14*(3), 281-307.

McGarr, O. (2009). The development of ICT across the curriculum in Irish schools: A historical perspective. *British journal of educational technology, 40*(6), 1094-1108. doi:10.1111/j.1467-8535.2008.00903.x

OFSTED. (2002). *ICT in schools: Effect of government initiatives*. London: Office for Standards in Education (O. f. S. i. E.).

OFSTED. (2004). *ICT in schools: The impact of government initiatives five years on*. London: Office for Standards in Education (O. f. S. i. E.).

Ottesen, E. (2006). Learning to teach with technology: authoring practised identities. *Technology, Pedagogy and Education, 15*(3), 275-290. doi:10.1080/14759390600923568

Ringstaff, C., & Kelley, L. (2002). *The learning return on our educational technology investment: A review of findings from research 2002*. San Francisco: WestEd. Retrieved from http://www.wested.org/online_pubs/learning_return.pdf

Webb, M. E. (2005). Affordances of ICT in science learning: implications for an integrated pedagogy. *International journal of science education, 27*(6), 705-735. doi:10.1080/09500690500038520

The effects and functions of speaker status in CALL-oriented communities

Judith Buendgens-Kosten[1]

Abstract. Do you know how to change your relationship status on Facebook? What about your language status? In most web 2.0 contexts, music preference or relationship status are more important than information about one's linguistic repertoire. In language learning communities and affinity spaces (Gee, 2004), however, language status is forefronted. This contribution will look at the function of 'native-speakerness' and 'language-learnerness' in a wide variety of CALL-oriented online communities and affinity spaces (online forum, massive open online course (MOOC), blogging community, other) from two different perspectives: (a) User settings: How is language status established in language learning communities? What affordances (e.g. user profile) are available for 'setting' one's language status, and what assumptions about native-speakerness underlie them? (b) Affordances: What effects do language status settings have on the user experience via such means as information filtering and availability of specific affordances? The paper aims to begin a discussion about the effect of language status attributions on learners as well as the pedagogical and linguistic assumptions behind the ways in which these services 'put the native speaker into the product'.

Keywords: native speaker, non-native speaker, blog, MOOC, forum, tandem.

1. Introduction

In most web 2.0 contexts, what languages you speak at which level and at which point in your life you acquired them are less important than your gender, age, or your music preference. In language learning communities and affinity spaces (Gee, 2004) though, your language status, specifically of what language(s) you

---

1. Goethe Universität Frankfurt, Frankfurt am Main, Germany; buendgens-kosten@em.uni-frankfurt.de.

How to cite this article: Buendgens-Kosten, J. (2014). The effects and functions of speaker status in CALL-oriented communities. In S. Jager, L. Bradley, E. J. Meima, & S. Thouësny (Eds), *CALL Design: Principles and Practice*; *Proceedings of the 2014 EUROCALL Conference, Groningen, The Netherlands* (pp. 29-34). Dublin: Research-publishing.net. doi:10.14705/rpnet.2014.000190

are a 'legitimate' native speaker and of which language(s) you are a learner, is forefronted.

In language learning contexts, being a native speaker is more than a mere description of a sociolinguistic fact. Native speakers are closely associated with authenticity (Buendgens-Kosten, 2013), and the presence of native speakers in a community is often highlighted in its advertising.

This paper looks at the functions of 'being a native-speaker' vs. 'being a language-learner' in a wide variety of language learning platforms (a blogging community, a MOOC, an online forum, a platform for finding tandem partners), focusing on two aspects:
- language status information;
- effect of language status on access to content or functions/affordances.

2. Method

For the purpose of this study, four online language learning services were analysed, three of which were online communities or affinity groups.

Lang-8 (Buendgens-Kosten, 2011) is a language learning blogging community (learners can choose from a broad range of languages offered). Language learners write blog posts in their target language and correct/comment on text written by learners in their native language.

SpanishMOOC is a MOOC teaching beginner Spanish. Learners watch interactive videos in the target language, watch instructional videos in English, and complete language drills and exercises. Learners can also interact with each other and with teachers.

How To Learn Any Language (HTLAL) is an online forum focussing on language learning. Users can discuss language learning and features of specific languages. Furthermore, there are sub forums dedicated to practicing specific languages, such as German or French, where all discussion is performed in the "theme-language" of that sub forum. HTLAL differs from the other communities by being a place where language learning is discussed, rather than primarily a place at which language learning is practiced.

ConversationExchange differs from the other three services discussed as it does not constitute an online community or affinity group. Learners go to

ConversationExchange to find partners for virtual or face-to-face language tandems by posting a short profile and by searching through existing profiles.

The discussion is based on the features these services had in the first half of 2014.

3. Discussion

The discussion will focus on language status information in user profiles and on how language status mediates access to affordances.

3.1. User settings

All four services allow or even require the inclusion of information about language status. Concerning native languages and target languages, they differ in how many languages can be named, if this information is mandatory, and if it is easy to change later on. See Table 1 and Table 2 for an overview.

Table 1. Overview of native language status treatment

language learning site	number of native languages	mandatory information?	easy to change?
Lang-8	1	mandatory	yes
SpanishMOOC	1 (from a small selection of options)	mandatory	no
HTLAL	multiple	voluntary	yes
ConversationExchange	multiple	mandatory	yes

Table 2. Overview of target language status treatment

language learning site	number of target languages	mandatory information?	easy to change?
Lang-8	2 (free account), multiple (premium account)	mandatory	yes
SpanishMOOC	Spanish only	NA	NA
HTLAL	multiple	voluntary	yes
ConversationExchange	multiple	mandatory	yes

At Lang-8 and ConversationExchange, language status-related information is part of the user profile, together with information such as country of origin, gender, or a descriptive text. HTLAL includes information about language status in what is called the "language profile" of the user. This information is displayed in an abbreviated form on the left side of each forum post by that user, and with additional information, if provided, on the language profile overview page.

Compared to the other services discussed, HTLAL has much more complex options for indicating language status. The main distinction is in languages a user "speaks" and languages he/she "studies". Any number of languages can be included in each category. To further specify this information, users can indicate native languages among the language spoken (marked by an asterisk), and add information about language level (e.g. "C2") to any language spoken or studied.

At SpanishMOOC, information about language status is requested during the early phase of the registration process. Only a very limited number of native languages are provided from which one can choose and the choice cannot be altered afterwards. The reason for this very limited selection will become clear in the next section, which discusses the affordances or functions that depend on language choice.

3.2. Affordances

In all four language learning services surveyed, language status information was, albeit to very different degrees, connected to access to information and functions.

The smallest effect could be observed at HTLA, where access to language profiles of other users was limited to those who had filled out their own language profile. The content of the language profile –what languages users speak, what languages they study– had no effect on access to content or software functions.

This looks quite different in Lang-8, where language settings determine which blog posts one can correct (those in one's native language) and which blog posts are suggested as reading material (those in one's native language and in the target languages). In Lang-8, one cannot "like" contributions but can give a "native speaker nod" –as long as one is a native speaker of the language in which the blog post was written. In ConversationExchange, potential tandem partners are not identified based on profile information of the person conducting the search, but based on the search criteria one enters in a search form. If a user accesses a profile the program deems not to be a good fit –because the person whose profile was accessed does not learn one of the user's native languages– it informs the user about this ("Please note that Pat is not learning your native language"), without limiting access to affordances such as contacting a person.

Within SpanishMOOC, access to software functions is determined by user group, not by language status. Only individuals with a "teacher" role can correct sentences by learners, but being a "teacher" is independent of a user's language status –being a native speaker does not make one a teacher, nor are teachers necessarily native speakers. In this MOOC, language status has another effect though. As mentioned above, only few languages can be chosen as native languages when registering for the learning platform (Instreamia) on which SpanishMOOC runs. One's choice of "native language" here influences the user interface language setting and the course material available. If one choses Spanish as native language, one receives a Spanish user interface, and SpanishMOOC becomes unavailable as course choice. If one choses English, the user interface is set to English and one can register for SpanishMOOC. Changing between languages requires creating a new account. Information about native language is also included in one's profile and visible to other users.

4. Conclusions

Users play different roles in the different communities, and the design of language status-related user data collected reflects this.

In Lang-8, for example, users are 'correctors' as well as learners, while in ConversationExchange they are tandem-partners. For both functions –to be allotted correction powers by the system and to be found by learners of their language(s)– an overview over the languages users speak is important. On both websites, access to any sub-pages is possible, but the ability to interact with them (e.g. by commenting, by contacting a person) is either controlled (Lang-8), or at least steered (at ConversationExchange). The assumption that a user's language status determines what material is helpful for him/her, and whom he/she can support with their learning is 'hard-coded' in the software.

Assumptions about speaker status itself have also been 'hard-coded' into the design of these language learning services: some see learners as monolingual, others as (potentially) plurilingual. In ConversationExchange –whose makers introduce themselves as "3 Italian polyglots from Venice who traveled the world and are fluent in Venetian, Italian, English, Spanish, PHP, SQL, Javascript" (ConversationExchange, n.d., para 1)– the number of native languages is not limited, while in Lang-8, each user can only be native speaker of one language. HTLAL, in turn, not only permits multiple native languages to be listed, but also allows for inclusion of languages "spoken" rather than "studied" that are non-native languages, and for the provision of additional information, specifically regarding skill level. One person equalling one native language (Lang-8) is contrasted with one person equalling multiple native languages (ConversationExchange) and with one person equalling multiple languages, native and non-native (HTLAL).

In SpanishMOOC, language status is less a statement of one's sociolinguistic background than a choice regarding the user interface language. Here, "native language" is equated with "preferred language".

The four services presented here demonstrate different ways to 'put the native speaker into the product'. Their designs reflect assumptions about what a native speaker is, and about the functions native speakers have in language learning. Each language status-related design decision shapes not only the underlying software structure, but also has an effect on user behaviour, and may impact the learning experience and learning outcomes.

References

Bündgens-Kosten, J. (2011). Blogging in the target language: Review of the 'Lang-8' online community. *Studies in self-access learning journal 2*(2), 97-99. Retrieved from http://sisaljournal.org/archives/june11/Bundgens-Kosten

Buendgens-Kosten, J. (2013). Authenticity in CALL: Three domains of 'realness'. *ReCALL 25*(2), 272-285. doi:10.1017/S0958344013000037

ConversationExchange. (n.d.). *Buy us a treat*. Retrieved from http://www.conversationexchange.com/buy-us-a-beer.php?lg=en

Gee, J. P. (2004). *Situated language and learning: A critique of traditional schooling*. New York: Routledge.

List of websites discussed

ConversationExchange: http://www.conversationexchange.com/index.php?lg=en
Lang-8: http://lang-8.com/
How To Learn Any Language: http://www.how-to-learn-any-language.com/forum/default.asp
SpanishMOOC: http://spanishmooc.com/

university of groningen

SNS for learners at beginner level: An alternative use of FB

Tiziana Carpi[1]

Abstract. Despite that previous studies have shown that the implementation of Social Network Sites (SNSs) into the classroom may bring several learning benefits, the focus has been mainly restricted to learners at intermediate language level with a focus on use of SNSs for fostering communicative competence or as class management. This project, implemented on a voluntary basis in a class of 103 first year students of Japanese L2 at an Italian University, challenged the use that has been made of SNSs so far and integrated Facebook for simple authentic language tasks. The study investigated: 1) students' perceptions and attitudes towards the use of Facebook (FB) to learn and practice Japanese script through digital devices, and 2) the potential benefits of FB in terms of language and cultural learning. Data were collected through questionnaires (pre and post project), language tasks and three language tests. Results show that students who participated in the FB project did not only provide very positive feedback but also performed better in the language test.

Keywords: social network sites, SNSs, Facebook, Japanese language learning, beginner students.

1. Introduction

In the last few years, SNSs have become part of today's learners' daily routine and an essential form of media literacy. With surveys reporting that 18% of Internet users are between 18-29 years old, and 90% of them have profiles on SNSs[2], it is

---

1. University of Milan, Italy; tiziana.carpi@unimi.it.
2. FB alone counts 800 million daily users (PewResearch Internet Project). Retrieved from http://www.pewinternet. org/fact-sheets/social-networking-fact-sheet/

How to cite this article: Carpi, T. (2014). SNS for learners at beginner level: An alternative use of FB. In S. Jager, L. Bradley, E. J. Meima, & S. Thouësny (Eds), *CALL Design: Principles and Practice*; Proceedings of the 2014 EUROCALL Conference, Groningen, The Netherlands (pp. 35-39). Dublin: Research-publishing.net. doi:10.14705/rpnet.2014.000191

not surprising that in recent years the use of SNSs in second language education has drawn the attention of an increasing number of researchers.

According to previous studies, benefits have been found in the development of communicative and socio-pragmatic competence, motivation and interpersonal relationships (McBride, 2009). However, in contrast with previous research, where target learners are at intermediate level and where SNSs have been mainly integrated for class management or as tools to foster communicative competence (Hitosugi, 2011), the present study has exploited the features of one of the most popular SNSs in a radically different way. FB was implemented in a project which, firstly, addressed absolute beginners with no prior knowledge of the L2 (Japanese) and secondly, aimed at helping students familiarize themselves and exercise with a different script, which exposed them to authentic language through Japanese websites.

The project aimed at investigating: 1) students' perceptions and attitudes towards the use of FB to learn and practice the Japanese script through digital devices, and 2) the potential benefits of FB in terms of language and cultural learning.

2. Method

2.1. Participants and the FB group

The participants of the project, which ran for ten weeks from October to December 2013, were absolute beginners (N=103, M=20.06 years) enrolled in the first year of a Japanese language course within the BA degree in Language and Cultural Mediation, University of Milan. The goal of the course (20 hours) was the introduction to the Japanese script: two *kana* syllabaries (*katakana* and *hiragana*), the first hundred *kanji* (chinese characters), and rōmaji, the system of transcription of the symbols into roman letters.

On a voluntary basis, the students were offered to take part in a project which included the use of FB in addition to class hours for activities related to Japanese language and culture learning. A closed FB group was created and half of the class (N=48) joined it.

2.2. Survey procedure

Data were collected in three stages: a) two questionnaires, one before and one at the end of the project, b) a total of 13 learning tasks posted on FB, and c) three language tests. In order to avoid non-spontaneous responses, it was emphasized that replying to tasks was absolutely optional.

The first questionnaire was administered to the whole class ($N=103$) before introducing the project, to gather information about students' overall attitude and perception of technology use in general, and specifically of FB for L2 and culture learning. The second questionnaire, administered at the end of the course and to which more than half of the class replied ($N=58$, including FB members), replicated some of the questions introduced in the first questionnaire, and further explored whether students who decided not to participate in the FB group, would have liked to join in the future. It also investigated potential worries concerning the implementation of FB for Japanese language and culture learning. The last section of this questionnaire was addressed only to FB members and explored their perception of participation in the FB project.

A set of 13 tasks was carefully designed in advance and posted weekly on the FB page. Students were suggested to do the tasks regularly, with no obligation. Most of them required students to go to specific Japanese websites, available only in the Japanese language (fast food chains, travel agencies, karaoke song playlists), choose one's favourite item (e.g. fast food menu, honeymoon destination, song and singer, etc.), and report it on posts using katakana and rōmaji. The goal was to help students practice reading and writing authentic Japanese.

At the beginning of the course, all the 103 students were informed that three language tests would be submitted during the classes but their attendance was optional. Students were required to write the transliteration of sentences from one script to the other (kanji into hiragana and vice versa, and katakana into rōmaji followed by translation). Because tasks on FB focused mainly on katakana use, only results of the test section related to katakana were taken into consideration for the subsequent data analysis.

3. Discussion

Data collected through the two questionnaires provide interesting clues about students' perception of FB use for language and culture learning. According to results from the first one ($N=103$), 92% of the students had a FB account. 72.8% said they were interested in using FB for learning Japanese language and culture and only a small percentage expressed to be doubtful (23.3%) or indifferent (3.6%) about it. While 56.9% of the total number of students took part in the FB group, 51.6% of the remaining students said they wished to participate in the future.

Furthermore, students declared an improvement on several aspects of language learning. Using a Likert scale, 78.8% of the participants fully or mostly agreed on saying that taking part in the FB project improved their language skills. Most of them (81.8%) thought that they deepened their interest in Japanese language and culture. 72.7% believed that they benefitted from participating to the FB group. 75.8% did not consider FB tasks took time away from their study and 79.8% did not think doing language practice with FB to be demotivating.

The majority (75.8%) reported that, thanks to FB, they improved the Japanese script using digital devices. In fact, while at the beginning only 38.8% declared they were able to write Japanese on the computer, at the end, the percentage raised to 79.3%. 78.8% asserted that FB helped them improve their ability to read katakana words as well as to memorize (75.8%) hiragana and katakana.

When asked whether students would have changed anything in the FB project, most answers reported their satisfaction over the task contents and delivery. Only a few mentioned the repetitive nature of some tasks.

Figure 1. Total score in the three katakana tests[3]

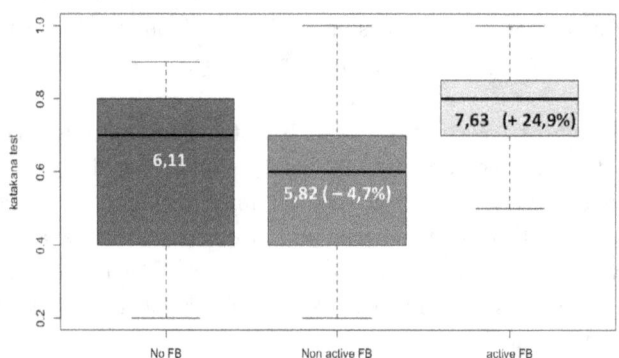

Database: N = 45 (only those who took all the three language tests, regardless their participation or not to FB group)

The most striking results emerge from the language tests. In this case, data were collected only from the students who took all the three tests ($N=45$). In order to evaluate the effect of participation in FB on learners' achievements, students were divided into three groups: those who did not join FB, those who did but were not

---

3. The results have been obtained through an ANOVA model controlling for gender, age, previous ability in reading and writing hiragana, katakana and kanji, computer skills and other individual characteristics to avoid pre-project bias.

active, and those who were active. Test results show that the total score in the three katakana tests obtained by the active FB members was 24.9% higher than those who did not join FB. However, those who joined FB but did not participate actively[4] scored 4.7% less than those who did not joined at all (Figure 1).

4. Conclusions

This study examined the effect of FB usage on beginner students of Japanese L2 since the very early stage of their learning. Data analysis showed that, besides students' very positive attitudes towards the use of FB to learn and practice Japanese language and culture, remarkable conclusions can be drawn from the test results: active FB members performed consistently better than those who were inactive. Improvements in their writing skills on the computer have also been found. Despite the voluntary nature of the FB project, 69% of the participants were active in their responses to tasks. Participants to FB enjoyed the project very much and expressed their willingness to join similar activities in classes at upper levels.

This study may support what Blattner and Lomicka (2012) advocate: "SNS should be integrated as an extension of the classroom so that language development can continue in a fun environment when students are working from other places" (p. 17).

Acknowledgements. I am grateful for The Japan Foundation for supporting my research and the project through a Fellowship for Ph.D. Candidate. I would also like to thank Prof. Kohji Shibano (Tokyo University of Foreign Studies) for his constructive comments.

References

Blattner, G., & Lomicka, L. (2012). *Facebook*-ing and the social generation: A new era of language learning. *Alsic* [Online], *15*(1). doi:10.4000/alsic.2413

Hitosugi, C. I. (2011). Using a social networking site in Japanese class. In E. Forsythe, T. Gorham, M. Grogan, D. Jarrell, R. Chartrand, & P. Lewis (Eds), *CALL: What's Your Motivation?* (pp. 72-83). Tokyo: JALT CALL SIG.

McBride, K. (2009). Social-networking sites in foreign language classes: Opportunities for re-creation. In L. Lomicka & G. Lord (Eds), *The next generation: Social networking and online collaboration in foreign language learning* (pp. 35-58). CALICO Monograph Series, 8. San Marcos, TX: CALICO.

---

4. Participants to the FB group were considered "active" if they had accomplished at least 25% of the total tasks.

university of groningen

Preliminary conclusions after the design and implementation of mobile learning apps for professionals

María Dolores Castrillo[1], Elena Bárcena[2], and Antonio Pareja-Lora[3]

Abstract. According to a recent research carried out by Aruba Networks (2014) in the US, the UK, France, Spain, Germany, Sweden, South Africa, Saudi Arabia and UAE, 86% of all respondents have two or more devices that can connect to the internet, and nearly two thirds (64%) already own three or more mobile devices with this feature; another 39% own four or more (p. 4). We live on the move, and this includes mobility, as well as working anytime, anywhere and lifelong learning. Thus, research on language teaching and/or learning should focus on the ways to get adapted to the specific new needs of our modern society (e.g. mobility). Accordingly, for instance, mobile-assisted language learning (MALL) activities should be app-based; "this is not a trend language educators can ignore" (Godwin-Jones, 2011, p. 8). In this paper, we present some preliminary results and conclusions after the design and implementation of some MALL apps carried out by the ATLAS research group. They have been developed in the context of the SO-CALL-ME project, in order to enable the members of ATLAS to explore the way in which students can improve their oral language skills "on the move".

Keywords: MALL, second language, foreign language, languages for special purposes, apps.

---

1. Facultad de Filología / ATLAS (UNED); mcastrillo@flog.uned.es.
2. Facultad de Filología / ATLAS (UNED); mbarcena@flog.uned.es.
3. Facultad de Informática (UCM) / ATLAS (UNED); aplora@ucm.es.

How to cite this article: Castrillo, M. D., Bárcena, E., & Pareja-Lora, A. (2014). Preliminary conclusions after the design and implementation of mobile learning apps for professionals. In S. Jager, L. Bradley, E. J. Meima, & S. Thouësny (Eds), *CALL Design: Principles and Practice; Proceedings of the 2014 EUROCALL Conference, Groningen, The Netherlands* (pp. 40-46). Dublin: Research-publishing.net. doi:10.14705/rpnet.2014.000192

1. Introduction

Recently, Aruba Networks (2014) undertook an analysis of the use of mobile devices in a number of countries from all over the world (USA, Spain, South Africa, Saudi Arabia, etc.), which gave rise to overwhelming data supporting its increase, such as the fact that 86% of all participants have two or more such devices connected to Internet, 64% have three or more, and 39% have four or more (p. 4). The fact is that the majority of us live 'on the move': mobile devices and our own mobility are part of everyday life, which allows us to work, learn, interact with each other and engage in entertaining activities almost anytime, anywhere. Regarding learning in particular, de Waard (2014) pointed out that "[m]obile learning (mLearning) is in perpetual beta" (p. 114). This observation, no doubt, applies to languages, since research on MALL is progressing at a good pace on the best practices around mobile devices as learning tools (Castrillo, Martín-Monje, & Bárcena, 2014; Wong, Chin, Tan, & Liu, 2010). Also, applications (apps) are viewed as an effective language learning formula as they can be used in a highly flexible way (individually or collaboratively), incorporating the user's own preferences and environment into the learning process and capturing their full undivided attention (Godwin-Jones, 2011). Although MALL is far from being mainstream in educational institutions at the moment, the authors agree with Godwin-Jones (2011) in that app-based learning "is not a trend language educators can ignore" (p. 8).

Taking this into account, the purpose of this paper is to present some preliminary results and conclusions driven from the design and implementation of some mobile-assisted language learning apps by the ATLAS research group. All these apps have been developed in the context of the SO-CALL-ME project (see the Acknowledgements). As presented in EUROCALL 2013 (Pareja-Lora et al., 2013), the SO-CALL-ME project was established to explore the way in which students can improve their oral language skills "on the move" by means of the MALL apps designed and developed within the ATLAS group. Hence, we present some initial conclusions following the implementation of some of the apps already developed.

The rest of this paper is divided into four sections: Section 2 outlines a general overview of SO-CALL-ME and the previous work done, presenting the methodological and pedagogical framework applied to develop the apps. Then, the main app features are described in Section 3. Section 4 discusses some relevant implementation details of these mobile learning apps, exploring the issues and problems faced, as well as other remarkable results. Finally, Section 5 provides a brief conclusion and sketches our planned future work.

2. MALL app development: a methodological and pedagogical framework

Previous work of the ATLAS research group, in which a number of English as a Foreign Language (EFL)-teaching apps were evaluated, has identified the need to strengthen the pedagogical framework of this kind of educational resource, that is, MALL apps (Arús, Rodríguez-Arancón, & Calle-Martínez, 2013; Martín-Monje, Arús, Rodríguez-Arancón, & Calle-Martínez, 2013; Pareja-Lora et al., 2013). The research goal of this assessment focused on the examination of the technical features and limitations of the most salient EFL MALL applications available, as well as on the evaluation of their pedagogic suitability.

To that end, a number of rubric-based evaluations of such apps were conducted (Arús et al., 2013). The most remarkable conclusions obtained after these evaluations are that (i) some apps that are attractive to students do not have a sound linguistic content and, hence, should not be used for language learning (or, at least, not autonomously), and (ii) most apps lack theoretical and methodological underpinnings. This represented a challenge that our group decided to face by engaging in the development of second language learning apps that are interesting, attractive and pedagogically sound at the same time.

In this light, the ATLAS group undertook the creation of a number of MALL applications in the broader context of language for specific purposes apps. These apps should (i) not be a mere mobile version of traditional online courses, (ii) provide quality teaching and practice, and thus, (iii) have a sound pedagogical, linguistic and methodological base. Therefore, a suitable methodology had to be chosen for their development. For this purpose, we decided to use the conceptual framework and methodology presented in Kukulska-Hulme (2012). This methodological framework was supplemented from a linguistic and pedagogical point of view with some suitable linguistic theories, such as the Systemic Functional Grammar (Arús, 2008; Halliday & Matthiessen, 2004) or the socio-linguistic theory (Canale & Swain, 1980), with an emphasis on meaning and communication, and a goal to develop learners' communicative competence.

3. Description of some ATLAS MALL apps developed so far

Here, we describe some of the apps developed so far by the ATLAS research group following the methodology presented above, namely (i) ANT, for oral comprehension practice through the news, (ii) FANCLUB, for the same skill, but through audio-books, (iii) Business App, focusing on listening comprehension and on teaching how to develop and perform successful business presentations, (iv) VIOLIN, for the audiovisual comprehension of videos, (v) VISP, for oral production, and (vi) Eating Out, a teaching resource for listening comprehension and communicative practice.

The following tables summarise the main characteristics of these apps. Firstly, Table 1 contains a brief description of the skills involved in each app. Secondly, Table 2 presents both (i) the resources used within each app in order to present and/or develop its different activities and (ii) the CEFR language level of the target users of the app. Finally, Table 3 shows the activities that each app includes.

Table 1. Skills involved in the use of the ATLAS apps

APP NAME	SKILL INVOLVED				
	Oral comprehension	Reading comprehension	Writing (text production)	Oral production	Other
ANT (Audio News Trainer)	YES	NO	NO	NO	
FANCLUB	YES	NO	NO	NO	
Business App	YES	YES	ADDRESSED	ADDRESSED	Audiovisual
VIOLIN	YES	NO	NO	NO	Audiovisual
VISP (Videoclips for Speaking Production)	YES	NO	YES	YES	Audiovisual

Table 2. Resources used within each ATLAS app and their corresponding CEFR language level

APP NAME	RESOURCES USED	USER'S CEFR LANGUAGE LEVEL
ANT (Audio News Trainer)	News provided by Internet radio issuers through RSS connection	A1-C1
FANCLUB	Prose fiction (free audiobooks) videos	A1-C1
Business App	E-voice simulator / YouTube video links	B1 Business people and students
VIOLIN	Video extracts from the TV-series "Friends" (length of the videos: 1'-3')	B1
VISP (Videoclips for Speaking Production)	Video extracts from the film "Moulin Rouge" (length of the videos: 5''-30'')	B1
Eating Out	Audio clip, performed by some ATLAS group members (length: 4' 20)	A2-B1

Table 3. Brief description of the activities included in each ATLAS app

APP NAME	DESCRIPTION OF ACTIVITIES
ANT (Audio News Trainer)	• Pre-questionnaire • New(s) selection (organized by level) • Listening • Comprehension and technical evaluation questionnaire
FANCLUB	• Audiobook selection • Listening (also fragmentary listening possible) • Comprehension quiz
Business App	• Learning goals specification (includes audio text) • Several activities of listening (several times if required) • Some activities that involve watching audiovisual materials (YouTube videos) • Several comprehension quizzes: "tick what you hear", "fill in the blanks", etc. • Automatically corrected exercises, including feedback

VIOLIN	• Warm-up (intro + open questions and/or new vocabulary to facilitate a better understanding)
	• 3 viewings of each "Friends" video: (1) selective hearing, (2) intensive monitoring, (3) global comprehension.
	• Instructions and activities for the 3 viewings:
	  • Viewing 1: Comprehension questions with 'sample answers' / multiple choice
	  • Viewing 2: Comprehension questions with 'sample answers'
	  • Viewing 3: Self-assessment rubric (meta-cognitive strategies)

VISP (Videoclips for Speaking Production)	• Introduction to audio description + sample video clip + questionnaire with personal data • Instructions + video viewings (as many times as desired) • Audio description of the video clip (scripting + reading recording) • Self-assessment rubric (meta-cognitive strategies)
Eating Out	• Listening comprehension, lexical and grammar-practice activities • Activities are adaptive • All activities automatically corrected by the application, including feedback

4. Results and discussion

As shown in Table 1, Table 2 and Table 3, only two of the applications focus on a particular domain (i.e. Eating Out, Business App), whereas most of them focus on a particular skill, in a domain-independent way. Besides, most of the applications provide some form of self-evaluation activities and focus on oral comprehension. Only some of them address oral and/or written production, for example. This last issue is mainly due to the fact that assessing and/or automatically correcting activities regarding these other skills is much more complicated than assessing oral comprehension. Since mobile apps are intended to provide autonomous learning (at least to some extent), it is important that MALL apps provide this function (automatic correction and/or evaluation of activities and exercises). This helps the users of the apps be aware of their own learning improvements and, hence, also keep them motivated. However, this does not mean that we are neglecting the production of apps that help practice these other skills with some appropriate self-evaluating and automatically corrected exercises. In fact, some preliminary research is being carried out towards this end. Finally, unfortunately, no statistics about the assessment of these apps by their users can be presented thus far either. Even though the apps have already been tested by the members of the research group, a large-scale evaluation of the apps (by a real set of users) is still pending. This evaluation will be carried shortly and will be published in the near future.

5. Conclusions

In this paper, we have presented some MALL applications developed within the ATLAS research group in the last months, in the context of the SO-CALL-ME project. Unlike most of the MALL applications developed so far by the members of our research group, the ATLAS mobile applications have been designed following solid sociological, pedagogical and linguistic methodologies and theories. We believe this makes these applications most convenient for the practice and learning of the elements (vocabulary, grammar) and skills (mainly oral comprehension) they deal with. However, unfortunately, this issue has not been assessed yet, since a formal evaluation of the apps presented in the paper is still pending (but will be carried out in the coming months). Besides, this set of applications is expected to grow in the future as well, since some research on other potential and supplementary applications is already being undertaken, in order to extend the types of skills covered by the applications developed until now.

Acknowledgements. The research described in this paper has been partly funded by the Spanish Ministry of Science and Innovation, Grant **FFI2011-29829**: **S**ocial **O**ntology-based **C**ognitively **A**ugmented **L**anguage **L**earning **M**obile **E**nvironment (**SO-CALL-ME**). We would like to thank the ATLAS (UNED) research group as well, for their constant inspiration, encouragement and support.

References

Aruba Networks. (2014). *Are you ready for #GenMobile. How a new group is changing the way we work, live and communicate*. Retrieved from http://www.arubanetworks.com/pdf/solutions/GenMobile_Report.pdf

Arús, J. (2008). Teaching modality in context: A sample lesson. *Odense Working Papers in Language and Communication, 29*, 365-380.

Arús, J., Rodríguez-Arancón, P., & Calle-Martínez, C. (2013). A pedagogic assessment of mobile learning applications. *Proceedings of the International Conference UNED – ICDE 2013 – Mobilizing Distance Education for Social Justice and Education* (pp. 630-643). Madrid: Universidad Nacional de Educación a Distancia.

Canale, M., & Swain, M. (1980). Theoretical bases of communicative approaches to second language teaching and testing. *Applied Linguistics, 1*(1), 1-47. doi:10.1093/applin/I.1.1

Castrillo, M. C., Martín-Monje, E., & Bárcena, E. (2014). Mobile-based chatting for meaning negotiation in foreign language learning. *Proceedings of the 10th International Conference on Mobile Learning. International Association for Development of the Information Society* (pp. 49-59).

De Waard, I. I. (2014). Using BYOD, mobile social media, apps, and sensors for meaningful mobile learning. In M. Ally & A. Tsinakos (Eds), *Increasing Access through Mobile Learning* (pp. 113-124). Vancouver: Commonwealth of Learning.

Godwin-Jones, R. (2011). Mobile apps for language learning. *Language Learning & Technology, 15*(2), 2-11. Retrieved from http://llt.msu.edu/issues/june2011/emerging.pdf

Halliday, M. A. K., & Matthiessen, C. M. I. M. (2004). *An introduction to functional grammar* (3rd ed.). London: Arnold.

Kukulska-Hulme, A. (2012). Language learning defined by time and place: A framework for next generation designs. In J. E. Díaz-Vera (Ed.), *Left to My Own Devices: Learner Autonomy and Mobile Assisted Language Learning. Innovation and Leadership in English Language Teaching, 6* (pp. 1-13). Bingley, UK: Emerald Group Publishing Limited.

Martín-Monje, E., Arús, J., Rodríguez-Arancón, P., & Calle-Martínez, C. (2013). REALL: rubric for the evaluation of apps in language learning. *Proceedings of ML13*.

Pareja-Lora, A., Arús, J., Martín-Monje, E., Read, T., Pomposo-Yanes, L., Rodríguez-Arancón, P., Calle-Martínez, C., & Bárcena-Madera, E. (2013). Toward mobile assisted language learning apps for professionals that integrate learning into the daily routine. In L. Bradley & S. Thouësny (Eds), *Proceedings of EUROCALL 2013: 20 years of EUROCALL: Learning from the Past, Looking to the Future* (pp. 206-210). Dublin: Research Publishing. doi:10.14705/rpnet.2013.000162

Wong, L.-H., Chin, C.-K., Tan, C. L., & Liu, M. (2010). Students' personal and social meaning making in a Chinese idiom mobile learning environment. *Educational Technology and Society, 13*(4), 15-26.

A case study on English language learners' task-based interaction and avatar identities in Second Life: A mixed-methods design

Julian ChengChiang Chen[1]

Abstract. English as a foreign language (EFL) learners' language use in 3-D virtual environments is a vibrant avenue that still deserves more research attention in the field of CALL. To contribute research and pedagogical implications to the current Second Life (SL) literature, this study aims to examine EFL adult learners' use of communication strategies during task-driven, voice-based negotiation, as well as to explore their avatar identities during their language practices in a task-based virtual course in SL. Operationalized by task-based interaction, quantitative results show that confirmation checks, clarification requests and comprehension checks are the most frequently used strategies. The interrelationship among task types, negotiation and strategy use is also established –jigsaw task prompts the most instances of negotiation and strategy use. Qualitative results drawn from triangulation of multiple data sources reveal that SL is endorsed as a promising learning environment owing to its simulated immersion, augmented reality, tele/co-presence and masked identities via avatars. This study demonstrates that implementation of task-based instruction can be maximized by 3-D simulated features in SL. It also implicates that 1) two-way directed tasks with convergent and single-outcome conditions will stimulate more cognitive and linguistic processes of negotiation involving interactional modifications, and 2) avatar identities can boost EFL learners' sense of self-image and confidence.

Keywords: task-based interaction, communication strategies, 3-D virtual environment, avatar identities.

---

1. chengchiang.chen@stonybrook.edu.

How to cite this article: Chen, J. C. (2014). A case study on English language learners' task-based interaction and avatar identities in Second Life: A mixed-methods design. In S. Jager, L. Bradley, E. J. Meima, & S. Thouësny (Eds), *CALL Design: Principles and Practice*; Proceedings of the 2014 EUROCALL Conference, Groningen, The Netherlands (pp. 47-51). Dublin: Research-publishing.net. doi:10.14705/rpnet.2014.000193

1. Introduction

Even though research has shown that the unique features (e.g., immersion, avatar presence, simulation) afforded by SL –a three dimensional virtual environment– have the potential to enhance learners' motivation, engagement and virtual identities (Cooke-Plagwitz, 2008; Dede, 2005), studies done on using interactionist theory as a theoretical framework to examine EFL learners' language use in SL are still scarce (cf. Peterson, 2005, 2006, 2010). The link between EFL learners' language acquisition in task-based interaction and virtual learning in SL still needs to be connected in current SLA literature (Kraemer, 2008). We need a better understanding as to 1) why EFL learners are drawn to SL, 2) how they perceive learning English in task-based interaction in SL versus real life (RL), 3) how they feel about using avatars to interact with other avatars in English, and 4) what kinds of features afforded by SL impact their language learning experiences and outcomes. Also, a full-blown virtual language course designed under the task-based design has not been fully documented in SL literature.

Motivated by the current English learning phenomenon where digital natives' learning styles are not accommodated in traditional English classes, this research also aims to uncover whether language instruction in SL can align with digital natives' learning styles in order to resolve the long existing digital divide (Prensky, 2005a, 2005b). As such, this study seeks to explore if SL can open up a new pedagogical fertile ground for English teaching and learning. To address these theoretical and pedagogical concerns, this case study raises two major research questions:

1. How do EFL learners use communication strategies to negotiate meaning during task-driven, voice-based interaction in SL?

2. What are EFL learners' attitudes toward using avatars to participate in a task-based virtual class in SL?

Situated in cognitive interactionist theory (Long, 1981, 1983) and driven by task-based language teaching (TBLT) (Doughty & Long, 2003), this study employs a concurrent mixed-methods design to better answer the research questions quantitatively and qualitatively.

2. Method

Nine adult EFL learners worldwide were recruited to participate in a 10-session virtual class in SL. Each virtual session had 90-minute contact hours and was conducted twice a week. Learners, in their avatar form, used voice chat to interact with peers in different communication tasks, such as opinion-exchange, jigsaw, information-gap and decision-making tasks. Also, capitalizing on the unique features afforded by SL, students had the opportunity to perform simulation-based and real-life-oriented tasks, such as using note cards to play an ice-breaker game in the first session, show-and-telling cultural clothing worn by their avatars, and collaborating with peers in a museum field trip project. Figure 1 shows a screen capture of students taking turns presenting their cultural outfits.

Figure 1. Show-and-tell on cultural clothing presented by learner avatars

Quantitative data were collected through participants' pre- and post-task-based interaction to examine how EFL learners use different communication strategies to resolve communication breakdown during negotiation of meaning in communicative tasks. Qualitative data were collected through students' journal entries to reflect on their perceptions about their learning experience in each SL virtual session. A pre-course survey was administered to gather their demographic information and attitudes toward English learning in SL before the course. A post-course survey was also distributed to probe their perceptions about their overall virtual learning experience and avatar identities in this task-based course, triangulated with a focus group interview and the researcher teacher's observation blog.

3. Results and discussion

Quantitative results showed that confirmation checks, clarification requests and comprehension checks were the three most frequently used strategies. Other types of strategy use were also found, such as a request for help, self-correction and topic shift, accompanied by another two newfound strategies that had not been previously documented in task-based research in 3-D multi-user virtual environments (MUVEs) (i.e., a metacognitive strategy and spelling out the word). Following Varonis and Gass's (1985) framework of negotiation of meaning, two types of negotiation routine were also identified: single-layered trigger-resolution sequence (standard negation routine in a four turn-taking discourse) and multi-layered trigger-resolution sequence (more complex routine that involves above four turn-takings). Additionally, the interrelationship among task types, negotiation and strategy use was also established in the study. That is, the jigsaw task prompted the most instances of negotiation and strategy use, followed respectively by information-gap task and decision-making task, whereas opinion-exchange task triggered the least.

Using grounded theory approach (Corbin & Strauss, 2008), three core themes emerged from qualitative data: 1) perceptions about factors that impact virtual learning experience in SL, 2) attitudes toward learning English via avatars in SL, and 3) beliefs about the effects of task-based instruction on learning outcomes in SL. Students in this study perceived SL as a potentially effective platform to empower their language learning. The immersive participation and augmented reality afforded by SL enabled them to interact with peers or other native English speakers in real time, without the burden and expenses of physical travelling. Being able to "teleport" to different life-like places in SL also allowed them to simulate various real-life scenarios and make learning more fun and meaningful. As such, their engagement, motivation, and sense of autonomy were enhanced.

Additionally, the telepresence realized in avatars also fostered their sense of belonging to the virtual community. Their masked identities through avatars also allowed them to "take risks" in speaking English without feeling the same shyness and embarrassment as would they in a real-life conversation discourse. Students' participation in the task-based virtual course also 1) showed longer retainment of engagement and motivation as well as spontaneous oral production through communication tasks, 2) fostered learner autonomy and investment of time and effort in language practices through culture-driven tasks, and 3) deepened real-life task experiences and knowledge and language acquisition through simulated tasks.

4. Conclusions

Drawn from both quantitative and qualitative results, this study implicates that 1) two-way directed tasks with convergent, obligatory, single-outcome conditions will stimulate more cognitive and linguistic processes of negotiation involving interactional modifications –which also leads to more complex and lengthy negotiation routine, 2) 3-D multimodal resources afforded by SL also provide additional visual support for EFL students' input acquisition and output modifications, 3) tasks that capitalize on SL features, students' cultural repertoire and world knowledge as well as simulate real-life tasks will make a difference in their virtual learning experiences, and 4) avatar identities boost their sense of self-image and confidence.

Despite unexpected technical glitches in SL that might challenge collecting consistent data for research in SL, it can be concluded that SL still has the potential to bring real life to the 3-D MUVE and empower both English teaching and learning. It is also time to teach and learn "outside the box" in the digital age.

References

Cooke-Plagwitz, J. (2008). New directions in CALL: An objective introduction to Second Life. *CALICO Journal, 25*(3), 547-557.

Corbin, J. M., & Strauss, A. L. (2008). *Basics of qualitative research: Techniques and procedures for developing grounded theory* (3rd ed.). Los Angeles, CA: SAGE.

Dede, C. (2005). Planning for Neomillennial learning styles. *EDUCAUSE Quarterly, 1*, 7-12.

Doughty, C. J., & Long, M. (2003). Optimal psycholinguistic environments for distance foreign language learning. *Language Learning & Technology, 7*(3), 50-80.

Kraemer, A. (2008). Formats of distance learning. In S. Goertler & P. Winke (Eds), *Opening doors through distance language education: Principles, perspectives, and practices*. CALICO Monograph Series (Vol. 7, pp. 11-42). San Marcos, TX: CALICO.

Long, M. H. (1981). Input, interaction, and second-language acquisition. *Annals of the New York Academy of Sciences, 379*, 259-278. doi:10.1111/j.1749-6632.1981.tb42014.x

Long, M. H. (1983). Native speaker/non-native speaker conversation and the negotiation of comprehensible input. *Applied Linguistics, 4*(2), 126-141. doi:10.1093/applin/4.2.126

Peterson, M. (2005). Learning interaction in an avatar-based virtual environment: A preliminary study. *PacCALL Journal, 1*, 29-40.

Peterson, M. (2006). Learner interaction management in an avatar and chat-based virtual world. *Computer Assisted Language Learning, 19*(1), 79-103. doi:10.1080/09588220600804087

Peterson, M. (2010). Learner participation patterns and strategy use in Second Life: An exploratory case study. *ReCALL, 22*(3), 273-292. doi:10.1017/S0958344010000169

Prensky, M. (2005a). Engage me or enrage me: What today's learners demand. *EDUCAUSE Review*, 61-64.

Prensky, M. (2005b). Listen to the natives. *Educational Leadership, 63*(4), 8-13.

Varonis, E., & Gass, S. M. (1985). Non-native/non-native conversations: A model for negotiating meaning. *Applied Linguistics, 6*(1), 71-91. doi:10.1093/applin/6.1.71

Fostering collaboration in CALL: Benefits and challenges of using virtual language resource centres

Liliana Cuesta Medina[1] and Claudia Patricia Alvarez[2]

Abstract. This paper presents the findings from a qualitative study on collaborative CALL design and implementation carried out with two groups of postgraduate language-teacher trainees who designed and piloted nine virtual language resource centres (VLRC) at 16 educational institutions of different levels and contents for an academic year. The project was conceived with the collaborative nature of online environments and the design principles of Paquette (2002) in mind. Data analysis revealed that both teacher trainees and their learners understood VLRCs as supporting the development of learner autonomy through the use of Web 2.0 technologies, various scaffolding agents, and instruction in learner strategies. The design of the VLRCs helped learners engage in collaborative projects related to their contexts and needs to achieve their learning objectives. However, some learners experienced technology-generated anxiety, which limited their usage of the VRLCs, as well as their engagement with and achievement in the collaborative activities planned. Likewise, some trainees experienced technostress stemming from lack of expertise with learning management systems (LMSs) and design of learning objects. Various possibilities for improving the design and implementation of VLRCs are recommended, such as including ICT training tutorials and activities that cater activities appropriate to a broader variety of learning styles and language skills.

Keywords: collaboration, CALL, virtual language resource centres, teacher education.

---

1. Universidad de La Sabana; liliana.cuesta@unisabana.edu.co.

2. Universidad de La Sabana; claudiap.alvarez@unisabana.edu.co.

How to cite this article: Cuesta Medina, L., & Alvarez, C. P. (2014). Fostering collaboration in CALL: Benefits and challenges of using virtual language resource centres. In S. Jager, L. Bradley, E. J. Meima, & S. Thouësny (Eds), *CALL Design: Principles and Practice; Proceedings of the 2014 EUROCALL Conference, Groningen, The Netherlands* (pp. 52-58). Dublin: Research-publishing.net. doi:10.14705/rpnet.2014.000194

1. Introduction

The ubiquitousness of Web 2.0 technologies and the possibilities provided by technology enable the creation of Virtual Resource Centres (VRC), online learning environments that offer learners access, synchronously or asynchronously, to a number of resources: instructors and tutors, subject matter experts, training managers and professors acting as designers (Paquette, 2002, p. 1). The same affordances can also be made available through VLRC, in which learners are granted access to collaborative learning practices and learning objects tailored to their language proficiency level, in addition to various types of interaction facilitated by the use of Web 2.0 tools (Alvarez & Cuesta, 2012). This paper examines the instructional design process followed in the creation of nine VLRCs. We elaborate on the infrastructure of the online environments and report on the collaborative learning practices carried out in the design and piloting of these VLRCs.

1.1. Instructional design process for VLRCs

The development of VLRCs drew upon learner needs identified by direct observations, informal interviews and the evaluation of learners' academic performance in the EFL subjects. This needs analysis revealed that the learners needed to strengthen their communicative skills and improve their learning autonomy through cognitive and meta-cognitive strategies as a means of "transferring responsibility for aspects of the language learning process such as setting goals, selecting learning strategies, and evaluating progress" (Cotterall, 2000, p.110). To meet these pedagogical needs, the teacher trainees were encouraged to follow a model based on Paquette's (2002) principles for creating virtual resource centres. Those principles were transferred to the VLRCs, as illustrated below.

1.2. Virtual resource centres

Virtual resource centres:

- represent learning systems centred on the learner. They foster the development of learner autonomy through learner strategy training;

- use distance and online instruction as assets to facilitate lifelong learning. The usage of metacognitive strategies (planning, monitoring and evaluating) (Appendix A) aids the development of a specific communicative skill enabling students to become more strategic, self-reliant, flexible, and productive in their learning endeavours (Scheid, 1993);

- contribute to the creation of a sense of community to increase student satisfaction through the inclusion of problem-solving activities that require learners to take roles (group leaders, providers, helpers, editors) and to participate in collaborative activities, even though participants belong to different surroundings and/or cultures;

- constitute a learning system that offers various ways of accessing and processing information. VLRCs allow for flexibility (i.e. learners need not follow a pre-selected path) and ubiquity (i.e. providing students with access whenever and wherever it is required);

- propose a constructivist pedagogy. Collaborative projects lead students to build understanding of a particular topic or context-related issue through student-centred learning activities involving negotiation of meaning and learning agent interaction (Alvarez & Cuesta, 2012);

- support the learning process through various seamlessly integrated resources, tools, and documents in a supportive scaffolding environment.

Figure 1. Supportive scaffolding in activity 1 LO1[3]

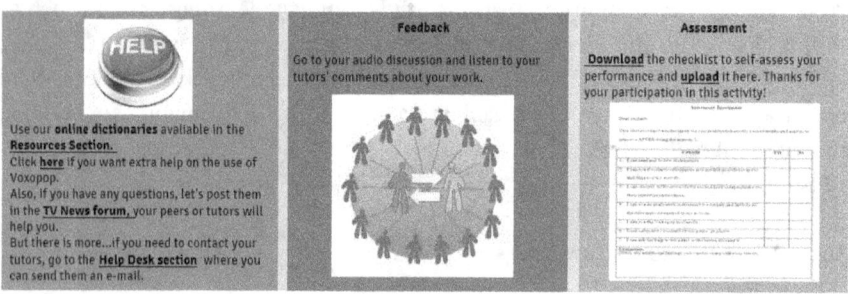

1.3. Components of VLRCs

VLRCs seek to provide students with extended learning practice opportunities related to the development and strengthening of a specific language skill or sub-skill and to the transfer of learning strategies to real-life application (e.g. strategies

---

3. Retrieved from http://budy12.wix.com/speakingcorner#!untitled/c1o4r

for public speaking, ESP, academic development and study opportunities, critical reflection on social and contextual issues). Open management systems that suited the targeted audience needs were selected by focusing on basic web design principles such as self-intuitive navigation, page layouts, text usage, and background colours and textures (Appendix A). To structure these centres, teachers included the components depicted in Figure 2, which were adapted depending on the target populations and their pedagogical needs for online learning (Siragusa, Dixon, & Dixon, 2007).

Figure 2. Components of the VLRCs

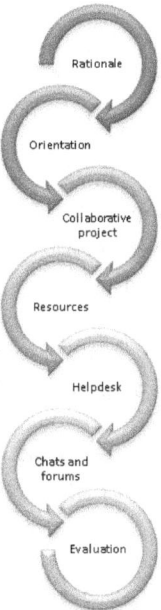

2. Method

In this qualitative study conducted in a private university setting, 16 teacher trainees working at primary, secondary, university, and technical levels in the private or public sector were required to create a set of nine VLRCs for groups of students of similar ages, linguistic needs, and proficiency levels, collaboratively or individually. The researchers, in the role of instructors, assisted the teacher trainees in selecting LMSs to host their VLRCs and structuring them to include the components suggested in the target course. All trainees were in-service teachers from elementary, secondary schools, and/or universities. The study examined several data sources (including questionnaires, surveys, and protocols). Data analysis was conducted using the grounded theory approach (Corbin & Strauss, 2008). Validity was ensured by following triangulation procedures in which a comprehensive use of qualitative data analysis strategies was present in all the stages of the study. These factors were then merged, examined, and theorised in the light of the main research question: *How might the usage of a VLRC facilitate effective collaborative learning practices?*

3. Discussion

3.1. Support source: blending interaction and autonomy development

In this study, the VLRC is understood as a catalyst that facilitates the development of collaborative learning practices through two main characteristics: autonomy and interaction. In this sense, the VLRC represents an opportunity to access and use various Web 2.0 technologies, customise learning experiences mediated by various scaffolding agents (e.g. peers, instructors, learning objects), and raise awareness regarding a different way to generate effective instructional processes, focused on the needs of the context. Data analysis showed that, in accordance with Little (1991), the first steps learners made towards autonomy depended on the development and exercise of capacities for detachment, critical reflection, decision making and independent action. Moreover, learners were able to gain awareness about their responsibilities to determine the purposes of their learning, as each monitored their respective progress and evaluated the outcomes. Trainees were able to make links between the different modes of interaction (Roblyer & Ekhaml, 2000) and learning opportunities offered in the VLRCs' collaborative environments, in which they self-accessed tools and procedures and were able to smoothly transmit these practices to their learners.

3.2. Mechanism to face the digital divide

The implementation of VLRCs served a myriad of purposes. Firstly, it was a mechanism to bridge the digital divide existing in many of the educational contexts where the VLRCs were implemented. In five of the participating institutions, learners had not previously had access to information technologies to assist education, either because the existing infrastructure was faultily used or because access to resources was limited.

Secondly, among the challenges encountered during the study, trainees reported various types of difficulties: technical, procedural, and attitudinal. They claimed to have limited experience in designing collaborative activities, even though they had previously received such training in their MA studies. They reported having only partial knowledge of relevant Web 2.0 tools and other target resources, as well as a lack of expertise in the technical management of the target LMS platforms. They thought that the design of collaborative learning activities was moderately difficult from an instructional point of view, either because they had not had sufficient experience in planning for collaboration or because they had misconceptions regarding what collaboration entailed. In their implementation stages, they agreed that when a design was faulty, their learners displayed limited participation and engagement in the language learning activities. Additionally, as they engaged in the process of design for collaboration, these various described challenges generated technostress, i.e. technology-generated anxiety behaviours in the trainees (Rosen & Weil, 1997).

4. Concluding remarks

The design and usage of VLRCs in diverse educational contexts provides teachers and learners with a variety of opportunities that can assist teachers to extend and improve their language learning practices. Even so, the present study also revealed several challenges and opportunities in the design and implementation of VLRCs that the language teacher must learn to take up effectively. The results of the present study suggest, firstly, that there is a need to shift paradigms with regards to collaborative work, which often remains unknown to practitioners as they confront the design, implementation, and even evaluation stages. Successful engagement with and openness to collaborative activities may often require specialised sequential training, awareness-raising, and involvement by different parties engaged in the process (trainees, learners, and institution's stakeholders), based on the target goals and required outcomes for the institution and the language classroom. It should be emphasized that this process might turn out to be time-consuming.

Additionally, for the implementation of VLRCs to be effective, collaborative activities should be planned to cater to various learning styles and language skills, according to the needs identified, and there should be a congruent plan for the use of novel technologies and pertinent features that might serve to capture and hold students' attention and interest (ref. interactivity, multimodal sources) throughout their language learning processes. This would also require the educational institution to generate policies for the effective inclusion of technology, viewing it as a source of support that assists language pedagogy. For us, the collaborative use of VLRCs suggests prospective language self-access initiatives as a complement to face-to-face language instruction or as a supplementary language learning plan for groups of learners who would access language learning through other means. Thus, we believe that being cognisant of what this process implies would assist both teachers and learners along the paths to be taken.

References

Alvarez, C., & Cuesta, L. (2012). Designing for online interaction: Scaffolded and collaborative interventions in a graduate-level blended course. *The EUROCALL Review, 20*(1), 1-9. Retrieved from http://eurocall.webs.upv.es/documentos/newsletter/papers_20(1)/02_alvarez.pdf

Corbin, J. A., & Strauss, A. (2008). *Basics of qualitative research* (3rd ed.). Thousand Oaks, CA: Sage.

Cotterall, S. (2000). Promoting learner autonomy through the curriculum: Principles for designing language courses. *ELT Journal, 54*(2), 109-117. doi:10.1093/elt/54.2.109

Little, D. (1991). *Learner autonomy: Definitions, issues and problems*. Dublin, Ireland: Authentik.

Paquette, G. (2002). *Handbook on information technologies for education and training: Designing virtual learning centers*. Berlin, Germany: Springer Verlag. Retrieved from http://hal.archives-ouvertes.fr/docs/00/19/06/67/PDF/Paquette-Gilbert-Chap16-2001.pdf

Roblyer, M., & Ekhaml, L. (2000). How interactive are your distance courses? A rubric for assessing interactivity in distance learning. *Online Journal of Distance Learning Administration, 3*(2). Retrieved from http://www.westga.edu/~distance/summer32.htm

Rosen, L. D., & Weil, M. M. (1997). *Technostress: Coping with technology @ work @ home @ play*. London, UK: Wiley.

Scheid, K. (1993). *Helping students become strategic learners: Guidelines for teaching*. Cambridge, MA: Brookline Books.

Siragusa, L., Dixon, K. C., & Dixon, R. (2007). Designing quality e-learning environments in higher education. *Proceedings ASCILITE 2007* (pp. 923 -935). Singapore. Retrieved from http://www.ascilite.org.au/conferences/singapore07/procs/siragusa.pdf

Appendix A. Virtual language resource centres

ECI expert: http://englisheci.weebly.com/
Keep Posted: http://keepposted.weebly.com/
Let's speak: https://sites.google.com/site/elbosquespeaksenglish/home
Maths Up: http://maths-up.webnode.es/
Reading Together: http://readingtogether.jimdo.com/
Speaking Corner: http://budy12.wix.com/speakingcorner
Unicor VLRC: http://unicorvlrc.webs.com/
Virtual English for us: http://virtualenglish4us.wix.com/corazonistaandics

university of groningen

Tableaux vivants as vehicles for cultural exchange

Joseph V. Dias[1]

Abstract. Intercultural simulations, such as Barnga (Thiagarajan & Steinwachs, 1990), along with the use of critical incidents (Gibson, 2002; Gropper, 1996), have long been a mainstay of intercultural communication courses and have found their way into English as a second language (ESL) and English as a foreign language (EFL) classrooms (Apedaile & Schill, 2007). In this paper, a computer-mediated communication (CMC)-enhanced cultural exchange project, which is in the spirit of these intercultural simulations, will be described and evaluated. In the process of the exchange project, conducted between universities and high schools in Japan and the United States, students in the respective settings exchanged word associations and tableaux vivants based on the same word prompts. A variety of web tools facilitated the project: the forms and spreadsheets available through Google Drive to gather the word associations; word cloud creation websites to visually represent the word associations; as well as online forums for the two groups to exchange impressions and interpretations. It was found that the exchange facilitated interesting insights and interpretations and allowed for the critical analysis of the concept of culture itself. Some of the artifacts produced through a series of these exchanges will be shown and applications of the project to tandem language learning will be explained.

Keywords: e-tandem, intercultural, tableau, CMC.

1. Introduction

Critical incidents (Gropper, 1996) and intercultural simulations, such as Barnga (Thiagarajan & Steinwachs, 1990), Journey to Sharahad (Darg, 1999) and An Alien Among Us (Powers, 1999), have played an important role in intercultural

---

1. giuseppedias@gmail.com

How to cite this article: Dias, J. V. (2014). Tableaux vivants as vehicles for cultural exchange. In S. Jager, L. Bradley, E. J. Meima, & S. Thouësny (Eds), *CALL Design: Principles and Practice*; Proceedings of the 2014 EUROCALL Conference, Groningen, The Netherlands (pp. 59-64). Dublin: Research-publishing.net. doi:10.14705/rpnet.2014.000195

communication courses, and they are occasionally used in ESL and EFL classrooms (Apedaile & Schill, 2007). They have been used with a wide variety of individuals: business people, missionaries, Peace Corps volunteers, diplomats, not to mention university students studying intercultural communication and foreign languages. These largely task-based simulations, which often involve role play, are intended to make participants more aware of their own cultural values, foster more positive attitudes toward the "other", help in identifying and avoiding stereotypes/ prejudice toward people of other cultures, facilitate the understanding of the sorts of problems that arise when communicating cross-culturally, and aid in navigating through culture shock smoothly and adjust to foreign host cultures with a minimum of tears and heartbreak.

This paper describes and evaluates a CMC-enhanced language and cultural exchange project, created in the spirit of the intercultural simulations noted above, which can be customized for use with students at practically any level or area of specialty. The project involves an exchange of word associations and tableaux vivants that are based on the same word prompts. Tableaux vivants are "living pictures" formed by a group of people who arrange themselves in a particular way, usually for dramatic effect. Concepts selected for the word associations/tableaux are negotiated by the teachers and students of the partner classes. Both word associations and tableaux are elicited to provide a wider range of artifacts to be used in subsequent discussions.

A variety of web tools facilitate the project: the digital affordances utilized in this project include Google Drive's spreadsheets and forms for the gathering of word associations, word cloud creation sites for visually representing the word associations, and forums for the groups to electronically exchange views and interpretations.

2. Method

2.1. Setting up the exchange

Partner classes for the exchange can be arranged through existing personal networks or by initiating an exchange request through online communities, such as those available on Edmodo (a learning management system with a Facebook-like interface2). If carried out as a formal class exchange project, the classes on each side of the exchange may have either a language or culture focus. The first exchange

---

2. https://support.edmodo.com/home#forums/20896730-follow-communities-and-connect-with-teachers

of this type attempted by the author, for example, involved a class of Japanese university students enrolled in an intercultural communication seminar and a class of American secondary school students studying Spanish. Students and teachers negotiated the concepts that were the basis of the word associations (which were to be transformed into word clouds) and corresponding tableaux vivants (which were photographed). The word clouds and the photos of the tableaux became the products and "conversation pieces" of the exchange.

2.2. Word associations

Members of the partner classes record their associations with the concepts selected. Concepts that lend themselves to a wide range of interpretations and representations are preferable. They might include, for example, "love", "sadness", "health", "happiness", "relationship", "peace", "future", and "endurance". They may be customized for exchange settings that share a specialization, such as business (Dias, 2014), in which case the concepts might consist of "honesty", "success", "fairness", "corruption", "trust", and "customer".

The forms feature of Google Drive (https://www.google.com/drive/index.html) can be used by students to record their associations to the concepts. Later, the words are transformed into tag clouds using tag cloud creation sites, such as Wordle (http://www.wordle.net/), Tagxedo (http://www.tagxedo.com/), or TagCrowd (http://tagcrowd.com/).

2.3. Creation of tableaux vivants

Students in the respective classes form groups of three or four. After being briefed about the meaning of tableau vivant, they discuss with fellow group members, for 5-7 minutes, how they will represent the concept(s) they were assigned; chosen from among the prompts previously given for the word associations. Depending on the size of the class and number of concepts, some groups may create multiple tableaux, which are subsequently photographed. A tableau for "innovate" might feature one learner forming a light bulb gesture with his hands over his head, while another learner appears to be snapping her fingers in a "eureka" moment. Every member of the same team must show a different way of representing the assigned concept through the tableau, so it is necessary for the members to discuss what the concept means to them and how they can display their interpretations as a group. The members may also opt to create one unified scene, such as two participants preparing to catch a third who is about to fall, representing trust, or a random assortment of differing interpretations.

2.4. Tableaux vivants juxtaposed with word clouds and exchanged

Juxtapositions of the tableaux and word clouds can be exchanged among the international partners through blog postings or by sharing PowerPoint files (see Figure 1).

Figure 1. Juxtapositions of tableaux vivants and word clouds

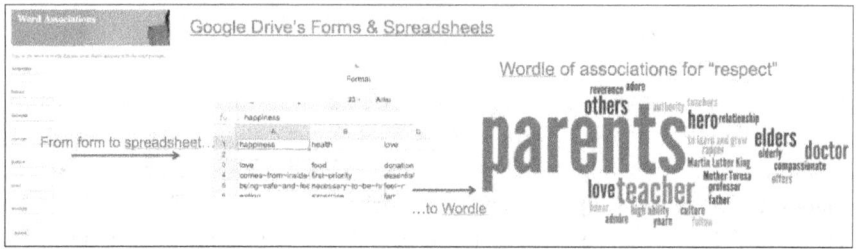

3. Discussion

Students enlarge their vocabulary by familiarizing themselves with the semantic fields encompassed by the word prompts. There are ample opportunities for speaking, as groups must negotiate what their tableaux will look like before performing them for the class. When one is called upon to express a concept through the body, by necessity, it becomes concrete and revealing. It is possible to arrive at the concept's core, confronting preconceptions, feelings, and ambivalences.

Through the relative sizes of words, the tag clouds reveal which ones appeared most frequently and, therefore, represent commonalities among members of the same group. In a written exchange carried out on a forum, groups may be asked to explain the thinking that went into their tableaux and relate it to the assortment of concepts in the corresponding word cloud.

Intergroup comparisons are the real focus of the exchange and similarities revealing common humanity are as significant as divergences that may indicate cultural differences. When comparing representations of "justice", for example, learners might observe that both include "scales of justice", showing that justice is connected with fairness for the two groups, whereas one might associate it more with punishment by showing someone being arrested in the tableau, while the others link it to superheroes (e.g. Ultraman) who provide deus ex machina solutions for the achievement of justice.

The exchange could be carried out as part of an e-tandem language learning project (Brammerts, 1996; O'Rourke, 2007), that is, an electronic exchange between two groups that are native speakers of the target languages that the partner class is learning.

4. Conclusions

Even if the activities described here do not give participating groups incredibly useful insights about their respective cultures, the practice provided in backing up claims about possible contributions of culture to behavior may reduce the predilection to stereotyping and cultural bias.

If this activity is done as an intercultural exchange with another group of business students, for example, as participants write and read analyses of the tableaux and word associations, they may have opportunities to make intercultural comparisons while at the same time reflect upon their own unconscious assumptions and values, leading them to speculate about the implications for business practices when different cultures come in contact.

One of the advantages of collaboration such as that described in this exchange project is that teachers and students on one side of the exchange who may be less well-versed in the technology necessary to accomplish the tasks, can help the other, providing additional opportunities for language and technological exchange.

References

Apedaile, S., & Schill, L. (2007). *Critical incidents for intercultural communication: An interactive tool for developing awareness, knowledge, and skills*. Edmonton, Alberta: NorQuest College. Retrieved from http://www.norquest.ca/NorquestCollege/media/pdf/centres/intercultural/CriticalIncidentsBooklet.pdf

Brammerts, H. (1996). Language learning in tandem using the Internet. In M. Warschauer (Ed.), *Telecollaboration in foreign language learning* (pp. 121-130). Honolulu: University of Hawaii Press.

Darg, P. (1999). *Journey to Sharahad*. Retrieved from http://globaledge.msu.edu/academy/course-content/exercises-and-simulations

Dias, J. V. (2014). Exploring business ethics through tableaux vivants. In C. S. C. Chan & E. Frendo (Eds), *New ways in teaching business English* (pp. 237-40). Alexandria, VA: TESOL.

Gibson, R. (2002). *Intercultural business communication*. Oxford: Oxford University Press.

Gropper, R. C. (1996). *Culture and the clinical encounter*. Yarmouth, Maine: Intercultural Press, Inc.

O'Rourke, B. (2007). Models of telecollaboration (1): eTandem. In R. O'Dowd (Ed.), *Online intercultural exchange: An introduction for foreign language teachers* (pp. 41-61). Clevedon: Multilingual Matters.

Powers, R. B. (1999). *An alien among us: A diversity game*. Yarmouth, Maine: Intercultural Press, Inc.

Thiagarajan, S., & Steinwachs, B. (1990). *Barnga: A simulation game on cultural clashes*. Yarmouth, Maine: Intercultural Press, Inc.

university of groningen

Designing a task based curriculum for intensive language training

Joost Elshoff[1]

Abstract. In this paper, I will report on the progress made in designing a curriculum for intensive language training, in which one-on-one instruction is combined with online exercises and drills to achieve an optimal blend of expertise and technology enhanced language learning. The Common European Framework of Reference (CEFR) has become a crucial tool for assessing language skills as well as for developing courses for students. Working with a very heterogeneous target group and teaching seven different languages in a five-day full immersion setting, it is crucial to continuously focus on the language tasks they need to perform in their target language. A task-based approach, in which language tasks are matched with their corresponding level according to the CEFR and categorized for industry specific domains, was designed and implemented for the development of new course materials. The focus is on combining receptive and productive language skills in realistic contexts, made available in an online learning environment as well as through authentic materials with assignments to promote a thorough understanding and the use of advanced language skills.

Keywords: CEFR, blended learning, task-based language learning, curriculum design.

1. Introduction

This paper discusses the steps taken in the last five years towards designing a task-based curriculum for communicative language learning and teaching in a blended environment. It is taking the best from both worlds: experienced native speaker teachers and technology that provides an environment in which students can boost

---

1. joost.elshoff@gmail.com.

How to cite this article: Elshoff, J. (2014). Designing a task based curriculum for intensive language training. In S. Jager, L. Bradley, E. J. Meima, & S. Thouësny (Eds), *CALL Design: Principles and Practice; Proceedings of the 2014 EUROCALL Conference, Groningen, The Netherlands* (pp. 65-71). Dublin: Research-publishing.net. doi:10.14705/rpnet.2014.000196

their language proficiency through authentic and relevant content and effective drills and exercises.

2. Institutional setting

2.1. History

Figure 1. Three crucial years in the history of the institute

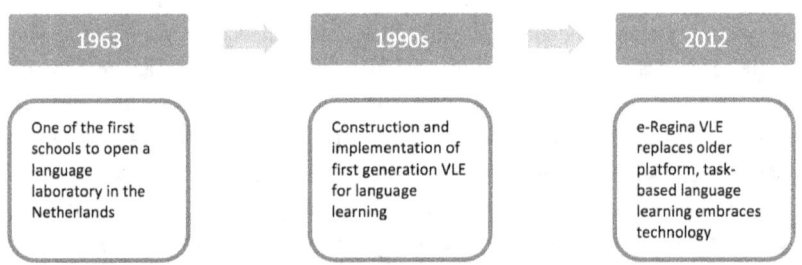

After opening the language laboratory in 1963, it did not take long to understand the importance of technology in language teaching. While the school primarily focused on missionaries and development workers travelling to distant parts of the world, the quality and results achieved in the Regina Coeli language laboratory quickly reached others, such as ambassadors, politicians and highly educated professionals (http://www.reginacoeli.com/about-us/the-nuns-of-vught.html).

Figure 2. The first language lab in Vught (1963)[2]

---

2. This picture is from the archives of Regina Coeli. Reproduced with kind permission from the board of directors (Harm-Jan Bouwknegt, Managing Director, and Esther van Berkel, Director of Studies).

2.2. View on language teaching

Students range from true beginners to near native speakers, and come from various parts of the world to boost their proficiency for their target language. Much of the original view on language teaching is still applied:

- students are individually taught by native speakers of the target language;
- all training programs are tailored to the specific needs of the student;
- teaching sessions alternate with study and practice in the language laboratory;
- all teaching occurs in an immersion setting, with a very limited use of support languages;
- form and correctness are as important as fluency;
- grammar in use and context, vocabulary and communication focus on language tasks the student needs to perform.

The old tape recorders, microphones and headsets were replaced by a virtual learning environments (VLE) in the 1990's, hosting learning materials for input and practice after every individual teaching session on the institute's network. By 2012, this VLE had seen a number of updates and was finally upgraded to e-Regina, incorporating audio, video and various new question and drill types.

In 2001, the language institute implemented CEFR for assessment and teaching. This framework is also used for the creation of 'integrated assignments', combining receptive and productive skills using authentic materials such as television programs, blogs and articles from newspapers and magazines.

3. CEFR, levels, tasks and domains

Designing realistic language tasks for our VLE is a challenging task, since the target we work with is heterogeneous, as can be seen in Figure 3. Furthermore, there are differences between target groups for languages taught at the institute: while the departments teaching English, German, French, Spanish, Portuguese and Italian mainly work with Dutch students, the students in Dutch language courses come from other countries. The Dutch department also works with very varying levels of proficiency, ranging from true beginners (0 - A1.1) to educative native (C1.1) and native speakers attending courses to hone specific skills such as academic or professional writing.

Other departments offer the same type of training, but to a more narrow range: most Dutch students studying a foreign language tend to be somewhat proficient in their target language. Also, whereas students studying Dutch plan to live and work in the Netherlands, most of their Dutch counterparts studying other languages tend to only need the target language in very specific situations, such as weekly international meetings or negotiations.

Figure 3. Student profile for 2012, no data available on 2013[3]

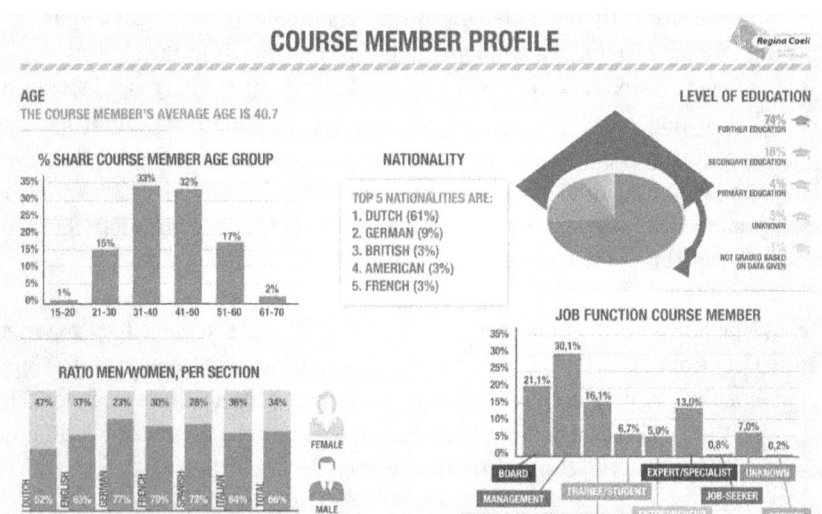

All of the elements described above were taken into account in designing a framework for curriculum and course material development. This approach to needs assessment (NA) is now used by all departments, and applied to their specific target groups:

- identify target group of students (nationality, mother tongue, age, and industry);
- identify domains of language (social, professional, role specific);
- describe language tasks based on CEFR levels for every domain;
- create instructional materials using or based on authentic materials.

All materials focus on a communicative approach to language learning in which the learner's need to communicate in specific situations is central. Assignments typically incorporate reading or listening/viewing tasks with processing tasks.

---

3. http://annualreport.reginacoeli.com

Table 1. Key competences related to CEFR levels as part of curriculum development framework

CEFR level	0 – A2.2	B1.1 – B2.1		B2.2 – C1
Key competence	describe	inform – instruct	motivate – argue	discuss – debate

Figure 4. Example of a domain used in teaching Dutch

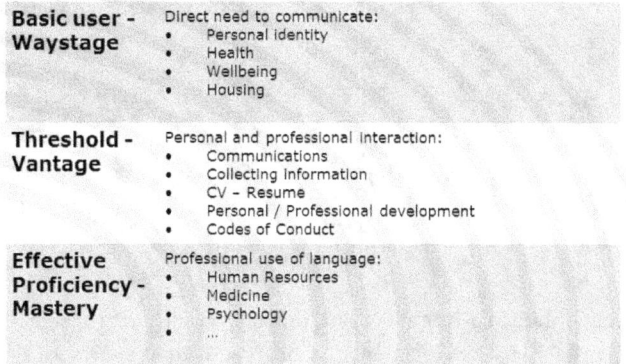

Tasks and assignments in the A-range of CEFR still focus on general topics of interest, such as personal living and employment situation, family, and hobbies. In the mid and high ranges of CEFR, we see a clear differentiation and specialization in learning needs and tasks; whereas the tasks and assignments in the social domain focus on situations anyone would need, the professional domains are more differentiated for industry, role and language tasks required.

4. CALL in the context of an intensive language training

The learner-centered approach to language training can only be effective because of the way learning technology has been incorporated in the curriculum. The blend of personal, one-on-one training and online processing in our online learning environment is key to ensure the results our students aim to achieve. The expertise offered by native speaker language trainers combines well with adequate exposure to the new structures and vocabulary in a student's target language. It also provides ample examples and relevant contexts for the student to practice with.

An intensive, five-day individual training typically consists of up to four 1-hour one-on-one sessions with a teacher and an equal number of sessions in e-Regina, as shown in Figure 5.

Figure 5. Neuner, Krüger, and Grewer's (1981) ABCD-model translated to a 5-day intensive training

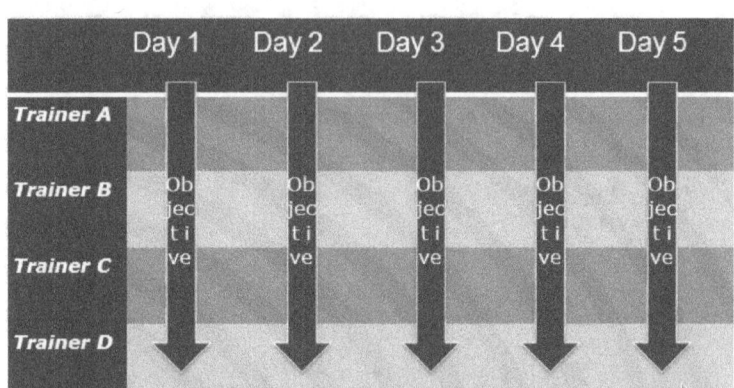

The time spent online in e-Regina is used to work on activities designed to optimize the learning effect, as key elements to be practiced are in series of exercises facilitating input, processing and active use in the target language, following the ABCD-model (Neuner, Krüger, & Grewer, 1981) in which new language elements are learned as follows:

- Input of new language elements through reading and/or listening.
- Guided processing through gap fill or matching exercises.
- Semi-guided processing through answering questions or finishing sentences.
- Conversation or discussion, role playing, and other more open exercises to be done with a teacher.

Stages A, B and C can be facilitated in a VLE, using a wide variety of activities, but stage D is best practiced with a teacher, since it requires direct and adequate feedback only a teacher can provide, although there are only a small number of activities that fall into this category.

5. Conclusions

Task-based language teaching in a communicative setting has been at the centre of the way Language Institute Regina Coeli has designed and developed its curriculum for over 50 years. Rooted in a long tradition of focusing on a student's learning needs and objectives and supported by modern technology, this approach provides the kind of clear results in as short a time as possible.

Needs assessment on multiple levels has always been key to design and develop the language learning experience that is the Regina Coeli approach. By thoroughly understanding our students' learning needs, we are able to create relevant communicative situations and materials for them to work with.

Technology plays a substantial part in optimizing language learning: the e-Regina VLE as well as the extensive library of exercises and authentic materials create an environment that facilitates both teachers and students before, during and after their intensive, individual language training.

Acknowledgements. I would like to thank Esther van Berkel (Director of Studies) and Truusje Franssen (Head of Dutch department) for giving me the opportunity to write and present this paper. Special thanks also go out to Suzanne Driessen (trainer and editor-developer of content integrated learning materials) for her support and for our discussions on educational innovation and e-learning. Last but not least, I would like to thank Annemieke Wagenaar (project lead) and Rob Blatter (trainer and consultant on instructional design) for their useful input and feedback.

References

CEFR. (2001). *Common European Framework of Reference for Languages: Learning, Teaching, Assessment*. Strasbourg: Language Policy Unit. Retrieved from http://www.coe.int/t/dg4/linguistic/Source/Framework_EN.pdf

Neuner, G., Krüger, M., & Grewer, U. (1981). *Übungstypologie zum kommunikativen Deutschunterricht*. Berlin: Langenscheidt.

university of groningen

Integrating CALL in ESOL classrooms: Understanding teachers' perspectives and meeting students' needs

Sara Farshad Nia[1] and Ronnie Davey[2]

Abstract. In line with the needs of the 21st century learners and dramatic improvements in schools' technological infrastructures, it is expected that the integration of digital tools into language learning courses would take a quicker pace and a smoother path. However, current research indicates that although this might be the case for foreign language learning courses, the situation differs for English Speakers of Other Languages (ESOL) classes in New Zealand schools. Despite the availability of various technologies, there is not much tendency for the integration of Computer Assisted Language Learning (CALL) tools into ESOL classrooms. Hence, this ongoing study explores the factors that contribute to the foregoing situation from ESOL teachers' perspectives in a New Zealand context. A series of in-depth interviews were conducted with a group of secondary school ESOL teachers. The initial thematic analysis of the data suggested that any meaningful integration of IT into ESOL environments requires active involvement of teachers, students, and policy makers. Such factors as teachers' professional identity, teacher education and professional development programs, school and ministry policies, and students' demography and their needs impacted ESOL teachers' choice in IT adoption. The findings of this study have significant implications for teachers, teacher educators, and policy makers alike as a more specialized focus on such challenging situations should be taken into consideration when educating ESOL teachers on the integration of CALL.

Keywords: ESOL, CALL, professional development, TPACK, policy making.

---

1. University of Canterbury; sara.farshadnia@pg.canterbury.ac.nz.
2. University of Canterbury; ronnie.davey@canterbury.ac.nz.

How to cite this article: Farshad Nia, S., & Davey, R. (2014). Integrating CALL in ESOL classrooms: Understanding teachers' perspectives and meeting students' needs. In S. Jager, L. Bradley, E. J. Meima, & S. Thouësny (Eds), *CALL Design: Principles and Practice*; Proceedings of the 2014 EUROCALL Conference, Groningen, The Netherlands (pp. 72-76). Dublin: Research-publishing.net. doi:10.14705/rpnet.2014.000197

1. Introduction

A plethora of literature exists on the factors contributing to teachers' uptake of information and communications technology (ICT) into their classrooms. Nevertheless, much of the related literature has tended to focus predominantly on teachers in general but factors impacting the IT adoption of ESOL/ESL teachers have remained understudied, especially in a New Zealand context (Ker, Adams, & Skyrme, 2013). This is significant mainly because the nature of the subject, students' demography, teachers' concerns and students' needs in such courses differ from any other course in the school.

In New Zealand, as in many other countries, ESOL is considered more of a support rather than a language learning course, and therefore, is relatively isolated compared to other disciplines. The system operates in a way that for greater language support, students are withdrawn from the mainstream courses into a smaller group from 3 to 12 hours a week, depending on their language needs. The student population in ESOL classes also varies from that of other classes, usually consisting of refugee, migrant, international fee-paying, and short-term visiting students. Aside from different language levels of students, each group has different needs and seeks a distinctive goal when attending ESOL. Therefore, given the foregoing context, this study aims at investigating the factors that contribute to ESOL teachers' ICT adoption and integration in New Zealand and how they reinforce and influence each other.

2. Method

This ongoing study falls within the domain of inductive research and utilizes a phenomenological approach so as to come to a holistic understanding of ESOL teachers' IT technology integration experiences in their schools. A mixed-method data collection approach was employed by conducting semi-structured interviews with 25 secondary ESOL teachers in New Zealand. The interviews were also followed by attending teacher cluster meetings, observing classes, and analyzing related documents such as online teacher forums and schools' ESOL policies.

3. Discussion

The objective of this research is to identify the factors which ESOL teachers perceive as important in their ICT integration. Among the six main themes emerging from the data, teacher awareness, teacher professional identity, and teacher supportive environment will be addressed in this paper.

3.1. Teacher awareness

Teachers' TPACK knowledge (Koehler & Mishra, 2009) or their awareness of the affordances and constraints of different digital tools in their subject area, such as language learning, was found to be of great significance to the participants. Relevant professional development courses, teachers' connections with colleagues and friends, and teachers' auto-didacticism are the three main interconnected elements that teachers highlighted as the main factors contributing to teacher awareness. The following quotations indicate teachers' confusion regarding both the selection and utilization of programs in their own context while highlighting the role of collegial connections:

> "Teachers don't know what to use. They don't know how it can be used. There is so much out there. You have to know what you want and what is gonna work in your classroom situation and that is the matter of just connecting with others" (Judy).

Similarly, the following teacher has emphasized her own enthusiasm and perseverance along with her connections as a factor in her technology uptake.

> "I do it in my own time because I am interested in it. I am a tweeter user big time and I am connected quite well with IT community, like outside of schools, and students at the university computer sciences. So, they are always coming up with "Hey! You should look at this", or, "Gosh! This is a new app", or "I am doing this", and so, if it catches my imagination, I look at it and think how I can use that" (Fay).

3.2. Teacher professional identity

Professional identity has been conceptualized in various ways through different sub-identities in the literature. Teachers' beliefs and their perceptions of their subject matter (Connelly & Clandinin, 1999), their relationship with students, their collegial interactions (Beijaard, Verloop, & Vermunt, 2000; Silva & Herdeiro, 2014), how teachers are being perceived by themselves and others (Ifanti & Fotopoulou, 2010), and the roles teachers feel they have to play (Ezer, Gilat, & Sagee, 2010) are some of the main features that shape teachers' professional identity and impact their practice.

Four main sub-themes emerged as significant in ESOL teachers' professional identity development and IT integration, namely, relative importance of the content topic, teacher role perceptions, beliefs about students, and beliefs about teaching and learning.

The following are respective examples of the above sub-themes, which further clarify the categorization:

> "Because I am not a course, I don't feel terribly valid and not really motivated" (Emily).

> "Lot of students, they just wanna pass, get their credits, get out the other side. So how am I gonna help them achieve that? Maybe it's not focusing on so much ESOL technology" (Elizabeth).

> "In myself, I didn't want the technology be an excuse for me to give up teaching. I said no, I want to connect with my students' world. It's the world they are in, Facebook and Twitter" (Jo).

3.3. Teacher supportive environment

Human technical and affective support and schools' supportive policies are the two main elements generating a supportive milieu. The immediate availability of a technician, colleague, family member, or techno-savvy student creates a supportive human atmosphere through which teachers can eliminate their fear of technology and enhance their IT integration experience. This is evident in the following statement by one of the teachers interviewed:

> "We are very lucky here. We have got an IT department and a help desk or often one or the other of us [teachers] is in the classroom next door and we usually run across or grab somebody and they can help us. We also have IT angels, a student who is quite good at IT, to help out" (Becky).

Schools' supportive policies include ministry and school ESOL policies with regards to ESOL position in the school, ESOL financial and technological support, assessment policies, material development policies, and ESOL teacher recruitment policies. The following are some of the examples corresponding to these factors:

> "Everyone is working in a group; they learn off each other, feed each other, to help this work for their department. The languages are doing the same. I have to do everything, I get frustrated and there is no one else there doing it with me" (Rebecca).

"ESOL is like the broom cupboard, because ESOL is usually seen as just an add-on, or something you can do without. ESOL is marginalized, we can push from below, but it needs to come from the top" (Nikki).

"The ESOL teachers are really struggling to find those resources that they really need to help them. People are not getting as much help as there could be from the system" (Sarah).

4. Conclusions

The aim of this study was to understand ESOL teachers' perceptions of the factors that contribute to their technology integration. The findings signify a need for recognition of ESOL teachers' role and position in schools, and the need for the implementation of supportive policies from the ministry and schools. These may include providing subject-related ESOL professional development opportunities, generating relevant material and resources, and more IT-compatible assessment procedures. The results indicate that although teachers value the integration of CALL into their syllabi, it is not among their top priorities, largely due to various problems they face, that are unique to their environment.

References

Beijaard, D., Verloop, N., & Vermunt, J. D. (2000). Teachers' perceptions of professional identity: An exploratory study from a personal knowledge perspective. *Teaching and Teacher Education, 16*(7), 749-764. doi:10.1016/S0742-051X(00)00023-8

Connelly, F. M., & Clandinin, D. J. (1999). S*haping a professional identity: Stories of educational practice*. New York: Teachers College Press.

Ezer, H., Gilat, I., & Sagee, R. (2010). Perception of teacher education and professional identity among novice teachers. *European Journal of Teacher Education, 33*(4), 391-404. doi:10.1080/02619768.2010.504949

Ifanti, A. A., & Fotopoulou, V. S. (2010). Undergraduate students' and teachers' perceptions of professional development and identity formation: A case study in Greece. *KEDI Journal of Educational Policy, 7*(1), 157-174.

Ker, A., Adams, R., & Skyrme, G. (2013). Research in applied linguistics and language teaching and learning in New Zealand (2006-2010). *Language Teaching, 46*(2), 225-255. doi:10.1017/S0261444812000535

Koehler, M. J., & Mishra, P. (2009). What is technological pedagogical content knowledge? *Contemporary Issues in Technology and Teacher Education, 9*(1), 60-70.

Silva, A. M., & Herdeiro, R. (2014). The work, perceptions and professional development of teachers. *Teaching Education, 25*(2), 184-201. doi:10.1080/10476210.2012.759554

Digital literacy and netiquette: Awareness and perception in EFL learning context

Sara Farshad Nia[1] and Susan Marandi[2]

Abstract. With the growing popularity of digital technologies and computer-mediated communication (CMC), various types of interactive communication technology are being increasingly integrated into foreign/second language learning environments. Nevertheless, due to its nature, online communication is susceptible to misunderstandings and miscommunications, which necessitates online learners' awareness of existing netiquette (i.e. network etiquette) rules (Shetzer & Warschauer, 2000). This paper, therefore, reports on a comparative study on the degree to which 75 English as a foreign language (EFL) learners and their 53 native English counterparts were familiar with netiquette rules and perceived them as useful. A netiquette familiarity test consisting of ten questions and a netiquette attitude questionnaire consisting of 30 Likert scale items were developed by the researchers based on Shea (1994), Hambridge (1995), and Gil (2006). It was pilot tested, validated, and administered to the participants. Results indicated that familiarity was low among the EFL learners and that they were not as much convinced of the necessity and usefulness of netiquette rules as the other group. The results suggest that despite the significance of the issue, scant attention is paid to preparing students for a 21st century language learning environment and integrating the ethics of CMC and netiquette into educating digitally literate EFL learners. The findings of this study are relevant to language teacher education, materials development, and interlanguage pragmatics.

Keywords: netiquette awareness, digital literacy, communication breakdown, e-politeness.

---

1. School of Teacher Education, University of Canterbury, New Zealand; sara.farshadnia@pg.canterbury.ac.nz.
2. School of Languages and Literature, Alzahra University, Iran; susanmarandi@alzahra.ac.ir.

How to cite this article: Farshad Nia, S., & Marandi, S. (2014). Digital literacy and netiquette: Awareness and perception in EFL learning context. In S. Jager, L. Bradley, E. J. Meima, & S. Thouësny (Eds), *CALL Design: Principles and Practice*; Proceedings of the 2014 EUROCALL Conference, Groningen, The Netherlands (pp. 77-82). Dublin: Research-publishing.net. doi:10.14705/rpnet.2014.000198

1. Introduction

Since communication via email, due to its cost-effectiveness and ease of access, has become a prevalent channel of communication, dealing with netiquette issues and the concept of e-politeness has immensely grown in significance, particularly among language learners (Chen, 2006). This is mainly because the netiquette of any particular online group embodies the culture and values of that group (Herring, 1996), and "the convenience brought by the computer-mediated communication does not guarantee effective intercultural communication" (Hsieh, 2009, p. 1). Therefore, to maintain successful communication, one should have a practical knowledge of norms of behaviour and adhere to specific patterns of social interaction and netiquette rules (Hymes, 1974; Saville-Troike, 2003). Notwithstanding the concern that such international "rules" have been formulated without consideration of the "beliefs/culture/comfort" of all stakeholders (Marandi, 2013), if language learners aim at being successful communicators, they have to become familiar with the online culture of the target language they are learning. Hence, this research aims at measuring the familiarity, awareness, and attitudes of online EFL learners and their native counterparts towards the online behaviour rules.

2. Method

A netiquette familiarity test (Reliability: 0.746) and a netiquette attitude questionnaire (Reliability: 0.827) are the instruments used in this study. The former consists of 17 questions: seven in the form of multiple-choice items, two true/false questions, and the remaining eight are open-ended essay-type questions. The overall format and content of the questionnaire was adapted from netiquette quizzes and web pages (Gil, 2006; Hambridge, 1995; Shea, 1994), originally designed for online applicants to test their netiquette knowledge. The questionnaire encompasses a wide range of diverse issues related to online communication such as observing email symbolism, respecting communicators' privacy, adopting an appropriate subject line, and avoiding personal or flaming emails.

The netiquette attitude questionnaire attempts to elicit participants' attitudes towards and beliefs about the necessity, adequacy and significance of netiquette rules. This questionnaire is composed of 30 six-point Likert scale questions. The first 13 questions deal with the adequacy of certain online behaviours and netiquette rules. The remaining questions deal with the necessity of performing particular actions or following particular rules. The questionnaires were administered to 75 non-native and 53 native speakers of English who were members of different online ESOL and language learning communities and mailing lists. Participation was voluntary and data collection was carried out in accordance with the human ethics requirements.

3. Discussion

3.1. Familiarity

The results of the familiarity of the participants with netiquette rules revealed that direct correlation existed between the level of scores and the participants' netiquette familiarity.

Table 1. Descriptive statistics results of the native/non-native English students on the netiquette familiarity scores

Score	English Language Learners (non-native)		Native English Speakers	
	Statistic	Std. Error	Statistic	Std. Error
Mean	3.51	.203	6.70	.215
Median	4.00		7.00	
Variance	3.091		2.446	
Std. Deviation	1.758		1.564	
Minimum	0		3	
Maximum	7		9	
Skewness	.012	.277	-.603	.327
Kurtosis	-1.062	.548	-.255	.644

According to Brown (1997), the amount of skewness and kurtosis are considered acceptable if their standard error times two is more than the absolute value of their statistics. According to the above assumption and based on Table 1, it can be observed that for both native and non native speakers the distribution is normal since the amount of skewness and kurtosis are considered acceptable as 0.277×2 > |0.012| and 0.548×2> |1.062| and 0.327×2 > |0.603| and 0.644×2> |0.255|. As the majority of the results supported the normal distribution of scores of both groups, an independent samples t-test was conducted on the native and non-natives' netiquette familiarity test results to see if a significant difference exists between the two sets of scores. Since Levene's Test for Equality of Variances in Table 2 did not indicate a significant difference in the variances ($F=2.686$, $p>0.05$), the equal variances assumption was accepted and the top line value was used. The results revealed that there was a significant difference between the non-native and native participants,

$t(126)=10.582$; $p<0.05$, and based on Table 1, since the mean score of the native English speakers was higher than that of English language learners (6.70>3.51), it can be concluded that the native participants were significantly more familiar with netiquette rules than the Language learners.

Table 2. Independent samples t-test on the familiarity netiquette test scores for English language learners and native English speakers

Score	Levene's Test for Equality of Variances		t-test for Equality of Means					95% Confidence Interval of the Difference	
	F	Sig.	t	df	Sig. (2-tailed)	Mean Difference	Std. Error Difference	Lower	Upper
Equal variances assumed	2.685	.104	10.582	126	.000	3.191	.302	2.595	3.788
Equal variances not assumed			10.798	119.427	.000	3.191	.296	2.606	3.777

3.2. Necessity and adequacy

The Chi-square test results on the attitude questionnaire (Table 4) revealed that there was a significant difference between both groups ($2=55.51$, $df=5$, $p<0.05$) and native participants gave significantly more weight to the necessity and adequacy of the netiquette rules (Table 3).

Table 3. Total results on the members' attitude towards the adequacy and necessity of netiquette rules

Group			Options							Total
			Very Appropriate/ Necessary	Appropriate/ Necessary	No Difference	Inappropriate/ Unnecessary	Totally Inappropriate/ unnecessary	Undecided		
Non-native	Count		463	698	203	230	47	159		1800
	Expected Count		533.8	685.0	211.5	203.3	39.3	127.1		1800.0
	% within Group		25.7%	38.8%	11.3%	12.8%	2.6%	8.8%		100.0%
	% within Options		50.8%	59.7%	56.2%	66.3%	70.1%	73.3%		58.6%
Native sp.	Count		448	471	158	117	20	58		1272
	Expected Count		377.2	484.0	149.5	143.7	27.7	89.9		1272.0
	% within Group		35.2%	37.0%	12.4%	9.2%	1.6%	4.6%		100.0%
	% within Options		49.2%	40.3%	43.8%	33.7%	29.9%	26.7%		41.4%
Total	Count		911	1169	361	347	67	217		3072
	Expected Count		911.0	1169.0	361.0	347.0	67.0	217.0		3072.0
	% within Group		29.7%	38.1%	11.8%	11.3%	2.2%	7.1%		100.0%
	% within Options		100.0%	100.0%	100.0%	100.0%	100.0%	100.0%		100.0%

Table 4. Chi-Square test results on attitudes towards netiquette

	Value	df	Asymp. Sig. (2-sided)
Pearson Chi-Square	55.514[a]	5	.000
Likelihood Ratio	56.577	5	.000
N of Valid Cases	3072		

Based on the results, the non-native speakers have a higher rate of unfamiliarity with netiquette rules and depicted less of a sense of necessity and usefulness for such rules in online environments. Therefore, it can be argued that the perceived usefulness of netiquette rules is positively related to the degree of familiarity with them. The results of this study support Wotruba, Chonko, and Loe's (2001) study on the positive relation that existed between perceived usefulness of ethics codes and the degree of familiarity with such codes. The results are also in line with the studies done on e-politeness and online intercultural communication. Biesenbach-Lucas (2007), who has examined e-politeness among native and non-native speakers, argued that native speakers create more polite messages towards their instructors than non-native speakers do. Studies on non-native students' writing request e-mails to their professors also showed lack of sufficient pragmatic knowledge to write appropriate emails (Chen, 2006).

4. Conclusions

This study is primarily concerned with the international communicative norms of behaviour in online communication, also known as netiquette rules. The results revealed that there exists a significant dearth of knowledge of such norms on the non-native English participants' part. Furthermore, it was also revealed that non-native speakers' perceived usefulness of such rules were also quite low. Thus, to compensate for the dearth of knowledge in this area, netiquette should be included and taught explicitly in classroom lessons (Shetzer & Warschauer, 2000). According to Wotruba et al. (2001), "when familiarity occurs, the code will begin to play a role in shaping the ethical climate and familiarity will allow the recognition of its usefulness as a guide to their behaviour" (p. 3). Therefore, the usefulness of netiquette rules as a tool in guiding online behaviour and the application of such codes of online behaviour will be strengthened as internet users become more familiar with the content and intentions of those codes.

References

Biesenbach-Lucas, S. (2007). Students writing emails to faculty: An examination of e-politeness among native and non-native speakers of English. *Language Learning and Technology, 11*(2), 59-81.

Brown, J. D. (1997). Skewness and kurtosis. *Shiken: JALT Testing & Evaluation SIG Newsletter, 1*(1), 20-23. Retrieved from http://www.jalt.org/test/PDF/Brown1.pdf

Chen, C. E. (2006). The development of e-mail literacy: From writing to peers to writing to authority figures. *Language Learning and Technology, 10*(2), 35-55. Retrieved from http://llt.msu.edu/vol10num2/pdf/chen.pdf

Gil, P. (2006). The famous netiquette quiz, level2. *About.com*. Retrieved from http://netforbeginners.about.com/library/quizzes2006/bl_netiquetteQL2.htm

Hambridge, S. (1995, October). RFC1855 (Netiquette Guidelines). *Intel Corp*. Retrieved from https://www.ietf.org/rfc/rfc1855.txt

Herring, S. C. (1996). *Computer-mediated communication: Linguistic, social and cross-cultural perspectives*. Amsterdam: Benjamins. doi:10.1075/pbns.39

Hsieh, S. C. (2009). *(Im)politeness in email communication: How English speakers and Chinese speakers negotiate meanings and develop intercultural (mis)understandings*. Unpublished doctoral dissertation, University of Birmingham, United Kingdom. Retrieved from http://etheses.bham.ac.uk/337/1/hsieh09PhD.pdf

Hymes, D. H. (1974). *Foundations in sociolinguistics: An ethnographic approach*. Philadelphia: University of Pennsylvania Press.

Marandi, S. S. (2013). Computer-assisted language learning. In R. Akbari & C. Coombe (Eds), *Middle East handbook of applied linguistics* (pp. 185-208). Dubai, United Arab Emirates: TESOL Arabia.

Saville-Troike, M. (2003). *The ethnography of communication: An introduction*. Malden, Mass: Blackwell. doi:10.1002/9780470758373

Shea, V. (1994). *Netiquette*. San Francisco: Albion Books

Shetzer, H., & Warschauer, M. (2000). An electronic literacy approach to network-based language teaching. In M. Warschauer & R. Kern (Eds), *Network-based language teaching: Concepts and practice*. New York: Cambridge University Press.

Wotruba, T. R., Chonko, L. B., & Loe, T. W. (2001). The impact of ethics code familiarity on manager behavior. *Journal of Business Ethics, 33*(3), 59-69. doi:10.1023/A:1011925009588

university of groningen

A context-aware solution in mobile language learning

Majid Fatahipour[1] and Mahnaz Ghaseminajm[2]

Abstract. Despite obvious benefits, some challenges exist in the way of sustainable utilization of mobile phone technology for language learning tasks. This paper shows how these challenges can be better addressed in the light of recent advancements in mobile phone technology, like context aware mobile learning, informed with a sound pedagogical basis for providing content. Since many models presented so far are either atheoretical or obtain their theory from fields other than language learning, we show how the Four Strands model (Nation, 2007) as an insider model can fit for this purpose, with its related tasks balancing the selected content used in customizing each learner profile, such as scanning data from background knowledge and location every few hours to trace if the user is following the same saved patterns and update the streamlined content when necessary. The resulting interactions are made possible and fit for the purpose through a novel context-aware framework which enables implementation of all Four Strands in language learning.

Keywords: context-awareness, mobile language learning, four strands model.

1. Introduction

The first time mobile phones are used for language learning purposes simply began with the utilization of SMS, i.e. text messaging. This was a good enough start at the time given the basic technology of those days. Its operation is so straightforward that it has still the most visible use in a country like Iran. There has been extensive research conducted on the use of mobile phones in language learning, which typically focused on SMS (e.g. Kennedy & Levy, 2008). Nowadays, we can go far beyond using SMS since it is only based on an early technology which under-

---

1. Islamic Azad University, Parand Branch, Tehran-Iran; majifata@yahoo.com.
2. Huddersfield University, Huddersfield, UK.

How to cite this article: Fatahipour, M., & Ghaseminajm, M. (2014). A context-aware solution in mobile language learning. In S. Jager, L. Bradley, E. J. Meima, & S. Thouësny (Eds), *CALL Design: Principles and Practice*; *Proceedings of the 2014 EUROCALL Conference, Groningen, The Netherlands* (pp. 83-87). Dublin: Research-publishing.net. doi:10.14705/rpnet.2014.000199

represents the potential of mobile language learning today and its use was not context aware. Moreover, as specified by Viberg and Grönlund (2012), most Mobile Assisted Language Learning (MALL) studies are experimental and small-scale, and most theories are used only in one or a few papers (p. 9). They further point out that this kind of approach raises the issue of the reliability of findings across changing technologies and over time; in terms of gained linguistic knowledge and skills, most attention is paid to learners' vocabulary acquisition, listening and speaking skills (Viberg & Grönlund, 2012, p. 9). Other components of language acquisition such as grammar, pronunciation and writing are not well-represented. As far as we know, a unified and comprehensive model that addresses language components in a balanced manner has not been employed.

2. Background and literature review

Intrusiveness, cost, practical technological constraints and pedagogical methodologies are the four factors challenging the success of mobile language learning tasks (Burston, 2014a, 2014b). In most MALL tasks, a series of regular or daily notifications intrude on learners' privacy because the users have little control or choice as long as they subscribe to the service. Apps, on the other hand, can be stored to wait for the user to take the initiative and use them. However, such 'push' or 'pull' pedagogical resources used to be expensive and each has their own disadvantages of intrusiveness and visibility (Kennedy & Levy, 2008). There are also plenty of practical technological constraints; a small screen would make it hard to work with, and graphics can be hard to present. The dependence on network spread and strength of transmission could also be another downside, as well as cost. Most apps are developed by computer specialists without employing insights from the field of language teaching. In spite of such limitations, mobile devices are still regarded as effective tools for distributing language learning materials to the learners. In this case, context-aware applications are non-intrusive and can be far less costly. A review of recent research on mobile apps on language acquisition shows that a wide-ranging investigation has been done. For instance, Hsu, Wang, and Comac (2008) found that the students' reception of mobile-accessible audioblog to submit and archive oral assessments have been more than its production. Oberg and Daniels (2013) found out that students show better performance when they use an iPod Touch at their own pace in classrooms.

The results of such research frequently points out optimism amongst learners towards the use of mobile technology in language learning or improving language ability. Less consideration "is devoted to individuals' language learning strategies and learning styles when employing mobile devices for their language learning"

(Viberg & Grönlund, 2012, p. 15). This is exactly where context awareness contributes the content which is streamlined to users' preferences and needs. The use of mobile technologies in learning grants several benefits such as flexibility, low cost-effectiveness, sizeability and user-friendliness, the features that researchers also consider to use in order to sustain language learning (Huang, Huang, Huang, & Lin, 2012).

3. Discussion

It is clear that a good theory should be multidisciplinary. One of the comprehensive language learning models that has captured the imagination of language teachers worldwide and been practiced in so many countries with promising results is Nation's (2007) Four Strands model. It encompasses all language skills and provides a unique classification that includes all skills and components of a language for the learner and recommends a realistic and balanced approach towards practicing and mastering all of them. The principle of the Four Strands is a comprehensive and widely accepted theoretical operationalization for language learning from which we have shown how it can fit in well with the requirements of mobile language learning. It posits that a well-balanced language course should have four equal strands: meaning focused input, meaning focused output, language focused learning, and fluency development (Nation, 2007). Meaning focused input includes activities such as "watching TV shows, movies, extensive reading, listening to radio or music or being a listener in a conversation" (De la Rouviere, 2012, para. 8). Meaning focused output is composed of activities such as diary keeping, note-writing, blogging, conversing, speech making as well as giving instructions. Language-focused learning is another strand that includes grammar, vocabulary, spelling, pronunciation and discourse – "deliberate learning can 'raise consciousness to help later learning' " (De la Rouviere, 2012, section 4, para. 2). Finally, the fluency development strand involves improving speed and spontaneity in all four skills. This is where our proposed context-aware mobile language learning framework comes in, to identify which content is most suitable for which learner in a given context. The above contents are based on the vocabulary learning framework in another language, initially proposed by Nation (2001).

In the next section, the architecture of context-aware mobile learning apps is explained. The summary of a sample of relating the learners' context to appropriate content, according to the Four Strands model, is shown in Table 1. The first column shows the Four Strands according to Nation's (2007) innovative and useful model. The second column is a list of possible topics and tasks to be fed into the learners' mobile device, stored in the data bank or content database. The last column also shows the most appropriate context for providing the content, divided between 'At home', when concentration is normally higher, and 'Commuting' mode, when noise of vehicles distracts the learners' attention.

Table 1. The relationship between Four Strands, topics and context

Strands	Possible Topics/Tasks	Context
Meaning focused output	diary keeping, note-writing, blogging, conversing, speech making as well as giving instructions	At home
Meaning focused input	"watching TV shows, movies, extensive reading, listening to radio or music or being a listener in a conversation" (De la Rouviere, 2012, para. 8)	Commuting
Language focused learning	grammar, vocabulary, spelling, pronunciation and discourse	Commuting
Fluency development	improving fluency in all four skills of the target language, making the learner quicker and more confident in using the language	At home

4. Conclusion

As a concluding remark, a framework for context-aware mobile learning apps is proposed. It initially consists of identifying the strands of learning and then defining tasks and topics according to this robust theoretical basis and matching those tasks and topics with different users' contexts. Thus, this study confirms the importance of focusing on user profiles, preferences, and learning styles of users to personalize the learning experience of users as was preliminarily mentioned in Fatahipour and Ghesemi Najm (2013). Following a context-aware framework informed by theory preserves the best gains from mobile language learning for students.

References

Burston, J. (2014a). A survey of MALL curriculum integration: What the published research doesn't tell. *CALICO Journal, 31*(3), 303-322. doi:10.11139/cj.31.3.303-322

Burston, J. (2014b). The reality of MALL project implementations: Still on the fringes. *CALICO Journal, 31*(1), 43-65. doi:10.11139/cj.31.1.103-125

De la Rouviere, N. (2012, June). The four strands of language learning. *Confused Laowai* [web blog]. Retrieved from http://confusedlaowai.com/2012/06/four-strands-language-learning/

Fatahipour, M., & Ghasemi Najm, M. (2013). Quality of sms-learning as a rapidly growing m-learning mode for foreign language learning. In *QScience Proceedings: Vol. 2013, 12th World Conference on Mobile and Contextual Learning (mLearn 2013), 30.* doi:10.5339/qproc.2013.mlearn.30

Hsu, H.-Y., Wang, S.-K., & Comac, L. (2008). Using audioblogs to assist English-language learning: An investigation into student perception. *Computer Assisted Language Learning, 21*(2), 181-198. doi:10.1080/09588220801943775

Huang, Y.-M., Huang, Y.-M., Huang, S.-H, & Lin, Y.-T. (2012). A ubiquitous English vocabulary learning system: Evidence of active/passive attitudes vs. usefulness/ease-of-use. *Computers and Education, 58*(1), 273-282. doi:10.1016/j.compedu.2011.08.008

Kennedy, C., & Levy, M. (2008). L'italiano al telefonino: Using SMS to support beginners' language learning. *ReCALL Journal, 20*(3), 315-330. doi:10.1017/S0958344008000530

Nation, P. (2001). *Learning vocabulary in another language.* Cambridge: Cambridge University Press. doi:10.1017/CBO9781139524759

Nation, P. (2007). The four strands. *Innovation in Language Learning and Teaching, 1*(1), 2-13. doi:10.2167/illt039.0

Oberg, A., & Daniels, P. (2013). Analysis of the effect a student-centred mobile learning instructional method has on language acquisition. *Computer Assisted Language Learning, 26*(2), 177-196. doi:10.1080/09588221.2011.649484

Viberg, O., & Grönlund, Å. (2012). Mobile assisted language learning: A literature review. *mLearn, CEUR Workshop Proceedings, 955* (pp. 9-16). Retrieved from CEUR-WS.org

university of groningen

Investigating an open methodology for designing domain-specific language collections

Alannah Fitzgerald[1], Shaoqun Wu[2], and Martin Barge[3]

Abstract. With this research and design paper, we are proposing that Open Educational Resources (OERs) and Open Access (OA) publications give increasing access to high quality online educational and research content for the development of powerful domain-specific language collections that can be further enhanced linguistically with the Flexible Language Acquisition System (FLAX, http://flax.nzdl.org). FLAX uses the Greenstone digital library system, which is a widely used open-source software that enables end users to build collections of documents and metadata directly onto the Web (Witten, Bainbridge, & Nichols, 2010). FLAX offers a powerful suite of interactive text-mining tools, using Natural Language Processing and Artificial Intelligence designs, to enable novice collections builders to link selected language content to large pre-processed linguistic databases. An open methodology trialed at Queen Mary University of London in collaboration with the OER Research Hub at the UK Open University demonstrates how applying open corpus-based designs and technologies can enhance open educational practices among language teachers and subject academics for the preparation and delivery of courses in English for Specific Academic Purposes (ESAP).

Keywords: corpus-based language learning, ESAP, OER, open access, user interface design, teacher education, British law reports corpus, MOOC.

---

1. Concordia University; alannahfitzgerald@gmail.com.
2. University of Waikato; shaoqunyw@gmail.com.
3. Queen Mary University of London; m.i.barge@qmul.ac.uk.

How to cite this article: Fitzgerald, A., Wu, S., & Barge, M. (2014). Investigating an open methodology for designing domain-specific language collections. In S. Jager, L. Bradley, E. J. Meima, & S. Thouësny (Eds), *CALL Design: Principles and Practice; Proceedings of the 2014 EUROCALL Conference, Groningen, The Netherlands* (pp. 88-95). Dublin: Research-publishing.net. doi:10.14705/rpnet.2014.000200

1. Introduction

More so than ever, we have increasing access to a range of authentic open content online, such as lectures and podcasts, e-books/textbooks, research publications, blogs, wikis, as well as free and open online tools for their linguistic analyses. Designing easy-to-use interfaces for the use of these linguistic tools is a key requirement for their uptake by non-expert users, namely learners, teachers, subject academics, instructional designers and language resource developers. The Open Educational Resources and Open Access movements within higher education provide a compelling opportunity for the development of derivative domain-specific language learning resources. The field of Computer Assisted Language Learning (CALL) is now presented with a large supply of interesting linguistic material relevant to specific subject areas, including text, supplementary images (slides), audio and video. Such material can be automatically analysed, enriched, and transformed into corpus-based resources that learners can browse and query in order to extend their ability to understand the language used, and help them to express themselves more fluently and eloquently in target subject domains.

Uses for domain-specific corpora in language learning and teaching are increasing in popularity (Gabrielatos, 2005; Stubbs & Barth, 2003). Salient lexico-grammatical patterns are easily identified and retrieved by corpus tools when corpora are derived from genres and certain types of document that predominate in domain-specific areas.

Many studies have been conducted into the perceived usefulness of corpora and concordancers for the search, analysis, retrieval and transfer of language items in language learning. Usability studies on the design and presentation of linguistic data by concordancers and corpus-based systems for uptake by language learners have not yet featured prominently in the research literature into CALL, however.

Collections in FLAX use an automated scheme that extracts recurrent grammatical patterns and phrases from text and presents them in an augmented text interface, designed for the non-expert corpus user (Wu & Witten, Forthcoming). Rather than relying on complex search commands to query corpora within involved concordancer interfaces (which have been designed by and for the corpus linguist), FLAX links relevant tools and resources into streamlined online interfaces for the language learner. For example, in the ESAP collections, FLAX connects to the open-source Wikipedia Miner toolkit to extract key concepts and their definitions from Wikipedia articles (Milne & Witten, 2013) to assist with reading and vocabulary as can be seen in Figure 1.

Figure 1. FLAX augmented text interface
with wikify function in Law Collections

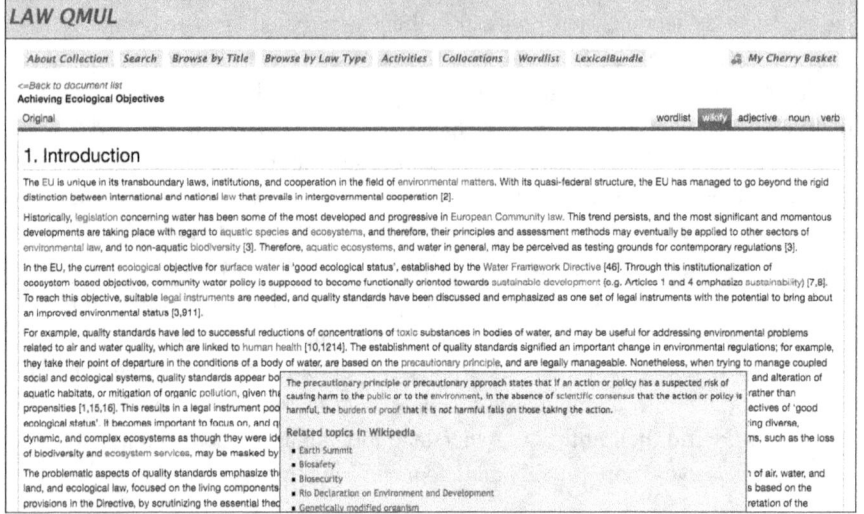

2. Method

2.1. Open domain-specific collections building in FLAX

"Use of OER leads to critical reflection by educators, with [...] improvement in their practice" (OER Research Hub, n.d., para. 1). This is one of a cluster of research hypotheses currently under investigation at the OER Research Hub for the development of open language corpora in FLAX in collaboration with Queen Mary University of London (QMUL).

Table 1. Type, number and source of items in the FLAX Law Collections

Type of media	Number and source of corpus items
Open Access Law research articles	40 Articles (DOAJ - Directory of OA Journals, with Creative Commons for the development of derivatives)
MOOC lecture transcripts/videos (streamed via YouTube/Vimeo)	4 MOOC Collections: Copyright Law (Harvard/edX), English Common Law (University of London/Coursera), Age of Globalization (Texas at Austin/edX), Environmental Law and Politics (OpenYale)
Podcast audio files/transcripts (OpenSpires)	10-15 Lectures (Oxford Law Faculty and the Centre for Socio-Legal Studies)
PhD Law thesis writing	50-70 EThoS Theses (sections: abstracts, introductions, conclusions) at the British Library (OA but not licensed Creative Commons – permissions granted by HEIs)
British Law Reports Corpus (BLaRC)	8.5 million-word corpus developed by María José Marín Pérez. Derived from free legal sources at the British and Irish Legal Information Institute (BAILII) aggregation website

Domain-specific law collections in FLAX were developed for ESAP students taking the Law Pathway on the summer pre-sessional and the Critical Thinking and Writing in Law In-Sessional programmes at QMUL. The law collections in FLAX are centred on the re-use of OER and OA research publications in the target domain of Law, as can be seen in Table 1. It is anticipated that these collections for legal English will be of use across both formal and informal language learning and translation contexts.

2.2. Formatting resources for use in FLAX

Text extracts of longer than 2-3,000 words are likely to halt or crash the FLAX server application, due to the quantity of text parsing that the FLAX server can efficiently process in a given time. Therefore, source texts have to be divided into sections of not more than 2-3,000 words in length.

Source articles are often downloadable in .pdf format, and are often accessible as full web documents. However, text extracts intended for upload to the FLAX website need to be marked up in HTML. Even with knowledge of HTML, the process of marking up each text extract is a time-consuming process. It was therefore decided to develop a web-based formatting tool, implemented using JavaScript, as can be seen in Figure 2 to ease the process of converting sections of text to HTML.

Figure 2. FLAX HTML resource formatting tool

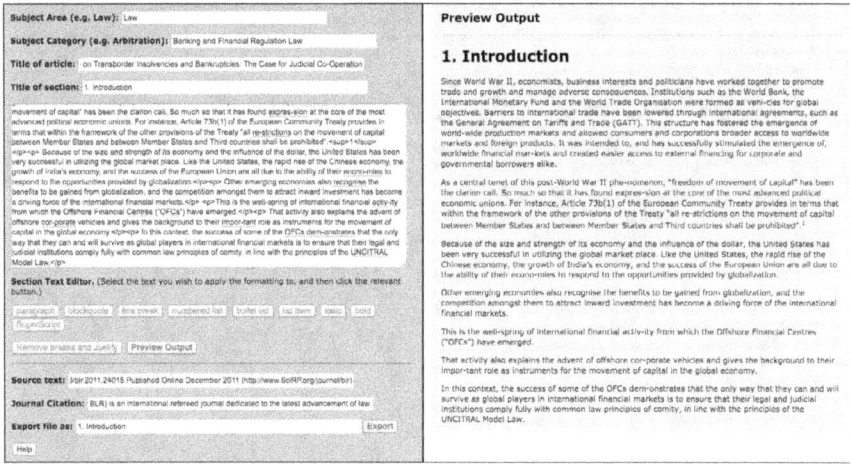

The user can paste copied text into a main text field, and paste/type the article title and section headings into labelled boxes. HTML tag buttons enable the user to insert tags at relevant points in the text in order to re-format as required. When the file is exported, using the 'Export' button, the tool generates the HTML file, using the text input by the user. The tool is still in early stages of development and can only handle basic text formatting functions. However, further iterations of the tool are planned (e.g. the inclusion of colour-coded tags for enhanced user readability; the ability to insert image links).

3. Discussion

3.1. Learning collocations in FLAX

Among other aspects of language, the ESAP for law collections in FLAX provide an excellent context in which to study collocations, a notoriously challenging aspect of English productive use even for quite advanced learners (Bishop, 2004; Nesselhauf, 2003).

Figure 3. Collocations in Law QMUL Collections linked to FLAX Wikipedia collocations database

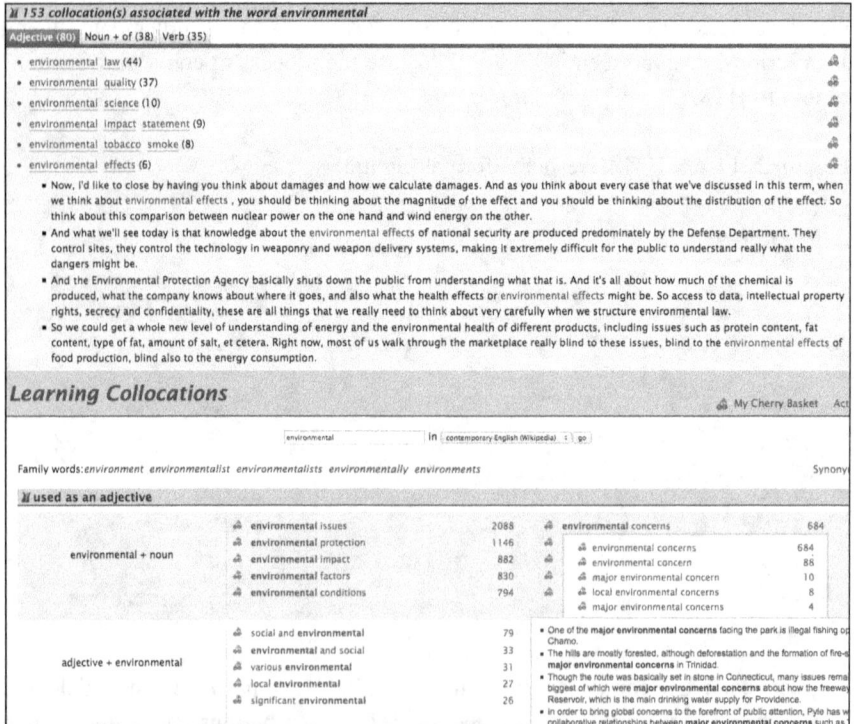

Figure 3 shows the result for the word *environmental*, which returns 153 collocations in the OpenYale lectures. Collocations are grouped under tabs that reflect the syntactic roles of the associated word or words: adjective (shown), noun + *of*, verb. The underlined words, *environmental* and *effects*, are hyperlinked to entries for those words in an external collocations database[4] built from a Wikipedia-derived corpus of 200 million articles. For example, clicking on the link for *environmental* generates a further collocations popup that lists *environmental issues*, *environmental protection*, etc., along with their frequency and their context in this much larger corpus.

3.2. Lexical bundles, word lists and natural language processing in FLAX

FLAX identifies "lexical bundles" used in the target ESAP law collections, which are multi-word sequences with distinctive syntactic patterns and discourse functions found in academic prose and lectures (Biber & Barbieri, 2007; Biber, Conrad, & Cortes, 2003, 2004). A typical pattern found in spoken corpora is *verb phrase + that* (*wanted to reemphasise/mention that...*).

Figure 4. FLAX open natural language processing of verb phrases in Law QMUL Collections

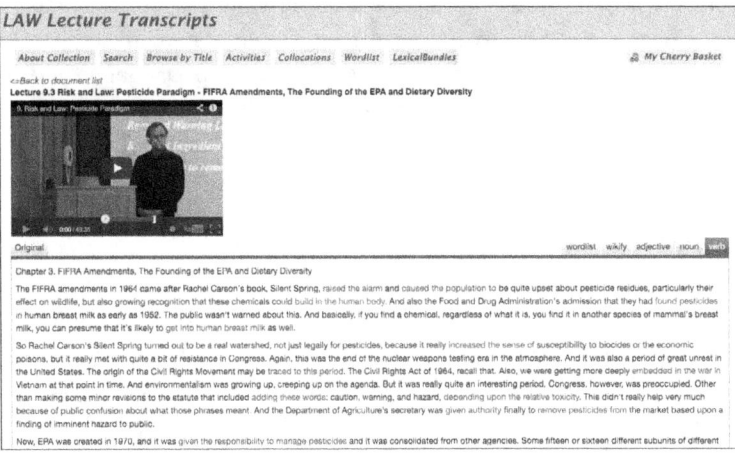

User-friendly interfaces have been developed in FLAX to enable learners to analyse collection documents against well-known word lists such as Coxhead's (2000) Academic Word List and West's (1953) General Service List. Topic-specific

---
4. The database is available at http://flax.nzdl.org/greenstone3/flax?a=fp&sa=collAbout&c=collocations

words are also extracted from the documents to highlight recurrent vocabulary and a keyword slider tool function has been designed to identify the keyness and frequency of certain lexical items as they occur in specific texts. Keyness refers to the frequency of words as they occur in specific documents as a text feature rather than in relationship to other words as a language feature in the case of collocations, for example. The FLAX system also uses Open Natural Language Processing for the syntactic tagging[5] of texts, as can be seen in Figure 4 with verb phrases from one of the environmental law lectures.

4. Conclusions

Content varies in terms of licensing restrictions, and FLAX has been designed to offer flexible linguistic support options for enhancing such content across both open and closed platforms. While we anticipate that this open methodology for domain-specific collections building in FLAX will be of value to language communities across formal and informal education, usage studies will be conducted at QMUL to suggest further directions for development.

Acknowledgements. We would like to thank the OER Research Hub, the Global OER Graduate Network, and The International Research Foundation (TIRF) for English Language Education Doctoral Dissertation Grant, for funding this research collaboration between the FLAX project at the University of Waikato in New Zealand, Concordia University in Canada, and Queen Mary University of London in the United Kingdom. We are particularly grateful to Dr. Saima Sherazi and William Tweddle at the Queen Mary Language Centre for their contributions with the planning of this project collaboration and with Dr. Sherazi's presentation of the work at the EuroCALL 2014 conference event.

References

Biber, D., & Barbieri F. (2007). Lexical bundles in university spoken and written registers. *English for Specific Purpose, 26*(3), 263-286. doi:10.1016/j.esp.2006.08.003

Biber, D., Conrad, S., & Cortes, V. (2003). Lexical bundles in speech and writing: An initial taxonomy. In A. Wilson, P. Rayson, & T. McEnery (Eds), *Corpus linguistics by the lune: A festschrift for Geoffrey Leech* (pp. 71-92). Frankfurt/Main: Peter Lang.

Biber, D., Conrad, S., & Cortes, V. (2004). If you look at ...: lexical bundles in university teaching and textbooks. *Applied Linguistics, 25*(3), 371-405. doi:10.1093/applin/25.3.371

---

5. See the OpenNLP system; http://opennlp.sourceforge.net

Bishop, H. (2004). The effect of typographic salience on the look up and comprehension of unknown formulaic sequences. In N. Schmidt (Ed.), *Formulaic sequences: Acquisition, processing, and use* (pp. 227-244). Philadelphia, PA, USA: John Benjamins. doi:10.1075/lllt.9.12bis

Coxhead, A. (2000). A new academic word list. TESOL Quarterly, 34(2), 213–238. Reprinted in 2007 in Corpus linguistics by W. Teubert & R. Krishnamurthy (Eds), *Critical concepts in linguistics* (pp. 123-149). Oxford, England: Routledge. doi:10.2307/3587951

Gabrielatos, C. (2005). Corpora and language teaching: Just a fling or wedding bells? Teaching English as a Second or Foreign Language, 8(4). Retrieved from http://tesl-ej.org/ej32/a1.html

Milne, D., & Witten, I. H. (2013). An open-source toolkit for mining Wikipedia. *Artificial Intelligence, 194*, 222-239. doi:10.1016/j.artint.2012.06.007

Nesselhauf, N. (2003). The use of collocations by advanced learners of English and some implications for teaching. *Applied Linguistics, 24*(2), 223-242. doi:10.1093/applin/24.2.223

OER Research Hub. (n.d.). *Hypothesis E – Reflection* [website]. Retrieved from http://oerresearchhub.org/collaborative-research/hypotheses/hypothesis-e-reflection/

Stubbs, M., & Barth, I. (2003). Using recurrent phrases as text-type discriminators. *Functions of Language, 10*(1), 61-104. doi:10.1075/fol.10.1.04stu

West, M. (1953). *A general service list of English words*. London: Longman, Green & Co.

Witten, I. H., Bainbridge, D., & Nichols, D. M. (2010). *How to build a digital library* (2nd ed.). Burlington, MA: Morgan Kaufmann.

Wu, S., & Witten, I. H. (Forthcoming). Transcending concordance: Augmenting academic text for L2 writing. Submitted to the *Journal of English for Academic Purposes*.

Effects of online translation on morphosyntactic and lexical-pragmatic accuracy in essay writing in Spanish as a foreign language

Kent Fredholm[1]

Abstract. The use of online translation (OT) is increasing as more pupils receive laptops from their schools. This study investigates OT use in two groups of Swedish pupils (ages 17-18) studying Spanish as an L3: one group (A) having free Internet access and the spelling and grammar checker of Microsoft Word, the other group (B) using printed dictionaries without Internet access. 112 Spanish essays were collected from the groups. Screencasts of 60 essay writings were recorded, and accompanied by a questionnaire and interviews to 13 pupils. The essays were analysed for morphological, syntactical and lexical accuracy. Significant differences between groups A and B were found for only a few error categories. Group B made a higher percentage of errors all-in-all, committed more mistakes regarding noun/adjective and noun/article agreement, whereas group A made more mistakes concerning verb mood, personal pronouns, and conjunctions. Many errors in group B can be explained by the fact that the pupils had no access to automatic corrective suggestions or automatic translation, as did group A. Flaws in OT can account for pronoun and syntactic errors in group A essays. The differences in correct use of verb mood and conjunctions are more difficult to explain and deserve further investigation.

Keywords: CALL, ICT, foreign language writing, grammar, accuracy, online translation.

---

1. Department of Language Education, Stockholm University; Kent.Fredholm@isd.su.se.

How to cite this article: Fredholm, K. (2014). Effects of online translation on morphosyntactic and lexical-pragmatic accuracy in essay writing in Spanish as a foreign language. In S. Jager, L. Bradley, E. J. Meima, & S. Thouësny (Eds), *CALL Design: Principles and Practice; Proceedings of the 2014 EUROCALL Conference, Groningen, The Netherlands* (pp. 96-101). Dublin: Research-publishing.net. doi:10.14705/rpnet.2014.000201

1. Introduction

As pupils' access to computers is increasing at schools investing in 1-1 projects in Sweden as well as other countries, their access to online resources is also increasing. This is evident in foreign language classes when it comes to writing in the studied language. Teachers are often heard complaining about pupils using online translation (OT) services, such as Google translate; however, the number of studies on pupils' use of OT in foreign language writing, especially concerning younger pupils, is still scarce, with exceptions from recent years such as Niño (2008, 2009), Steding (2009), Garcia and Pena (2011), and O'Neill (2012). Teachers' and pupils' ideas of OT are often based more on personal beliefs and prejudices, rather than on detailed data. The present study, part of a Ph.D. project on pupils' use and perception of ICT in foreign language learning, examines the effects of OT on grammatical, syntactic, lexical and pragmatic features of Spanish essays written by pupils at the Swedish upper secondary school.

2. Methods and participants

2.1. Participants and data collection

Two groups studying Spanish as a foreign language were investigated during the autumn semester of 2013 as they wrote four essays on text genres present in the Swedish national curriculum for foreign languages (Skolverket, 2013). The pupils, ages 17-18, had studied Spanish for five years prior to the study. Both groups used their laptops to write and both had access to printed dictionaries. One group (henceforth "A") had free access to the Internet and to the spelling and grammar checkers of Microsoft Word, whereas the other group ("B") was not allowed to use any online resources. Group A mainly chose to use Google translate and the similar site Lexikon24; a few Google searches for background information on different topics were also made. In all, 57 pupils handed in 112 essays, 84 from group A and 28 from group B. The fact that several group B pupils had not followed instructions during the writing sessions, using Internet resources despite being told not to, disqualified many of their essays from the analysis.

Each of the four writing tasks were distributed via the school's learning management system, where the pupils also handed in their essays. They were given thirty minutes to write, with an additional five minutes to read instructions and to save their work. They were also asked to record their screens as they were writing, using screencast-o-matic.com. Thirty-three pupils managed to do so, handing in screencasts of 60 essay writings.

After the final essay writing session, the pupils were also asked to fill out a questionnaire, and thirteen pupils were interviewed. The questions asked focussed on the pupils' choice of writing strategies and technology use and will not be further commented on here.

2.2. Measures of morphosyntactic accuracy

Morphological or grammatical accuracy was measured as the mean number of morphological errors per essay, regarding verbs, noun/adjective and noun/article agreement, pronouns, and prepositions. Errors of word order, clause and sentence structuring, the use of adjectives instead of adverbs or vice-versa, and the use of conjunctions were counted to measure syntactic accuracy.

2.3. Measures of lexical-pragmatic accuracy

The lexical accuracy was measured as the ratio of context inadequate words to the total amount of words, and the amount of misspelled words (following the definitions of Rimrott & Heift, 2005, p. 21).

Pragmatic accuracy regarded the choice of context appropriate words, idiomatic expressions, and the inconsistent use of personal pronouns and corresponding verb endings, with an incoherent alternation of 2nd and 3rd person as form of address, present in many of the group A essays.

The data received were entered in SPSS and submitted to a t-test. The significant (and in a few cases near-significant) differences between the groups thus revealed will be commented on in the following section.

3. Results

The most striking result of the present study is the low number of significant differences between the groups, as far as morphology and syntax are concerned. Bigger differences, mainly regarding complexity, could be found on clause and sentence levels, where group B produced fewer sentences, fewer independent clauses and a smaller amount of correct sentences; the differences are, however, also quite small in these fields, albeit significant.

On the whole, group B made more errors ($p=.012$), but many of these are smaller mistakes such as noun/adjective or noun/article agreement, and misspellings. Taking into account the pupils' Spanish grades from the previous year, the differences both within and between the groups are clearly correlated to grade level, high-achievers from both groups performing better, producing fewer errors, longer texts and more complex sentence structures.

3.1. Morphosyntactic accuracy

As for morphology, significant differences were found concerning the use of verb mood, where group A performed more errors ($p=.007$), as well as noun/adjective agreement (near significant, $p=.052$) and noun/article agreement ($p=.001$), both showing more errors in group B.

Group A produced more syntactic inaccuracies than group B. These inaccuracies regard minor errors as the appropriate choice of conjunctions (a near significant difference, $p=.057$), and more important syntactic errors affecting entire clauses or sentences, often rendering them difficult or impossible to understand ($p=.036$).

Significant differences were also found in the ratio of correct sentences to the total number of sentences, group A rating higher ($p=.013$). The accuracy on sentence level refers to both morphological and syntactic accuracy as well as the absence of misspellings. In numbers, the differences are quite small, group A on average producing 11.90 sentences per essay out of which 3 correct, and group B 10.57 sentences, out of which 2 correct. The differences are more clearly referable to grade levels than to technology use.

3.2. Lexical and pragmatic accuracy

Group B made many more spelling errors than group A, which is natural as they did not have any help other than dictionaries, and, furthermore, often chose not to consult these as it was considered too time-consuming or too difficult to find the words or to understand the dictionary entries.

Pupils of group A commented that they felt that the Spanish spelling and grammar checker of Microsoft Word (that was not used in group B) had helped them to correct many mistakes. This seems plausible as far as misspellings are concerned, but less so for grammatical errors, which were still numerous. Many of the spelling errors were automatically corrected by Word (especially missing accents and erroneous use of capital letters), and these corrections do not seem to have attracted pupils' attention; therefore, their belief that the spelling checker helped them to learn Spanish orthography better must be taken with a pinch of salt.

In the first essay, written as a reply to a fictitious 19-year-old boy asking for advice on his friends' overconsumption of alcohol, group A switched frequently between formal and informal forms of address (using the Spanish *tú* and *usted* and their corresponding 2nd and 3rd person verb endings). This was seen to a much lesser extent in group B. The majority of these inconsistencies were clearly due to the use of OT, as Google translate often –but not always– translated the Swedish *du* (2nd person) to Spanish *usted* (3rd person).

4.   Discussion and conclusions

Apart from the few areas where significant differences could be seen, the use of OT does not seem to have affected writing performance in any decisive way, neither improving it nor giving worse results than had it not been used. Group A essays were slightly longer and contained a few more complex sentences and fewer errors, but almost none of the 112 essays can be considered well-written. Only one of the 57 pupils managed to use the technology effectively, producing texts in a Spanish appropriate for the level of instruction.

If the purpose of intermediate level foreign language writing is considered strictly as text production and nothing more, the present study can neither recommend nor discourage the use of OT, as its effects seem hardly discernable. The role of writing in the foreign language classroom needs, however, to be taken into greater consideration; most teachers would hopefully say that its purpose is to practice and improve pupils' abilities to use the language, and in that case, OT should probably be used sparingly, as suggested by researchers stating that it does not improve language learning (Garcia & Pena, 2011; Niño, 2008, 2009; O'Neill, 2012; Steding, 2009). This is, nevertheless, an area that needs further research rather than a priori sentiments of rejection. Considering the difficulties among the pupils' of the present study to produce grammatically and pragmatically coherent texts or, indeed, sentences, the Swedish school needs to reconsider first and foremost the place foreign language writing should have in foreign language teaching, and only secondly what role OT and other technologies should play in this.

References

Garcia, I., & Pena, M. I. (2011). Machine translation-assisted language learning: Writing for beginners. *Computer Assisted Language Learning, 24*(5), 471-487. doi:10.1080/09588221.2011.582687

Niño, A. (2008). Evaluating the use of machine translation post-editing in the foreign language class. *Computer Assisted Language Learning, 21*(1), 29-49. doi:10.1080/09588220701865482

Niño, A. (2009). Machine translation in foreign language learning: Language learners' and tutors' perceptions of its advantages and disadvantages. *ReCALL, 21*(2), 241-258. doi:10.1017/S0958344009000172

O'Neill, E. M. (2012). *The effect of online translators on L2 writing in French*. Unpublished Doctoral Dissertation. Urbana-Champaign: University of Illinois.

Rimrott, A., & Heift, T. (2005). Language learners and generic spell checkers in CALL. *Calico Journal, 23*(1), 17-48.

Skolverket. (2013). Ämne - Moderna språk. *Skolverket*. Retrieved from http://www.skolverket.se/laroplaner-amnen-och-kurser/gymnasieutbildning/gymnasieskola/mod?tos=gy&subjectCode=mod&lang=sv

Steding, S. (2009). Machine translation in the German classroom: Detection, reaction, prevention. *Die Unterrichtspraxis/Teaching German, 42*(2), 178-189.

Encouraging self-directed group learning through an e-portfolio system

Eri Fukuda[1], Mitsuko Suzuki[2], Shinichi Hashimoto[3], and Hironobu Okazaki[4]

Abstract. In this study, the researchers examined how 64 university students engaged in self-directed group learning and used a self-developed e-portfolio system. A six-week event was held where the students made entries to the e-portfolio individually each week, received feedback from advisors, studied in groups on a voluntary basis, and reflected on their group learning as a team. The data was collected from various sources including the pre- and post-TOEIC (Test of English for International Communication) or TOEFL (Test of English as a Foreign Language) test scores, group learning reflection sheets, a questionnaire, and follow-up interviews with two participants. Significant score improvements were observed in the TOEIC test results. Although the number of submitted reflection sheets did not correlate with the increase in the students' test scores, the data suggests that group learning and reflection had strengthened students' learning motivation. Moreover, mutual support from group members encouraged the participants to continue studying. Though scheduling remained the major obstacle to the collaborative process, by adding group learning to individual learning and record keeping in the e-portfolio, the students found English learning enjoyable and useful as they were able to identify gaps in their knowledge previously overlooked. This article ends with the areas to be considered for future projects.

Keywords: e-portfolio, group learning, autonomous learning, test preparation.

---

1. Chugoku Junior College; efukuda@cjc.ac.jp.
2. Soka High School; smitsuko1129@gmail.com.
3. The University of Electro-Communications; heiwanian@gmail.com.
4. Akita Prefectural University; okazaki@akita-pu.ac.jp.

How to cite this article: Fukuda, E., Suzuki, M., Hashimoto, S., & Okazaki, H. (2014). Encouraging self-directed group learning through an e-portfolio system. In S. Jager, L. Bradley, E. J. Meima, & S. Thouësny (Eds), *CALL Design: Principles and Practice; Proceedings of the 2014 EUROCALL Conference, Groningen, The Netherlands* (pp. 102-106). Dublin: Research-publishing.net. doi:10.14705/rpnet.2014.000202

1. Introduction

Electronic portfolios (e-portfolios) are increasingly used in tertiary education. As Fitch, Peet, Reed, and Tolman (2013) pointed out, "portfolios can foster the integration of [...] self-reflection, group learning, and assessment" (p. 37) which could consequently maximize students' learning outcomes. The e-portfolio system of the present study was created and utilized at a private Japanese university to support students' autonomous language learning. The uniqueness of this self-developed e-portfolio system lies in an interactive function which allows communication between a learner and advisor. Through this system, students are not only able to record their reflections on their own language learning, but also receive weekly feedback from a trained advisor.

The current study attempted to incorporate group learning into autonomous learning assisted by the e-portfolio. As previous research has indicated, cooperative learning enhances group members' self-efficacy and motivation (Dörnyei & Ushioda, 2011). University students in this study formed groups of four and voluntarily studied toward a common goal to obtain a higher TOEIC or TOEFL ITP test score. After generating a study plan, students engaged in both group and self-language learning. Group learning reflection sheets were kept in paper form while individual learning reflections were recorded in the e-portfolio. Weekly feedback from an advisor was provided for only those who made e-portfolio entries.

2. Method

2.1. Participants

In the current study, the data was collected from 64 students (16 teams). Originally, 19 teams applied for the project, two teams did not take part in any e-portfolio or group learning. In addition, one team neither held a group learning session nor reported their progress in the e-portfolio system after the first week. Thus, these three groups were excluded from the data. There were 31 students who had acquired TOEIC scores in the 400s, 18 students in the 500s, and three in the 600s. For the TOEFL ITP scores, there were 11 students who were in the 400 range and one in the 500 range.

2.2. Procedure

The following sets of data were collected in the current research: the students' pre- and post-TOEIC or TOEFL ITP scores, two kinds of group learning reflection sheets, a questionnaire, and interviews. The event was held in the fall semester of 2013 for six weeks. The students were required to take the same tests as the pre- and post-assessments.

Two kinds of group learning reflection sheets were available: weekly and daily reflection sheets. One worksheet was used to share individual learning in the previous week. The other was used to describe what the participants learned together on the day of group learning. The students were allowed to use this latter sheet as many times as they studied together.

A post-sessional questionnaire was devised for the present research to inquire about the students' insight into the effectiveness of the project. Eleven students cooperated with the questionnaire survey. The questionnaire included five Likert-scale type questions asking to rate how the e-portfolio and group learning assisted their learning and affected their level of motivation. In addition, three open-ended questions were incorporated to elicit further information.

Lastly, follow-up interviews were conducted with two participants in Japanese.

3. Result and discussion

Overall, 121 individual e-portfolio entries and 115 group learning sessions were reported in the project. First of all, the results of the pre- and post-test were compared in order to assess students' progress. In case of the TOEFL test takers, although their scores slightly improved from the pre- (M=465.1, SD=30.7) to post-test (M=490.6, SD=50.6), the result of paired-samples t-test indicated that there was no significant score improvement over the six weeks, $t(10)$= 1.98, p>.05.

As for the TOEIC test takers, their average test scores significantly increased from the pre- (M=496.9, SD=68.0) to post-test (M=525.3, SD=87.3), $t(39)$=, p<.05. The number of e-portfolio entries and group reflection sheets did not correlate with either the TOEFL test, $r(9)$= .36, p>.05, or TOEIC test score increase, $r(38)$=.03, p>.05. Perhaps, frequency of reflections is not directly related to the language learning outcomes. To further investigate the effectiveness of the project, the focus was shifted to what the students actually wrote in their reflections.

According to the daily group learning reflection sheets, the students spent time preparing for the TOEIC or TOEFL tests for 52.63% of the time. As the tests require a wide range of linguistic knowledge, vocabulary learning accounted for 21.05% of the responses and grammar 18.75%. Although knowledge-based learning is often challenging for language learners, through group learning, the participants encouraged each other, as their responses in the questionnaires show.

One of the Likert-scale type questions was on the effects of keeping records of group learning over the individual record keeping in the e-portfolio. An item included in this question asked whether sharing individual learning done in the previous week and writing down each member's comments on the weekly group reflection sheet promoted English learning in synergy with the e-portfolio. The students showed relatively strong agreement with the item ($M=4.45$, $SD=0.52$). Another item contained in this question was whether the group record keeping made learning interesting, which gained general agreement ($M=4.18$, $SD=0.6$). Also, the respondents less agreed that there was only slight differences between individual and group record keeping ($M=2.27$, $SD=1.10$).

The second Likert-scale type item questioned how group learning affected the participants. The students agreed that group learning made learning more interesting ($M=4.27$, $SD=0.65$). Moreover, the majority thought group learning was useful ($M=4.55$, $SD=0.69$). Finally, the prominent result was found in the item on the increase of motivation in English learning. Although only 11 students responded to the questionnaire, the result showed students' highly positive perception toward group learning ($M=4.64$, $SD=0.50$).

In fact, more than 10% of the individual e-portfolio entries contained the efficiency of group learning. Most students reported that group learning allowed them to notice their own progress as well as areas of further improvements. For instance, one of the students checked vocabulary with her team members and mentioned, "Even if I thought I had memorized [the words] perfectly, I couldn't define several words in a question format. I want to continue studying like this in groups".

Furthermore, in the open-ended questions, the respondents reported that team members encouraged each other and regained motivation through studying in group even when their motivational level decreased. One student wrote in the questionnaire, "We were able to accomplish things that I would have probably given up if I had been on my own".

Finally, a drawback of this project would be a scheduling difficulty. A student noted, "When [all the members] were unable to attend a group learning session, our motivation diminished or the number of meetings declined". Thus, additional assistance for scheduling was needed.

4. Implications and conclusion

Integration of group learning and e-portfolios does not automatically guarantee synergetic effects. As the participants reported difficulties arranging group learning sessions, organizers should recommend students to find team members who are available during the same time periods. The students should reach an agreement on specific times and days to congregate. In addition, although the following procedure should not be mandatory since the purpose of the kind of project is to support autonomous learning, at the first orientation, the organizers could provide a weekly schedule for participants to fill out time periods for group learning sessions so that each group member can officially agree on the schedule. Once this particular obstacle is solved, the project will be even more successful in the future.

References

Dörnyei, Z., & Ushioda, E. (2011). *Teaching and researching motivation* (2nd ed.). Harlow: Longman.

Fitch, D., Peet, M., Reed, B. G., & Tolman, R. (2008). The use of eportfolios in evaluating the curriculum and student learning. *Journal of Social Work Education, 44*(3), 37-54. doi:10.5175/JSWE.2008.200700010

university of groningen

Supporting content and language integrated learning through technology

Ana Gimeno-Sanz[1], Caoimhín Ó Dónaill[2], and Kent Andersen[3]

Abstract. This paper describes Clilstore and how this tool can support Content and Language Integrated Learning (CLIL), which involves teaching a curricular subject through the medium of a foreign language, as was evidenced through data collected from two surveys conducted with secondary school teachers from various European countries.

Keywords: content and language integrated learning, Clilstore, tools for CLIL teachers project.

1. Introduction

Content and Language Integrated Learning was recognised as a teaching methodology by the Commission of the European Communities in its Communication No. 449 on Promoting Language Learning and Linguistic Diversity: An Action Plan 2004-2006, published in 2003. In this past decade we have witnessed how CLIL has steadily rooted its teaching principles and is slowly becoming a dominant methodology in all sectors of education that are sensitive to bilingual education. Research and reflective practice literature is currently abundant and CLIL is the focus of an increasing amount of empirical studies proving the methodology's worth. In line with this trend, the EU-funded *Tools for CLIL Teachers* project has developed an online authoring tool to support the implementation of CLIL. This tool, which is known as Clilstore, facilitates being able to automatically link every word in a text to freely available online dictionaries

---

1. Universidad Politécnica de Valencia, Spain; agimeno@upvnet.upv.es.

2. University of Ulster, Northern Ireland, UK; c.odonaill@ulster.ac.uk.

3. Syddansk Erhvervsskole Odense, Denmark; ka@sde.dk.

How to cite this article: Gimeno-Sanz, A., Ó Dónaill, C., & Andersen, K. (2014). Supporting content and language integrated learning through technology. In S. Jager, L. Bradley, E. J. Meima, & S. Thouësny (Eds), *CALL Design: Principles and Practice; Proceedings of the 2014 EUROCALL Conference, Groningen, The Netherlands* (pp. 107-112). Dublin: Research-publishing.net. doi:10.14705/rpnet.2014.000203

in a wealth of languages. Clilstore's features are particularly enhanced when videos and their transcripts are embedded into the system from one of the many streaming video applications currently available. The units created within Clilstore become part of an ever-growing repository for learners and teachers alike.

2. Methodology

2.1. Content and language integrated learning

The EU's policy on multilingualism mentioned above states that CLIL implicates teaching a curricular subject through the medium of a language other than that normally used. The subject can be entirely unrelated to language learning, delivered in a bilingual context, or include a language learning component serving a dual purpose: that of the subject matter and that of a foreign language. CLIL has steadily been on the rise for the past 20 years and this trend is continuing, judging by the amount of literature currently available.

Teachers who adopt the CLIL methodology are specialists in a discipline other than the foreign language. They are by definition proficient speakers of the target language and very often collaborate with language teachers. The crucial factor here is that the learners acquire new knowledge with regard to the subject matter whilst simultaneously practising and acquiring the foreign language. However, it is commonly the content of the curricular subject that determines the types of activities used and the methodologies and teaching approaches to be followed.

2.2. Clilstore, Multidict and Wordlink

Clilstore is a simple-to-use, yet extremely powerful, authoring tool that enables teachers to create materials based on the integration of streaming video embedded from external sources, together with a repository of ready-made materials for teachers and learners alike. The materials currently available in Clilstore amount to 1,133 units, covering all 6 levels (A1 to C2) of the *Common European Framework of Reference for Languages* in 47 different languages.

Clilstore is built on two interconnected tools, that is, Multidict and Wordlink. Both tools can function as stand-alone resources or within Clilstore. Multidict is a dictionary interface allowing quick monolingual or bilingual searches in over 100 language combinations. Wordlink is the software interface that can connect most webpages, word by word, to existing free online dictionaries. It allows users to automatically link any of the words that appear within a text included in a Clilstore unit to a vast selection of dictionaries, thereby supporting learners when reading online as immediate dictionary consultation is guaranteed.

In Figure 1 we can see the typical layout of a Clilstore unit. The unit belongs to the repository of units for learners of Spanish at a B2 level of proficiency and includes the entire script of a YouTube video describing the features and uses of graphene. The use of Wordlink has automatically associated all of the words in the script to Multidict, thereby linking them to all the available online monolingual and bilingual dictionaries. As we can see in the illustration below, the word "tejidos" (tissues) has been selected; this triggers the Multidict dictionary interface to appear on the right hand side of the screen (default mode). The parameters of the word being looked up can be pictured below: 1) the source language, 2) the target language for translation, and 3) the selected online dictionary. It is not necessary to re-enter the search term in order to switch between dictionaries (Gimeno, Ó Dónaill, & Zygmantaite, 2013).

Figure 1. Sample Clilstore unit

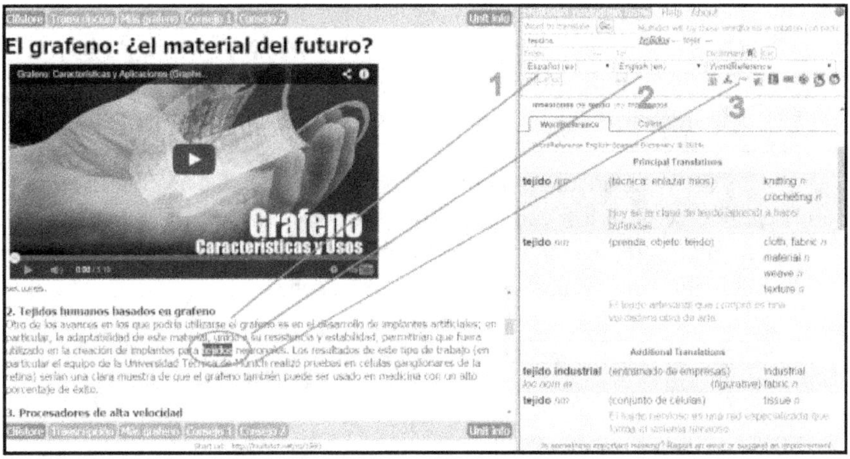

3. Discussion

In order to validate Clilstore and its integral modules, Multidict and Wordlink, and to determine a) to which extent training courses focusing on the use of Clilstore can become helpful to develop CLIL skills and b) to which extent Clilstore was helpful in achieving this, three members of the *Tools for CLIL Teachers* project participated in a European-wide teacher training course and conducted a survey based on pre-course and post-course opinion questionnaires. In the initial questionnaire, the questions were geared towards discovering the participant's prior knowledge about CLIL, their readiness to adopt such a methodology and their attitude towards using ICT in their teaching practice. This survey unveiled a general lack of awareness regarding the theories underlying CLIL and the practicalities involved in adopting this methodology; lack of knowledge as to ICT resources that are available to support the teacher and a tendency to use practices firmly grounded on a teacher-centred approach. The final survey intended to collect data regarding their level of confidence in applying a number of CLIL attributes in their teaching, the degree to which they thought CLIL relies on ICT, and their perception of learner versus teacher-centred approaches, after having completed the two-week course.

The participants consisted of 30 secondary school teachers from nine different European countries teaching subjects ranging from Electronics, Telecommunications, Computing and ICT to Geography, History, Science, Music and Art. They all held certificates accrediting a B2 level or higher of English proficiency.

Regarding their opinion of the CLIL concept in general after completing the course, the entire class was favourable to applying this methodology in their teaching. The following are a few comments that we think are worth mentioning because they summarise the overall impression:

- "The CLIL methodology is useful to improve the students' motivation in learning because it involves the use of different means of communication and it integrates a wide variety of pedagogical methodologies. The lessons built in this way are more interesting for students".

- "[CLIL] is a new methodology based on multimodality and scaffolding, which is very useful".

- "In my opinion CLIL is a good method to transfer content and language, even if you have to create all your lessons and it is a big job".

- "I think CLIL is a very ambitious concept. If it works, it is perfect for the students but I think it takes a lot of time for CLIL to work with students, and it takes a lot of time for teachers to prepare lessons".

From these comments we can elicit several conclusions that were, in general, common to the whole group: a) teachers perceive CLIL as a means of motivation for students because it involves using multiple approaches to teaching, b) it assimilates multimodality in learning, and c) it caters for a variety of learning styles. As can be seen, the main drawback is related to the amount of extra work and time that has to be invested in preparing suitable lessons in order to adapt their subject matter to the CLIL methodology.

Regarding the degree of confidence in applying CLIL after taking the course, 48.15% state that they are *confident* and 18.58% state that they are *very confident* in developing learning outcomes for both language and subject matter. If we consider the sum of these two statements, over 65% of the participants perceive CLIL as an optimal methodology to teach both content and language. The participants' confidence to provide multimodal input and distributing it evenly across their CLIL units increased to levels of *very confident* (48.15%) and *confident* (40.74%), adding up to nearly 90%. Self-confidence in being able to incline the balance towards student-centred learning rather than teacher-centred learning was another of the attributes where the course had helped participants gain assertiveness: *very confident* (33.33%) and *confident* (51.85%), adding up to a total of 85% of the participants. Additionally, 77.8% of the respondents claimed that the introductory course on CLIL and the use of Clilstore had changed their views on teacher-centred versus learner-centred learning and provided the following explanations:

- "Students should be more involved in their learning".

- "Yes, I will try to apply more student-oriented education".

- "In Italy the widespread methodology is teacher-centred; so I have learnt different ways of teaching and, in the end, a dramatic change in the way of thinking and planning lessons".

- "The tools that I have learnt are very interesting, but it is necessary [to] employ a lot of time to build the lesson, because in my case there are very few existing materials. And it is a huge effort to create the material in English".

- "Using these tools changed my views on learning-centered approaches".

As we can see, in a number of cases, the course encouraged teachers to change their focus from teaching to learning and their will to incorporate methods to support the learner and increase their involvement in the process, despite the amount of work that creating *ad-hoc* materials may imply in areas where there are less ready-made resources available.

Regarding how reliant CLIL is on ICT, again the views of the respondents coincided considerably. 29.63% stated that CLIL relied *very strongly* and 55.56%, *strongly*, adding up to over 85% of the group. 11.11% were *neutral* and 3.70% *disagreed* entirely and thought that CLIL could be put into practice independently of ICT. One of the respondents commented that CLIL "is not necessarily reliant [on ICT]. There are lots of things that can be done without it, especially Wordlink as it just helps to understand a text, it doesn't teach understanding skills".

When asked about the usefulness of the Clilstore system to design units for CLIL in their own subject, nearly 85% of the respondents rated it as *high* or *very high*.

One of the general remarks –which can be summarised in the following opinion: "It is necessary to have a global planning to state the main principles and practice[s] of CLIL in Europe. It is not a good idea that each teacher uses CLIL as they consider the best way"– points, in our opinion, to one of the key factors that can cause teachers to hesitate putting CLIL into practice, i.e. the fact that subject specialists need well-developed methodological guidelines to support the implementation of CLIL in the classroom and the backing of language specialists to provide support in terms of foreign language learning.

4. Conclusions

Evidence drawn from the post teacher training course questionnaire leads us to believe that a) teachers are willing to adopt CLIL in their classes and to collaborate with language specialists to put this dual-focus methodology into practice, and b) Clilstore is perceived as a useful tool in order to create, publish and deliver learning materials that aid in conducting dual-focused teaching by supporting content learning as well as foreign language learning.

Reference

Gimeno, A., Ó Dónaill, C., & Zygmantaite, R. (2013). *Clilstore Guidebook for Teachers*. Retrieved from http://www.languages.dk/archive/tools/guides/ClilstoreGuidebook.pdf

Learning strategies and motivation among procrastinators of various English proficiency levels

Yoshiko Goda[1], Masanori Yamada[2], Takeshi Matsuda[3], Hiroshi Kato[4], Yutaka Saito[5], and Hiroyuki Miyagawa[6]

Abstract. Our research project focuses on learning strategies and motivation among academic procrastinators in computer assisted language learning (CALL) settings. In this study, we aim to compare them according to students' levels of English proficiency. One hundred and fourteen university students participated in this research project. Sixty-four students determined to be procrastinators were the focus of this research, and we analyzed their learning strategies and motivation based on their English proficiency (i.e. TOEIC-IP scores). The students were categorized into four groups: under-300s ($n=17$), 400s ($n=22$), 500s ($n=21$), and over-600 ($n=4$). The learning strategies and motivation of the students were collected with a researcher-created 5-point Likert questionnaire consisting of 33 items. The group differences were discriminately analyzed for each item of the questionnaire. The results showed that students who think that the amount to be learned is too large and those who tire easily may ultimately have inefficient and ineffective learning results. The research findings should be significant for teachers and researchers attempting to discriminate between active and passive procrastinators in order to predict their performance and match them with suitable learning supports.

Keywords: procrastinator, learning strategies, motivation, English proficiency level.

---

1. Kumamoto University; ygoda@kumamoto-u.ac.jp.
2. Kyushu University; mark@mark-lab.net.
3. Shimane University; mat@hirc.aoyama.ac.jp.
4. The Open University in Japan; hiroshi@kato.com.
5. Former Tsukuba University; kyoui94@gmail.com.
6. Aoyama Gakuin University; miyagawa@si.aoyama.ac.jp.

How to cite this article: Goda, Y., Yamada, M., Matsuda, T., Kato, H., Saito, Y., & Miyagawa, H.. (2014). Learning strategies and motivation among procrastinators of various English proficiency levels. In S. Jager, L. Bradley, E. J. Meima, & S. Thouësny (Eds), *CALL Design: Principles and Practice; Proceedings of the 2014 EUROCALL Conference, Groningen, The Netherlands* (pp. 113-118). Dublin: Research-publishing.net. doi:10.14705/rpnet.2014.000204

1. Introduction

The purpose of this research is to analyze and compare learning strategies and motivation among procrastinators of different English proficiency levels who are engaged in computer-assisted language learning (CALL). Thanks to the advancement of technology, the use of CALL designed to include in face-to-face instruction and outside-the-classroom e-learning has increased, and such blended education requires more self-regulated learning. In this research project, we focused on students' behavior while they were engaged in blended learning. Specifically, the characteristics of procrastinators were examined in connection with their English proficiency levels.

It is said that about 70% of university students are procrastinators (Schouwenburg, Lay, Pychyl, & Ferrari, 2004), and procrastination has been viewed as a negative factor in terms of academic success (e.g. Hussain & Sultan, 2010; Tan et al., 2008). Academic procrastination has often been viewed as being related to a lack of self-regulated learning (e.g. Wolters, 2003). However, procrastination may not always have negative effects on learning, and some procrastinators use procrastination intentionally as a result of their self-regulation.

Chu and Choi (2005) introduced the concept of active and passive procrastination. Passive procrastination is considered as non-purposeful academic postponing as a result of a lack of planning, motivation, attention, and self-regulation. Active procrastination, on the other hand, is an intentional decision to procrastinate and the ability to complete the assigned tasks by their deadlines because of strong motivation under time pressure. If students are active procrastinators, then they may not need much support from the instructor to complete their assignments and tasks by the deadlines. Our research project's goal is to categorize learners into types and to match the categories with the types of e-learning support they require.

In our previous research related to learning behavior types in CALL courses (Goda, Yamada, Matsuda, Kato, & Saito, 2013), seven learning behavior types were found: (1) procrastination, (2) learning habit, (3) random, (4) diminished drive, (5) early bird, (6) chevron, and (7) catch-up. When the learning types and their English proficiencies were compared, learning type (1) was significantly lower in terms of proficiency than learning type (2) (Type (1): $N=145$, $M=432.48$; Type (2): $N=9$, $M=582.78$). This implies that being in the learning habit category may lead to higher levels of English proficiency and that procrastinators may have inefficient and ineffective learning strategies. However, we assume that learning type (1) includes both active and passive procrastinators. In order to provide effective learning support to individuals in CALL, the procrastinators should be categorized further and differentiated into a support-necessary group and a support-unnecessary group. Students with higher English proficiency levels were assumed to use procrastination intentionally as active procrastinators.

2. Method

2.1. Participants

In this research project, 114 undergraduate students who registered for a CALL course at a university in Japan during the spring semester of 2013 participated. Sixty-four students were categorized as having learning type (1), procrastination, and their learning strategies and motivation were analyzed based on their English proficiency levels. English proficiency was operationally defined as the TOEIC-IP score, and four groups were created based on students' TOEIC-IP score levels: under-300s, 400s, 500s, and over-600. There were 17, 22, 21, and 4 students in these groups, respectively.

2.2. Course description

The targeted CALL course was a one-credit mandatory class provided to sophomores at the university. The semester began in April and ended in July of 2013, and there were 15 lessons over the semester. As the main material for the course, Newton e-Learning (TLT training Soft/TOEIC®TEST) was employed to encourage students' self-paced mastery learning of English. Once a week, students were required to come to the classroom to have a face-to-face class and study the materials outside the classroom.

2.3. Data collection and analysis

The students' perceived learning strategies and motivation were obtained via a researcher-developed questionnaire. The questionnaire consisted of 33 5-point-Likert-scale items related to learning strategy and motivation. The items were selected and created based on three dimensions (cognitive, affective, and behavioral) of self-regulated learning (Wolters, 2003). The questionnaire included 16 cognitive and meta-cognitive, eleven affective, and six behavior and context items.

The questionnaire was implemented at the end of the first class, and the TOEIC-IP was conducted during the 9th week of the semester. The learning behavior types were categorized into seven groups using the method of Goda et al. (2013), visualizing the learning progress from the beginning to the end of the semester. The descriptive statistics for learners' behavior types and TOEIC-IP scores were reported first. The students in the procrastination group were categorized into four groups (under-300s, 400s, 500s, and over-600). Then, the discriminant analyses were performed for the groups' questionnaire responses related to learning strategies and motivation.

3. Results

3.1. Descriptive statistics

The learning behaviors of the 114 students were categorized into seven types, (1) procrastination, (2) learning habit, (3) random, (4) diminished drive, (5) early bird, (6) chevron, and (7) catch-up, based on their actual learning progresses. The numbers of students in each category were 64, 6, 3, 12, 2, 11, and 8, respectively. There were eight students who studied too little, merely accessing the learning materials once and/or dropping out. They did not match any of the learning behavior types. Since the learning strategies and motivation of the procrastinators were the focus of this research, the 64 procrastinators' responses on the questionnaire were further analyzed.

The grand mean of all participants ($N=114$) on the TOEIC-IP was 486.71, and the mean of the 64 students in the procrastination group was 459.53. The procrastinators were further categorized into four groups based on their TOEIC-IP scores: under-300s ($n=17$), 400s ($n=22$), 500s ($n=21$), and over-600 ($n=4$). The means and standard deviations of each question item regarding the learning strategies were calculated based on the English proficiency groups. The results showed that the most extreme mean values (i.e. the highest mean among the four groups) were observed for the under-300s or over-600 groups.

3.2. Inferential statistics

The discriminant analyses of the four groups on all question items resulted in two significant items (Questions 15 and 25) and two marginally insignificant items (Questions 4 and 28) (Q4: $F_{(3,60)}=2.544$, $p=.065$, Q15: $F_{(3,60)}=3.559$, $p=.019$, Q25: $F_{(3,60)}=4.718$, $p=.005$, Q28: $F_{(3,60)}=2.518$, $p=.067$). Table 1 shows the results regarding significance and marginal insignificance on Tukey's post-hoc tests. Table 1 also provides the question items, mean differences, and probabilities. The under-300s group significantly differs from the 400s on the questions 15 and 25. This implies that students who think that the amount to learn is too great and tire easily might ultimately have inefficient and ineffective learning results. To discriminate between the under-300s and the over-600 groups, Q28 might be useful.

Table 1. Significant results of post-hoc Tukey analyses

	Question	(I) TOEIC_ Level	(J) TOEIC_ Level	Mean Difference (I-J)	S.E	p	95% CI Lower	95% CI Upper
Q4	I want to finish an assignment as soon as possible.	Under-300s	400s	-0.43	0.22	0.23	-1.02	0.16
			500s	-0.53†	0.23	0.10	-1.13	0.07
			Over-600	-0.79	0.39	0.18	-1.81	0.23
		400s	500s	-0.10	0.21	0.96	-0.66	0.46
			Over-600	-0.36	0.38	0.77	-1.36	0.63
		500s	Over-600	-0.26	0.38	0.90	-1.26	0.74
Q15	The assigned amount of learning per day is too much to catch up.	Under-300s	400s	.733**	0.26	0.04	0.04	1.43
			500s	0.59	0.27	0.14	-0.12	1.29
			Over-600	-0.18	0.45	0.98	-1.38	1.02
		400s	500s	-0.15	0.25	0.94	-0.81	0.51
			Over-600	-0.91	0.44	0.18	-2.08	0.27
		500s	Over-600	-0.76	0.45	0.33	-1.94	0.42
Q25	I get tired easily.	Under-300s	400s	.880**	0.25	0.00	0.22	1.54
			500s	0.66*	0.25	0.05	0.00	1.33
			Over-600	0.97	0.43	0.12	-0.16	2.10
		400s	500s	-0.22	0.24	0.79	-0.84	0.40
			Over-600	0.09	0.42	1.00	-1.02	1.20
		500s	Over-600	0.31	0.42	0.88	-0.80	1.42
Q28	I don't feel rushed until the deadline is nearing.	Under-300s	400s	0.26	0.25	0.71	-0.39	0.91
			500s	0.07	0.25	0.99	-0.59	0.72
			Over-600	1.10*	0.42	0.05	-0.01	2.22
		400s	500s	-0.20	0.23	0.84	-0.81	0.42
			Over-600	0.84	0.41	0.19	-0.25	1.93
		500s	Over-600	1.04†	0.42	0.07	-0.06	2.13

Note. * $p < .05$, ** $p < .01$, † $p < .10$.

4. Discussion and conclusions

The results imply that among procrastinators, those who thought there was too much material to learn and those who easily became tired of things may ultimately have inefficient and ineffective learning. Those passive procrastinators need more support to help them control their cognitive, affective, and behavioral regulation within this context. In contrast, active procrastinators may feel rushed long before the deadline, although they do not concentrate their studies within the period just before the deadline. Because of the unease or tension caused by not studying early, active procrastinators may use learning strategies and motivation control to concentrate on the contents and learn them effectively. This tension may also play an important role in procrastination research.

In this research project, a researcher-developed questionnaire was used to collect data, and other questionnaires related to learning strategies and motivation should be employed for data collection. TOEIC-IP scores were adopted to categorize the learners in terms of English proficiency, assuming that students with higher levels of proficiency would have better learning skills and more motivation and that this would be a useful way to separate active and passive procrastinators. This underlying assumption should be examined using different samples and contexts in future research.

Acknowledgements. This work was supported by JSPS KAKENHI Grant Number 24300289.

References

Chu, A. H. C., & Choi, J. N. (2005). Rethinking procrastination: Positive effects of "active" procrastination behavior on attitudes and performance. *The Journal of Social Psychology, 145*(3), 245-264. doi:10.3200/SOCP.145.3.245-264

Goda, Y., Yamada, M., Matsuda, T., Kato, H., & Saito, Y. (2013). e ラーニングにおける学習行動の分類 [Categorization of learning behavior in e-Learning] (pp. 867-868). *Proceedings of the 29th Annual Conference of JSET*.

Hussain, I., & Sultan, S. (2010). Analysis of procrastination among university students. *Procedia Social and Behavioral Sciences, 5*, 1897-1904. doi:10.1016/j.sbspro.2010.07.385

Schouwenburg, H. C., Lay, C., Pychyl, T. A., & Ferrari, J. R. (2004). *Counseling the procrastinator in academic settings*. Washington, D.C.: American Psychological Association. doi:10.1037/10808-000

Tan, C. X., Ang, R. P., Klassen, R. M., Yeo, L. S., Wong, I. Y. F., Huan, V. S., & Chong, W. H. (2008). Correlated of academic procrastination and students' grade goals. *Current Psychology, 27*(2), 135-144. doi:10.1007/s12144-008-9028-8.

Wolters, C. A. (2003). Understanding procrastination from a self-regulated learning perspective. *Journal of Educational Psychology, 95*(1), 179-187. doi:10.1037/0022-0663.95.1.179

university of groningen

Evaluation of a web conferencing tool and collaborative tasks in an online Chinese course

Sijia Guo[1]

Abstract. This case study aims to explore the best practice of applying task-based language teaching (TBLT) via the web conferencing tool Blackboard Collaborate in a beginners' online Chinese course by evaluating the technical capacity of the software and the pedagogical values and limitations of the tasks designed. In this paper, Chapelle's (2001) criteria for CALL task appropriateness are adopted and adapted to evaluate five tasks designed for an online environment in terms of practicality, language learning potential, learner fit, authenticity and positive impact. In the second semester, 2013, eight BA on-campus students who enrolled in an introductory Chinese language course agreed to participate in this project. Five fortnightly one-hour online sessions were conducted, which included two jigsaw tasks, two decision-making tasks and one information-gap task. Learners' interaction in the online sessions has been recorded and transcribed for a deep investigation of learners' negotiation actions in peer-peer interaction. Their experiences of using Blackboard Collaborate and tasks were recorded in in-depth interviews and pre and post-session questionnaires.

Keywords: CALL evaluation, TBLT, web conferencing, SLA, second language acquisition, online Chinese teaching.

1. Introduction

The popularity of task-based language teaching in the context of computer-mediated communication (CMC) has drawn increasing attention from both researchers and language teachers (Thomas & Reinders, 2010). A great number of studies have been conducted to investigate the use of audio/video or web conferencing tools and their

---

1. sijia.guo@mq.edu.au.

How to cite this article: Guo, S. (2014). Evaluation of a web conferencing tool and collaborative tasks in an online Chinese course. In S. Jager, L. Bradley, E. J. Meima, & S. Thouësny (Eds), *CALL Design: Principles and Practice*; *Proceedings of the 2014 EUROCALL Conference, Groningen, The Netherlands* (pp. 119-126). Dublin: Research-publishing.net. doi:10.14705/rpnet.2014.000205

influence on learners' interaction and task design (e.g. Hampel, 2006; Hampel & Stickler, 2012; Rosell-Aguilar, 2005). However, there is a lack of research into how to evaluate the appropriateness of web conferencing tools and tasks. This study was performed with the purpose of bridging the gap by proposing a set of criteria for web conferencing-based collaborative tools. The paper will present findings from an empirical study in this context.

1.1. Literature review

Creating optimal conditions to maximise the efficiency of task-based instructions has been one of the key concerns of second language acquisition (SLA) research (e.g., Hampel, 2006; Hampel & Stickler, 2012; Rosell-Aguilar, 2005). From a cognitive point of view, Skehan (1998) summarises and proposes five guidelines for implementing effective task-based instruction. Based on these guidelines, Chapelle (2001) proposes a set of criteria for CALL tasks evaluation.

1.2. Criteria for evaluating the appropriateness of web conference-based collaborative tasks

In the study, Chapelle's (2001) six criteria for CALL tasks appropriateness and Wang's (2008) criteria for evaluating meaning-focused videoconferencing tasks have been used as guidelines for evaluation.

Table 1. Criteria for evaluating web conferencing tools and collaborative tasks

Criteria	Descriptions
Practicality	The fit between tasks and the affordance of the web-conferencing tool(s) to support collaborative tasks completion.
Language learning potential	<ul><li>The extent to which learners' attention is directed toward the forms of the language while engaging in meaning-based tasks.</li><li>Learners' improvement in the target language, especially in communicative competence.</li><li>The appropriateness of tasks in facilitating collaborative learning.</li></ul>
Learner fit	The fit between learners' characteristics and tasks' characteristics, such as: <ul><li>The fit between the level of the difficulty of the tasks and the level of proficiency of the learners.</li><li>The fit between the amount of opportunity for engagement or interaction with learners' expectation.</li></ul>
Authenticity	The degree of correspondence between the web conferencing-based activities and target language activities of interest to learners outside the classroom.
Positive impact	The positive effects of the web conferencing-based tasks on those who participate in it (e.g. the impact of the multimodal environment, the impact on learners' confidence in learning, etc.).

The criteria for evaluating web conferencing tools and collaborative tasks in the current study are summarised in Table 1 above.

2. Method

In this study, the predominant purpose was to evaluate the appropriateness of the web conferencing tool and the collaborative tasks designed (Egbert, Chao, & Hanson-Smith, 1999; Larsen-Freeman & Long, 1991; Long, 1996; Pica, 1994; Spolsky, 1989). A case study approach was adopted to apply the proposed criteria to evaluate both software and pedagogical values of the tasks (Yin, 2009). As Jamieson and Chapelle (2010) state, today's pressing question is "to what extent a particular type of CALL material can be argued to be appropriate for a given group of learners at a given point in time" (p. 2).

2.1. Context of the study

In the second semester (from August to November 2013), eight BA on-campus students who enrolled in an introductory level Chinese language course participated in the current study. Five fortnightly one-hour online sessions were conducted through the web conferencing tool Blackboard Collaborate (see Figure 1).

Figure 1. A screenshot of Blackboard Collaborate online session

Blackboard Collaborate is a web conferencing tool that enables users to communicate with each other via video, audio, text chat, feedback tools (e.g. emoticons, raise-up hand and polling) and whiteboard (see Guo, 2013 for more details).

2.2. The tasks and data collection

Underpinned by interactionist SLA and sociocultural theories, the five collaborative tasks aimed at reinforcing vocabulary and grammar learning and at facilitating learners' communicative competence. Following the task typology proposed by Pica, Kanagy, and Falodun (1993), the five tasks included: two jigsaw tasks, two decision-making tasks and one information-gap task (see Table 2). Figure 1 is a snapshot of the jigsaw task-describing an accident.

Table 2. Summary of tasks and data collection

	Week	Task type	Topic
1	Week 2	Information-gap	Applying for a Chinese visa
2	Week 4	Decision making	Buying clothes and sending it to China
3	Week 6	Jigsaw task	Maps and showing directions
4	Week 10	Decision making	Planning for a trip
5	Week 12	Jigsaw task	Describing an accident

The participants' experiences of using Blackboard Collaborate and tasks were recorded through in-depth interviews, pre and post-session questionnaires.

3. Results and discussion

3.1. Practicality

According to Chapelle (2001), practicality refers to the degree of easy implementation of a CALL task in a certain language teaching setting, including the availability of hardware and software, and the assistance offered by knowledgeable personnel to deal with any unforeseen issues. Findings from the interviews indicated that the affordance of Blackboard Collaborate was satisfactory to support the collaborative tasks completion.

The audio and video quality during the online sessions received positive feedback from the participants. However, echoing the findings in Wang's (2004) study, Internet bandwidth microphone quality was the major limitation. The installation and use of the software was easy and straightforward.

3.2. Language learning potential

Following Chapelle (2001), language learning refers to "the extent to which the activity can be considered to be a language learning activity rather than simply an opportunity for language use" (p. 55). Further, she differentiates language learning and language use as "the extent to which the task promotes beneficial focus on form" (p. 55). In the current study, language learning potential is measured by both focus on form and learners' improvement in Chinese and collaborative learning as below.

3.2.1. Focus on Form

In the follow-up questionnaires, the participants were asked to write down expressions, grammar structures and vocabulary they remembered in the online sessions. The answers primarily focused on grammar structures, vocabulary and certain expressions intensively used in the online sessions, such as "请再说一遍" (Please say it again); "…(English word) 中文怎么说" (How do you say … in Chinese?) "停，走错了！" Stop! You took the wrong way (in the 4th online session).

3.2.2. Improvement in Chinese

The data analysis of interviews and the follow-up survey indicated that the participants perceived that their Chinese proficiency had improved throughout the online sessions, particularly in listening and speaking. One student mentioned in the interview: "I think the fluency has been improved for certain. And also I'm being able to apply the grammar structures in practice. That's just a big thing for me".

3.2.3. Collaborative learning

Results from the interviews showed that the implementation of tasks in the web conferencing based online environment has great potential in stimulating collaborative learning. All the participants preferred collaborative learning rather than individual learning in the context of online language learning, which is contradictory to Wang's (2008) findings.

3.2.4. Learner fit

The participants' perceptions of task difficulty were varied depending on their Chinese proficiency, topic familiarity and task instructions. For example, Student

5 said, "I like the 3rd and 5th online sessions were straightforward and we know what to do. No much thought in deciding things". However, all of them admitted the tasks were challenging in a good way.

In terms of engagement, the majority of participants confirmed that they felt engaged in the online sessions. The participants' feedback suggested that learners' engagement increased when they were used to the online learning environment and higher academic rewards could make participation more attracting.

3.3. Authenticity

When designing the tasks, authenticity was one of the most important concerns. Certain topics, which might be closely related to the learners' real life, were selected. For example, applying for a Chinese visa to participate in a language exchange program, how to fill out a Visa application form; how to ask and show directions, go shopping, etc. In the interviews, all the participants confirmed that the tasks were practical in different ways. Particularly, one student reported her experience of applying the expressions in the 3rd session (showing directions) to help a Chinese lady take a train in Sydney.

3.4. Positive impact

The online sessions have shown a number of positive impacts on the participants, including:
- it created a less pressured environment to learn and practice the target language;
- learners felt more confident to use the target language;
- learners felt more confident to use technology to study a foreign language;
- the positive feedback and encouragement received from peers and the teacher made them feel more confident;
- learners felt they had more opportunities to study between lectures and tutorials.

4. Conclusions

This study proposed a set of criteria for evaluating the appropriateness of web conference-based collaborative tasks and provided empirical evidence of the implementation of the criteria from percipients' perceptions. The findings, which are context specific, showed that the web conferencing tool Blackboard Collaborate, and the five collaborative tasks designed for the particular teaching environment, had great potential in stimulating learner-learner interaction, facilitating their SLA and learner fit.

We are aware of the limitations of the study. Firstly, the findings and arguments were based on the data collected from a small cohort. Secondly, all the participants were on-campus students. The results for distance learners might be different. Further studies should investigate a comparison of results of online tutorials for on-campus students and distance students.

Acknowledgements. We would like to thank the Faculty Partnership Project (FPP) team members from Learning and Teaching Centre (LTC) at Macquarie University who contributed to the online sessions' design and implementation. We would also like to thank all the students who participated in the project. Thank you for your contribution and feedback.

References

Chapelle, C. (2001). *Computer applications in second language acquisition: Foundations for teaching, testing and research*. Cambridge: Cambridge University Press.

Egbert, J., Chao, C. C., & Hanson-Smith, E. (1999). Computer-enhanced language learning environment: An Overview. In J. Egbert & E. Hanson-Smith (Eds), *Computer-enhanced language learning*. Alexandria, VA: TESOL Publications.

Guo, S. (2013). Applying web-conferencing in a beginners' Chinese class. *Paper presented at the Electric Dreams, Proceedings ascilite 2013, Sydney*.

Hampel, R. (2006). Rethinking task design for the digital age: A framework for language teaching and learning in a synchronous online environment. *ReCALL, 18*(1), 105-121. doi:10.1017/S0958344006000711

Hampel, R., & Stickler, U. (2012). The use of videoconferencing to support multimodal interaction in an online language classroom. *ReCALL, 24*(2), 116-137. doi:10.1017/S095834401200002X

Jamieson, J., & Chapelle, C. A. (2010). Evaluating CALL use across multiple contexts. *System, 38*(3), 357-369. doi:10.1016/j.system.2010.06.014

Larsen-Freeman, D., & Long, M. H. (1991). *An introduction to second language acquisition research*. London: Longman.

Long, M. H. (1996). The role of the linguistic environment in second language acquisition. In W. C. Ritchie & T. K. Bhatia (Eds), *Handbook of research on language acquisition. Vol. 2: Second language acquisition* (pp. 413-468). New York: Academic Press.

Pica, T. (1994). Research on negotiation: What does it reveal about second language learning conditions, processes, and outcomes? *Language Learning, 44*(3), 491-527. doi:10.1111/j.1467-1770.1994.tb01115.x

Pica, T., Kanagy, R., & Falodun, J. (1993). Choosing and using communication tasks for second language instruction and research. In G. Grookes & S. M. Gass (Eds), *Tasks Language Learning: Integrating Theory and Practice* (pp. 9-34). Clevedon: Multilingual Matters.

Rosell-Aguilar, F. (2005). Task design for audiographic conferencing: Promoting beginner oral interaction in distance language learning. *Computer Assisted Language Learning, 18*(5), 417-442. doi:10.1080/09588220500442772

Skehan, P. (1998). *A cognitive approach to language learning*. Oxford: Oxford University Press.

Spolsky, B. (1989). *Conditions for second language learning: Introduction to a general theory*. Oxford: Oxford University Press.

Thomas, M., & Reinders, H. (2010). *Task-based language learning and teaching with technology*. London: Bloomsbury Academic.

Wang, Y. (2004). Supporting synchronous distance language learning with desktop videoconferencing. *Language Learning & Technology, 8*(3), 90-121.

Wang, Y. (2008). *Distance language learning and desktop videoconferencing: A Chinese language case study*. Saarbrücken, Germany: VDM Verlag Dr. Müller.

Yin, R. K. (2009). *Case study research: Design and method* (4th ed.). Thousand Oaks, CA: Sage.

university of groningen

A follow-up study of the Facebook project for Japanese university students: Has it been enhancing student interaction, learner autonomy, and English learning?

Mayumi Hamada[1]

Abstract. This is a follow-up study of the Facebook (FB) project conducted from October 2011 to January 2013. The purpose of the project was to investigate how FB can help Japanese university students improve their English, and determine whether FB can facilitate student interaction and learner autonomy by integrating FB activities into English lessons. In the first semester, the students started to use FB for their English study. The results showed that the students' overall reaction to FB was positive and the project developed their English ability and facilitated learner autonomy to some extent. In the following year, the students were given an opportunity to exchange information and opinions with American university students. It was found that the project encouraged the students to become interested in learning about cultural differences. The project also facilitated learner autonomy to a larger extent and helped improve the students' English ability, especially in regard to grammar and vocabulary. In this study, I will present further results of the project based on a survey conducted one year after the project ended. I will also discuss whether and how FB has been facilitating learner autonomy, English learning, and student interaction in the absence of teacher-directed assignments.

Keywords: Facebook, learner autonomy, motivation, writing.

---

1. University of Marketing and Distribution Sciences, Kobe, Japan; mayumi_hamada@red.umds.ac.jp.

How to cite this article: Hamada, M. (2014). A follow-up study of the Facebook project for Japanese university students: Has it been enhancing student interaction, learner autonomy, and English learning? In S. Jager, L. Bradley, E. J. Meima, & S. Thouësny (Eds), *CALL Design: Principles and Practice*; *Proceedings of the 2014 EUROCALL Conference, Groningen, The Netherlands* (pp. 127-133). Dublin: Research-publishing.net. doi:10.14705/rpnet.2014.000206

1. Introduction

With advances in communication technologies, social networking sites (SNS) have become an indispensable communication tool. Facebook is one of the most visited sites and has reached more than 1.23 billion users worldwide by the end of 2013 (Kiss, 2014). As Prichard (2013) argued, since FB can provide a positive experience to second language learners, FB has great potential for language learning in EFL environments as a platform and link to the world.

I therefore decided to conduct a FB project with Japanese university students in order to investigate the effect of FB on English learning, student interaction, and learner autonomy. In the first semester of the project, the main goal was to help students get in the habit of writing regularly in English on FB. It was found that the project could facilitate learner autonomy and English learning to some extent. However, it was also found that most students were reluctant to make foreign friends on their own (Hamada, 2012). In the second and third semester, the students were provided with an opportunity to exchange information and opinions with American university students. It was found that the project encouraged the Japanese students to become interested in learning about cultural differences and initiating interaction with others. The project also facilitated learner autonomy and helped improve the students' English ability, especially in regard to grammar and vocabulary. The project ended in January 2013. Since then no FB assignments have been given to the students and FB activities have been entirely left up to individual students, without any control or supervision by the teacher.

This study aims to investigate the effect of the FB project on the Japanese students in the absence of teacher supervision, examining how or if student interaction, learner autonomy, and English learning have been taking place. This research investigates the following three questions.

Since the FB project ended, how has it influenced:

- student interaction?
- learner autonomy?
- the students' English learning?

2. Methodology

The FB project was conducted from October 2011 to January 2013. The participants were 13 freshmen at the University of Marketing and Distribution Sciences

(UMDS) in Japan. A closed group was formed on FB and students were assigned homework to be used for evaluation and grading.

In the fall semester of 2011 the homework assignment consisted of a weekly topic for consideration, and all students wrote about the same topic within 4-6 lines. In the spring and fall semester of 2012 the project was conducted with the collaboration of Portland State University (PSU). A writing task was assigned to both PSU and UMDS students every week, and all students wrote about the same topic.

The project ended at the end of January 2013. At that time the number of UMDS participants was 11. A year later a survey was administered to collect feedback from UMDS students concerning their FB activities. Ten students out of 11 replied to the survey.

3. Results

Figure 1. Question 1

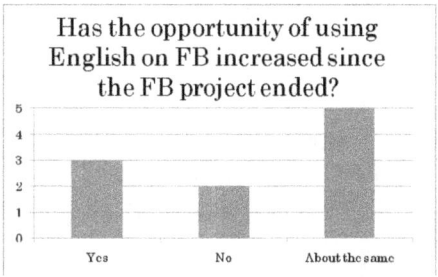

In response to Question 1, two students stated "No" (Figure 1). This indicates that eight students have continued to use English on Facebook.

Figure 2. Question 2

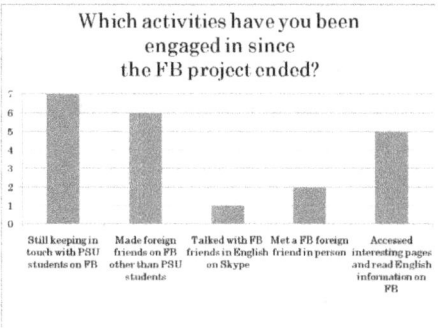

Concerning Question 2, seven students were still keeping in contacting with PSU students by reading their posts and posting comments (Figure 2). Six students found more friends on FB, other than the PSU students, on their own. Only one student did not do any of the activities.

Figure 3. Question 3

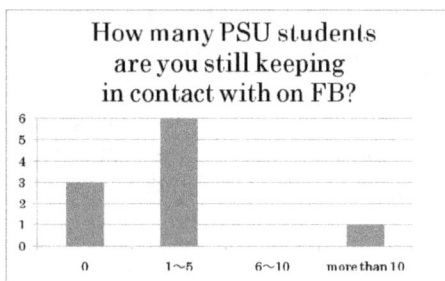

As for Question 3, it was found that all students except one had at least one foreign friend on FB (Figure 3). The three students who made more than 30 foreign friends studied abroad after the project ended.

Figure 4. Question 4

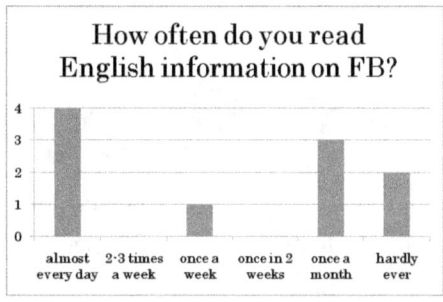

Figure 5. Question 5

As regards Question 4 there was significant variance; four students commented that they read English information on FB almost every day while five students read no more than once a month (Figure 4). The kind of English information they were getting on FB was updates on their friends' status, foreign news reports, news about favorite artists, and information about American TV dramas or movies.

Concerning Question 5, it was found that nobody was posting comments more often than once every two weeks (Figure 5). Six students out of 10 replied they hardly ever posted comments.

Figure 6. Question 6

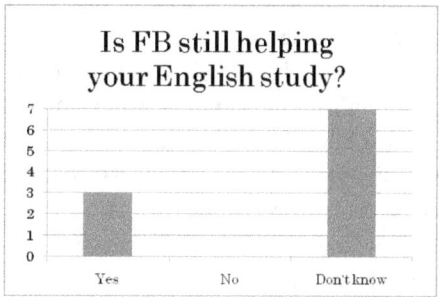

To Question 6, three students agreed that FB was still helping them study English, while seven students were not sure about the effect of FB on their study of English (Figure 6). However, nobody answered "No".

4. Discussion

The overall results indicate that the project has had a positive impact on the students since the end of the period of active teacher supervision.

Concerning research question one, the findings strongly suggest that the project has influenced student interaction to a large degree. The survey showed that 70% of the students were still in touch with the PSU students on FB even one year after the project ended, indicating that the project was successful enough to encourage lasting interaction without the teacher's supervision.

As for research question two, the survey indicates the project has greatly facilitated learner autonomy. According to the survey, opportunities for using English on FB have either increased or at least have been the same for 80% of the students since the project ended. It was observed that the students have been voluntarily engaged in various activities; finding new foreign FB friends other than PSU students, getting English information on FB, or even meeting FB friends in person. These findings indicate that FB has stimulated the students' intrinsic motivation and that English has become a medium for using FB.

Another finding was that the students hardly posted comments, in contrast to reading activities. The same tendency was also found in Hamada's (2013) previous study. As Schalow (2011) pointed out, Japanese people may be "inhibited learners" who are afraid of making mistakes.

As regards research question three, the findings suggest that the project stimulated English learning, especially in the area of reading and vocabulary acquisition. It is assumed that incidental learning has occurred through various FB activities in English. This may explain the finding that 70% of the students were not sure about the effect of FB on their English study; they were not really conscious of language learning because they used English not for "mandatory" assignments, but for fun. Furthermore, reading activities on FB can be considered as "extensive reading," especially for the four students who read English information on FB almost every day. Reading activities may have increased reading speed and promoted reading fluency, as Day and Bamford (2002) claimed. It is difficult however, to measure a direct correlation between the FB project and improvement in English language skills since other variables were also involved.

5. Conclusion

This study examined the results of my follow-up study of the FB project to investigate the potential of FB for enhancing student interaction, learner autonomy, and English learning. It was found that the project was effective enough to cause lasting student interaction even one year after the project ended. The project also facilitated autonomous learning, motivating students to voluntarily engage in various FB activities in English in the absence of assignments or direct supervision by a teacher. It was also suggested that the project helped the students continue to use English on FB, and possibly improved their English language skills. The findings suggest that FB can be a very effective tool to enhance English learning and learner autonomy once the teacher sets up a comfortable and safe environment for the students and helps them make a habit of using English on FB. It is unknown how long the students will continue to use English on FB or what kind of learning outcome will be produced in the long run. It is expected, however, that the students will continue to regard FB as interesting and beneficial. It is hoped it will also broaden their views and knowledge as a result of reading English information and communicating with people throughout the world. It will therefore provide the means to improve English ability without a sense of "studying English".

Acknowledgements. I would like to thank my colleague, Thomas Schalow, for his constructive comments.

References

Day, R. R., & Bamford, J. (2002). Top ten principles for teaching extensive reading. *Reading in a Foreign Language, 14*, 136-141.

Hamada, M. (2012). A Facebook project for Japanese university students: Does it really enhance student interaction, learner autonomy, and English abilities? In L. Bradley & S. Thouësny (Eds), *CALL: Using, Learning, Knowing, EUROCALL Conference, Gothenburg, Sweden, 22-25 August 2012, Proceedings* (pp. 104-110). Dublin: Research-publishing.net. doi:10.14705/rpnet.2012.000035

Hamada, M. (2013). A Facebook project for Japanese university students (2): does it really enhance student interaction, learner autonomy, and English abilities? In L. Bradley & S. Thouësny (Eds), *20 Years of EUROCALL: Learning from the Past, Looking to the Future. Proceedings of the 2013 EUROCALL Conference Évora, Portugal* (pp. 98-105). Dublin: Research-publishing.net. doi:10.14705/rpnet.2013.000145

Kiss, J. (2014, February 4). Facebook's 10th birthday: From college dorm to 1.23 billion users. *The Guardian*. Retrieved from http://www.theguardian.com/technology/2014/feb/04/facebook-10-years-mark-zuckerberg

Prichard, C. (2013). Training L2 learners to use SNSs appropriately and effectively. *CALICO Journal, 30*(2), 204-225. doi:10.11139/cj.30.2.204-225

Schalow, T. (2011). Building an online learning community in Japan: The challenge of distributed learning in a social network. In S. M. Thang, K. Pramela, F. F.Wong, L. K. Lin, M. Jamilah, & M. Marlyna (Eds), *Language and Cultural Diversity* (pp. 89-105). Serdang: Universiti Putra Malaysia Press.

university of groningen

Linking CALL and SLA: Using the IRIS database to locate research instruments

Zöe Handley[1] and Emma Marsden[2]

Abstract. To establish an evidence base for future computer-assisted language learning (CALL) design, CALL research needs to move away from CALL versus non-CALL comparisons, and focus on investigating the differential impact of individual coding elements, that is, specific features of a technology which might have an impact on learning (Pederson, 1987). Furthermore, to help researchers find possible explanations for the success or failure of CALL interventions and make appropriate adjustments to their design, these studies should be conducted within the framework of second language acquisition (SLA) theory (Pederson, 1987). Despite this, a recent review found that broad CALL comparisons are still common and studies focusing on individual coding elements are rare (Macaro, Handley, & Walter, 2012). Moreover, few studies make links with SLA and few measure linguistic outcomes using measures developed in the field of SLA. One reason for this may be difficulty in obtaining the instruments used in SLA research. The IRIS database is introduced as one way of addressing this problem.

Keywords: research methods, instruments, second language acquisition, open access.

1. Introduction

It is our conviction that more basic CALL research, and replications thereof, are required to construct a reliable evidence base upon which future CALL software can be designed. Basic CALL research refers to research which allows us to develop an understanding of what specific features of digital environments create

---

1. Department of Education, University of York; zoe.handley@york.ac.uk.

2. Department of Education, University of York; emma.marsden@york.ac.uk.

How to cite this article: Handley, Z., & Marsden, E. (2014). Linking CALL and SLA: Using the IRIS database to locate research instruments. In S. Jager, L. Bradley, E. J. Meima, & S. Thouësny (Eds), *CALL Design: Principles and Practice*; Proceedings of the 2014 EUROCALL Conference, Groningen, The Netherlands (pp. 134-139). Dublin: Research-publishing.net. doi:10.14705/rpnet.2014.000207

conditions and engage learners in processes that promote SLA, as well as what task variables promote SLA.

CALL research, however, is largely failing to do this, and what we have instead is an accumulation of studies whose findings cannot easily be connected to those of studies in the broader field of SLA, or even other studies within CALL itself. Firstly, broad atheoretical CALL vs non-CALL comparisons –comparing CALL software with 'pen-and-paper' or 'traditional' classroom activities– are still common in the CALL evidence base (Macaro et al., 2012). In such studies, the experimental condition tends to differ in multiple ways from the control condition, and as a consequence it is not possible to determine to which feature of the software any observed differences should be attributed.

Secondly, most CALL research is not grounded in SLA theory (Macaro et al., 2012). Grounding CALL research in SLA theory helps researchers to identify possible explanations for the effectiveness of particular manipulations of CALL environments and make appropriate adjustments to their design to better support language acquisition (Pederson, 1987).

Thirdly, the outcome measures employed in many CALL studies were developed for the specific purposes of the study in question and often differ from those commonly used in SLA research (Macaro et al., 2012). This is problematic because failure to engage in instrumental replication, i.e. to use the outcome measures employed in previous research, limits the comparability of studies (Polio, 2012).

Finally, methods are frequently not adequately reported to permit replication, and in particular, instruments are often not provided (Macaro et al., 2012). Replication is, however, a cornerstone of scientific enquiry, necessary to ensure the construction of a reliable evidence base (Polio, 2012).

In summary, current approaches to CALL research "are encouraging an accumulation of vaguely inter-connected research findings rather than the construction of knowledge across independent studies" (Porte, 2013, p. 12) upon which future CALL software can be designed.

In response to this, we introduce some different forms that basic research and replication might take in CALL research, and introduce IRIS (www.iris-database.org), a digital repository of instruments, materials and stimuli used to elicit data in SLA research, as a resource to facilitate replication and promote the design of comparable studies.

2. Basic CALL research

As said, we believe that more basic CALL research is required to allow us to construct an evidence base upon which to design future CALL. Basic CALL research refers to research designed "to discover something about how students best learn a language", which "provid[es] explanatory data and add[s] to the theoretical bases for second language learning" (Pederson, 1987, p. 125). It might take one of three forms: (1) exploratory research, (2) observational research, or (3) narrowly focused experimental research. Exploratory research is characterised by ethnographic studies in which researchers observe and interview students about their naturalistic use of CALL software with a view of identifying hypotheses regarding what features of digital environments create conditions and engage learners in processes that promote second language acquisition (Pederson, 1987). This might also be achieved through design-based research (see Yutdhana, 2008) and educational engineering (see Colpaert, 2006). Observational research refers to studies which log the processes that students engage in during software use and explore the relationship between software use and learning gains. Narrowly focused experimental studies isolate out specific coding elements, i.e. specific features of a technology which might have a differential impact on learning, and explore hypotheses grounded in SLA theory and research.

3. Replication in CALL

Further to more basic CALL research, replication is also required. Exact replications, in which researchers attempt to copy the original study as closely as possible using identical subjects, conditions, and instruments, among other things, should be conducted, where possible, to allow the confirmation of the reliability of findings (Polio & Gass, 1997). Instrumental replications, approximate replications in which the same outcome measures as used in previous research are employed, permit comparisons of findings across studies. Conceptual replications in which findings are tested using a different study design, are essential to demonstrate the external validity of findings, i.e. "to see if the results hold for a different population, in a different setting, or for a different modality" (Polio & Gass, 1997, p. 502), in a context in which there is so much individual variation in success.

Replication in CALL research has, however, largely been neglected, with the exception of a number of studies which have replicated findings of SLA research (Chun, 2012). Instrumental replication is, however, essential to enable us to connect the findings of different CALL studies with one another and studies in the broader field of SLA, and construct an evidence base upon which to base the design of future CALL software.

The problem, however, is that CALL research is not adequately reported to permit instrumental replication, let alone exact replication (Macaro et al., 2012). Instruments, including background questionnaires, measures of proficiency, instruments for data elicitation and pre- and post-tests, and coding frameworks (Polio & Gass, 1997), are rarely provided in CALL studies, and often barely discussed in the methods sections of research articles (Macaro et al., 2012). While it is always possible to contact authors to request materials, researchers can be difficult to track –they move– and they may not always be able to easily locate materials used in their past research (Marsden & King, 2013; Marsden & Mackey, 2014).

4. The IRIS database

Instruments for Research into Second Language Learning and Teaching (IRIS) is an open access digital repository of materials used to collect data in research on second and foreign language acquisition. All instruments held on the database have been used to collect data for a peer-reviewed publication, i.e. a peer-reviewed journal or conference proceedings, and edited book, or a successful doctoral thesis. The database is searchable along a number of dimensions including instrument type, linguistic feature, and learner proficiency, and materials can be downloaded and re-used, mostly held under a Creative Commons Attribution Non-Commercial Share-Alike licence.

It is also possible for researchers to upload their own instruments to the database for use by other researchers. In fact, 23 top ranking journal editors are now encouraging uploads, and IRIS currently holds over 850 documents bundled into approximately 280 instruments. The coverage of the database is wide, with over fifty instrument types, and over forty research areas represented.

As a research area, CALL is currently underrepresented with only two instruments, in comparison with morphosyntax (grammar) for which there are over 100. In line with current interests in computer-mediated task-based language learning, however, a variety of tasks are held on the database which might be re-used and adapted. These include tasks designed to investigate learners' use of communication strategies (García Mayo, 2005), elicit specific morphosyntactic forms (Mifka Profozic, 2012), and examine the impact of task complexity on the extent to which focus is on form or meaning (Révész, 2011).

5. Conclusion

Current approaches to CALL research comparisons have resulted in "an accumulation of vaguely inter-connected research findings" (Porte, 2013, p. 12). To provide a reliable evidence base upon which to base future CALL design, more basic research, and replications thereof, are necessary. Instrumental replication is particularly important to permit researchers to build on the findings of previous research. To permit such comparisons, CALL researchers are encouraged to contribute instruments to the IRIS database. With 4,600 downloads to date and references to the publications in which the instruments have been used, having materials on IRIS increases the visibility of research.

Acknowledgements. IRIS is directed by Emma Marsden (York, UK) and Alison Mackey (Georgetown, USA / Lancaster, UK), and is funded by the Economic and Social Research Council and the British Academy.

References

Chun, D. (2012). Review article: Replication studies in CALL research. *CALICO Journal, 29*(4), 591-600.

Colpaert, J. (2006). Pedagogy-driven design for online language teaching and learning. *CALICO Journal, 23*(3), 477-497.

García Mayo, M. (2005). Interactional strategies for interlanguage communication: Do they provide evidence for attention to form? In A. Housen & M. Pierrard (Eds), *Investigations in instructed second language acquisition* (Studies on Language Acquisition Series). Mouton de Gruyter.

Macaro, E., Handley, Z. L., & Walter, C. (2012). A systematic review of CALL in English as a second language: Focus on primary and secondary education. *Language Teaching, 45*(1), 1-43. doi:10.1017/S0261444811000395

Marsden, E., & King, J. (2013). The instruments for research into second languages (IRIS) digital repository. *The Language Teacher, 37*(2), 35-38.

Marsden, E. J., & Mackey, A. (2014). IRIS: A new resource for second language research. *Linguistic Approaches to Bilingualism, 4*(1), 125-130. doi:10.1075/lab.4.1.05mar

Mifka Profozic, N. (2012). *Oral corrective feedback, individual differences and L2 acquisition of French past tenses*. Unpublished doctoral dissertation. University of Auckland.

Pederson, K (1987). Research on CALL. In Smith, W. F. (ed.), *Modern media in foreign language education: Theory and implementation* (pp. 99-131). Lincolnwood, Illinois: National Textbook Company.

Polio, C. (2012). Replication in published applied linguistics research: A historical perspective. In Porte, G. (ed.), *Replication research in applied linguistics* (pp. 47-91). Cambridge: Cambridge University Press.

Polio, C. & Gass, S. (1997). Replication and reporting. *Studies in Second Language Acquisition, 19*(4), 499-508. doi:10.1017/S027226319700404X

Porte, G. (2013). Who needs replication? *CALICO Journal, 30*(1), 10-15. doi:10.11139/cj.30.1.10-15

Révész, A. (2011). Task complexity, focus on L2 constructions, and individual differences: A classroom-based study. *The Modern Language Journal, 95*(4), 162-181. doi:10.1111/j.1540-4781.2011.01241.x

Yutdhana, S. (2008). Design-based research in CALL. In Egbert, J. L. & Petrie, G. M. (Eds). *CALL research perspectives* (pp. 169-178). Mahwah, NJ: Lawrence Erlbaum.

Underspecification-based grammatical feedback generation tailored to the learner's current acquisition level in an e-learning system for German as second language

Karin Harbusch[1], Christel-Joy Cameran[2], and Johannes Härtel[3]

Abstract. We present a new feedback strategy implemented in a natural language generation-based e-learning system for German as a second language (L2). Although the system recognizes a large proportion of the grammar errors in learner-produced written sentences, its automatically generated feedback only addresses errors against rules that are relevant at the learner's current L2 acquisition stage. This approach is motivated by the results of two recent studies into German as L2 teaching in classroom situations. Both studies observed that the acquisition stages that L2 learners go through during L2 acquisition are similar to developmental stages for German as first language (L1), with only slight differences depending on the learner's native language (French or Italian). The individual acquisition stages often deviate from the organization of the L2 instruction lessons used in the classroom. They also found that attempts to teach L2 rules which surpass the learner's current acquisition stage are futile. Our system emulates the observed acquisition stages, and the feedback it provides only addresses errors that are 'teachable' at the learner's acquisition stage; the learner is not notified of errors that are beyond this stage. The computational approach to obtain the desired error-diagnostic behavior is based on underspecifications of the system's grammar rules.

Keywords: ICALL, e-learning, natural language generation, grammar teaching, German as a second language (L2), personalized feedback.

---

1. University of Koblenz-Landau, Koblenz, Germany; harbusch@uni-koblenz.de.
2. University of Koblenz-Landau, Koblenz, Germany; cameran@uni-koblenz.de.
3. University of Koblenz-Landau, Koblenz, Germany; johanneshaertel@uni-koblenz.de.

How to cite this article: Harbusch, K., Cameran, C.-J., & Härtel, J. (2014). Underspecification-based grammatical feedback generation tailored to the learner's current acquisition level in an e-learning system for German as second language. In S. Jager, L. Bradley, E. J. Meima, & S. Thouësny (Eds), *CALL Design: Principles and Practice*; *Proceedings of the 2014 EUROCALL Conference, Groningen, The Netherlands* (pp. 140-145). Dublin: Research-publishing.net. doi:10.14705/rpnet.2014.000208

1. Introduction: developmental stages in L2 acquisition

In research on Intelligent Computer-Assisted Language Learning (ICALL), grammatical/linguistic-awareness teaching figures prominently (cf. Meurers, 2013; Roehr, 2007). Generating appropriate feedback is essential in any e-learning system for second language (L2) learning (cf. a recent empirical study by Kartchava, 2012). Many authors advocate personalized feedback (Vasilyeva, 2007), i.e. different learners receive different information, and learners have the possibility to choose the feedback that suits their needs or preferences best. An indispensable prerequisite in such systems is an appropriate user model enabling the system to take the student's knowledge and 'cognitive readiness' (Varnosfadrani & Ansari, 2011) into account when providing corrective feedback.

In a study of grammar errors in written essays by 220 French-speaking learners of L2 German in primary and secondary schools in Geneva/Switzerland, Diehl, Christen, Leuenberger, Pelvat, & Studer (2000) report that even under classroom conditions, pupils go through acquisition stages similar to those observed in first language (L1) acquisition. Crucially, these acquisition stages do not always reflect the organization of the L2 instruction lessons taught in the classroom.

Diehl et al. (2000) identify three "strands" in L2 grammar acquisition (see Table 1). None of the consecutive steps in any strand can be left out –no deviation is vertically possible. Horizontal alignment within each strand reflects the personal acquisition level of the learner. Diehl et al. (2000) interpret their results as strong support for Pienemann's (1989) teachability hypothesis, i.e. grammar instruction has only a chance to be effective if it dovetails with natural acquisition orders and strategies. Ballestracci (2005) argues in the same vein, based on error analyses and classifications of German essays written by Italian-speaking students.

Table 1. The three strands of acquisition levels according to Diehl et al. (2000)

(1) Verbal Morphology	(2) Verb Placement	(3) Case Marking in Noun Phrases
I Preconjugative Phase *(Infinitives)*	I Main Clauses *(Subject-Verb)*	I One-Case-System *(only Nominative forms)*
II Conjugation of Regular Verbs in Present Tense	II Coordinated Main Clauses Wh- and Yes/No-Questions	II One-Case-System *(arbitrary distribution of Nominative/Dative/Accusative forms)*
III Conjugation of Irregular Verbs in Present Tense; Modal Verb + Infinitive	III Correct Topological Assignment of Verbs *(Left and Right Verb Bracket)*	III Two-Case-System Nominative + Object cases *(N-Forms + arbitrarily distributed Dative/Accusative forms)*
IV Auxiliaries + Participles	IV Subordinate Clauses	IV Three-Case-System
V Past Tense	V Inversion *(X-Verb-Subject)*	
VI Remaining Forms		

2. U-COMPASS: generating feedback tailored to the learner's acquisition level

Based on the empirical findings mentioned above, we tailor the feedback delivered by our e-learning system (called U-COMPASS) to the personal acquisition level of the learner –an input parameter to be set by the teacher.

In a drag-and-drop manner, the learner freely constructs phrases/sentences in German. In order to identify the learner's current problem, the student's and the system's generation process become aligned. For any action by the learner, e.g. adding/inflecting word forms or (re-)arranging word order, a natural language paraphrase generator calculates whether the linguistic construction is correct (for details, see Harbusch & Kempen, 2011). Linguistic nomenclature and levels of detail depicted by the system can be set by the teacher. Figure 1 is a screenshot taken during the construction of sentence (1) by an advanced learner exercising word order rules in main and subordinate clauses (cf. phase IV/V in strand (2) of Table 1). The figure illustrates part of the structure underlying sentence (1) in terms of the syntactic formalism of Performance Grammar (PG) (Kempen & Harbusch, 2002). The teacher has selected a German nomenclature (e.g. Kopf 'Head'). Phrasal node labels are suppressed; instead, colors distinguish phrase types, For instance, a modifier in pink can only bind a leaf node with the same color option.

(1) Was will der kleine Junge dass ich ihm allenfalls baue
   What wants the little boy that I him at best build
   'What does the little boy want me to build for him at best'

PG distinguishes three aspects of the structure of sentences: dependency relations (grammatical functions), constituent structure, and linear order. The dependency relations and the constituent structure together form the hierarchical (or dominance) structure. The dependency relations include functional relations: SB=Subject, OA=Accusative Object, DA=Dative Object, etc.). The constituent structure comprises word categories (parts of speech) and word groups (the various types of phrases and clauses). PG is lexicalized, i.e. every constituency rule is associated with a lexical anchor consisting of at least one word form (cf. Harbusch & Kempen, 2011).

Selecting a word form in the lexicon activates a so-called treelet (cf. dependency relations in the second layer of nodes in Figure 1). Linear order is computed in terms of topology-based declarative rules (not spelled out here; see Harbusch & Kempen, 2002). Stretchable rectangular grey boxes represent topologies; they are depicted around the head of a treelet. Within each box, the learner puts the nodes of the corresponding treelet in the desired order. Example (1) illustrates a case where the wh-pronoun 'what' –which is the filler of the Direct Object (OA) of *baue* 'build' in the complement clause (KOMP-S)– gets fronted in the main-clause topology of *will* 'want'. Basically, the core system recognizes any grammatical error by matching student actions against the system's grammar rules. The student is notified of any rule violation through traffic-light colors: Red warns against a "hard" error (e.g. an attempt to attach an Adjective as head of the Subject NP), while yellow signals a "soft" error –one that is provisionally accepted by the system but can be corrected at a later time (as in Figure 1).

Figure 1. Screenshot depicting part of the construction of sentence (1). The treelet of *allenfalls* 'at best' in the right lower corner has been selected from the lexicon at the left but is not yet integrated into the overall structure. The system has spotted a word order error in the subordinate clause and notifies the student by printing the misplaced nodes in yellow (cf. word ordering of "baue ihm" in the KOMP-S clause)

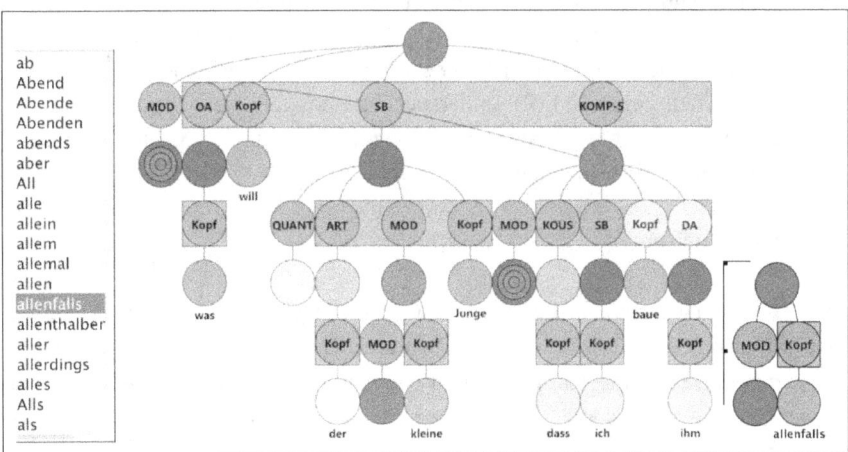

The aforementioned empirical results (Section 1) suggest that feedback on learner errors is effective only if it is in tune with the learner's current acquisition level. Hence, U-COMPASS should "overlook" errors that are beyond this level (and thus are currently unteachable). One way to obtain this behavior is by the introduction of malrules (e.g. Fortmann & Forst, 2004).

A malrule tells the system to provisionally treat an ill-formed structure as correct. Therefore, the system distinguishes three types of diagnosis: (1) correct structures,

(2) incorrect structures rescued by malrule application, and (3) remaining errors resulting from a mismatch with the grammar rules (including malrules). U-COMPASS contains malrules for the typical errors outlined in Table 1 and gives feedback only if a malrule is applied. For instance, the malrule dealing with phase I of strand (3) assigns CASE=Nominative to any grammatical function –although the core system's PG rule only allows CASE=Nominative for the Subject but not the (In-)Direct Object. For learners in phase II, a malrule allows the case options Nominative/Dative/Accusative to be applied to any grammatical function. In phase III, (In-)Direct Objects still allow CASE= Dative/Accusative whereas the Subject is restricted to Nominative. In Phase IV, the full set of rules of the core system is applied without invoking malrules.

Within the PG formalism, the various malrules needed to deal with the three strands of Table 1 can be stated very succinctly by allowing underspecifications for the correct rules. This means modifying the grammar rules in such a way that they overgenerate, i.e. produce certain ill-formed constructions, as desired by the acquisition stages. In the above-mentioned example, the CASE fillers in the treelets have specific underspecification settings (e.g. the Direct Object, which requires CASE=Accusative, has an UNDERSPEC_CASE= Nominative/Dative/Accusative if phase II in strand (3) is the parameter setting for the learner's acquisition stage). For linearization, i.e. strand (2), underspecifications tell the system not to apply specific topological rules during certain acquisition stages, e.g. up to phase V, checks of Subject-Verb-Inversion are suppressed.

3. Conclusions

In our e-learning system for L2=German, we have implemented a feedback strategy that only notifies the learner of errors that are 'teachable' at the current personal acquisition level of the learner, and overlooks any other errors (which will be brought to the learner's attention only at a later stage of acquisition). This strategy is inspired by the results of recent empirical studies in German as an L2 teaching.

We are preparing a first evaluation of U-COMPASS in a classroom. Moreover, we use the data material collected in the two cited empirical studies to automatically set up language games where the learners are invited to correct authentic errors at their current acquisition level.

Acknowledgements. We would like to thank Gerard Kempen for fruitful discussions on the COMPASS system, and for his comments on an earlier version of this paper.

References

Ballestracci, S. (2005). *Zum DaF-Erwerb ausgewählter grammatischer Strukturen der deutschen Sprache bei italophonen Studierenden der Pisaner Facoltà di Lingue e Letterature Straniere.* PhD thesis, Università di Pisa, Italy.

Diehl, E., Christen, H., Leuenberger, S., Pelvat, I., & Studer, T. (2000). *Grammatikunterricht: Alles für der Katz?* Tübingen: Niemeyer.

Fortmann, C., & Forst, M. (2004). An LFG Grammar Checker for CALL. In R. Delmonte, P. Delcloque, & S. Tonelli (Eds), *Procs. of the InSTIL/ICALL2004 Symposium, Venice.*

Harbusch, K., & Kempen, G. (2002). A quantitative model of word order and movement in English, Dutch and German complement constructions. *Procs. of the 19th COLING, Taipei.*

Harbusch, K., & Kempen, G. (2011). Automatic online writing support for L2 learners of German through output monitoring by a natural-language paraphrase generator. In M. Levy, F. Blin, C. Bardin Siskin, & O. Takeuchi (Eds), *WorldCALL: International Perspectives on Computer-Assisted Language Learning Routledge Studies in Computer Assisted Language Learning* (pp. 128-143). New York: Routledge.

Kartchava, E. (2012). *Noticeability of corrective feedback, L2 development and learner beliefs.* PhD Thesis, Université de Montréal, Canada.

Kempen, G., & Harbusch, K. (2002). Performance Grammar: A declarative definition. In M. Theune, A. Nijholt, & H. Hondorp (Eds), *CLIN 2001* (pp. 148-162). Amsterdam: Rodopi.

Meurers, D. (2013). Natural language processing and language learning. In C. A. Chapelle (Ed.), *Encyclopedia of Applied Linguistics* (pp. 1-13). Oxford, UK: Blackwell.

Pienemann, M. (1989). Is language teachable? Psycholinguistic experiments and hypothesis. *Applied Linguistics, 10* (1), 52-79. doi:10.1093/applin/10.1.52

Roehr, K. (2007). Metalinguistic knowledge and language ability in university-level L2 learners. *Applied Linguistics, 29*(2), 173-199. doi:10.1093/applin/amm037

Varnosfadrani, A. D., & Ansari, D. N. (2011). The effectiveness of error correction on the Learning of morphological and syntactic features. *World Journal of English Language, 1*(1), 29-40. doi:10.5430/wjel.v1n1p29

Vasilyeva, E. (2007). Towards personalized feedback in educational computer games for children. In *Procs. of the Sixth conference on IASTED International Conference Web-Based Education, Chamonix.*

Task design for intercultural telecollaboration in secondary schools: Insights from the EU project TILA

Petra Hoffstaedter[1] and Kurt Kohn[2]

Abstract. Our contribution focuses on synchronous oral telecollaboration in secondary schools. With reference to the EU project TILA, aspects of task design and implementation are discussed against the backdrop of issues of technological quality in connection with class organisation in computer labs. Case study evidence is provided in favour of the integration of telecollaborative out-of-class activities.

Keywords: telecollaboration, intercultural communication, language learning, secondary schools, TILA.

1. Introduction

The EU project TILA[3] (www.tilaproject.eu) explores the use of telecollaboration for intercultural communication and language acquisition in secondary schools (Jauregi, Melchor-Couto, & Vilar Beltrán, 2013). Tasks are designed as blended learning "ensembles involving combinations of environments and technological media", including face-to-face interaction, independent work at home, and "synchronous and asynchronous interaction in the web" (Kohn & Hoffstaedter, 2014, p. 3). The project's innovative ambition, however, is clearly set on synchronous oral communication in the 3D virtual world of OpenSim and on the

---

1. Steinbeis-Transferzentrum Sprachlernmedien; petra.hoffstaedter@gmail.com.
2. University of Tübingen; kurt.kohn@uni-tuebingen.de.
3. The EU project TILA has been funded with support from the European Commission. This publication reflects the views only of the author, and the Commission cannot be held responsible for any use which may be made of the information contained therein.

How to cite this article: Hoffstaedter, P., & Kohn, K. (2014). Task design for intercultural telecollaboration in secondary schools: Insights from the EU project TILA. In S. Jager, L. Bradley, E. J. Meima, & S. Thouësny (Eds), *CALL Design: Principles and Practice; Proceedings of the 2014 EUROCALL Conference, Groningen, The Netherlands* (pp. 146-150). Dublin: Research-publishing.net. doi:10.14705/rpnet.2014.000209

videoconferencing platform BigBlueButton. This is in keeping with assumptions regarding crucial interdependencies between language learning, communication and telecollaboration. Following Sociocultural Theory (Swain, Kinnear, & Steinman, 2010), we posit that communication is more than a language learning objective; it is a mediating environment that fundamentally influences and shapes the direction of learning and the very formation of the learner's communicative competence. Successful language learning thus requires rich and authentic communication practice, preferably beyond the inevitable limitations of even the most communicative classroom. This is where synchronous oral telecollaboration comes in with its potential for intercultural contact and communication, and thus for authenticated and incidental intercultural language learning.

2. The stony path from potential to reality

Turning potential into reality can be quite a challenge. The first phase of TILA pilot activities helped shape our understanding of some of the technological and organisational problems involved in implementing synchronous oral telecollaboration in secondary schools.

While the technological infrastructures available in secondary schools are sufficient for written synchronous (e.g. chat) and written asynchronous (e.g. forum, blog) telecollaboration (Kohn & Warth, 2011), the conditions for synchronous oral telecollaboration are far less satisfactory. Participant observation and teacher feedback made it clear that in many of the OpenSim and BigBlueButton exchanges, the sound quality was not sufficient to ensure pedagogically sustainable communicative interaction. In many cases, sound disturbances and breakdowns in both environments tended to reduce communication to 'survival exchanges' (e.g. "Can you hear me?"). The pupils' surprisingly positive feedback can be interpreted as encouraging evidence of the high motivational potential of oral telecollaboration; it must not, however, weaken our concern for technological quality, which is a necessary condition for the pedagogical success of any telecollaborative event.

The technological quality of synchronous oral telecollaboration is closely linked to issues of class organisation. Since learning and teaching in schools is traditionally based on class-size groups (with ad-hoc sub-groupings) in face-to-face mode at fixed times, organisation of telecollaboration exchanges between entire classes and within set class hours thus seems to be the natural candidate. However, forms of organisation geared to face-to-face classroom communication are not necessarily suitable for purposes of synchronous oral telecollaboration. Full-class meetings, e.g. via videoconferencing, offer only limited options, in particular one-to-many or one-to-one with classmates providing background support. By contrast, communication in small groups or between pairs opens up a significantly richer array of naturally relevant types of communicative interaction. The obvious solution thus seems to be to 'shepherd' the pupils to the computer lab, where they team up with their partner class in small parallel telecollaboration groups. Such a set-up, however, often suffers from noise disturbances because of lack of communicative privacy and a temporary network overload with detrimental effects on sound/video quality. Shortcomings of parallel telecollaboration can, of course, be avoided by taking a few 'telecollaboration pupils' temporarily out of the class. But while this is feasible for exploration purposes in a project context, it cannot provide a model for sustainable pedagogical action. A more promising pedagogical solution would be to shift the focus of attention and extend telecollaboration to include homework and other forms of out-of-class activities.

All in all, the sound pedagogical integration of synchronous oral telecollaboration requires careful adaptation of concepts and strategies of class organisation. Easy and ready-made solutions should not be expected; there needs to be developmental room for 'learning to teach' and 'learning to learn'.

3. Telecollaboration task design and implementation

In keeping with the overall blended learning approach and also in order to ensure pedagogical integration into the overall curriculum, telecollaboration tasks in TILA "are not designed as isolated units but rather as more or less complex task ensembles organised in pedagogical macro phases from 'preparatory' to 'main' to 'follow-up'" (Kohn & Hoffstaedter, 2014, p. 3).

The preparatory phase typically involves subtasks that help prepare the ground for the main telecollaborative task. This may concern, for instance, getting to know each other, knowledge development, or making oneself familiar with telecollaboration tools. Preparatory tasks can be face-to-face or online, synchronous or asynchronous, individual or collaborative. The main phase focuses on intercultural communicative interactions in synchronous (BigBlueButton, OpenSim) and/or asynchronous (forum, blog) environments. These activities give the entire task ensemble its pedagogical and telecollaborative focus. In the follow-up phase, pupils engage in subtasks designed to secure learning results. They can again be face-to-face or online, synchronous or asynchronous, individual or collaborative.

In a first case study, pupils and teachers from a French and a German school[4] engaged in successive telecollaboration exchanges to explore the potential of OpenSim for intercultural communicative learning experiences. Each exchange was set around learning stations in the form of French or German posters and had a special thematic focus, i.e. waste disposal, vegetarian diet, fashion, or Europe. French/German pairs of pupils walked from one poster to the next; they discussed the pictures and questions presented in the language used on the poster.

The 'tandem' format enabled the pupils to help each other understand the message conveyed and to find appropriate expressions. Each event was supported by preparatory and follow-up activities in face-to-face and forum/blog/wiki modes. The assessment by teachers and pupils regarding the tasks' communication and learning potential was positive. The posters stimulated communication and discovery of intercultural differences. Pupils favoured topics like fashion where they were able to talk about themselves and their likes and dislikes. The developmental set-up enabled valuable insights and improvements from one exchange to the next. At the same time, however, class organisation proved to be complex and taxing; communication was impeded by low sound quality and background noise due to parallel telecollaboration pairs in the computer labs.

Because of these problems, a second case study with pupils and teachers from a Dutch and a French school[5] was conducted to explore telecollaborative out-of-class exchanges as part of the pupils' collaborative homework assignments. The exchanges were designed as pair conversations in 'lingua franca' format; pairs of French/Dutch pupils with German as the target language met in BigBlueButton, each from their home PCs, to discuss topics such as 'drinking age', 'dress code in school', 'a day without mobile phones', or 'where our clothes are made'. Pupils who felt uncomfortable with this task or did not have the required technological infrastructure at home discussed the same topics with a peer in a Moodle forum. In a follow-up activity, the pupils were asked to write a summarising protocol in a wiki as input for the final discussion in class. The outcomes were highly encouraging. Natural and fluent conversations conforming to the pupils' respective levels of proficiency clearly demonstrate the pedagogical validity and technological feasibility of the homework approach.

---

4. Cathérine Felce, College La Cerisaie, Charenton-le-Pont, France; Hajo Zenzen, Gymnasium Saarburg, Germany.

5. Cathérine Felce, College La Cerisaie, Charenton-le-Pont, France; Helga Frömming, Berlage Lyceum, Amsterdam, Netherlands.

4. Conclusions

Synchronous oral telecollaboration has a promising potential for intercultural communication and language learning in secondary schools. In the commonly chosen in-class approach with parallel telecollaboration groups in a computer lab, communication is however often seriously handicapped by issues of class organisation, poor sound/video quality and too little communicative privacy. To ensure pedagogically sustainable implementation of synchronous oral telecollaboration tasks, it is thus of key importance to look beyond the computer lab and integrate out-of-class options, in particular collaborative homework activities. Evidence from our case study strongly supports this solution, which is also in line with a blended learning approach.

Acknowledgements. We would like to thank our teachers Cathérine Felce, Helga Frömming and Hajo Zenzen for their creative expertise and enthusiastic commitment.

References

Jauregi, K., Melchor-Couto, S., & Vilar Beltrán, E. (2013). The European project TILA. In L. Bradley & S. Thouësny (Eds), *20 years of Eurocall: Learning from the past, looking to the future. Proceedings of the 2013 Eurocall Conference, Évora, Portugal* (pp. 123-128). Dublin/Voillans: Research-publishing.net. doi:10.14705/rpnet.2013.000149

Kohn, K., & Hoffstaedter, P. (2014). *WP 3 research: Specification of TILA research studies*. Retrieved from http://www.tilaproject.eu/moodle/mod/page/view.php?id=1496

Kohn, K., & Warth, C. (Eds). (2011). *Web collaboration for intercultural language learning. A guide for language teachers, teacher educators and student teachers*. Münster: Monsenstein und Vannerdat (eBook).

Swain, M., Kinnear, P., & Steinman, L. (2010). *Sociocultural theory in second language education: An introduction through narratives*. Clevedon: Multilingual Matters.

university of groningen

Challenges and opportunities for business communication: A Facebook approach conundrum

Chung-Kai Huang[1], Chun-Yu Lin[2], and Daniel Steve Villarreal[3]

Abstract. Facebook is currently one of the most popular platforms for online social networking among university students. The ever-growing prevalence of Facebook has led business educators to explore what role social networking technology might play in business training and professional development. Nonetheless, much is left to be learned about how Facebook is influencing student learning in the area of business communication. This paper examined the effect on learners' satisfaction of incorporating Facebook into business communication courses. A total of 147 undergraduate students from a national university in Taiwan participated in this web-supported study. To analyze the students' reflection quantitatively, a survey was employed. The findings showed that the incorporation of Facebook into coursework effectively assisted students' learning of business communication. Facebook worked as the social glue that connected students together in a learning community, provided opportunities for sharing, and transformed students' learning attitudes towards their business presentation projects. Students deepened their understanding of content knowledge learning not only from the class input but also via peer feedback activities on Facebook. In addition to the benefits gained, care should be taken not to over-privilege Facebook. Weighing the balance between social networking practice on Facebook and face-to-face interaction in class, pedagogical suggestions and recommendations are addressed for future pedagogical use and research direction.

Keywords: business communication, Facebook, web-supported learning.

---

1. Department of International Business, National Taipei University of Business, Taiwan; hck2005@ntub.edu.tw.
2. Department of Business Administration, National Taipei University, Taiwan; chunyu@mail.ntpu.edu.tw.
3. Center for General Education, National Defense Medical Center, Taiwan; interpreterman@aol.com.

How to cite this article: Huang, C.-K., Lin, C.-Y., & Villarreal, D. S. (2014). Challenges and opportunities for business communication: A Facebook approach conundrum. In S. Jager, L. Bradley, E. J. Meima, & S. Thouësny (Eds), *CALL Design: Principles and Practice; Proceedings of the 2014 EUROCALL Conference, Groningen, The Netherlands* (pp. 151-157). Dublin: Research-publishing.net. doi:10.14705/rpnet.2014.000210

1. Introduction

The advance of digital technologies and social media has provided opportunities for business educators to develop new approaches to educational training in higher education (Alavi, Yoo, & Vogel, 1997). Today's students are exposed to ubiquitous Web 2.0 technologies (García-Ruiz, Fernández, & Pulido, 2014). Due to this wave, business educators are incorporating social media and technology, extending their capabilities to assist students in knowledge sharing, project collaborating and polishing targeted skills and expertise (Crews & Stitt-Gohdes, 2012). Thus, blended learning has revolutionized traditional lecture-based business communication classrooms.

Facebook is recognized for its potential in formulating online learning communities and motivating students to learn. Facebook, originally established for social networking, has received considerable attention in education because of its accessibility, convenience, and flexibility (Bowman & Akcaoglu, 2014; Prescott, 2014). Business communication is a specialized area of communication. Thus, business communication practitioners must consider the communication processes' key elements: messages, senders, receivers, feedback, context, challenge and interference as well as understand business requirements (Francis, Stricker, Russell-Dempsey, Morrison, & Winzenburg, 2009).

In this study, Facebook is used to archive students' class presentations, share their presentation materials from Prezi and allow them to provide constructive peer feedback for the presented business topics. Practicing pertinent real-world related business issues via a structured video- and text-based format enables students to practice varied business communication modes. Reflective writing activities help students think critically about business communication's key elements and write concisely (Decarie, 2010). Consequently, this study employs the following research questions. First, what is the relationship between learners' perceptions about course effectiveness, perceived usefulness, ease of use, the peer feedback system and satisfaction respectively? Second, does perceived ease of use affect the relationships among learners' perceptions about course effectiveness, usefulness, the peer feedback system, and satisfaction?

2. Method

This quantitative survey study investigated relationships among students' perceptions regarding the dimensions of course, technology, environment, and their satisfaction in a business communication class incorporating Facebook. The effect of perceived ease of use on the relationships was examined. The study site was a Taiwanese national university's business school, ranked as one of Taiwan's best vocational-tracked institutions. Participants are generally highly motivated and self-regulated. The questionnaire items were selected to elicit learner satisfaction and underlying variables. The conceptual framework was replicated from Huang's (2012) research study.

Table 1. Questionnaire items, means and standard deviation (N=147)

Construct/Variable	Number of Items	$M(SD)$
Learner Satisfaction (LS)	6	4.14(.54)
Course Effectiveness (CE)	6	4.14(.50)
Perceived Usefulness (PU)	4	3.67(.70)
Peer Feedback System (PFS)	14	3.40(.45)
Perceived Ease of Use (PEU)	3	4.43(.51)

The data were collected during the 2013 fall semester. The quantitative analyses had three main aspects. The purpose of the descriptive statistic analysis was to analyze the distribution of participants' basic information in order to obtain a preliminary understanding of their basic characteristics and responses to the five variables (Table 1). The correlation analysis and simple regression analysis addressed the first three research questions and determined which factors correlated with learner satisfaction. The hierarchical regression answered the fourth research question.

3. Discussion

The survey was distributed to all business communication students with 147 replies received (98% response rate). Of the 147 completed surveys, 20 males (13.6%), and 127 females (86.4%). Seventy (47.6%) participants were seniors; seventy-seven (52.4%) were juniors. One hundred and forty-two (96.6%) of them were international business majors, four (2.7%) were finance majors, and one (0.7%) was information science (see Table 2 for detail: overall, heterogeneous sampling).

Table 2. Demographic information about respondents (N=147)

Categories	Number	Percentage
Gender	147	100
Male	20	86.4
Female	127	13.6
School Years	147	100
Senior	70	47.6
Junior	77	52.4
Major	147	100
International Business	142	96.6
Finance	4	2.7
Information Science	1	0.7

In the correlation analysis, a Pearson product-moment was adopted to assess the inter-factor correlations (Table 3). A simple correlation and a simple regression measured the relationships among perceived learner satisfaction and each factor. The results showed that all three antecedent variables and one moderating variable, and the outcome variable had significant relationships. Course effectiveness was positively correlated with learner satisfaction ($r=.47$, $p<.01$), perceived usefulness was positively correlated with learner satisfaction ($r=.46$, $p<.01$), peer feedback system was positively correlated with learner satisfaction ($r=.36$, $p<.01$), and perceived ease of use was positively correlated with learner satisfaction ($r=.34$, $p<.01$).

Table 3. Simple correlation between variables

Variables	LS	CE	PU	PFS	PEU
LS	—				
CE	.47**	—			
PU	.46**	.57**	—		
PFS	.36**	.42**	.55**	—	
PEU	.34**	.23**	.25**	.31**	—

*$p < .05$ **$p < .01$

We examined the moderating effect of perceived ease of use on the relationships between learners' perceptions regarding course, usefulness, and technology, and their satisfaction with this course. Table 4, Model 1 includes three independent variables: course effectiveness, perceived usefulness, and the peer feedback system. This model accounted for 53.2% of the variance in learners' satisfaction ($R^2=.532$). Course effectiveness had a significant positive effect on learner satisfaction ($\beta=.293$, $p<.01$), and the peer feedback system also had a significant positive effect on learner satisfaction ($\beta=.230$, $p<.05$). However, perceived usefulness had no significant effect on learner satisfaction. Model 2 includes all three independent variables and the moderating item (PEU). This model accounted for 56.7% of the variance in learner satisfaction ($R^2=.567$). Course effectiveness had a significant positive effect on learner satisfaction ($\beta=.273$, $p<.01$), peer feedback system had a significant positive effect on learner satisfaction ($\beta=.214$, $p<.05$), and perceived ease of use had a significant positive effect on learner satisfaction ($\beta=.207$, $p<.01$). However, perceived usefulness had no significant effect on learner satisfaction.

Model 3 includes all three independent variables, the moderating item (PEU) and the three interaction items. This model accounted for 57.0% of the variance in learners' satisfaction ($R^2=.570$). Course effectiveness had a significant positive effect on learner satisfaction (β=.269, p<.01), peer feedback system had a significant positive effect on learner satisfaction (β=.206, p<.10), and perceived ease of use had a significant positive effect on learner satisfaction (β=.210, p<.01). However, perceived usefulness had no significant effect on learner satisfaction. None of the three interaction items had a significant effect on the relationship between learners' perceptions about courses, usefulness, technology, and their satisfaction.

Table 4. Examination of moderating effect of perceived ease of use (N=147)

Predictors	Model 1	Model 2	Model 3
CE	.293***	.273***	.269***
PU	.112	.066	.057
PFS	.230**	.214**	.206*
PEU		.207***	.210***
CE * PEU			.069
PU * PEU			-.008
PFS* PEU			-.016
R^2	.532	.567	.570
Adj R^2	.283	.321	.325
ΔR^2	.268	.302	.291
F	18.820	7.972	.238

Dependent variable: Learner satisfaction, *p < .10, **p < .05, ***p < .01

4. Conclusions

The results showed that the students' perceptions about course effectiveness, feedback system, and ease of use of Facebook had a positive effect on their satisfaction with the course. However, learners' perceived usefulness did not significantly affect on their satisfaction. Furthermore, learners' perceived ease of use of Facebook did not have a significant effect on the relationships among their perceptions about the course, usefulness, technology, and their satisfaction with this course.

Based on the proposed research questions and the correlational results obtained, a course can be designed to teach business communication, while considering and incorporating the appropriateness regarding Facebook's technology affordance and functions. Effective teaching and learning objectives and activities play an important role in students' attitudinal responses. Regarding Facebook's pedagogical usefulness, due to its social media features, a Facebook platform helps promote students' reading and writing interchange by cultivating their communication competencies. Students appreciate the supplementary online learning on Facebook as they become more active learners. Additionally, a peer feedback system should be organized, as students perform online tasks and receive feedback from other learners. By connecting with classmates, students will better understand about their drawbacks and strengths in their business communication skills.

The hierarchical recession indicates no significant relationship between the perceived usefulness of Facebook and learner satisfaction. A possible reason may be the lack of authentic business communication-like exercises. Course effectiveness, perceived ease of use and peer feedback system lead to the positive increase of learners' course satisfaction. Furthermore, the findings also suggest that Facebook's perceived ease of use has no moderating effect on altering learners' course satisfaction. For today's digital native university students, social media is closely tied to daily life; they grasp Facebook's interfaces and features. This might explain the insignificance of the interaction among perceived ease of use of Facebook and course effectiveness, perceived usefulness and the peer feedback system.

For future curriculum design, a Facebook-utilizing learning design promises to provide teachers with a framework that will enable them to design effective, quality learning experiences for business communication students. Instructors should document teaching activities and scaffold processes on Facebook, reflect students' practice of learning and share instructional design that potentially improve teaching quality in business communication. For future research design, replication of this study in other university subjects or cultural contexts may furnish deeper understanding of the challenges and opportunities of implementing Facebook.

Acknowledgement. We cordially thank the Ministry of Science and Technology for the foreign travel grant to present our preliminary results in EUROCALL 2014 at the University of Groningen, Netherlands.

References

Alavi, M., Yoo, Y., & Vogel, D. R. (1997). Using information technology to add value to management education. *Academy of management Journal, 40*(6), 1310-1333. doi:10.2307/257035

Bowman, N. D., & Akcaoglu, M. (2014). "I see smart people!": Using Facebook to supplement cognitive and affective learning in the university mass lecture. *The internet and higher education, 23*, 1-8. doi:10.1016/j.iheduc.2014.05.003

Crews, T. B., & Stitt-Gohdes, W. L. (2012). Incorporating Facebook and Twitter in a service-learning project in a business communication course. *Business Communication Quarterly, 75*(1), 76-79. doi:10.1177/1080569911431881

Decarie, C. (2010). Facebook: Challenges and opportunities for business communication students. *Business Communication Quarterly, 73*(4), 449-452. doi:10.1177/1080569910385383

Francis, C., Stricker, J., Russell-Dempsey, G., Morrison, K., & Winzenburg, K. (Eds). (2009). *Projects in speech communication*. Logan, IA: Perfect Learning.

García-Ruiz, R., Fernández, N. G., & Pulido, P. C. (2014). Competency training in universities via projects and Web 2.0 tools: Analysis of an experience. RUSC. *Universities and Knowledge Society Journal, 11*(1), 61-75.

Huang, C.-K. (2012). *Learner satisfaction with blog- and wiki-supported writing in an EFL course in Taiwan*. Doctoral dissertation, University of Texas at Austin. Retrieved from https://repositories.lib.utexas.edu/bitstream/handle/2152/ETD-UT-2012-08-6197/HUANG-DISSERTATION.pdf?sequence=1

Prescott, J. (2014). Teaching style and attitudes towards Facebook as an educational tool. *Active Learning in Higher Education, 15*(2), 117-128. doi:10.1177/1469787414527392

university of groningen

Contextual language learning: Educational potential and use of social networking technology in higher education

Chung-Kai Huang[1], Chun-Yu Lin[2], and Daniel Steve Villarreal[3]

Abstract. This study investigates the potential and use of social networking technology, specifically Facebook, to support a community of practice in an undergraduate-level classroom setting. Facebook is used as a tool with which to provide supplementary language learning materials to develop learners' English writing skills. We adopted the technology acceptance model to examine students' initial expectations and perceptions of, and attitudes toward the use of Facebook as a learning platform for sharing of knowledge and class experiences. Data were collected both qualitatively and quantitatively from 18 students who were enrolled in a semester-long English writing course at a public university in Taiwan. Findings indicate that Facebook provides an easy-to-use interface for learners to leverage the social networking skills that are part and parcel of their everyday world and to generate shared knowledge among each other within a small group environment. Given the fact that college-age students are already proficient with Facebook and other social media, language teachers should take advantage of that situation by incorporating Facebook into classrooms. It is also suggested that language teachers consider their expected learning objectives and outcomes while utilizing Facebook for its educational purposes and meaningfulness.

Keywords: Facebook, social networking, knowledge sharing, language learning.

---

1. Department of International Business, National Taipei University of Business, Taiwan; hck2005@ntub.edu.tw.
2. Department of Business Administration, National Taipei University, Taiwan; chunyu@mail.ntpu.edu.tw.
3. Center for General Education, National Defense Medical Center, Taiwan; interpreterman@aol.com.

How to cite this article: Huang, C.-K., Lin, C.-Y., & Villarreal, D. S. (2014). Contextual language learning: Educational potential and use of social networking technology in higher education. In S. Jager, L. Bradley, E. J. Meima, & S. Thouësny (Eds), *CALL Design: Principles and Practice; Proceedings of the 2014 EUROCALL Conference, Groningen, The Netherlands* (pp. 158-164). Dublin: Research-publishing.net. doi:10.14705/rpnet.2014.000211

1. Introduction

The improvement of information and communication technologies has resulted in the emergence of online social communities (Ito et al., 2008). In today's knowledge-based society, the necessity of sharing knowledge assets in a global or electronic collaborative fashion is not necessarily inevitable (Chu & Kennedy, 2011). In the twenty-first century's world of global citizenship, the adoption of web tools can boost participation in global citizenship; web-based technology lends itself to facilitating both teachers and learners taking advantage of learning opportunities. Furthermore, the Internet can enhance educational administrators' effectiveness (Ajjan & Hartshorne, 2008). Today, with economic, social, and cultural policies being driven by the need for globalization and bounded by contextual constraints, education faces a changing era of new technologies of information and communication, and rapid construction and sharing of diverse knowledge.

Social networking technologies now provide more effective tools for communication in educational contexts by facilitating personal interaction and enhancing a sense of community among students (Brady, Holcomb, & Smith, 2010). For example, Facebook usage is growing significantly, due to its accessibility and capacity to deliver educational information to students (Roblyer, McDaniel, Webb, Herman, & Witty, 2010). In Taiwan, English is learned as a foreign language since it is not generally used outside of language classrooms. In foreign language education, Facebook-mediated pedagogy can help sustain active participation, as Facebook allows instructors to design meaningful environments. They can do so by engaging learners in the use of target languages, along with access to multimedia, authentic material and on-demand course references and support (Blattner & Lomicka, 2012). In spite of these benefits, evidence shows that some students still struggle to see the value of social networking technologies for learning and teaching (Bennett, Bishop, Dalgarno, Waycott, & Kennedy, 2012). Therefore, this study provides an overview of educational potential and use of social networking technology in higher education, and describes the methodology used specifically in language classrooms. We also summarize the implementation experiences of the instructor and students involved and present the key findings as well as practical recommendations for researchers and educators.

2. Method

The instructional design is based on contextual learning, a constructivist-driven teaching and learning concept (Imel, 2000). Being a prevalent social networking technology, Facebook is widely used by today's young students worldwide. After posting, friends can read and respond immediately. Therefore, it is convenient and fun to communicate and share thoughts. By incorporating Facebook in course management, instructors can present information in such a way that students are able to construct meaning based on their experiences (Wang, Woo, Quek, Yang, & Liu, 2012). In this study, we explored how students used and made sense of Facebook. We have observed this pedagogical practice since 2012. Findings of this research were drawn from our preliminary results from a semester-based implementation of Facebook at a public Taiwanese university in the first year of research. Eighteen Taiwanese students who enrolled in a junior English course with a focus on writing participated in this study.

The Facebook presence was a private group so that only invited student members could participate. We considered previous work (Shiu, Fong, & Lam, 2010) about Facebook and its uses in education. The following are our research questions: (1) How do instructors utilize and react to using Facebook in a university-level language course design for educational purposes? (2) What are student perceptions and attitudes towards Facebook use within the context of a university-level language course?

Mixed methods were employed to assess the data from qualitative and quantitative perspectives. The survey questionnaire and the open-ended questions addressed to the students were adopted from Huang (2012), considering the contextual learning environment in which Facebook was used. The modified questionnaire consisted of the following major categories: course dimension, technology dimension, environmental dimension and learner dimension. Descriptive analysis (e.g. mean, standard deviation, frequency distribution) was conducted using the SPSS statistical software package version 16.0 for the sixteen valid surveys collected. Based on the predetermined themes, open-ended comments were grouped into categories; initial succinct points were included in the results to support findings.

3. Discussion

The teaching goal of this language course was to help students cultivate their English writing knowledge and skills through the use of Facebook in addition to the required genre practice of writing. Because the instructor specializes in technology-assisted learning, he believes that setting up a customized Facebook group page could provide opportunities to share knowledge, exchange information and communicate with classmates according to the thematic discussion issues. His teaching philosophy is influenced by his doctoral and master's programs' training. He indicated his viewpoints about technology-supported curriculum and instruction as he applied Facebook for pedagogical applications.

In traditional physical classrooms, it might be difficult for students to continue their learning in a self-regulated and contextual approach because of certain factors: number of students, time constraints, or lack of intrinsic motivation from the learners. Followed by the classroom activities, Facebook helps connect students to structured learning tasks and enables them to produce formative feedback, along with reflections on given assignments (see Figure 1).

Figure 1. Facebook online discussion

As a young professor, the instructor has more recent exposure to digital technologies than older professors, and he keeps up with very up-to-date information. On the Facebook page of his class, he sorted out theme-based questions for discussion and helped students improve their critical thinking by sharing their knowledge collectively in a written feedback format. Students were able to apply knowledge to cultivate their writing and their problem-solving skills. Along with gaining knowledge in writing skills, students were encouraged to share their own ideas in writing and interact with others when performing writing assignments. Facebook's characteristics facilitate students' communication because students can post and receive messages in a one-to-one and in a one-to-many mode.

This supplementary process reinforces the contextualization by adding the educational value of adopting Facebook in educational settings –levels of communication and collaboration increase, as do deeper levels of reflection. The instructor also reported positive effects on observing student engagement in the Facebook-supported network. A Facebook group provides better motivation for students to perform writing tasks due to the blended instructional design of onsite course teaching and Facebook community interaction. Table 1 shows the mean scores and standard deviation among the selected variables based on the five-point Likert scale: learner satisfaction (LS), course effectiveness (CE), perceived usefulness (PU), perceived ease of use (PEU), peer feedback system (PFS), learner community support (LCS) and instructor response timeliness (IRT).

The results show that the participating students were highly satisfied with the design of the Facebook-supported learning community, especially with the course's effectiveness and perceived usefulness of the functions that Facebook provides.

Table 1. Profile of student response to the survey

	LS	CE	PU	PEU	PFS	LCS	IRT
Mean	4.61	4.71	4.41	3.50	3.21	2.95	4.63
S.D.	0.45	0.38	0.60	0.49	0.44	0.70	0.50

Writing tasks are read by the instructor and peers. Their reflections can present strengths and weaknesses of the texts they read or video clips they watch. Observation by peers can raise students' awareness of improving their writing accuracy in an implicit way. Nonetheless, since there was no direct corrective feedback received from the instructor and other peers focusing on the writing per se, the students cannot benefit from using the form-based feedback as guides for improving their grammatical mistakes, word usage and content revision. Teacher feedback on students' writing is critical in a traditional classroom, as it is when the writing is completed in Facebook. Although writing can be enhanced from peers' constructive comments, students still prefer teacher feedback. Finally, the instructor claimed that "it would be advantageous if Facebook could customize its reply function by providing a threaded response underneath each original post". In this way, tagging the person who leaves the original message is not necessary and discussion centered on the same topics can be grouped together. Overall, Facebook has contributed to the effectiveness of course design and promoted learners' satisfaction about the teaching of English writing.

4. Conclusions

Today's higher educational community has gradually adopted social networking technologies into curriculum design. Facebook is used frequently by university students and may be a potential tool to integrate into university courses. Such education-oriented social networking technologies provide viable tools for educators hoping to expose students to the potential educational opportunities and meaningful inquiries in subject domain learning. Findings from this study help to provide an overview of some initial research on the use of Facebook as a contextual interactive environment in educational settings. Both the instructor and students are receptive to incorporating Facebook as an academic platform, having identified the potential benefits and drawbacks of using Facebook.

In addition to the perceived "benefits through enhanced communication, interaction and flexibility in course content delivery" (Irwin, Ball, Desbrow, & Leveritt, 2012, p. 1230), this study can suggest how to better utilize Facebook to meet the needs of instructors and students. Equally important, concerns over student privacy and safety in Facebook for education-based purposes also needs to be addressed by imposing limits regarding the community's accessibility. Social networking technology, as stated by Irwin et al. (2012), "is well-received [; however], it is still unclear if and how Facebook can enhance student learning outcomes. Continued investigation of Facebook use in [higher] education may provide further insight" into pertinent issues as well as effectively organize established community support aligned with the curriculum development and course teaching goals (p. 1230).

Acknowledgement. We cordially thank the Ministry of Science and Technology for the foreign travel grant to present our preliminary results in EUROCALL 2014 at the University of Groningen, Netherlands.

References

Ajjan, H., & Hartshorne, R. (2008). Investigating faculty decisions to adopt Web 2.0 technologies: Theory and empirical tests. *The internet and higher education, 11*(2), 71-80. doi:10.1016/j.iheduc.2008.05.002

Bennett, S., Bishop, A., Dalgarno, B., Waycott, J., & Kennedy, G. (2012). Implementing Web 2.0 technologies in higher education: A collective case study. *Computers & Education, 59*(2), 524-534. doi:10.1016/j.compedu.2011.12.022

Blattner, G., & Lara Lomicka. (2012). Facebook-ing and the social generation: A new era of language learning. *Alsic, 15*(1). doi:10.4000/alsic.2413

Brady, K. P., Holcomb, L. B., & Smith, B. V. (2010). The use of alternative social networking sites in higher educational settings: A case study of the e-learning benefits of Ning in education. *Journal of Interactive Online Learning, 9*(2), 151-170.

Chu, S. K.-W., & Kennedy, D. M. (2011). Using online collaborative tools for groups to co-construct knowledge. *Online Information Review 35*(4), 581-597. doi:10.1108/14684521111161945

Huang, C.-K. (2012). *Learner satisfaction with blog- and wiki-supported writing in an EFL course in Taiwan*. Doctoral dissertation, University of Texas at Austin. Retrieved from https://repositories.lib.utexas.edu/bitstream/handle/2152/ETD-UT-2012-08-6197/HUANG-DISSERTATION.pdf?sequence=1

Imel, S. (2000). *Contextual learning in adult education, practice application brief no. 12*. ERIC Clearinghouse on Adult, Career, and Vocational Education, 2000. Retrieved from http://eric.ed.gov/?id=ED448304

Irwin, C., Ball, L., Desbrow, B., & Leveritt, M. (2012). Students' perceptions of using Facebook as an interactive learning resource at university. *Australasian Journal of Educational Technology, 28*(7), 1221-1232.

Ito, M., Horst, H., Bittanti, M., Boyd, D., Herr-Stephenson, B., Lange, P. G., Pascao, C. J., & Robinson, L. (2008). *Living and learning with new media: Summary of findings from the digital youth project*. Chicago: The John D. and Catherine T. MacArthur Foundation.

Roblyer, M. D., McDaniel, M., Webb, M., Herman, J., & Witty, J. V. (2010). Findings on Facebook in higher education: A comparison of college faculty and student uses and perceptions of social networking sites. *The internet and higher education, 13*(3), 134-140. doi:10.1016/j.iheduc.2010.03.002

Shiu, H., Fong, J., & Lam, J. (2010). Facebook – Education with social networking websites for teaching and learning. In P. Tsang, S. S. Cheung, V. K. Lee, & R. Huang (Eds), *Hybrid learning* (Vol. 6248, pp. 59-70). Berlin Heidelberg: Springer.

Wang, Q., Woo, H. L., Quek, C. L., Yang, Y., & Liu, M. (2012). Using the Facebook group as a learning management system: An exploratory study. *British Journal of Educational Technology, 43*(3), 428-438. doi:10.1111/j.1467-8535.2011.01195.x

university of groningen

EFL learners' perceived use of conversation maintenance strategies during synchronous computer-mediated communication with native English speakers

Atsushi Ino[1]

Abstract. This study investigated the perceived use of conversation maintenance strategies during synchronous computer-mediated communication with native English speakers. I also correlated the relationships of the strategies used with students' speaking ability and comprehensive proficiency level. The research questions were: (1) how were the learners' perceived use of conversation maintenance strategies related with one another?; and (2) what were the relationships of those strategies with learner's speaking ability and English proficiency? During the semester, the participants participated in five synchronous computer-mediated communication sessions in total. Each of the teachers listened to three presentations during each 50 minutes session. During one period, the teacher interacted with the learners, especially after each presentation, asking questions and giving some comments. Significant correlations were found between keeping eye contact and asking questions to the teacher, between keeping eye contact and taking action/showing attitude to continue conversation, and between keeping eye contact and readiness to help peers. It was also found that asking questions to the teacher and readiness to help peers were strongly correlated. These results seemed to mean that keeping eye-contact was a crucial conversation maintenance strategy in videoconferencing synchronous computer-mediated communication (SCMC).

Keywords: EFL learners, videoconferencing, SCMC, strategies, speaking ability, English proficiency.

---

1. Hosei University, Japan; iino@hosei.ac.jp.

How to cite this article: Ino, A. (2014). EFL learners' perceived use of conversation maintenance strategies during synchronous computer-mediated communication with native English speakers. In S. Jager, L. Bradley, E. J. Meima, & S. Thouësny (Eds), *CALL Design: Principles and Practice*; Proceedings of the 2014 EUROCALL Conference, Groningen, The Netherlands (pp. 165-171). Dublin: Research-publishing.net. doi:10.14705/rpnet.2014.000212

1. Introduction

1.1. Problem

In the Japanese English as a foreign language (EFL) environment, the learners at university level have few chances of authentic output and interaction in English. Although they have a fair amount of vocabulary and grammatical knowledge gained through competitive entrance examinations to universities, they are weak in applying their linguistic knowledge to performance. Even after they enter university, they still have few opportunities to speak English for authentic communication.

1.2. Solution

Videoconferencing, an oral mode of SCMC, seemed a solution for such a situation. It has been found that it enhances learner's ability of native/non-native speaker interactions, which leads to the promotion of L2 acquisition process as well as motivation to learn an L2, especially for beginner level learners (Jauregi, de Graaff, van den Bergh, & Kriz, 2012).

Therefore, the researcher decided to provide the students the opportunities to have videoconferencing through Skype with native English speakers regularly during a semester. Concretely, in each videoconferencing session, each group of three learners gave a 10 minute presentation to a native English speaking teacher. They then had a discussion with the teacher about the content each student presented. Interactions during the sessions seemed to be a crucial opportunity to have real conversations with native English speakers.

1.3. Conversation maintenance strategies

To see the progress of the learners' speaking performance, what the researcher operationally called 'conversation maintenance strategies' was adopted. Actually, communication strategies could be the term which broadly includes various kinds of strategies to avoid and make up for communication breakdowns (Long, 1983).

Among the typically referred line up of communication strategies (e.g. Smith, 2003), the one called 'conversational continuants' (Lee, 2001) or 'supportive move' (Zuengler, 1989) was regarded as an important strategy for beginner L2 speakers. Since oral SCMC frequently urges the teacher to check the learners' comprehension of exchange, responsive moves taken by the learners seemed important to maintain conversation between the teacher and the learners, for example, keeping eye contact through the camera and clearly verbalizing listeners' responses such as acknowledgement.

1.4. Research questions

This study investigated perceived use of conversation maintenance strategies during synchronous computer-mediated communication with native English speakers as an indicator of motivation to learn L2. I also examined the relationships of the strategies used with speaking ability and comprehensive proficiency level. Thus, the research questions were: (1) how were the learners' perceived use of conversation maintenance strategies related with one another?, and (2) what were the relationships of those strategies with learner's speaking ability and English proficiency?

2. Method

2.1. Participants

The participants were 21 Japanese university students majoring in Economics. During the semester, the participants participated in five synchronous computer-mediated communication sessions in total. Two Filipino native-like English teachers were in charge of seven groups of two or three Japanese EFL learners. The teachers listened to three presentations during 50-minute-sessions each. During one session, the teacher had interactions with the learners, especially after each presentation, asking questions and giving some comments.

2.2. Data collection procedure

Speaking ability was assessed through an interview test following the format of an *Eiken* (*Eiken* Foundation of Japan) test for Japanese learners of English, which consists of reading aloud, comprehension questions, picture narration with criteria of content and grammatical accuracy and open-ended Q&A (two different topics). In each of the tasks, three raters evaluated the learner performance on a five point scale ($a=.78$). The sum of the evaluation in each task was adopted as the speaking ability score.

To obtain the learners' perception of conversation maintenance strategies, a questionnaire was given after the sessions which asked whether they could actually put the strategies into practice.

To measure English proficiency level, CASEC (Computerized Assessment System for English Communication), a computerized test of English, was used. It is an adaptive test based on Item Response Theory by which it is able to accurately test a student's English ability in a short amount of time. It was developed by The Japan Institute for Educational Measurement (JIEM). It consists of four sections: vocabulary, expressions in conversation situations, listening comprehension, and dictation. Each section has 15 questions with 250 points being a perfect score. This makes the total score 1000 points. The test takers took between 40 and 60 minutes to complete the test.

3. Results

3.1. Descriptive statistics

The means of each question were calculated based on the post SCMC reflection questionnaire, which was conducted after the first, third, and fifth sessions. The participants responded with YES (3) / In between (2) / No (1) (see Table 1).

Table 1. Mean scores in strategy use

Questions		M (/3)	SD
Q1	Could you keep eye contact with your teacher?	2.65	0.46
Q2	Could you speak loud enough?	2.77	0.39
Q3	Could you ask some questions to the teacher?	2.26	0.47
Q4	Could you use expressions showing your comprehension? e.g. Uh-huh. Yes. OK. I see. All right. Me, too. Really? That's great/nice/wonderful/etc.	2.76	0.33
Q5	Did you use "echoing" or "shadowing" techniques to continue the conversation or clarify the part that you could not understand? e.g. A: I like Kyoto very much. →B:Oh, you like Kyoto a lot! A: You bet! →B: You bet? →A: Oh "you bet," means "you're right".	2.02	0.60
Q6	Did you ask some questions to the teacher?	2.49	0.51
Q7	Did you take action/show your attitude to continue the conversation?	2.68	0.45
Q8	Did you ACTIVELY listen to the interaction of your group members?	2.77	0.37
Q9	Were you always ready to help other members and speak at any time?	2.45	0.58

3.2. RQ1: How were the learners' perceived use of conversation maintenance strategies related with one another?

Based on the questionnaire results, the relationships between the strategies were examined with Pearson Correlation Coefficients. Significant correlations were found between keeping eye contact (Q1) and asking questions to the teacher (Q6) ($r=.61$, $p<.01$), between keeping eye contact (Q1) and taking action/showing attitude to continue conversation (Q7) ($r=.49$, $p<.05$), and between keeping eye contact (Q1) and readiness to help peers (Q9) (r=.47, p<.05). It was also found that questioning the teacher (Q3) and readiness to help peers (Q9) were strongly correlated (r=.70, p<.01).

3.3. RQ (2): What were the relationships of those strategies with the learner's English speaking ability and proficiency level?

Descriptive statistics of the speaking test are displayed in Table 2. The sum of the average total score by the three raters was 55.2 (SD=18.4). Mean score of the proficiency test was 614.4 points out of 1000. The correlation coefficient between the mean speaking score and mean proficiency test score was .61 (p<.05).

Table 2. Evaluation of each speaking test task by three raters

Rater	Reading aloud			Comprehension Q			Picture Narration			Vocabulary & Grammar		
	A	B	C	A	B	C	A	B	C	A	B	C
M	3.7	3.3	3.6	2.4	1.9	2.6	3.5	2.4	3.7	3.4	2.3	3.4
SD	0.58	0.46	0.59	0.86	0.65	0.81	0.93	0.68	1.06	0.68	0.56	0.81

Rater	Q&A			Q&A			Total			SUM
	A	B	C	A	B	C	A	B	C	
M	3.2	2.7	3.7	3.4	2.5	3.7	19.5	15	20.7	55.2
SD	1.25	0.58	1.19	1.24	0.68	1.06	3.74	1.92	4.3	18.4

Table 3. Correlation coefficients of speaking ability and proficiency with the strategies

	Q1	Q2	Q3	Q4	Q5	Q6	Q7	Q8	Q9
Speaking ability	.227	.282	.432**	-.045	.314	.300	.339	.197	.329
CASEC	-.107	.153	-.135	.207	.411**	.353	.263	-.043	.027

Table 4. Results of CASEC test

	Vocabulary	Expressions	Listening	Dictation	Total
M	159.8	149.9	158.1	146.7	614.4
SD	23.5	15.0	22.7	17.4	57.4

Based on this data, it was found that speaking ability was correlated with (Q3) asking questions to the teacher (r=.43, p<.05). Other strategies did not show any significant relationship with speaking ability (Table 3). Concerning the relationship with the proficiency score (CASEC, see Table 4), (Q5) using echoing/shadowing had a significant relationship (r=.41, p<.05).

4. Discussion

A significant correlation between maintaining eye contact and asking questions to the teacher seemed natural because it is common to look at the interlocutor when asking questions. This result indicates that videoconferencing was quite close to face to face conversation. Other strategies which related to eye contact, such as taking action/showing attitudes to continue the conversation and readiness to help peers, were also an indication of the extent to which the learners focused on the teacher's utterances through the camera to maintain conversation.

Another interesting finding was the fact that questioning the teacher and readiness to help peers were strongly correlated. This phenomenon was also close to face to face conversation because the learners who were eager to ask questions to the teacher were eager to help peers, or the learners who were eager to help peers were eager to ask questions to the teacher.

This result could be related to another finding that speaking ability was correlated to asking questions to the teacher. This means the good speakers were more likely to ask questions, possibly because of the less cognitive burden to do so. Thus, they could help peers.

The last finding was that the learner's English proficiency level had a significant relationship with using echoing or shadowing of the teacher's expressions to continue the conversation. This strategy use implicated that repeating the teacher's utterances in conversation was used often by highly proficient learners. This strategy was used the least among the learners, as seen in the descriptive statistics (Table 1). However, this fact indicated that only high proficiency learners with a strong listening ability and articulation automaticity could use the strategy.

5. Conclusions

In this study, videoconferencing mode of synchronous computer-mediated communication was investigated, shedding light on how the learners maintain conversation with native speaker teachers. The perceived use of eye contact was implied to be a crucial conversation maintenance strategy, especially in videoconferencing SCMC, exactly like face to face communication. Also, high speaking ability extended the strategy use not only between the learner and the teacher but also to peers, which indicated that the social aspect of conversation maintenance was also of concern for the learners. In terms of variety of strategies used, the least used strategy, echoing or shadowing the teacher's expressions to continue conversation, was mostly used by highly proficient learners. These findings indicated the improvement of speaking ability and overall English proficiency level help expand the repertoires of conversation maintenance strategies.

References

Jauregi, K., de Graaff, R., van den Bergh, H., & Kriz, M. (2012). Native non-native speaker interactions through video-web communication, a clue for enhancing motivation. *Computer Assisted Language Learning Journal, 25*(1), 1-19. doi:10.1080/09588221.2011.582587

Lee, L. (2001). Online interaction: Negotiation of meaning and strategies used among learners of Spanish. *ReCALL, 13*(1), 232-244. doi:10.1017/S0958344001000829a

Long, M. H. (1983). Native speaker/non-native speaker conversation and the negotiation of comprehensible input. *Applied Linguistics, 4*(2), 126-141. doi:10.1093/applin/4.2.126

Smith, B. (2003). The use of communication strategies in computer-mediated communication. *System, 31*, 29-53. doi:10.1016/S0346-251X(02)00072-6

Zuengler, J. (1989). Assessing an interaction-based paradigm: How accommodative should we be. In M. R. Eisenstein (Ed.), The dynamic interlanguage: Empirical studies in second language variation (pp. 49-67). New York: Plenum Press. doi:10.1007/978-1-4899-0900-8_4

Medical students' perceptions of using mobile phones for their English study

Jun Iwata[1], Yuko Tamaki[2], Wang Shudong[3], John Telloyan[4], Yuri Ajiki[5], and John Clayton[6]

Abstract. The authors conducted a needs analysis to investigate their medical students' needs and preferences for using mobile devices for their English study. The analysis showed the students' expectations of mobile learning were very high and two-thirds of them were interested in building medical English terminology through mobile learning. Then, the authors created mobile learning content designed mainly for helping their students review medical terminology. The content was delivered to 242 students twice a week during the period from July 2013 to January 2014. The authors then conducted a survey on their students' perceptions of the content delivered. It revealed that half of the students found the content useful for their English study and about two-thirds of them found the content level to be appropriate. However, the log analysis showed that only an average of 9.5 % of the students worked on the medical quizzes. This result suggests that achieving a high degree of student involvement in their autonomous mobile learning is difficult and it is necessary for teachers to further investigate ways to enhance students' motivation for mobile learning.

Keywords: mobile learning, English for Medicine, students' perceptions, ESP, motivation.

---

1. Shimane University; j_iwata@med.shimane-u.ac.jp
2. Shimane University; tamaki@soc.shimane-u.ac.jp
3. Shimane University; wangsd@soc.shimane-u.ac.jp
4. Shimane University; telloyan@med.shimane-u.ac.jp
5. Shimane University; yajiki@med.shimane-u.ac.jp
6. Waikato Institute of Technology; John.Clayton@wintec.ac.nz

How to cite this article: Iwata, J., Tamaki, Y., Shudong, W., Telloyan, J., Ajiki, Y., & Clayton, J. (2014). Medical students' perceptions of using mobile phones for their English study. In S. Jager, L. Bradley, E. J. Meima, & S. Thouësny (Eds), *CALL Design: Principles and Practice; Proceedings of the 2014 EUROCALL Conference, Groningen, The Netherlands* (pp. 172-178). Dublin: Research-publishing.net. doi:10.14705/rpnet.2014.000213

1. Introduction

Amidst the rapid progression of internationalization, English is becoming increasingly important for Japanese students to prepare for their future career. This is especially true of medical/nursing students due to growing demand for them to use English at conferences and/or workshops and increasing opportunities for them to communicate with other medical staff and patients in English. However, the curricula at medical schools in Japan are so extensive that the time allocated for English classes is quite limited. Therefore, language teachers at medical schools are expected to not only improve their English curricula, but also offer effective and attractive self-study courses and materials which help enhance students' independent and autonomous study.

Since 2007, the authors have been evaluating their current teaching practices and modifying the structure and content of their English classes by applying a blended-learning model using Moodle, a popular open source Learning Management System (Iwata, Tamaki, & Clayton, 2011). They have also started to design a range of self-study materials by using mobile devices, which are expected to be a useful tool for enhancing students' autonomous study (Bakay, Bulut, & Delialioglu, 2013). The authors' key goals for the use of mobile devices such as mobile phones, smart phones and tablets were firstly to give learners more opportunities to practice their medical English skills by providing them with ongoing access to a range of useful learning resources, and secondly to help enhance student's learner autonomy by using mobile devices.

2. Students' needs and preferences for mobile learning

The authors conducted a needs analysis in July 2013 to investigate their medical students' needs and preference for using mobile devices for their English study by asking the following three questions:

- Have you used your mobile device for study purposes?
- Do you think mobile learning will be effective?
- What topics would you like to study with your mobile devices?

The results obtained from Questions (1) and (2) indicate that 59.6% students have used mobile devices for their study and 62.9% students expected mobile learning to be effective. The results from Question (3), as seen in Table 1, show that students prefer vocabulary building and one-third (35.0%) of the students would like to study medical terms.

Table 1. Preferred topics (*N*=242)

	number	%
General terms	163	67.9%
Medical terms	**84**	**35.0%**
TOEIC/ TOEFL exercise	67	27.9%
General conversation	59	24.6%
Medical conversation	**40**	**16.7%**
Grammar exercises	35	14.6%
Reading exercise	27	11.3%

3. Creating and delivering mobile learning content

3.1. Creating mobile learning content

The authors created a total of 54 mobile learning units for reviewing medical terminology in 2013, expecting the content would help students review medical vocabulary they had studied in class and enhance their self-study. Each unit consisted of 5 multiple-choice quizzes taken out of 1,000 basic medical terms including body parts, symptoms, abbreviations, prefixes and suffixes. Figure 1 shows a sample content for reviewing major terms related to psychiatry.

Figure 1. Quiz form

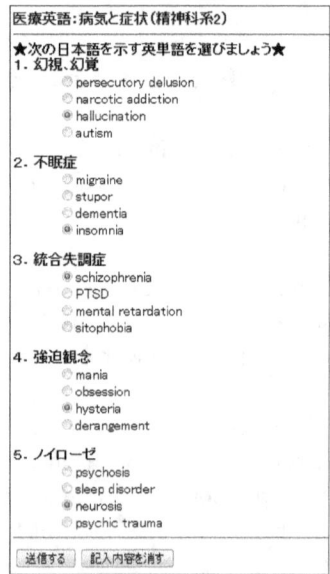

Students answered multiple-choice questions by clicking radio buttons on their mobile devices and then clicking a "Send" button. After that the feedback form including answers, points, and comments was shown as illustrated in Figure 2. The feedback was designed to be helpful and informative for students by giving detailed comments on each targeted term and other options.

Figure 2. Feedback

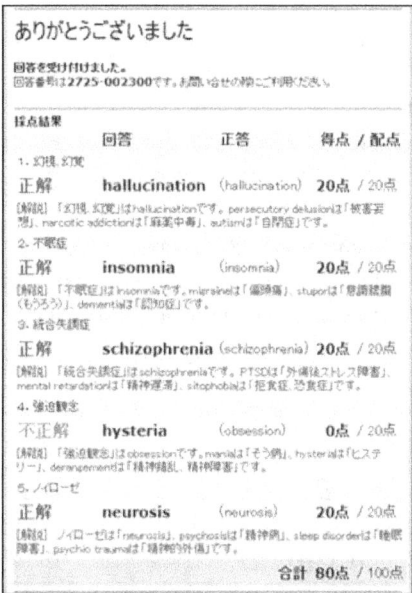

3.2. Delivering mobile learning content

The content created by the authors was delivered to a total of 242 recipients, most of whom were first-year medical and nursing students. All students were voluntary participants in the study of mobile learning. Details concerning content delivery are as follows.

(1) System: "InterCussion", web-based system (paid).

(2) Recipients: 242 medical and nursing students of Shimane University, Japan.

(3) Mobile devices students used: smart phones (78.8%), tablets (5.8%), mobile phones (5.0%), other devices (10.2%).

(4) Frequency: twice a week (Tuesdays and Fridays at noon).

(5) Duration: 7 months (July 2013 – January 2014).

4. Evaluation

The authors conducted a survey on their students' perceptions of the content delivered and 120 recipients answered the survey (response rate: 49.6%). It revealed that about half of the students found the content effective for their English study, as shown in Table 2. The majority of them found the difficulty level of the content appropriate, as shown in Table 3. With regard to the twice-a-week frequency of content delivery, 60.8% students thought it moderate and 21.8% students thought it was too often and that 'once-a- week' was more desirable.These results indicate that in general, learners seemed to think that the mobile learning content was effective and the frequency of delivery was appropriate. However, enhancing learner autonomy, one of the key drivers of this study of mobile learning, was still not successful as the number of the participants who actually tried the medical term quiz was quite low at only 9.5% on average, with 18.2% the maximum and 5.8% the minimum.

Table 2. Effectiveness (*N*=120)

	number	%
Very effective	8	**6.7%**
Effective	46	**38.3%**
Neither	37	30.8%
Not so effective	7	5.8%
Not effective at all	0	0 %

Table 3. Difficulty level (*N*=120)

	number	%
Too difficult	1	0.8%
A little difficult	28	23.3%
Appropriate	75	**62.5%**
A little easy	3	2.5%
Too easy	1	0.8 %

5. Discussion

While students' expectations of mobile learning were high, their readiness for mobile learning still seems to be low. This may suggest that achieving a high degree of student involvement will continue to be quite difficult no matter how much interest students demonstrate in mobile learning (Kwon, 2013).

The results from the evaluation of the mobile learning content left the authors two challenges to solve. Firstly, they need to modify the content and delivery system to better suit students' needs and preferences. Secondly, they need to investigate what factors affect learners' motivation and autonomy in mobile learning context and they need to seek ways to increase student's motivation for mobile learning.

6. Conclusions

The initial findings from the survey on medical students' needs and preferences of mobile learning indicate that most students were interested in studying English vocabulary with their mobile devices and they expected mobile learning to be effective for their English study. The survey results on students' evaluations of the content delivered show that the majority of them found the content effective for improving medical English language skills and the level of the content appropriate. However, the data analysis revealed that the students' actual use of the content was at a low level of 9.8% on average, which illustrates a need for further analysis.

The authors are conscious that further investigation on how their mobile learning content actually helps learners improve their medical English skills/knowledge and how the content helps them become motivated to study autonomously is required. However, the authors believe further practice of creating and delivering mobile learning content and development of measures for evaluating these practices would be valuable in monitoring the effectiveness of their mobile learning content and enhancing mobile learning for the purpose of teaching English for medicine.

Acknowledgements. This research was partially supported by the Ministry of Education, Science, Sports and Culture, Grant-in-Aid for Scientific Research (C), 24501189, 2012-2014.

References

Bakay, S., Bulut, I. H., & Delialioglu, O. (2013). English as a foreign language (EFL) students' readiness and perceptions towards mobile learning. *EDULEARN13 Proceedings* (pp. 251-257).

Iwata, J., Tamaki, Y., & Clayton, J. (2011). Integrating Moodle-based activities into teaching English for medicine: Instructional design and students' perceptions. In G. Weir., S. Ishikawa, & K. Poonpol (Eds), *Corpora and language Technologies in Teaching, Learning and Research* (pp. 39-49). Glasgow: University of Strathclyde.

Kwon, Y. A. (2013). Study of college EFL learners' continued use of and the perceptual changes toward mobile-assisted language learning. In *Proceedings of the 2013 WorldCALL, Global perspectives on computer-assisted language learning* (pp. 153-155).

university of groningen

An intelligent tutoring system for learning Chinese with a cognitive model of the learner

Michał Kosek[1] and Pierre Lison[2]

Abstract. We present an intelligent tutoring system that lets students of Chinese learn words and grammatical constructions. It relies on a Bayesian, linguistically motivated cognitive model that represents the learner's knowledge. This model is dynamically updated given observations about the learner's behaviour in the exercises, and employed at runtime to select the exercises that are expected to maximise the learning outcome. Compared with a baseline that randomly chooses exercises at user's declared level, the system shows positive effects on users' assessment of how much they have learnt, which suggests that it leads to enhanced learning.

Keywords: intelligent tutoring systems, cognitive model, Bayesian networks, zone of proximal development.

1. Introduction

We present an intelligent tutoring system with a probabilistic model of user's knowledge of words and constructions, which chooses exercises that are most likely to maximise the learning outcome. It consists of English-to-Chinese translation tasks, which accept a large number of alternative translations and give interactive feedback when the provided answer is incorrect.

---

1. Department of Informatics, University of Oslo; michalkk@student.iln.uio.no.
2. Department of Informatics, University of Oslo; plison@ifi.uio.no.

How to cite this article: Kosek, M., & Lison, P. (2014). An intelligent tutoring system for learning Chinese with a cognitive model of the learner. In S. Jager, L. Bradley, E. J. Meima, & S. Thouësny (Eds), *CALL Design: Principles and Practice*; Proceedings of the 2014 EUROCALL Conference, Groningen, The Netherlands (pp. 179-184). Dublin: Research-publishing.net. doi:10.14705/rpnet.2014.000214

1.1. Structure of an exercise

Figure 1 shows an ongoing session with the program. Underlined words can be clicked to look them up in the MDBG English-Chinese dictionary[3]. In the first attempt the student used an incorrect construction, so the relevant fragment was highlighted in red.

After the second attempt, the system indicated a construction that was missing. The hint contained a hyperlink to the dictionary, which was clicked by the student, and a dictionary entry showed up on the right-hand side. Then the student used the construction from the dictionary. The feedback shows another missing construction; the exercise is unfinished.

Figure 1. Exercise in progress

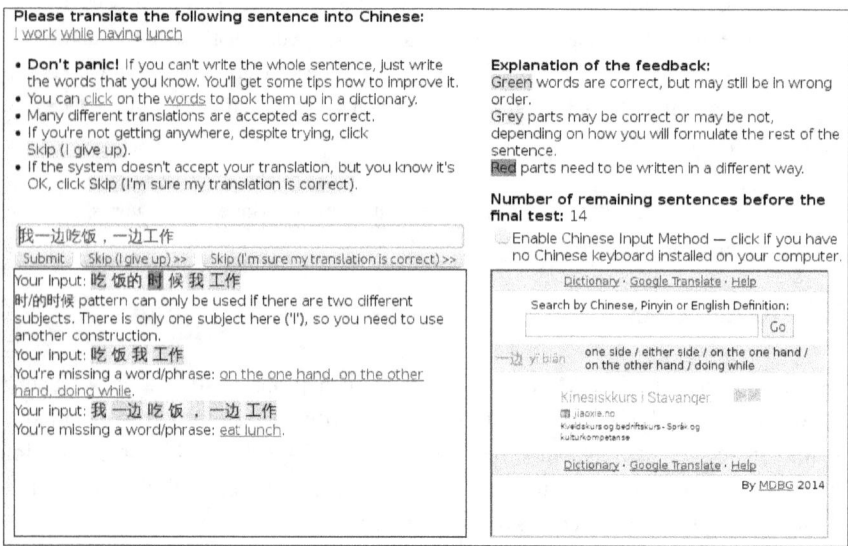

The system leads the user towards an answer that is closest to the input according to the BLEU score (Papineni, Roukos, Ward, & Zhu, 2002). A large number of correct answers are accepted: different possible orders of constituents are allowed, and synonyms are recognised. The user can skip the exercise when she doesn't know the correct answer despite the hints, and when she knows that her answer is correct, despite the system saying otherwise.

---

3. http://www.mdbg.net

1.2. Selecting next exercise

Our research focuses on selecting exercises that are most beneficial to the user. This requires modelling the user's knowledge of words and grammatical constructions (both called *constructions* here), understood as pairs of one or several forms and a specific meaning. Users' knowledge is only partially observable through their interaction with the program; therefore a probabilistic student model is used. Its core is a set of random variables, one per construction. The probability of knowing a construction is updated as the program gathers indirect evidence.

Before starting the exercises, the users assess their Chinese proficiency, and take a character recognition test, which determines the approximate number of Chinese characters they know. These data provide indirect evidence about which constructions are likely to be known –someone who scores high in the test will more likely know difficult words than someone who scores low. Afterwards, every exercise provides additional evidence. The user clicking on a word to check its translation indicates that she probably does not know it. Giving up and skipping to the next exercise indicates that probably some of the constructions in the sentence are unknown.

These pieces of evidence are represented in a Bayesian network (Pearl, 1988), letting the system reason about the learner's knowledge. Figure 2 presents a fragment of the network, relevant to the exercise shown before. The white nodes are hidden: the user's actual level and her knowledge of words are not directly observable. The grey nodes contain observable evidence: self-assessment, results of the character test, dictionary lookups and the exercise status (completed successfully or skipped). After the self-assessment and the character test, the values in the three top nodes are updated, and these changes are propagated into the hidden nodes. After each exercise, information about word lookups and the exercise status is used to update the hidden nodes.

The information about the user's knowledge is used to select an exercise that that will probably maximise the learning outcome. The system selects sentences that are most likely to lie within the Zone of Proximal Development (ZPD) (Vygotsky, 1978). Here, ZPD consists of sentences that the user would not translate without help, but would translate given the dictionary and system's hints. The sentence cannot be too easy (if everything is known, nothing will be learnt), or too difficult (with many unknown words, the user probably will not remember them). The next sentence is therefore chosen by an influence diagram (Pearl, 1988) that assigns lowest utility to sentences with all known constructions, and highest utility to sentences with some unknown constructions –but not too many.

Figure 2. Fragment of the Bayesian network

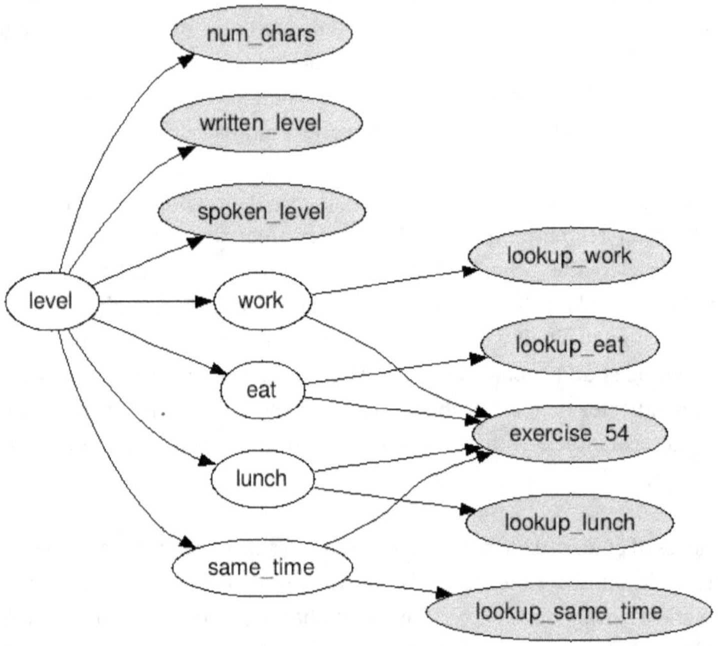

2. Method

2.1. Parameter initialisation

We created 94 exercises, containing 91 constructions selected as learning targets, repeated among different exercises, with 3 constructions per exercise on average. 60 learners of Chinese were invited to assess their level, take the character test and do randomly chosen exercises.

The analysis of self-assessment, character test results, lookup ratio and skip ratio revealed four clusters of users that we called A, B1, B2 and C, to indicate rough correspondence with the CEFR levels (Council of Europe, 2001). There was not enough data to differentiate sub-levels of A and C. We assumed that the character test results were normally distributed within each group, and estimated the distribution of the number of known characters given the user's actual level.

We divided constructions into difficulty classes: for every user level X, class X contains constructions that were looked up by some users whose level is X, but not by those at higher levels. The constructions that were never looked up were removed from the learning target list, being too easy. Common conditional probability tables were created for each class. Classes B2 and C were merged during the evaluation, because the latter contained only three constructions.

2.2. Experiment

The goal of the experiment was to investigate the effects of using the cognitive model to select the exercises. The baseline used users' self-assessment of their written proficiency, and selected random exercises at that level. The level of an exercise was defined as the highest level of a construction that appears in that exercise.

The participants were recruited at Chinese language classes, online forums and, because of relative scarcity of Chinese L2 learners, by snowball sampling. 60 people used the program online, 33 of them went through all selected exercises and submitted a post-test and questionnaire. 24 participants were left after discarding two native Chinese speakers and those who had used the system before the experiment. The participants were randomly assigned to the system or baseline, their level was assessed, and they took the character test, and did 14 exercises. The system used the influence diagram to select the exercise with the highest utility, while the baseline chose a random unseen exercise at the user's declared level.

The post-test contained a stratified random sample of constructions to translate, with 6 random items from each of 3 strata: A, B1, B2+C. The questionnaire asked the users about subjective difficulty of the exercises and how much they had learnt. Post-test results and answers to the former question did not show significant differences, while answers to the latter showed statistically significant differences ($p<.05$) between the users of the system and the baseline, shown in the last row of Table 1.

The subjective effects could be compared for whole populations that submitted the questionnaire. As for the objective measures, the evaluation had to be done separately for every level, to satisfy an assumption that users' prior knowledge is similar. Hence, the lack of difference in the objective measures may have been caused by small sample sizes. An experiment with more participants is needed to investigate this.

The system currently models user's knowledge only during one session. Ways of separating short-term and long-term knowledge in the model must be investigated. No constructions are retained forever without repetition, but repeating same words during every session is suboptimal, therefore a forgetting model is important for a vocabulary tutor.

Table 1. Evaluation results

		System (15 participants)		Baseline (9 participants)	
	User level	Mean	SD	Mean	SD
Post-test results (number of correct answers)	A	15.33	2.81	14.25	1.48
	B1	16.75	1.09	17.75	0.43
	B2	18.00	0.00	18.00	0.00
	C	18.00	0.00	n/a	n/a
Subjective difficulty assessment (too easy or too difficult=0, right level=1)		0.53	0.50	0.44	0.50
Users' subjective assessment of how many items they've learnt (none=0, few=1, some=2, a lot=3)		1.53	0.88	0.89	0.57

3. Conclusions

We have presented a system that stores probabilistic information about users' knowledge of words and constructions on the basis of evidence collected, which is used to select exercises that are most beneficial to the user. Our experiment has shown positive effects of the system on users' assessment of how much they have learnt. Larger and longer-term experiments must be conducted to determine a possible difference in objective measures.

Acknowledgements. We would like to thank Jan Tore Lønning for his help with editing and proofreading the draft version of this article.

References

Council of Europe. (2001). *Common European Framework of Reference for Languages: Learning, teaching, assessment.* Cambridge: Cambridge University Press.
Papineni, K., Roukos, S., Ward, T., & Zhu, W. J. (2002). BLEU: A method for automatic evaluation of machine translation. *Proceedings of the 40th Annual Meeting on Association for Computational Linguistics* (pp. 311-318).
Pearl, J. (1988). *Probabilistic reasoning in intelligent systems.* San Francisco: Morgan Kaufmann.
Vygotsky, L. S. (1978). *Mind in society: The development of higher psychological processes.* Cambridge: Harvard University Press.

university of groningen

Language learning 2.0 – international collaboration made easy

Tuula-Harriet Kotikoski[1] and Natasha Doshi[2]

Abstract. The Internet has become part of our daily life and serves as a source of knowledge as well as a space for interaction. E-learning is thus a vital element in teaching, and digital media offer not only the possibility to support the individual learning processes of students, but also to foster multilingualism and to immerse into authentic learning environments. In this paper, the project "JAMK-VUAS online learning" will be described and reflected upon in detail, i.e. its aims, outcomes, lessons learned, learning styles, and Internet platforms. In addition, a brief outlook on future areas/topics/themes for such online collaborations, which need to be beneficial and fruitful for all parties involved, will be presented.

Keywords: e-learning, online interaction, authentic learning environment, multilingualism.

1. Introduction

Internationalisation has become an integral part across university campuses around the globe. Besides the mobility of students, lecturers and administrative staff, the implementation of international projects is often encouraged as another tool to increase the internationalisation level within higher education institutions (c.f. de Wit, 2013; EUA, 2013). This aspect is both a great contribution and a challenge for the English classroom, where such projects can easily be implemented and should be beneficial for all parties involved. This article is a work-in-progress study that aims to explore some possibilities of enriching individual English courses by providing local students the chance to cooperate with students from another

---

1. Jyväskylä University of Applied Sciences (JAMK), Finland; tuula.kotikoski@jamk.fi.
2. Vorarlberg University of Applied Sciences (VUAS), Austria; natasha.doshi@fhv.at.

How to cite this article: Kotikoski, T.-H., & Doshi, N. (2014). Language learning 2.0 – international collaboration made easy. In S. Jager, L. Bradley, E. J. Meima, & S. Thouësny (Eds), *CALL Design: Principles and Practice; Proceedings of the 2014 EUROCALL Conference, Groningen, The Netherlands* (pp. 185-190). Dublin: Research-publishing.net. doi:10.14705/rpnet.2014.000215

linguistic and cultural background using English as a lingua franca and completing real-life-tasks with the opportunity of receiving direct feedback (c.f. Marsh, 2002).

2. Method

When starting international co-operation with a partner university, the first item on the agenda is understanding your partner. One way to get to know how the partner university operates is to visit each other, the simplest means for this is to arrange teacher exchanges. With Erasmus support this was possible and it was a natural way to meet and discuss the curricula and possibilities of implementing courses together. Both authors (from JAMK and VUAS) participated in teacher exchange and in addition, there were the student exchanges, during which both sides learnt more about the students, their ways of learning and different teaching methods.

JAMK University of Applied Sciences is located in Central Finland, Jyväskylä and has 8,000 students and over 30 degree programmes. JAMK has only one compulsory English course for all degree students on bachelor level, 4 ECTS at present. They also offer one compulsory Swedish course, 4 ECTS and provide elective courses in Spanish, German, French, Italian, Russian, Chinese, Japanese, Each One Teach One (language tandem) and Language Café. One important aspect that was also taken into account when trying to find common areas of interest was JAMK's "Internationalisation at Home", i.e. international semesters in all degree programs (30 ETCS – English-medium courses).

At VUAS, which is situated in Austria's most western part, there are about 1000 students and degrees can be completed in engineering, business, IT, media design and social work (both bachelor and master). English is compulsory in all programs (5-6 semesters, 12-15 ECTS) and the courses are content-based. Other languages are offered as electives, mostly Spanish, Italian, Turkish, Mandarin, and Russian; in addition "international semesters" (integral part of the "Internationalisation at Home"-strategy) are realised in all degree programs (about 30 ETCS with English-medium courses).

These significant differences between VUAS and JAMK were the reason why the following JAMK course was chosen for the pilot project: English for Working Life (3 ECTS). This course contains the following units: business communication, talking about yourself and your studies, job application process, and intercultural communication. This course is offered both as a face-to-face or an online implementation. Due to the teaching commitment of the involved lecturer, the following two courses at VUAS were an option for joint activities: Applications (second semester of InterMedia, BA) and Intercultural Communication (elective course on Master level for students from all disciplines).

3. What we want(ed) to achieve

The aims we hoped to achieve were to increase international co-operation on different levels: both students and staff exchanges, learn from each other, offer students and lecturers international experience and new learning styles as well as find out whether collaboration actually works. We also hoped that collaborating on small projects might lead to bigger (possibly EU-funded) projects with a larger number of partners.

3.1. Pilot project

The online projects started with the idea of taking our first steps on a small scale, and the first project started in November 2012: 18 master students from VUAS who had chosen the elective course "Intercultural Communication" and 18 engineering students (ICT, 2nd year) from JAMK participated in this project. As a pre-assignment for the three-day intensive block, the Austrian students were asked to find out as much as possible about Finnish culture. For this, they just received a short email with a short description of the task and the contact details of the Finnish partners. At this stage, the students had never met their lecturer and had not spent any time in class to discuss the task. In most cases, the VUAS students sent emails to the JAMK students with ready-made questions about Finnish culture, which then were either discussed via email or via Skype using English as the common language. The underlying aim of this activity was to reflect on communication styles and stereotypes, which was then done together in class when students at VUAS actually met for their elective course.

The evaluation of this first pilot project, which was carried out on both sides in the form of questionnaires and interviews, showed that students were faced with mostly the following challenges:

- The IC course at VUAS took place only on three days (no face-to-face contact before online activity) during a weekend, therefore the timetable had to be tight.

- JAMK students did not take a similar course, their English course only contained some elements of intercultural communication; however, it was only one unit among many.

- The time-frame had to be carefully considered; we did not want to spend too much or too little time on this task.

- The students' levels of language skills were very heterogeneous.

- The age levels were also different: there were both bachelor and master students, full-time and part-time students, as well as mature students.

- The students represented different cultures; at VUAS there were Austrian, German, French, Indian, US-Austrian, Russian, and Czech-German students participating in the course, whereas the students at JAMK were Finnish.

- One issue that caused anxiety was the actual contact with a "stranger" and what to say or do when the contact had been established.

- Skype conversation was also considered stressful and students were shy and nervous at the beginning.

- For the Finnish students, understanding the task and reflecting on its outcome was the most difficult task.

The outcomes at VUAS after the 3-day course on intercultural communication were mostly positive. The students were surprised by the task and were very eager to discuss intercultural issues with their Finnish counterparts. Some students mentioned that they had a two-hour talk on Skype. The students learnt to take notes based on discussions and prepared well for the online discussion. The Austrian students became more aware of differences in communication styles. The theory learnt was applied to practice and this task served as an ideal opening for intercultural communication and, in particular, stereotypes. JAMK students' attitude was also very positive and they suggested another similar task for next year's students. They enjoyed the authenticity of the situation and appreciated the opportunity to use the language in a natural context with peers in another country. This pilot experiment supported the Finnish students' course content very well: the students learnt to introduce themselves, talk about themselves and life in Finland. After the small talk phase, they moved on to discuss intercultural communication issues utilising social media (c.f. Stanley, 2013).

There were also negative comments: some VUAS students did not receive any response to their email even after the lecturers sent reminders. Skype was regarded

Language learning 2.0 – international collaboration made easy

as scary and intimidating and many students mentioned that emails would have been easier. Not all Finnish students got an Austrian counterpart either, as the group sizes were quite different. As the Finnish students study only one semester, it is challenging to find the perfect time for the Austrian contact and match the course content in both universities. Since this was a pilot study, the two lecturers noticed during their reflection and evaluation period that preparation time should have been longer and that one needs to carefully plan such activities as not only academic calendars can be quite different, but that also differences in working styles, communication styles, time-management, etc. can be rather challenging.

3.2. Second project

The second project, which was implemented in spring 2013, focused on the job application process, with special emphasis on CV writing, which was an important content in both universities and their English courses. The core question here was "can an outsider understand my CV?". This time, the teams had more in common as all students were on bachelor level with similar degree programs and age groups. Both teams had a short introduction to the activity and they were asked to tell about their university and home-town to get started. Both VUAS and JAMK groups received guidance on how to get in touch with their partner students, how to write a proper email, how to handle the task and the time was now announced already at the beginning of the course with information on the given time-frame. The teachers offered students continuous support if they needed it.

This time, the outcomes at VUAS were very positive. According to the feedback given in surveys and in direct form in class, the students were eager to complete the task and showed great interest in Finland and the Finnish people. The task was clear, it was a helpful activity, easy to manage and not too time-consuming. There were some concerns such as self-confidence issues, e.g. "How do I pronounce this Finnish name?", "Will they know who I am?", "What shall I write in this first email?", "I need to check them on Facebook first" or "Can you [teacher] check my work first?".

The outcomes at JAMK were also positive, which was demonstrated in their written evaluation of this second project. For the teacher, this was an excellent project; emails had just been discussed and written in class. This task with VUAS was a hands-on project with authentic material and peer feedback on CVs. The students were concerned that they might not get a reply from anyone or that they might not understand the Austrian students. The timetable was critical again since the Finnish students' course was almost finished and they were worried about "What if they write to me when I am already working and the term has finished?". Of course, they also wanted to get their grades as soon as possible.

4. Conclusion

The collaboration between VUAS and JAMK continues this fall with another small project and new themes/topics are constantly being explored by the involved teachers, who both feel that –even though small and easy to implement– these joint activities are worth the effort and enrich the learning environment of the involved students and are thus very beneficial for both institutions.

The course evaluations on both sides, as well as individual statements and comments from students involved, show that using such online projects is a great opportunity to improve the learning environment and change the dynamics of existing courses. In general, one can say that students were more motivated to complete the given tasks, which was mostly due to the interactive part. This enabled new possibilities for authentic materials and assignments. From the perspective of the lecturers, it seems that the involved students profited not only on linguistic and content-specific aspects but also on social aspects, which is another reason to continue such online-projects in the future and increase the learning opportunities in this direction for even more student groups.

References

De Wit, H. (Ed.). (2013). *An introduction to higher education internationalisation*. Milan: Vita e Pensiero.
EUA – European University Association (2013). *Internationalisation in European higher education: European policies, institutional strategies and EUA support*. Bruxelles: The European Union.
Marsh, D. (2002). *CLIL/EMILE – The European dimension: Actions, trends and foresight potential*. Bruxelles: The European Union.
Stanley, G. (2013). *Language learning with technology – Ideas for integrating technology in the language classroom*. Cambridge: Cambridge University Press.

Guiding learners to near native fluency in English through an adaptive programme of activities which includes phoneme and prosody analysis

Alistair Lawson[1], Ann Attridge[2], and Paul Lapok[3]

Abstract. Many students of English language find pronunciation difficult to master. This work in progress paper discusses an incremental and iterative approach towards developing requirements for software applications to assist learners with the perception and production of English pronunciation in terms of phonemes and prosody. It was found that prompts for eliciting target pronunciation should include a visual indication of the meaning of the target word or phrase in addition to the sound, and that the learners should be led through a hierarchy of words. This should start with phonemes of simple (one syllable) words, and adaptively build up to prosody of two syllable words, then increasing the syllables in the target words as the learner improves. A simple representation of prosody was developed and found to be intuitive by students for comparing their pronunciation to that of a native speaker. Students considered that an analysis time of within one second for phonemes and prosody was considered "real time", and requested integration with social media for both enabling competition and celebration of achievement.

Keywords: MALL, ESOL, pronunciation, prosody, feedback.

---

1. Institute for Informatics and Digital Innovation, Edinburgh Napier University; a.lawson@napier.ac.uk.
2. K2L Ltd United Kingdom.
3. Institute for Informatics and Digital Innovation, Edinburgh Napier University.

How to cite this article: Lawson, A., Attridge, A., & Lapok, P. (2014). Guiding learners to near native fluency in English through an adaptive programme of activities which includes phoneme and prosody analysis. In S. Jager, L. Bradley, E. J. Meima, & S. Thouësny (Eds), *CALL Design: Principles and Practice; Proceedings of the 2014 EUROCALL Conference, Groningen, The Netherlands* (pp. 191-195). Dublin: Research-publishing.net. doi:10.14705/rpnet.2014.000216

1. Introduction

This project aims to address pronunciation problems of English language learners. Many students of English at all levels find pronunciation difficult to learn. Though important for comprehension and fluency, pronunciation is seen by many as being given the least attention in language learning (e.g. Gilakjani, Ahmadi, & Ahmadi, 2011). Achievement of near native fluency involves the ability to reproduce English prosody in terms of pitch, intensity, and duration, in addition to basic phonemic competence. However, current pronunciation software tools mainly address phonemic difficulties and give little or no analytical feedback, or too much feedback, such as complex graphs of speech waveforms and spectrograms, but in a way that pays little attention to problems with prosody. This work in progress paper reports on the preliminary results of a project entitled Protalk, which includes phonemic diagnosis but also takes the learner forward by analysing and giving usable feedback on prosody problems. The project, with a view to developing mobile apps, is being carried out in an iterative and incremental software development approach (e.g. Demetris, Farnum, Markel, & Rosenhan, 2012) with a focus on user experience design and evaluation, market research, and with a multidisciplinary team of language teachers, software engineers, games developers, and marketing professionals.

2. Method

The first stage of user evaluation focussed on intelligibility of prompts used to illicit the pronunciation of target words or phrases by the student. This focussed solely on prosody and investigated ten subjects (five intermediate to advanced, and five beginners), whose pronunciation of a set of predetermined words, phrases and sentences were benchmarked against a set of native speaker recordings in order to establish the following:

- The extent to which the learner benefitted from audio only or audio plus text as a prompt to pronouncing the words, in order to establish the feasibility of training ear and vocal apparatus without text-based prompts.

- To what extent the learner's pronunciation was affected by their understanding of the words they were pronouncing in order to establish the most effective learning methodology when using de-contextualised speech segments.

The second stage of user evaluation involved investigating how to present the potentially complex feedback in such a way that learners understand, engage and are motivated to improve. This used mock-ups of a mobile application, and the paths that a student would take through the learning experience. Ten further subjects took part in this analysis. A set of simple visual symbols was devised which represent pitch, intensity, duration, and give learners instant visual feedback on all three parameters in a simple, clear manner that avoids information overload, which can occur with existing methods of displaying waveforms and spectrograms.

In parallel with these two evaluations, a cloud-based web service API (Application Programming Interface) was developed to allow analysis of speech recorded by the learners to be analysed for phonemic accuracy, and for pitch, intensity, and syllable duration. The development of this web service API was carried out in an iterative and incremental manner taking account of the findings of the user-centred evaluations, two of which are reported here. In addition, a market validation was conducted and the findings incorporated into the design requirements.

3. Results

The first evaluation identified the use of audio as the prime focus, but some learners expressed a preference for the written word. As a result, the option of accessing the text after the audio was included in the design of the mobile application. The second finding indicated that for all students it was beneficial for pronunciation to understand the meaning of the target speech segment.

Additional findings from the first evaluation (with the beginners group) firstly made it obvious that it was necessary to devise an adaptive system to determine the individual phonemes that learners were struggling with in one or two syllable words before moving on to analysing prosody alongside phonemic diagnosis in more complex words and phrases. The market validation report also confirmed the need to include phonemic analysis as a starting point. There was a need to (1) provide contextualisation and aid understanding through illustration (using images) and access to dictionary support as required, and (2) cater for different levels of students by creating sets of words appropriate to their lexical knowledge.

The findings of the second evaluation (for the intermediate level group) were that pronunciation was the most challenging part of language learning (as compared to learning vocabulary and grammatical structure). This evaluation confirmed that most students wanted to master the phonemes first before moving on to improving their prosodic ability. The division of words into syllable groups, and progressing through levels from two, to three, to four syllable words was thought to be helpful in building up prosodic competence. Feedback was also received on the look and feel of the application, and in particular the representation of prosody, but also included requesting the use of animations in addition to static images to help give the meaning of the target words, and make the app more attractive and engaging. A simple representation of prosody was developed and found to be intuitive by students for comparing their pronunciation to that of a native speaker. Integration with social media was requested by students for competing against other learners or celebrating achievement, as was the ability to track performance over time. A response time for analysis of the speed recordings of within one second was considered to be "real time" by users.

4. Discussion and future work

The main areas of challenge relating to the development of this kind of mobile app included:

- the design of intelligible prompts for eliciting the target pronunciation;
- the design of the appropriate learning paths through a hierarchy of target pronunciations;
- the quantity of feedback required by the learner;
- the quality of feedback required by the learner;
- the speed of feedback required by the learner.

The current project focusses on providing feedback in relation to phonemic pronunciation and three components of prosody: loudness, pitch and duration of syllable for individual words. Future work will involve investigating how to include phrases and sentences. The accuracy of the analysis results provided by the Web service API requires evaluation and benchmarking against a database of words and phrases that have been accurately tagged for phonemic and prosodic features. The robustness, scalability and security of the webservice will also need to be evaluated.

Applications of this technology include mobile apps (e.g. for single words), call centre training (e.g. customised scripts), and a children's adventure game (e.g. to engage children in mastering English pronunciation).

5. Conclusions

The user centred approach was useful in determining requirements for assisting learners with the perception and production of English pronunciation. Prompts for eliciting target pronunciation should include a visual indication (such as pictures or animations) of the meaning of the target word or phrases in addition to the sounds. Learners should be led through a hierarchy of words, starting with phonemes of one syllable words as the target, and adaptively building up to that prosody of two syllable words, then increasing to three syllable words, and so on, as the learner improves. A simple representation of prosody was developed and found to be intuitive by students for comparing their pronunciation to that of a native speaker. An analysis time of within one second for phonemes and prosody was considered "real time" by students. Integration with social media for both enabling competition and celebration of achievement was requested by participants.

Acknowledgements. This work results from the Protalk project funded by the UK Technology Strategy Board.

References

Demetris, C., Farnum, C., Markel, J., & Rosenhan, S. (2012, June 4). Developing UX agility: Letting go of perfection. *UX Matters*. Retrieved from http://www.uxmatters.com/mt/archives/2012/06/developing-ux-agility-letting-go-of-perfection.php

Gilakjani, A., Ahmadi, S., & Ahmadi, M. (2011). Why is pronunciation so difficult to learn? *English Language Teaching, 4*(3), 74.

university of groningen

Corpus-based learning of Cantonese for Mandarin speakers

John Lee[1] and Tak-Sum Wong[2]

Abstract. This paper reports our experience in using a parallel corpus to teach Cantonese, a variety of Chinese spoken in Hong Kong, as a second language. The parallel corpus consists of pairs of word-aligned sentences in Cantonese and Mandarin Chinese, drawn from television programs in Hong Kong (Lee, 2011). We evaluated our pedagogical approach with Mandarin-speaking students at a university course. For each student, we first diagnosed the set of Cantonese words with which s/he experienced difficulties. Then, on a web-based interface, the student independently searched in the parallel corpus for sentence pairs involving this set of Cantonese words, and analysed the translations and usage examples. Our experiments showed that, in both the short- and long-term, the corpus-based pedagogical method helped students better retain their knowledge of difficult Cantonese words.

Keywords: parallel corpus, language acquisition, Cantonese, Mandarin.

1. Introduction

Since its return to China in 1997, Hong Kong has received a large number of visitors from mainland China to study and work in the city. There has thus been a marked increase in the need to teach Cantonese, the Sinitic variety spoken in Hong Kong, to the mainland Chinese, most of whom speak Mandarin Chinese as their first language. Since both languages are developed from Middle Chinese, they share many cognates with strong, regular phonological correspondence. Nonetheless, they are not mutually intelligible.

---

1. Department of Linguistics and Translation, City University of Hong Kong; jsylee@cityu.edu.hk.

2. Department of Linguistics and Translation, City University of Hong Kong; tswong-c@my.cityu.edu.hk.

How to cite this article: Lee, J., & Wong, T.-S. (2014). Corpus-based learning of Cantonese for Mandarin Speakers. In S. Jager, L. Bradley, E. J. Meima, & S. Thouësny (Eds), *CALL Design: Principles and Practice; Proceedings of the 2014 EUROCALL Conference, Groningen, The Netherlands* (pp. 196-201). Dublin: Research-publishing.net. doi:10.14705/rpnet.2014.000217

Spoken by more than 55 million people, Cantonese is the "most widely known and influential variety of Chinese other than Mandarin" (Matthews & Yip, 2011, p. 3). Because Cantonese is a predominantly spoken language, it is relatively difficult for learners to find written samples of the language. Example sentences in textbooks are often artificially created, and do not always reflect the most colloquial or current usage. In this paper, we explore the use of a parallel corpus of Cantonese and Mandarin Chinese (Lee, 2011) as bilingual teaching material. The corpus contains more than 8000 Cantonese-Mandarin sentence pairs; the Cantonese sentences are transcriptions of television programmes, while the Mandarin sentences are the corresponding subtitles. In addition, the Cantonese and Mandarin words in each sentence pair are aligned. An example is shown in Table 1.

While computer-assisted language learning (CALL) for Mandarin has been much investigated (e.g. Shei & Hsieh, 2012; Yang & Xie, 2013), less attention has been paid to acquisition of Cantonese as a second language. Most previous studies have focused on pronunciation (Ki, 2006; Shī, 2002; Wong, 2010; among others), while research in vocabulary acquisition has been limited to contrastive studies of the correspondence between these two languages (e.g. Zeng, 1991). This paper is the first to evaluate the use of parallel corpus for teaching Cantonese to Mandarin speakers. In a classroom experiment, we show that our corpus-based pedagogical method significantly improved the students' Cantonese proficiency.

Table 1. Examples of word-aligned Cantonese-Mandarin sentence pairs from the parallel corpus used in our study (Lee, 2011)

Cantonese	俾 *béi*	你 *néih*	偷 *tāu*	咗 *jó*
Mandarin	被 *bèi*	你 *nǐ*	偷 *tōu*	了 *le*
Gloss	PASS	2SG	'steal'	**perfect.aspect.particle**
Translation	"[It's been] stolen by you"			
Cantonese	大件事 *daaihgihnsih*	喇 *la*		
Mandarin	糟糕 *zāogāo*	了 *le*		
Gloss	'terrible'	**mood.particle**		
Translation	"[That's] terrible!"			

The Mandarin *le* has different Cantonese counterparts in different contexts. As a perfect aspect particle, its Cantonese equivalent is *jó* (top sentence); as a mood particle, however, its Cantonese equivalent is *la* (bottom sentence, Table 1).

One can for example search sentences using Cantonese or Mandarin keywords, and view word alignments between Cantonese-Mandarin sentence pairs (Lee, Hui, & Yeung, 2013)

2. Experiment

2.1. Research question

Beyond the textbook, language teachers often want to employ authentic examples from contemporary media as pedagogical material in the classroom. Because Cantonese is a predominantly spoken language, it can be difficult to find such examples for Cantonese in the written form. In this study, we explore the use of a recently compiled parallel corpus of Cantonese and Mandarin Chinese (Lee, 2011) for this purpose. We have developed a web interface (Figure 1) to facilitate independent learning of Cantonese by Mandarin-speaking students. Students can retrieve sentences containing particular Mandarin or Cantonese keywords, view the Mandarin-Cantonese sentence pairs, and study the word alignments (Lee et al., 2013). In this paper, we investigate the extent to which this corpus-based method enhances the teaching of Cantonese as a second language.

Figure 1. The web interface used in the CALL session in our study

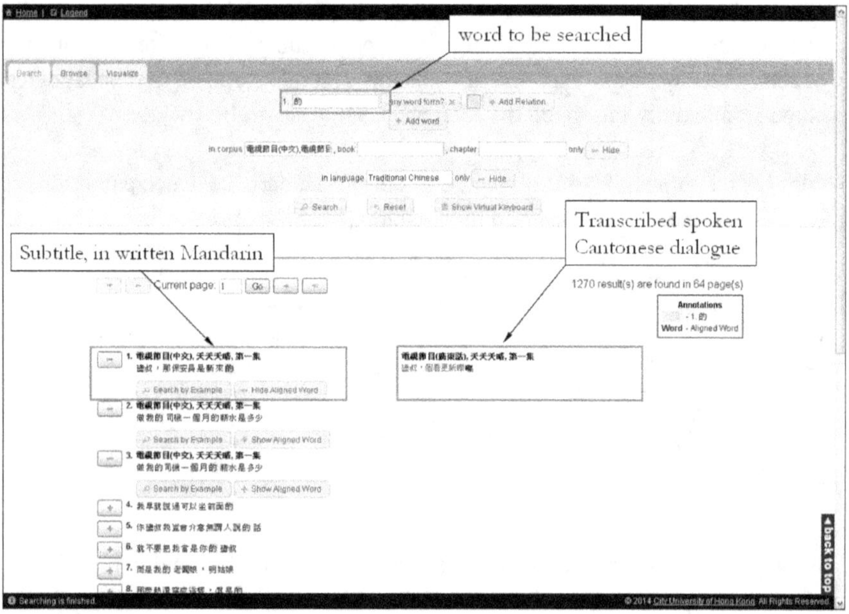

2.2. Experiment design

The evaluation took place at a 13-week course, *Cantonese Communication Skills for Putonghua Speakers*, offered at City University of Hong Kong. In total, 34 students participated, of which 27 completed all four tasks. All were Mandarin-speaking undergraduate students. Before taking this course, most had little knowledge of Cantonese.

During the 7th week, we administered a pre-test, which contained 24 Mandarin sentences, each with one word underlined. The students were asked to translate the underlined word into Cantonese. We chose Mandarin words (e.g. the word *le* in Table 1) that had at least two different translations in Cantonese (*jó* and *la*), depending on context. Specifically, the test assessed each student on 12 Mandarin words, each appearing in two sentences requiring two different Cantonese translations. Overall, for 47.8% of these words, the students gave incorrect Cantonese translations in at least one of the two contexts; we collected these words to be used in our CALL experiment.

Two weeks later, each student completed a CALL session, using the web interface of the parallel corpus shown in Figure 1. Given a list of Mandarin words, the student was asked to search for sentences in which they appear, retrieve the original transcribed Cantonese utterance, and analyse the meanings and functions of the Cantonese words to which they were aligned. We personalised the list for each student, by randomly selecting half of the Mandarin words which the student failed to translate correctly in the pre-test (henceforth, the "CALL set"), and excluding the other half as control (the "non-CALL set").

Immediately after this session, we administered a post-test to measure the short-term effect of the session. As in the pre-test, the student was asked to translate the same 24 Mandarin words, although in different sentences and contexts. After three weeks, we administered a delayed post-test, using the same Mandarin words but again in different contexts, to measure the long-term effect.

2.3. Experimental results

A summary of our experimental results is given in Table 2. To ensure there is no significant difference in the students' previous knowledge about the words in the CALL and non-CALL sets, we first compare their performance on these two sets in the pre-test. The students correctly translated 38.0% of the words in the CALL set, and 36.8% in the non-CALL set. The difference in their performance on the two sets is not significant[3].

---

3. By chi-square test, $\chi^2=0.36$, $p>0.05$, $d.f.=1$

In the post-test, after the CALL session, student performance on both sets improved substantially. Even for words in the non-CALL set, which were not involved in the CALL session, the score rose to 69.4%. The students likely noticed some of these words in the sentences they browsed, and learned about their usage as a side effect. Meanwhile, the score on the CALL set increased even more sharply, to 86.7%. Hence, even with the beneficial side effect, student performance on the CALL set was significantly higher[4] than on the non-CALL set. These figures suggest that the corpus-based pedagogical approach was very effective in the short-term.

In the delayed post-test, as expected, student performance on the CALL set decreased slightly to 83.7%, while the non-CALL set increased to 74.3%. However, the score on the CALL set remained significantly better[5] than that of the non-CALL set. These results suggest that the use of the parallel corpus also improved students' Cantonese proficiency in the long-term.

Table 2. Average student score for Mandarin-to-Cantonese translation, divided into the CALL set (those words that are studied in the CALL session) and the non-CALL set (the rest)

Average score	CALL set	Non-CALL set
Pre-test	38.0%	36.8%
Post-test	86.7%	69.4%
Delayed post-test	83.7%	74.3%

Scores on the former set were significantly higher than on the latter set in the post-test and delayed post-test. In all three tests, there were 166 words in the CALL set and 144 in the non-CALL set.

3. Conclusions and future work

We have investigated the effect of a corpus-based pedagogical method for teaching Cantonese as a second language. This method centers on a personalised computer-assisted language learning session, where each student actively searched in a parallel corpus (Lee, 2011) and learned about usage of Cantonese words for which s/he previously failed to master. Compared to the pre-test, the students demonstrated significantly higher proficiency in Cantonese in the post-test; the long-term effect, as measured in the delayed post-test, is also strong.

---

4. By chi-square test, $\chi^2=0.99$, $p<0.0005$, $d.f.=1$

5. By chi-square test, $\chi^2=0.84$, $p<0.05$, $d.f.=1$

For future work, we would like to enrich the corpus by providing pronunciation information, and to use the interface to teach Cantonese grammar.

References

Ki, W. W. (2006). *Computer-assisted perceptual learning of Cantonese tones*. Paper presented at the 14th International Conference on Computers in Education, Peking, Nov 30-Dec 4.

Lee, J. (2011). Toward a parallel corpus of spoken Cantonese and written Chinese. In *Proceedings of the 5th International Joint Conference on Natural Language Processing* (pp. 1462-1466), Chiang Mai, Thailand, November 8–13, 2011.

Lee, J., Hui, Y. C., & Yeung, C. Y. (2013). Toward a digital library with search and visualization tools. In *Proceedings of the 6th Language and Technology Conference*.

Matthews, S., & Yip, V. (2011). *Cantonese: A comprehensive grammar* (2nd ed.). London: Routledge.

Shei, C., & Hsieh, H.-P. (2012). Linkit: A CALL system for learning Chinese characters, words, and phrases. *Computer Assisted Language Learning*, 25(4), 319-338. doi:10.1080/09588221.2011.589390

Shī, Z. (2002). *Guǎngzhōu yīn Běijīng yīn duìyìng shǒucè* 廣州音北京音對應手冊 [A handbook on the correspondence between Cantonese pronunciation and Pekinese pronunciation]. Canton: Jinan University Press.

Wong, T.-S. (2010). *A pilot study on the outcome of teaching phonological correspondence in Cantonese class for Mandarin speakers*. Paper presented at the 2010 Annual Research Forum of the Linguistic Society of Hong Kong (LSHK-ARF 2010), Hong Kong. Retrieved from http://www.lshk.org/arf2010/doc/LSHK-ARF_2010_abstracts_2.0.pdf

Yang, C., & Xie, Y. (2013). Learning Chinese idioms through iPads. *Language, Learning & Technology, 17*(2), 12-23.

Zeng, Z. (1991). *Colloquial Cantonese and Putonghua equivalents* (3rd ed.) (S. K. Lai, Trans.). Hong Kong: Joint Publishing (Hong Kong) Company Limited.

Collaborative enquiry through the tabletop for second/foreign language learners

Mei Lin[1], Anne Preston[2], Ahmed Kharrufa[3], and Zhuoran Kong[4]

Abstract. Interactional communicative competence and higher-order thinking have been well documented as two of the biggest challenges for second/foreign language learners (EFL learners). This paper evaluates the use of digital tabletops as tools for problem-solving tasks in groups. The evaluation is based on a preliminary study of an application of the use of Digital Mysteries task with EFL learners in a Higher Education institution. It focuses more specifically on the extent to which collaborative learning platforms provided by interactive tabletops can promote and support the application of both thinking and linguistic skills for EFL learners. Based on an interdisciplinary perspective which draws from instructed second language learning and human-computer interaction fields, the evaluation considers moment-to-moment multimodal interaction of three groups of Chinese English language learners with and around the completion of the Digital Mysteries task. It seeks to identify what specific affordances in the design might benefit EFL learners in terms of thinking skills, interactional competence and linguistic performance, and by the same token, what might not. This paper concludes with a number of suggestions about how technologies designed for collaborative enquiry might be repurposed for higher-order thinking and language learning.

Keywords: digital table, enquiry, interactional competence, higher order thinking.

---

1. mei.lin@ncl.ac.uk.
2. anne.preston@newcastle.ac.uk.
3. ahmed@reflectivethinking.com.
4. kzr1123@163.com.

How to cite this article: Lin, M., Preston, A., Kharrufa, A., & Kong, Z. (2014). Collaborative enquiry through the tabletop for second/foreign language learners. In S. Jager, L. Bradley, E. J. Meima, & S. Thouësny (Eds), *CALL Design: Principles and Practice; Proceedings of the 2014 EUROCALL Conference, Groningen, The Netherlands* (pp. 202-208). Dublin: Research-publishing.net. doi:10.14705/rpnet.2014.000218

1. Introduction

Research on communicative competence stresses the role of negotiation for meaning and students' participation in oral communication. Participation and group tasks, however, do not automatically lead to negotiations for meaning. Digital Tabletops are an emerging technology offering good potential as a collaborative learning platform. A tabletop is a large horizontal display that allows students to interact with its contents directly using pens or touch. This technology is unique in combining the benefits of face-to-face collaborative learning that usually takes place around traditional tables with advantages gained from using computer technology (e.g. regulating the task, interaction with and around the tabletop, and logging the session for reflection).

Digital Mysteries (Kharrufa, Leat, & Olivier, 2010) is a tool for the development and assessment of students' higher-order-thinking. The pedagogical design was based on Moseley et al.'s (2005) thinking skills framework, and structures the completion of the Mysteries in three stages (Figure 1): reading (information gathering), grouping (building understanding) and sequencing (productive thinking). The Grouping stage focuses on developing meaning and organising ideas into groups while the sequencing stage puts a strong focus on reasoning and understanding causal relationships (through the use of the arrow shaped sticky tape).

Figure 1. Digital Mysteries three-stage structure and its mapping to Moseley et al.'s (2005) thinking skills model

STRATEGIC AND REFLECTIVE THINKING		
A dedicated reflection stage, reflection prompts at stage boundaries, the use of an ill-defined task in a collaborative environment		

COGNITIVE SKILLS		
Information-gathering: Reading stage	*Building understanding:* Grouping stage	*Productive thinking:* Sequencing and webbing stage, answering the question
Focus on reading, experiencing, recognizing, comprehending, and recalling information	Focus on classifying and organizing information (group tool), identifying relation (sticky tape), representing and sharing ideas (note tool and discussions), etc.	Focus on reasoning and understanding causal relationships (the arrow sticky tape and normal sticky tape, the need to build a layout that reflects the students' reasoning), problem solving, and creative thinking

Students are asked to solve open-ended mysteries based on a number of data slips via multiple pen-based interactions. Direct interaction with the application enables students to scale, move, group and regroup, and sequence in order to make sense of causal relationships of the different pieces of information. By physically manipulating data slips, students not only engage in the task, but will make their thinking visible on the tabletop and available for self and collective reflection and evaluation (Leat & Nichols, 2000).

An overall enforced structure is designed to help students go through the stages that correspond to progressing levels of thinking, i.e. reading, grouping, and reasoning. This study sought to identify what specific affordances a pen-based version of the Digital Mysteries tabletop application might benefit EFL learners in terms of collaboration and higher order thinking, and what might not.

2. Method

2.1. An interdisciplinary approach

The evaluation adopts an interdisciplinary approach which considers moment-to-moment multimodal interaction of three groups of Chinese EFL learners. The interactions were considered through the lens of three perspectives: Reasoning skills in the light of the Jewell's (1996) Reasoning taxonomy; interactional competence and linguistic performance, guided by a conversation analysis for SLA approach, and interaction with the pedagogical-technological design of the user interface (Cummins, 2008; Kharrufa, Olivier, & Leat, 2010).

2.2. Synchronised audio and video files with transcripts

The completion of the Digital Mysteries were audio and video recorded for the three groups (Groups A, B, and C). Extracts were identified and synchronised with video logs. Synchronisation allowed examination of triggers of interaction (verbal and non-verbal) and of the extent to which this collaborative learning platform promoted and supported the application of both thinking and language learning skills for EFL learners.

2.3. Analysis

An initial three way independent analysis of the multimodal data was conducted. The authors then exchanged views on observed performance and outcome, linking to the underlying design of the tabletop and Digital Mysteries.

3. Discussion

The findings suggested that although the students completed the same task with the same built-in structure for the stages, variations were observed among the three groups. Group A followed the three stages to the letter, though their answer to the question 'Why Gail's weekly shopping takes 40-minutes longer?' was less satisfactory compared with that of Group B and C. Group C demonstrated a higher level of cognitive awareness in terms of sorting and sequencing the information from the outset. They produced longer sequences of talk involving negotiation for meaning and reasoning, and arrived at a more logical answer to the question than Group A, though less satisfactory than Group B. Group B divided jobs of reading and sorting at the first two stages, spent more time on sequencing and reflecting, and made the most logical argument.

In terms of the role of the tabletop in mediating the task completion, direct interaction using the pens allowed students to engage with the organisation of the information (Figure 2).

Figure 2. Group C: sorting

It was evident in more than one instance that the ability to enlarge the slips prompted reading aloud, encouraged discussions around its content, and pulled students together in the task. All the information visible on the table provided a space of learning (Walsh, 2011) to scan information, search for links between them, reflect on their thinking and make necessary changes (Figure 3). This facility made a high–cognitive-demand activity manageable (Cummins, 2008) with regard to both thinking and speaking in a foreign language.

Figure 3. Group B: Checking final layout of reasoning

In addition, labelling groups of slips and sequencing generated a lot of talk of clarifications, differentiation of causes, reasons or effects, and evaluation or re-examination of their decisions. This resulted in a move to higher-order thinking. There was evidence of sequences consisting of proposals, acceptance, checking, and dispute to further the discussion (Jewell, 1996). As the thinking skills advanced, so did the organisation of the talk. Long and complex stretches of turn-taking reflected students' interactional competence mediated by the table. Many examples implied the use of discourse markers. For instance, 'maybe' was used to seek confirmation or make comments during proposals. 'This' and 'that' were used as a way to signal joint attention to slips. The striking number of occurrences of 'this' in all three groups leads to the conclusion that it is used as an economic device in terms of working memory to spare more space for a speedy and fluent discussion of reasons as shown in Extract 1.

Extract 1: Group C

      423   Gao: Also in the next, **this** lead to **this**.

      424   Wan: **This** is maybe useful.

      425   Hao: I think **this** one is the reason, can be the reason for these two.

It is interesting to note a potentially close link between the use of the table and multimodal behaviour and thinking where postures could demonstrate 'thinking' and also 'interthinking' (Littleton & Mercer, 2013). Here, although there was no 'talk' as such, there was still language processing going on (Table 1).

Table 1. Discourse markers used by students in solving Digital Mysteries

Discourse markers/stems	Group A	Group B	Group C
This	44	96	120
Maybe	10	33	22
I think	20	25	34
I don't think	0	6	0
Do you think…	0	15	1
What do you think	0	6	3
Why	7	25	14
Because	6	19	30
Reasons	12	27	43
Logic	0	11	0

From a thinking skills perspective, students were going through stages of gathering and processing information, and seeking relationships between various slips. Sometimes the gathering and processing information were integrated with no clear separation. In terms of reasoning skills, argument construction called for critical evaluation of ideas proposed by others in the group (Jewell, 1996). In some cases, solutions were 'on-hold'. Students did not reach a satisfactory solution but carried on with the activity until more information was available or noticed, making them rethink previous decisions.

From a language learning perspective, grouping and sequencing encouraged students reading and/or re-examining the slips at least more than once. This recycling of information helped EFL learners internalise the language they encountered.

4. Conclusions

This study investigated how digital technology might support EFL learners when engaged in higher-order thinking tasks. Our findings suggest that digital tabletop technologies hold a number of benefits for EFL learners engaged in collaborative enquiry. Importantly, these benefits comprise learning behaviours as they happen 'on' and 'off' the tabletop. Learners demonstrated a development in thinking critically as well as operationalising linguistic and interactional competences with, around and through the technology. How this type of activity might enhance learning in the longer-term is a fruitful next line of enquiry.

References

Cummins, J. (2008). BICS and CALP: Empirical and theoretical status of the distinction. In B. Street & N. H. Hornberger (Eds), *Encyclopaedia of Language and Education* (2nd ed.) (Volume 2: Literacy) (pp. 71-83). New York: Springer Science + Business Media LLC.

Jewell, P. (1996). *A reasoning taxonomy for gifted education*. In M. T. McCann & F. Southern (Eds), *Fusing talents: Proceedings of the 6th national conference on gifted education Australian association for the education of the gifted and talented.*

Kharrufa, A. S., Leat, D., & Olivier, P. (2010). Digital Mysteries: Designing for learning at the tabletop. In *Proceedings of the ACM International Conference on Interactive Tabletops and Surfaces 2010, Saarbrücken, Germany, November 7-10, 2010, ITS'10.*

Kharrufa, A. S., Olivier, P., Leat, D. (2010). Learning through reflection at the tabletop: A case study with Digital Mysteries. In *Proceedings of World Conference on Educational Multimedia, Hypermedia and Telecommunications, Toronto, Canada June 28-July 2, 2010* (pp. 65-674).

Leat, D., & Nichols, A. (2000). Brains on the table. Diagnostic and formative assessment through observation. *Assessment in Education: Principles, Policy & Practice, 7*(1), 103-121.

Littleton, K., & Mercer, N. (2013). *Interthinking: Putting talk to work*. Oxon: Routledge.

Moseley, D., Baumfield, V., Elliot, J., Gregson, M., Higgins, S., Miller, J., & Newton, D. (2005). *Frameworks for thinking*. Cambridge: Cambridge University Press. doi:10.1017/CBO9780511489914

Walsh, S. (2011). *Exploring classroom discourse: Language in Action*. London: Routledge.

PETALL: A European project on technology-mediated TBLT

António Lopes[1]

Abstract. The Common European Framework of Reference (CEFR) lays strong emphasis on task-based language teaching (TBLT). However, this approach constitutes a challenge for many foreign language teachers, not so much because they are not familiar with the approach or its benefits, but because of the requirements and practical conditions to be met. Most national curricula are clear about the importance of TBLT. The reality of the classroom does not mirror it. The consortium, coordinated by the University of Algarve, is constituted by Higher Education Institutions and secondary schools working in tandem from ten countries (Germany, Greece, Hungary, Italy, the Netherlands, Portugal, Serbia, Spain, Turkey, and the UK). The consortium proposes to build on the outcomes of previous Comenius projects, extending previously acquired knowledge to other partners and constructing a transnational strategy for information and communications technology (ICT)-based task design management. This entails setting up regional networks to promote the languages of the partners involved in the project.

Keywords: LLP transversal project, technology-mediated TBLT, linguistic diversity, teacher training.

1. Introduction

PETALL stands for **P**an-**E**uropean **T**ask **A**ctivities for **L**anguage **L**earning and is a Transversal Key Activity 2 (Languages) project funded by the European Commission. The main objective of the project (2013-2016) is to provide the teaching community with examples of good practices in which ICT is used in the language classroom to serve productive purposes and in a target-oriented way, as

---

1. University of Algarve; alopes@ualg.pt.

How to cite this article: Lopes, A. (2014). PETALL: A European project on technology-mediated TBLT. In S. Jager, L. Bradley, E. J. Meima, & S. Thouësny (Eds), *CALL Design: Principles and Practice; Proceedings of the 2014 EUROCALL Conference, Groningen, The Netherlands* (pp. 209-213). Dublin: Research-publishing.net. doi:10.14705/rpnet.2014.000219

propounded by the CEFR. Coordinated first by the University of Amsterdam, and later by the University of Algarve, it involves a total of ten countries.

2. Background to the project

Despite the emphasis that the CEFR places on TBLT, the approach still represents a challenge for many teachers. They may be familiar with the concept and its communicative benefits, since tasks are usually learner-centred and involve problem-solving procedures or the development of products, which helps learners meet practical challenges, facilitates interaction and makes them responsible for the outcomes of the communication process. However, some requirements and conditions are difficult to meet. The national curricula of many countries are clear about the importance of adopting a task-based approach in foreign language learning. The reality of the classroom, however, does not live up to that standard. Tasks may be rather accessible and intelligible in their design, but the ways in which they can be incorporated into classroom routines and effectively integrated into lesson planning present teachers with methodological and practical problems, which may be discouraging. As a result, they prefer to revert to conventional teaching practices in which they feel more confident and less exposed to the contingencies of real-time communication between learners.

Surveys conducted within the scope of the Comenius project ETALAGE revealed that the reluctance of teachers to revert to TBLT resulted from lack of support and the relatively low levels of collaboration between teachers. An added difficulty detected was related to the inadequacy of the ETALAGE tasks to the specific needs of the classes in each country. The process of adaptation of some ETALAGE tasks proved time-consuming and, given the specific characteristics of their design, sometimes demanded the introduction of significant changes (Lopes, 2012).

3. Seeking solutions

One of the conclusions drawn from ETALAGE was that the international potential of the tasks, their ability to travel well and to be shared by teachers across Europe without too much entropy, should be furthered through cross-cultural task design management. This called for the creation of regional networks for methodological reflection and joint implementation of tasks. The collaborative work between teachers in different national settings, in particular the ones which rely on communicative exchange across cultural and geographic divides, is a prerequisite to circumvent some of the limitations identified in the previous project. Examples are complications that resulted from the adaptation process, the lack of support and dialogue between peers, and the challenge of designing and implementing tasks that might make the best of the diversity of cultural experiences in each country.

4. Relevant literature

Only in recent years have researchers paid closer attention to the integration of ICT into TBLT. Authors like Ellis (2003), Nunan (2004), and Willis and Willis (2001) have contributed to the development of the theoretical and methodological framework of TBLT, but usually technology-mediated contexts have been left aside. The features of such contexts demand a specialized approach, as the uses of language have also evolved to meet the rapidly changing prerequisites, constraints and potentials of ICT. In 2010, Thomas and Reinders edited a volume of studies dedicated to technology-mediated TBLT, encompassing such matters as intercultural exchanges with the application of computer-mediated communication (CMC), network-based CALL, synchronous and asynchronous CMC, teacher education, and virtual-world networking environments, aspects which PETALL intends to cover.

5. Aims and objectives

The project seeks to:

- encourage collaborative work between teachers in different countries and teacher trainers by setting up regional networks for the development of ICT-based tasks;

- facilitate access to technology-mediated tasks that travel well, securing the quality of communicative exchange across cultural and geographic divides;

- promote mutual understanding and awareness of linguistic and cultural diversity through ICT-based TBLT;

- enhance the quality of teacher education in technology-mediated TBLT.

At a methodological level, the consortium members further aim to explore the following aspects:

- the dynamics of transnational collaborative work between teachers in task design and management;

- the way evaluation tools can leverage both the quality of teacher education in technology-mediated TBLT and the effectiveness of task-based language learning;

- the aspects that guarantee that the tasks proposed by the project travel.

6. Methodology

PETALL will pool the expertise of 10 tandems of teacher education institutes and practice schools to select samples of good practice of ICT-based tasks. Each tandem will select four task activities, two in cooperation with the tandem in one neighbouring country and two in cooperation with the tandem in the other neighbouring country. Tasks will be tried out by pupils in the practice schools of the tandem and of those of the other tandems so as to assure that they "travel well". Each tandem will also produce its training course.

The project is divided into six phases; the first being devoted to the selection and adaptation of learning tasks, which will be revised in the course of the second phase after try out and evaluation by end users and independent experts. The third one is devoted to the design of the training courses, which will be revised in the course of the fourth phase after try out and evaluation by end users and independent experts . The final year will be devoted to translation of the products first in English and then in all the languages of the consortium and their publication.

7. Impact, dissemination, exploitation

As mentioned by Curriculum for Excellence (n.d.), "[o]ne of the key aims of modern languages teaching is to develop young people's 'communicative competence' so that they are able to use and enjoy the language effectively in real situations and for a range of relevant purposes in work and leisure throughout their life" (p. 173). PETALL will allow teachers to use and adapt a set of tasks that are intrinsically interesting and motivating. PETALL tasks will allow students to develop a range of competences which go beyond the mere development of language skills and will promote the development of competences such as the use of ICT, enquiry skills, critical thinking, creative thinking, communication, collaborative working and interpersonal relationships, problem solving, decision making, organisation, management and leadership.

PETALL tasks and the information gleaned from the implementation and analysis of the success of the tasks with target groups (teachers, trainers, schools, policy makers, students) will be shared with the profession in a number of contexts. Initially, project partners share their experiences with colleagues in their own, as well as neighbouring, institutions. Subsequently, this will be followed by presentations and papers at regional, national and international conferences, and refereed articles in professional publications. This engagement with a task-based learning approach and the pan-European nature of the project should lead to further research and collaborative development work within the project team and with the contacts made in the implementation and dissemination of the tasks.

The communication channels used for the PETALL project are the development of a website, production of brochures and posters, participation in scientific meetings, courses and publication of articles in journals, conference proceedings, lectures, etc.

A crucial element in the dissemination of the results is translation into different languages. This is a major venture as all the national samples of good practice and courses are to be translated into the project language (English) and into the other national languages prior to being uploaded in the website.

References

Curriculum for Excellence. (n.d.). *Education Scotland* [website]. Retrieved from https://www.educationscotland.gov.uk/Images/all_experiences_outcomes_tcm4-539562.pdf

Ellis, R. (2003). *Task-based language learning and teaching*. Oxford: Oxford University Press.

Lopes, A. (2012). Changing teachers' attitudes towards ICT-based language learning tasks: the ETALAGE Comenius project (the Portuguese case). *The EUROCALL Review, 20*(1), 100-103.

Nunan, D. (2004). *Task-based language teaching*. Cambridge: Cambridge University Press. doi:10.1017/CBO9780511667336

Thomas, M., & Reinders, H. (Eds). (2010). *Task-based language learning and teaching with technology*. New York: Continuum.

Willis, D., & Willis, J. (2001). Task-based language learning. In R. Carter & D. Nunan (Eds), *The Cambridge guide to teaching English to speakers of other languages* (pp. 173-179). Cambridge: Cambridge University Press. doi:10.1017/CBO9780511667206.026

university of groningen

Effects of summary writing on oral proficiency performance within a computer-based test for integrated listening-speaking tasks

Zhihong Lu[1] and Yanfei Wang[2]

Abstract. The effective design of test items within a computer-based language test (CBLT) for developing English as a foreign language (EFL) learners' listening and speaking skills has become an increasingly challenging task for both test users and test designers compared with that of pencil-and-paper tests in the past. It needs to fit integrated oral proficiency tasks into the framework of quantitative psychometric testing modes. It also needs to meet higher demands of test takers living in today's digitized world. To test if summary writing in integrated listening-speaking tasks is beneficial to EFL learners in decreasing their anxiety in the follow-up speaking task, a fifteen-week experiment was carried out at a CALL-based English audio-video speaking class (EAVSC). To measure the effects, both pre- and post-tests along with follow-up surveys were carried out. Analyses of correlated data show that there is a positive correlation between EFL learners' performance of summary writing and that of the follow-up oral test item, i.e. the personal statement.

Keywords: summary writing, anxiety, item design, personal statement.

1. Introduction

Anxiety in the process of any test can be an unavoidable psychological factor which distracts test takers from their performance and usually affects their test results. Previous studies and classroom observations show that anxiety usually has negative effects on EFL learners' performance in a test, especially in a speaking

---

1. Beijing University of Posts and Telecommunications, China; luzhihong@bupt.edu.cn, zhihonglu2013@aliyun.com.
2. Beijing University of Posts and Telecommunications, China; 739960735@qq.com, wyf_8873@126.com.

How to cite this article: Lu, Z., & Wang, Y. (2014). Effects of summary writing on oral proficiency performance within a computer-based test for integrated listening-speaking tasks. In S. Jager, L. Bradley, E. J. Meima, & S. Thouësny (Eds), *CALL Design: Principles and Practice*; *Proceedings of the 2014 EUROCALL Conference, Groningen, The Netherlands* (pp. 214-219). Dublin: Research-publishing.net. doi:10.14705/rpnet.2014.000220

test. Breeze (2004) states that, according to Fulcher's (2003) conclusion, in order "to provide a valid speaking test, it is necessary to capture the relevant aspects of speaking on the one hand, and prevent interference in the score from irrelevant factors, on the other" (para. 3).

In today's digitized world, conducting computerized integrated listening-speaking tasks can be even more challenging for EFL learners. As Grant, Huang, and Pasfield-Neofitou (2013) indicate, "while traditional modes of learning continue to remain important, relevant, and in demand, all disciplines need to embrace the challenges and opportunities online and blended learning bring" (p. 2).

Summary writing, a content-based task type, can be used to simultaneously test two or more language skills: listening and writing, or reading and writing. However, there is not much research concerning the issue, neither on the combination of summary writing with listening-based integrated tasks, nor on the process of conducting oral productive tasks in EFL classroom practice.

This study aimed at finding out if such innovative item design can minimize the negative effects of EFL learners' anxiety in a listening-based speaking task.

2. Method

2.1. Research questions

The specific research questions were:

- Is there a positive correlation between EFL learners' performance of summary writing and that of the personal statement?

- Is summary writing helpful to decrease EFL learners' anxiety in their follow-up oral output?

2.2. Research design

This study was carried out at the first author's EAVSC for non-English majors and lasted for fifteen weeks from February 25th to June 3rd, 2014. Two administrative classes were randomly divided into two groups: an experimental class and a control class. The course was conducted in a digital lab, which made it possible to do synchronous oral communication, random grouping, and speech recording and collecting. All the students were required to do their pre- and post-tests through a self-developed web-based English language skills training system (see Figure 1), and data about their learning and responses to the various activities could be collected automatically.

The integrated listening-speaking test design was as follows: firstly students were given video/audio-based listening material and the media was played several times. During the period, students were required to do several listening comprehension tasks which included short-answer questions, multiple choices, true or false, sentence completion, constructing questions, and finally summary writing of the same material in five minutes. This was followed up with a one-minute personal statement about the same material (see Figure 1).

Figure 1. A screenshot of the post-test on the teacher's interface of the system

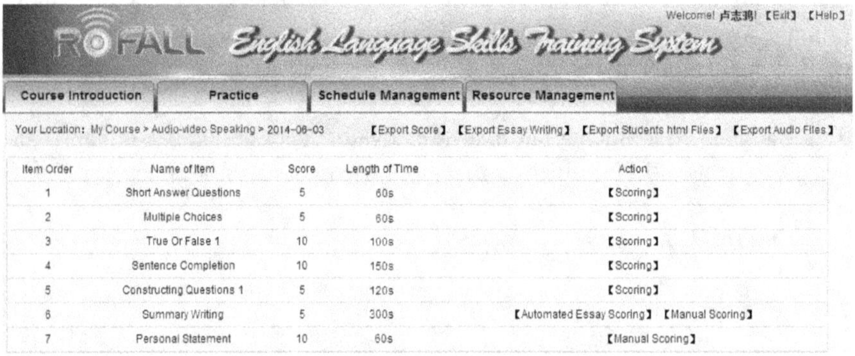

Item Order	Name of Item	Score	Length of Time	Action
1	Short Answer Questions	5	60s	【Scoring】
2	Multiple Choices	5	60s	【Scoring】
3	True Or False 1	10	100s	【Scoring】
4	Sentence Completion	10	150s	【Scoring】
5	Constructing Questions 1	5	120s	【Scoring】
6	Summary Writing	5	300s	【Automated Essay Scoring】【Manual Scoring】
7	Personal Statement	10	60s	【Manual Scoring】

To measure the effects of summary writing on oral proficiency performance, pre- and post-tests were carried out. In the pre-test, students in both classes were not required to do summary writing. During the fifteen-week period, the students in the experimental class were trained to be familiar with the above test mode and they were required to complete summary writing before the speech recording in post-test, while those in the control class were not. The study focused on whether summary writing had positive effects on decreasing anxiety in the oral production. As such, we intended to find out if there was a significant difference in anxiety between the two tests.

2.3. Instruments

One integrated listening-speaking test and two questionnaires, which include an anxiety scale of personal statement, were assigned to both classes. Additionally, some items about the effect of summary writing on the degree of anxiety in the personal statements were added to the questionnaire for the experimental class during the post-test.

2.4. Data collection

All the students' personal statements were rated on the basis of IELTS Speaking Band Descriptions by two teachers to minimize bias. 51 (31 from the experimental class and 24 from the control class) copies of feedback from each questionnaire were collected and counted as valid.

2.5. Data analysis

Data was processed by using SPSS 17.0:

- Pearson correlation tests were used to illustrate the correlation between the score of the summary writing and personal statements.

- Descriptive statistics (mean, standard deviation, percentage) were used to analyze the anxiety scale and the students' feedback in the experimental class with respect to the effect of summary writing on anxiety in the personal statements.

- Paired sample t-test was employed to find out if there is a significant difference in students' anxiety in each class between the pre- and post-tests.

3. Discussion

3.1. Summary writing and personal statements

As shown in Table 1, there exists a positive correlation between students' score of summary writing and that of the personal statements in the experimental class.

Table 1. Correlation between the summary writing and personal statements

		Personal statement
Summary writing	Pearson Correlation Coefficient	.549*
	Significance(two-tailed)	.001
	N	31

*: Correlation is significant at the 0.01 level (2-tailed).

3.2. Analysis of two questionnaires

A paired sample t-test for the anxiety scale of the personal statements was used to measure if there was a significant difference in students' anxiety between the pre- and post-tests in both classes. The results show that there were no significant differences in both classes, with a level of significance value of 0.98 ($t=-0.24$, $df=23$, $p>0.05$) in the control class, and 0.08 ($t=1.84$, $df=26$, $p>0.05$) in the experimental class.

A paired sample t-test for the anxiety scale with respect to coherency and logic in the personal statements shows that there were no significant differences between the two tests in both classes, with a level of significance value of 0.15 ($t=1.49$, $df=23$, $p>0.05$) in the control class and 0.07 ($t=1.89$, $df=26$, $p>0.05$) in the experimental class.

Concerning the anxiety scale with respect to language expressions in the personal statements, items #4 and #11 in both questionnaires, i.e "*in the process of doing the personal statement, I felt so nervous that I forgot the words and expressions I had known before*" and "*in the process of doing the personal statement, I was too nervous to utter words and sentences*", were of particular interest. A paired sample t-test shows that the mean score of #4 in the experimental class pre- and post-tests were 3.70 and 3.11 respectively, with a level of significance value of 0.00 ($t=3.17$, $df=26$, $p<0.05$). The mean score of #11 in the experimental class pre- and post-tests were 3.67 and 3.19 respectively, with a level of significance value of 0.01 ($t=2.80$, $df=26$, $p<0.05$). Meanwhile, the p value of #4 and #11 in the control group was 1.00 ($t=0.00$, $df=23$, $p>0.05$) and 0.37 ($t=0.91$, $df=23$, $p>0.05$) respectively. This confirmed that the difference between the two tests in the experimental class was significant while in the control class it was not.

A paired sample t-test for the anxiety scale with respect to short-term memory loss in the personal statements shows that there were no significant differences between the two tests in both classes, with a level of significance value of 0.83 ($t=-0.22$, $df=23$, $p>0.05$) in the control class and with a level of significance value of 0.40 ($t=0.85$, $df=26$, $p>0.05$) in the experimental class.

The feedback from effect of summary writing on anxiety in the personal statements in the experimental class shows that most students felt that summary writing was helpful to ease their anxiety.

4. Conclusions

This study leads to the following conclusions:

- There is a positive correlation between EFL learners' performance of summary writing and that of the personal statements within a computer-based test for integrated listening-speaking tasks.

- In a listening-based oral test, summary writing, to a certain degree, may help in lowering EFL learners' anxiety in the process of oral performance since it can enable them to feel prepared in discourse organization before speech, especially in language expression.

However, in this study, some limitations still remain that may have biased the results:

- The number of subjects involved was not big enough to meet the statistic requirement for a reliable outcome.

- The relevant factors that may affect EFL learners' anxiety were not fully considered.

- The questionnaires may not include all the possible effects of summary writing on EFL learners' anxiety in the personal statements.

Acknowledgements. This study is part of the humanities and social sciences project "Research on Multidimensional Assessment for a Web-based English Audio-video Speaking Course" (12YJA740052), supported by the Ministry of Education in China. We would like to thank Prof. Fuan Wen and his technical team for their support in the course of the study, and Beijing Rainier Network Science and Technology for giving us permission to include screenshots of the system in use in this paper. We would also like to thank all the editors of the proceedings for their constructive comments and suggestions in the process of revising this paper.

References

Breeze, R. (2004). *Book review of Testing Second Language Speaking*, Glenn Fulcher (2003), Harlow: Pearson Longman, Pp. xxi + 288, ISBN 0-582-47270-9. TESL-EJ, 8(1). Retrieved from http://tesl-ej.org/ej29/r5.html

Fulcher, G. (2003). *Testing second language speaking*. Harlow: Pearson Longman.

Grant, S., Huang, H., & Pasfield-Neofitou, S. (2013). Language learning in virtual worlds: The role of foreign language and technical anxiety. *Journal of Virtual Worlds Research, 6*(1), 1-9.

Telecollaborative desktop-videoconferencing exchange: The case of Mark

Véronique Martin[1]

Abstract. This presentation is a case study of the Intercultural Communicative Competence (ICC) development of Mark, one of ten American students engaged in a desktop-videoconferencing telecollaborative exchange with a class of French students. Due in part to its inherent complexity, this context has not been widely researched. To observe ICC development, I used a combination of a priori categories based on the "Attitude" component of Byram's (1997) model, that is, the willingness to show value to one's partner or relativize one's self, and a set of emerging themes (Boyatzis, 1998) gathered from the data. The video-recorded sessions are analyzed in conjunction with data from background surveys, autobiographies, journal entries, and email exchanges. This methodology sheds light on the behavioral choices of a participant who, despite a high level of engagement and motivation, does not appear to take advantage of the exchange for the purpose of ICC development, a behavior that I noticed in other members of his class. While linguistic development can be observed, there is little display of "self-relativizing" and "valuing others" (Byram, 1997, p. 34). These results raise the question of how the methodology could be modified to better foster ICC development in students like Mark, or whether it is even possible to reach this goal within such a mediated environment.

Keywords: telecollaboration, intercultural communicative competence, desktop-videoconferencing.

1. Introduction

This presentation reports on the case of Mark, an American student majoring in French, who was enrolled in a fifth semester French conversation course, when

---

1. University at Albany, State University of New York; martinv49@gmail.com.

How to cite this article: Martin, V. (2014). Telecollaborative desktop-videoconferencing exchange: The case of Mark. In S. Jager, L. Bradley, E. J. Meima, & S. Thouësny (Eds), *CALL Design: Principles and Practice*; Proceedings of the 2014 EUROCALL Conference, Groningen, The Netherlands (pp. 220-224). Dublin: Research-publishing.net. doi:10.14705/rpnet.2014.000221

he took part with his classmates in a semester-long telecollaborative exchange. The overall objective was to investigate if and how students were able to take advantage of the online mediated multimodal environment to engage in a learning and socialization process with a French partner and show evidence of intercultural communicative development. Mark was paired with a French student who he had expressed an interest in working with to complete a collaborative project. Personal information shared at the beginning of the study indicated that he intended to become a French teacher and that he had an extensive travel experience and some Francophone ancestry (Haitian grandfather). He also declared himself "interested" and "curious" in knowing more about Francophone cultures and "very interested" in the opportunity to speak with native French students.

Students engaged in a series of one-on-one desktop videoconferencing sessions in the course of the exchange. This complex and less researched learning environment was selected because it provides both the immediacy of authentic interaction with access to many channels to support it (visual, audio, chat, online access to dictionaries and sites, etc.), and constitutes a good platform to support meaningful and personal intercultural exchanges. This choice of technology was not without risks. Indeed, the potential for tensions and conflict linked to video-based intercultural interaction had been raised previously (O'Dowd, 2006). However, in this exploratory study, the intention was not to avoid possible miscommunication or conflict; they were viewed rather as natural occurrences and possible learning moments in these exchanges. Still, measures were taken to foster a comfortable intercultural learning environment, such as in and out of class preparatory work with the participants and a careful pairing process.

2. Method

2.1. Study procedure

The study spanned the entire French conversation course and included three phases: 1) preparation for the exchange with in-class readings and discussions on intercultural variation and information exchanges between the transatlantic partners; 2) online collaborative sessions in the lab with written contacts between sessions; and 3) presentations and debates in class.

The study adopted a qualitative approach to data collection and analysis. Two tasks were assigned during the online sessions: an elective introductory questionnaire and a required collaborative debate preparation with a PowerPoint presentation. In addition, students completed background surveys, wrote autobiographies, and kept journals in which they wrote reflectively about the sessions and their own presentations. These instruments were selected to generate and collect data over the course of the semester that could provide an in-depth look at the intercultural exchange.

2.2. Data analysis

In order to investigate intercultural communicative development, the "Attitude" factor from Byram's (1997) model of Intercultural Communicative Competence was chosen. A hybrid method of analysis was then employed to examine the data. It was comprised of Byram's (1997) a priori list of attitudinal objectives as well as categories aligned with the goal of "relativizing self" and "valuing others" (p. 34), gathered through a process of emerging themes (Boyatzis, 1998) based on the students' recorded interactions. This methodological choice, which sets this study apart from others, was made in an effort to determine and clarify what could count as observable attributes of "Attitudes" in this multimodal telecollaborative exchange, and consequently to reflect more closely the actual mediated processes in the data with regard to ICC learning.

Mark was one of three participants selected for this in-depth study through a process of qualitative sampling. Byram's (1997) attitude objectives and the data-driven themes were used to code his three recorded and transcribed online sessions. This analytic process provided an in-depth picture of his interaction with his partner and in particular, his willingness to show value to him or relativize himself as well as his unwillingness to show these behaviors, coded as "lack of" or absence of "Attitudes", over the course of the exchange.

3. Discussion

A close analysis of Mark's recordings triangulated with other data sources yielded a markedly different picture than the one that initially emerged from the field notes. The data gathered from the survey, Mark's verbal comments and written reflections as well as my observations of the sessions, first suggested that he was eager to participate, to improve his language skills, and to interact with a French discussion partner. As a serious student and experienced traveler, he appeared well poised to take advantage of the intercultural learning environment. However, the combing of the recorded sessions for displays of attitudes of curiosity and openness through "self-relativizing" and "valuing others" (Byram, 1997, p. 34), as first steps towards "decentering" (Byram, 1997), indicated otherwise. His overall production of attitudes during the three sessions was limited both in number and in type of attitudes produced: only five of the ten coded categories were present in his discourse. In the first two sessions, he also displayed a strong tendency to self-prioritize, evidenced by the higher presence of coded instances of "lack of value" for his partner. The main collaborative task work did not fulfill its mediational function, in the sense that Mark flouted the guidelines and did not produce any of the attitudes which were specifically targeted by this task. It is also telling that he chose to skip the initial task which was not mandatory, but still strongly recommended, in which he was meant to gather information about his partner and help develop a more personal connection, something he was not especially interested in.

4. Conclusions

The general evolution of the exchange did not show significant signs of development in Mark's ability to show openness and curiosity towards his partner or a greater ability to relate to him as person as opposed to a task partner. Unlike other participants who successfully used the online mediated environment and collaborative task work to develop their intercultural communicative competence, the choice of methodology did not lead to development and therefore does not seem to be a good choice in the case of Mark.

Despite his high level of motivation, engagement and stated enjoyment of the exchange, the data indicates that his sole goal seemed to be the opportunity to practice his language skills with a native speaker and improve his level of proficiency. This observation highlights the effect of students' agencies, that is, of their personal interests, experiences and motives and goals when engaging in these exchanges and how these affect their intercultural learning potential. Addressing these issues and strengthening the pre-exchange preparatory work in order to better clarify the goals of telecollaborative exchanges might be a good way to assist participants like Mark.

Finally, despite the lack of "Attitudes" in Mark's discourse, he was able to develop both culture-specific interactional conventions and remedial strategies to avoid conversation breakdowns, convey meaning and adjust to his partner's mediation both in French and in English. This indicated that he was able to develop "skills of discovery and interaction", another factor of Byram's (1997, p. 33) models of ICC.

Acknowledgements. I am grateful for the valuable collaboration of my French colleague, Véronique Rahimi, during the past seven years of regular telecollaborative exchanges. I am also indebted to the committed group of students who took part in the exchange.

References

Boyatzis, R. E. (1998). *Transforming qualitative information: Thematic analysis and code development.* Thousand Oaks, CA: Sage Publications.

Byram, M. (1997). *Teaching and assessing intercultural communicative competence.* Clevedon, UK: Multilingual Matters.

O'Dowd, R. (2006). The use of videoconferencing and emails as mediators of intercultural student ethnography. In J. Belz & S. Thorne (Eds.), *AAUSC 2005: Internet-mediated intercultural foreign language education.* Boston, MA: Thomson Higher Education.

university of groningen

Seamless integration of desktop and mobile learning experience through an ontology-based adaptation engine: Report of a pilot-project

Marco Mercurio[1], Ilaria Torre[2], and Simone Torsani[3]

Abstract. The paper describes a module within the distance language learning environment of the Language Centre at the Genoa University which adapts, through an ontology, learning activities to the device in use. Adaptation means not simply resizing a page but also the ability to transform the nature of a task so that it fits the device with the smallest effectiveness loss with respect to the ability the activity is meant to develop. In our environment, activities are tagged with a language-related ability so that an exercise which would not be usable on a given device can be transformed so as to be both usable and to maintain its original language learning potential. Following previous analyses of the most technical features of the engine, this paper will report on a pilot project, and the design and testing of an English course whose activities are transformable thanks to reasoning mechanisms based on the ontology. Our analysis will focus on the most important issues that have arisen during the development of the course.

Keywords: mobile language learning, ontology, distance language learning.

1. Introduction

A major point of interest in mobile technology is its supposed ability to bring language learning outside the classroom by exploiting networking along with mobility (Kukulska-Hulme & Shield, 2008). Our project, however, is more

---

1. University of Genoa, Italy; marco.mercurio@unige.it.
2. University of Genoa, Italy; ilaria.torre@unige.it.
3. University of Genoa, Italy; simone.torsani@unige.it.

How to cite this article: Mercurio, M., Torre, I., & Torsani, S. (2014). Seamless integration of desktop and mobile learning experience through an ontology-based adaptation engine: Report of a pilot-project. In S. Jager, L. Bradley, E. J. Meima, & S. Thouësny (Eds), *CALL Design: Principles and Practice; Proceedings of the 2014 EUROCALL Conference, Groningen, The Netherlands* (pp. 225-229). Dublin: Research-publishing.net. doi:10.14705/rpnet.2014.000222

institution-oriented and aims at making language learning content on a web-based platform also available to mobile devices. Adapting content from desktop computers to mobile devices is a thorny matter because of, for example, the physical features of the devices, which influence the way learners approach activities (Huang & Lin, 2011).

To accomplish the task of adapting content to different devices, we developed an ontology capable of determining the best way to transform an activity given a) the physical features of the device, b) the language ability the activity aims to train and c) the activity's task type. In our contribution, we report the results of a pilot project in which we designed a short language course which was attended on mobile phones without adaptation and on mobile phones with adaptation.

An environment, called CliRe, was designed at the Language Centre of the Genoa University to allow teachers to develop their own courses by building and combining language learning activities. Each activity is enriched by metadata (e.g. duration and ability). By using these data, users know how much time is needed to perform a learning unit and which abilities it aims at developing. The activities contained in the platform are used as a part of different courses. The Italian Ministry of Education is funding language courses for secondary school teachers to prepare them for Content and Language Integrated Learning (CLIL) teaching. A part of these courses is to be held online and the Language Centre is in charge for these online, forty-hour courses for the Liguria Region. These are interactive courses in which learners use part of the platform content. The platform, therefore, allows for a precise estimate as regards the duration of the content supplied with the course so that learners' activities and actual work can be assessed and evaluated in detail.

Our interest in mobile technology is that it could be an effective way to also deliver content in the learners' spare time, which could be an advantage to adult professional learners. Our project, therefore, is more formal and institution-centered if compared with many experiments on mobile learning which aim at integrating informal, social and mobility issues into language learning.

2.   Analysis and discussion

A major issue in mobile assisted language learning (Chinnery, 2006) is that the physical features of a device have a profound impact on its use for an activity; screen dimension and input method can make the execution of an activity hard if not impossible (Stockwell, 2012).

Content adaptation to a device's features, therefore, is a fundamental step if an activity is to be performed on a mobile device. Adaptation, however, is not simply a matter of screen dimensions or usability, but potentially entails profound transformations as, for instance, a certain input method (e.g. writing letters in a gap fill exercise) would be difficult to use on a given device. Input method, on the other hand, influences the type of task to be performed; task type, in turn, influences the kind of activity that can be done. As might be expected, some activities are more fitted than others for learning a given language ability: text reading and multiple choice questions are comprehension exercises, while sentence reconstruction is suited for morphosyntax exercises. Not all activity types can be performed on all devices.

We adopted Heift's (2003) distinction amongst task (i.e. the action the learner performs, e.g. click a button, enter some text, etc.) and type (i.e. the actual exercise, e.g. multiple choice, gap filling, etc.), and integrated into our platform an ontology-driven adaptation engine that, whenever an activity is accessed through a mobile device, determines whether the device is physically suited for that activity. In case it is not, the engine tries to transform the activity so that a suited input method and task are found for the device, but allows for an activity type which is suited for the language ability attributed to the original activity.

The ontology is made of several interacting components:
- input method and its fitness for a task;
- task and its fitness for an activity;
- activity type and its fitness for an ability.

To be able to transform activities, we formalised these interactions in an ontology. A special exercise syntax, named Proteus, was designed to allow exercises to be transformed from one type into the other; so far, exercises in this format can be rendered into gap filling form, multiple choice, matching and sentence reconstruction types.

For instance, a listening activity is made up of an audio file and a gap filling exercise. The engine will determine if the device is fitted for a) audio playback and b) a text-entering task. In case the device is not fitted for such tasks, the engine will transform the activity so that it is fitted for the device (device/task) and for the ability (activity/language ability); in this case, the gap filling exercise would be transformed into a multiple choice for devices in which text entering is assessed as non (or hardly) usable. In case the gap filling type was part of a writing activity, it would be transformed into a reconstruction exercise.

To test our engine, we designed a short course on collocations which was administered to two groups of students; the first group accessed the course without adaptation while the second group accessed a course whose activities were adapted for their devices. As the course was centered on lexis, most of the exercises were formally simple (e.g. matching between collocation and meaning) and did not contain multimedia elements, so that our engine would only work on exercise transformations.

3. Conclusion

The results of our experimentation, fully illustrated in Mercurio, Torre, and Torsani (2014), show that adapted content yields better results as regards task execution time and user perception of usability. A caveat, however, seems to be in order: usability is only one side of the matter and some work remains as regards actual usage and its potential for language learning.

In particular, the following areas will be the subject of our next experimentations:

- Formal transformation. We need further tests to determine whether the Proteus format can successfully transform activity types into one another and not only perform formal transformations; in other words we need to determine if the format is capable of actually transforming an exercise into another equally difficult exercise.

- Adherence between activity types and language learning ability. We need to verify whether our transformation engine can also successfully apply to other activity types (e.g. including multimedia) targeted at different language abilities.

- Long-term effectiveness. We need to ascertain whether success in our tests is due to the experimental setting or users are actually interested in performing activities in their spare time and, in this case, whether this format actually makes activities appealing to learners.

References

Chinnery, G. M. (2006). Emerging technologies. Going to the mall: mobile assisted language learning. *Language learning & technology, 10*(1), 9-16.

Heift, T. (2003). Drag or type, but don't click: A study on the effectiveness of different CALL exercise types. *Canadian Journal of Applied Linguistics/Revue canadienne de linguistique appliquée, 6*(1), 69-85.

Huang, L. L., & Lin, C. C. (2011). EFL learners' reading on mobile phones. *The JALT CALL Journal, 7*(1), 61-78.

Kukulska-Hulme, A., & Shield, L. (2008). An overview of mobile assisted language learning: From content delivery to supported collaboration and interaction. *ReCALL, 20*(3), 271-289. doi:10.1017/S0958344008000335

Mercurio, M., Torre, I., & Torsani, S. (2014). Responsive web and adaptive web for open and ubiquitous learning. *Proceedings of the Conference on Technology Enhanced Learning, Graz, Austria.*

Stockwell, G. (2012). Mobile-assisted language learning. In M. Thomas, H. Reinders, & M. Warschauer (Eds), *Contemporary computer-assisted language learning* (pp. 201-216). New York: Bloomsbury Academic Publishing.

Partial and synchronized captioning:
A new tool for second language listening development

Maryam Sadat Mirzaei[1], Yuya Akita[2], and Tatsuya Kawahara[3]

Abstract. This study investigates a novel method of captioning, partial and synchronized, as a listening tool for second language (L2) learners. In this method, the term partial and synchronized caption (PSC) pertains to the presence of a selected set of words in a caption where words are synced to their corresponding speech signal, using a state-of-the-art automatic speech recognition (ASR) technology. The system automatically selects words/phrases which are likely to hinder the learner's listening comprehension and discards the rest. To evaluate the system, the performance of 58 Kyoto University students was assessed by a listening comprehension test on TED talks, under three conditions: no caption, full caption and PSC. Analysis of results revealed that while reducing the textual density of captions to less than 30%, PSC realizes comprehension performance as well as the full caption condition. Moreover, it gains higher scores compared to other conditions for a new segment of the same video without any captions. The findings suggest that PSC can be incorporated into CALL systems as an alternative method to enhance L2 listening comprehension.

Keywords: listening comprehension, partial and synchronized caption, word frequency, speech rate, ASR, CALL.

1.   Introduction

In recent years authentic audio/visual materials have become more accessible, increasingly used by L2 learners. While these resources provide rich content and

---

1. Kyoto University; maryam@ar.media.kyoto-u.ac.jp.

2. Kyoto University; yuya@media.kyoto-u.ac.jp.

3. Kyoto University; kawahara@i.kyoto-u.ac.jp.

How to cite this article: Mirzaei, M. S., Akita, Y., & Kawahara, T. (2014). Partial and synchronized captioning: A new tool for second language listening development. In S. Jager, L. Bradley, E. J. Meima, & S. Thouësny (Eds), *CALL Design: Principles and Practice; Proceedings of the 2014 EUROCALL Conference, Groningen, The Netherlands* (pp. 230-236). Dublin: Research-publishing.net. doi:10.14705/rpnet.2014.000223

reflect real-world language, they often entail complex listening comprehension skills (Rogers & Medley, 1988). To facilitate the comprehension of these materials, adding captions is considered as an effective solution. Along with its effectiveness, captioning has received critical attention for bringing too much textual assistance and impeding the development of listening strategies (Pujolà, 2002; Vandergrift, 2004).

The type of captioning may influence the effect of this assistive tool on language learning. Although the conventional full captioning method is still the mainstream of contemporary education, other methods such as keyword/paraphrase captioning have drawn some attention (Garza, 1991). Moreover, the advances of the ASR technology have enabled the generation of synchronized captions. Unlike the typical captions where chunks of words appear on the screen, in synchronized captions the emergence of words on the screen is concurrent to the speaker's utterance. This method fosters word recognition, but promotes word-by-word decoding known as a hindering strategy.

With the purpose of providing adequate textual assistance to L2 listeners while encouraging them to use their listening skills, this study introduces a new method of captioning, partial and synchronized captioning (Figure 1).

Figure 1. Screenshot of PSC on a TED talk made from the original transcript "how we motivate people how we apply our human resources"

In this method, the original transcript is automatically reduced to a partial caption, which includes only a selected set of words/phrases (partialization). Particular to this method, each word in the caption is synchronized to its respective speech signal (synchronization).

2. Partial and synchronized caption

PSC focuses on assisting the listeners to cope with aural input difficulties without constantly referring to the verbatim caption. To this end, a system was developed based on two main modules: synchronization and partialization (Figure 2). These two are complementary and their integration counteracts the demerits of one another. For instance, synchronized captioning neatly presents the word boundaries, but it is criticized for promoting dependence on caption and encouraging word-by-word decoding. Partial captioning builds on the synchronized caption to avoid over-reliance on reading, however, the irregular and salient appearance of the words in this caption is only handled by the alignment feature of synchronized captioning (Table 1).

Figure 2. Data flow and main modules of the system

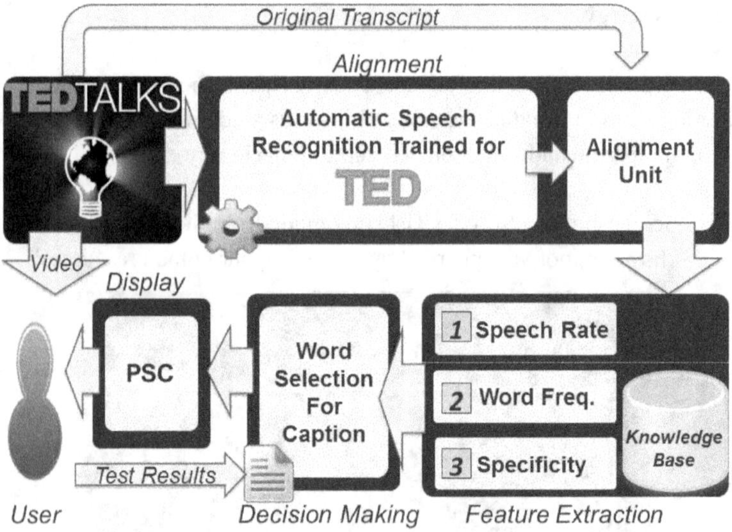

2.1. Synchronized caption

Selecting TED talks as the medium of this study, an ASR system was trained by the TED corpus and employed to make alignment. This provides accurate alignment in word level, which in turn enables text-to-speech mapping and fosters word recognition. Synchronized captioning, although in favor of many language learners, has several disadvantages that are alleviated in partial captioning.

2.2. Partial caption

In the partial captioning process, the system selects a subset of words that are likely to be incomprehensible for L2 listeners. This type of captioning attempts to actively mediate the comprehension by bringing a sort of scaffold. As a result, learners' current level of competence should be taken into account when preparing captions. A prudent choice to define credible criteria for selecting the target words is to consider major obstacles of listening comprehension as follows.

2.2.1. Speech rate

High speech rate can negatively affect listeners' comprehension of both native and non-native speakers (Griffiths, 1992; Wingfield, 2000). The proposed method precisely calculates the speech rate of words in syllables per second and represents words/phrases uttered faster than the normal rate of speech or the tolerable rate for the learner.

2.2.2. Word frequency

When listening to an audio, unfamiliar words often confine listeners' attention and impede comprehension. To address this issue, the proposed method selects the difficult words and presents them on screen while masking the rest. The frequency of words in written/spoken corpora is a reliable measure to assess word difficulty. The study measured the frequency of each word using the word family lists based on British National Corpus (Nation & Webb, 2011) and Corpus of Contemporary American English (Davies, 2008-). We also handled instances such as academic words (Coxhead, 2000), proper names and interjections.

Table 1. Comparison of caption methods

Caption Type \ Advantage	Full Caption	Keyword Caption	Proposed Partial Caption	Synchronized Caption	PSC
Aid word boundary detection	✓			✓	✓
Speech-to-text mapping				✓	✓
Avoid over-reliance on reading		✓	✓		✓
Avoid being distractive	✓			✓	✓
Automatic	✓		✓	✓	✓
Adjustable to learners' knowledge			✓		✓
Adjustable to the content		✓	✓		✓

3. Evaluation

Given the novelty of the method, the following questions have been investigated to evaluate the system:

- Do captioned videos result in better comprehension compared to non-captioned ones?

- Can PSC substitute the conventional full-text captioning?

- Does PSC help the learner comprehend the video later without any captions?

The participants of this study were 58 Japanese students enrolled in CALL courses at Kyoto University, ranging from 19 to 22 years old. Videos of American speakers were selected from the TED website (www.TED.com) and trimmed to approximately 5-minute meaningful segments. The Vocabulary Size Test (Nation & Beglar, 2007) was used to evaluate the participants' vocabulary reservoir.

The students were grouped into three proficiency levels based on their TOEIC or CASEC scores: beginners, pre-intermediates and intermediates. In each group, the learners' vocabulary size and their tolerable rate of speech were evaluated to generate PSC. Thus, for each group a particular PSC was generated with a different percentage of words to be shown, ranged from 20% to 30% of the original transcript. The students watched the videos under three conditions: no caption (NC), full caption (FC) and PSC. The experiment had two parts: first, the students watched 70% of the video under one of the above conditions and took a listening test; next, the subjects watched the rest of the same video (30%) without caption (presuming a real-world situation) and took another test.

4. Results and discussion

The result of one-way ANOVA test on the first part (70%) revealed a significant difference between NC ($M=35.7$, $SD=14.7$) condition and PSC ($M=52.9$, $SD=19.4$) or FC condition ($M=54.2$, $SD=17.3$) at $p<.05$. This answers the first research question by showing that the students' scores on PSC condition are significantly higher than NC condition. However, no significant difference was found between the score on PSC and FC condition in this part [$F(1, 57)=25$, $p=.62$]. The findings provide the answer to the second research question and suggest that PSC leads to the same level of comprehension as FC while providing less than 30% of the transcript.

In the second part of the experiment (30% without caption), the best scores were gained when the learners first watched videos with PSC [$F(2,118)=20.5$, $p<.05$] compared to other conditions. The results provide a positive answer to the third research question and suggest the effectiveness of PSC on preparing the learners for real-world situations. Although this is a short-term enhancement partly because of adaptation to the video, this finding is still valuable.

A Likert-scale questionnaire reflected positive learner feedback on PSC. However, learners were skeptical about substituting FC by PSC.

5. Conclusion

The study introduced a smart type of captions that allows the use of limited textual clues and promotes listening to the audio in order to comprehend the material. The findings highlighted the positive effect of this method in enhancing listening comprehension by presenting less than 30% of the text. Given the nature of listening skills, however, a long-term experiment is required to evaluate the overall listening improvement of the L2 learners.

Acknowledgements. We would like to thank Mark Peterson for his inspiration and brilliant comments and Kourosh Meshgi for his invaluable assistance.

References

Coxhead, A. (2000). A new academic word list. *TESOL quarterly, 34*(2), 213-238. doi:10.2307/3587951

Davies, M. (2008-). *The Corpus of Contemporary American English: 450 million words, 1990-present*. Retrieved from http://corpus.byu.edu/coca/

Garza, T. J. (1991). Evaluating the use of captioned video materials in advanced foreign language learning. *Foreign Language Annals, 24*(3), 239-258. doi:10.1111/j.1944-9720.1991.tb00469.x

Griffiths, R. (1992). Speech rate and listening comprehension: Further evidence of the relationship. *TESOL Quarterly, 26*(2), 385-390. doi:10.2307/3587015

Nation, I. S. P., & Beglar, D. (2007). A vocabulary size test. *The Language Teacher, 31*(7), 9-13.

Nation, I. S. P., & Webb, S. A. (2011). *Researching and analyzing vocabulary*. Boston: Heinle Cengage Learning.

Pujolà, J. T. (2002). CALLing for help: Researching language learning strategies using help facilities in a web-based multimedia program. *ReCALL, 14*(2), 235-262. doi:10.1017/S0958344002000423

Rogers, C. V., & Medley, F. W. (1988). Language with a purpose: Using authentic materials in the foreign language classroom. *Foreign Language Annals, 21*(5), 467-478. doi:10.1111/j.1944-9720.1988.tb01098.x

Vandergrift, L. (2004). 1. Listening to learn or learning to listen? *Annual Review of Applied Linguistics, 24*, 3-25. doi:10.1017/S0267190504000017

Wingfield, A. (2000). Speech perception and the comprehension of spoken language in adult aging. In D. Park & N. Schwarz (Eds), *Cognitive Aging: A Primer* (pp.175–195). Philadelphia, PA: Psychology Press.

university of groningen

Modelling typical online language learning activity

Carlos Montoro[1], Regine Hampel[2], and Ursula Stickler[3]

Abstract. This article presents the methods and results of a four-year-long research project focusing on the language learning activity of individual learners using online tasks conducted at the University of Guanajuato (Mexico) in 2009-2013. An activity-theoretical model (Blin, 2010; Engeström, 1987) of the typical language learning activity was used to analyse and interpret data. The study revealed (1) problems for learners to move beyond the task's objective (i.e. making a video) to attain the set language learning outcomes (e.g. developing speaking skills), and (2) the prevalence of orality over literacy in learning practices. Methodologically, a sample of 10 learners individually engaged with a purpose-built task. This was followed up by stimulated recall sessions (Gass & Mackey, 2000). The resulting video data was segmented using the concept of *disturbances* (Montoro & Hampel, 2011, p. 124; adapted from Engeström & Sannino, 2011), that is, deviations in learner behaviour from teacher expectations. Twenty-three dimensions and six processes were used to categorise data. A major systemic *contradiction* (Engeström, 2001), stemming from institutional and societal mass-production and efficiency-oriented practices, emerged, which partly led learners to take an other-than-language-learning orientation associated with, for instance, their underuse of learning tools and an over reliance on memory, perception, oral instruction and private speech.

Keywords: CALL, online tasks, activity theory, language learning, modelling.

---

1. DICIS, University of Guanajuato; cmontoro@me.com.
2. FELS, Department of Languages, The Open University; Regine.Hampel@open.ac.uk.
3. FELS, Department of Languages, The Open University; Ursula.Stickler@open.ac.uk.

How to cite this article: Montoro, C., Hampel, R., & Stickler, U. (2014). Modelling typical online language learning activity. In S. Jager, L. Bradley, E. J. Meima, & S. Thouësny (Eds), *CALL Design: Principles and Practice*; *Proceedings of the 2014 EUROCALL Conference, Groningen, The Netherlands* (pp. 237-240). Dublin: Research-publishing.net. doi:10.14705/rpnet.2014.000224

1. Introduction

In the context of an unprecedented expansion of and demand for the provision of English language learning and teaching opportunities at the University of Guanajuato (Mexico), a four-year (2009-2013) research project was launched to look into the language learning activity of individual learners using online tasks in a self-access centre.

After modelling the typical online language learning activity in this context, data analysis results revealed a systemic contradiction blocking the movement from the pursuit of the language task's objective (i.e. making a video) to the attainment of language learning outcomes (e.g. developing speaking skills). Most learners completed the task following the most direct route, paying scant attention to learning tools and learning opportunities, relying heavily on orality instead (e.g. private speech) and resisting a more literacy and text-based approach.

2. Method and results

Following a cultural-historical activity-theoretical (CHAT) approach (Engeström, 1987; Leontiev, 1978; Vygotsky, 1987), the unit of analysis in the study was the language learning activity system (see Montoro & Hampel, 2011 for details). Building upon work by Blin (2010), the system was refined to achieve a model of the typical language learning activity that applies to this context. Next, extensive video data was analysed. It consisted of video-recorded and computer-tracked individual sessions with a sample of ten intermediate language learners at a higher-education institution who engaged with a purpose-built online task followed by stimulated recall (SR) (Gass & Mackey, 2000) sessions to discuss their performance.

Data was segmented using the concept of *disturbances* or "deviations in learner behaviour from the language teacher-designer's expected course of events" (Montoro & Hampel, 2011, p. 124; adapted from Engeström & Sannino, 2011). Later, 23 dimensions (e.g. inner speech-private speech, technological affordances), grouped under six main processes (e.g. mediation by tools, orientation), were used to categorise the data and characterise the language learning activity.

Qualitative and quantitative results revealed the existence of a major systemic *contradiction* (i.e. an instance of a "historically accumulating structural tensions within and between activity systems"; Engeström, 2001, p. 137) affecting the transition from the learner to the immediate, practical objective of the task and ultimately to the attainment of more general language learning outcomes. Institutional and societal forces based on mass-production and efficiency-oriented practices were reflected in the 'getting things done' approach and in an aversion to errors and tool-use shown by most learners.

3. Discussion

An other-than-language-learning orientation to the task meant several learners understood *what* they were doing (i.e. making a video to introduce themselves in English) but, because they derived their motivation from sources other than improving their English, they cared less about what they were doing this *for*, which resulted in poor language learning gains. This orientation affected the system in various ways, such as in the observed underuse of learning tools, the emergence of a hidden curriculum with self-imposed rules and the need for support from the community.

For instance, learners overwhelmingly prefered 'hearing' (from others and from themselves through private, self-addressed speech) to reading when learning, and relied on memory, on knowledge existing 'in their heads', rather than on text-based sources such as dictionaries and their own written notes. This explains why they would rather 'find' information (on *Google translate*, for instance) instead of 'searching' for information. Learners seemed to operate orally at the level of perception and memory instead of using higher psychological skills (e.g. problem solving) that require advanced literacy skills (e.g. summarising, reformulating).

4. Conclusions

To conclude, learners in this context are in need of more opportunities to work within their zone of proximal development (Vygotsky, 1978) with more capable peers or teachers. The focus must be placed firmly on language learning and learner development to assist learners in their efforts to make the transition from orality to literacy, from memory and perception to higher psychological functions using more complex learning support tools.

A number of concepts can help in this regard, such as *dynamic assessment* (Lantolf & Poehner, 2011), fusing instruction and assessment, and practical applications of activity theory such as the *miniature cycles of expansive learning* (Engeström, 1999) and the *change laboratory methodology* (Engeström, Virkkunen, Helle, Pihlaja, & Poikela, 1996), notwithstanding the potential value of CALL tasks and SR as teaching-learning-researching tools.

Acknowledgements. We would like to thank *PROMEP*, *SEP*, *DICIS* and the University of Guanajuato in Mexico, and the Open University in the UK for much needed funding and support. We are also grateful to Yrjö Engeström, Annalisa Sannino, Anu Kajamaa and all the CRADLE colleagues in Helsinki for being wonderful hosts during a three-month research visit. We also acknowledge the anonymous reviewers, colleagues and participants in the study for their time and effort.

References

Blin, F. (2010). Designing cybertasks for learner autonomy: Towards an activity theoretical pedagogical model. In M. J. Luzón, M. N. Ruiz-Madrid, & M. L. Villanueva (Eds), *Digital Genres, New Literacies, and Autonomy in Language Learning* (pp. 175-196). Newcastle upon Tyne: Cambridge Scholars Publishing.

Engeström, Y. (1987). *Learning by expanding: An activity-theoretical approach to developmental research*. Helsinki: Orienta-Konsultit.

Engeström, Y. (1999). Innovative learning in work teams: Analyzing cycles of knowledge creation in practice. In Y. Engeström, R. Miettinen, & R.-L. Punamäki (Eds.), *Perspectives on Activity Theory* (pp. 377-404). Cambridge: Cambridge University Press. doi:10.1017/CBO9780511812774.025

Engeström, Y. (2001). Expansive learning at work: Toward an activity theoretical reconceptualization. *Journal of Education and Work, 14*(1), 133-156. doi:10.1080/13639080020028747

Engeström, Y., & Sannino, A. (2011). Discursive manifestations of contradictions in organizational change efforts: A methodological framework. *Journal of Organizational Change Management, 24*(3), 368-387. doi:10.1108/09534811111132758

Engeström, Y., Virkkunen, J., Helle, M., Pihlaja, J., & Poikela, R. (1996). The change laboratory as a tool for transforming work. *Lifelong Learning in Europe, 1*(2), 10-17.

Gass, S. M., & Mackey, A. (2000). *Stimulated recall methodology in second language research*. Mahwah, NJ: Lawrence Erlbaum Associates.

Lantolf, J. P., & Poehner, M. E. (2011). Dynamic assessment in the classroom: Vygotskian praxis for second language development. *Language Teaching Research, 15*(1), 11-33. doi:10.1177/1362168810383328

Leontiev, A. N. (1978). *Activity, consciousness, and personality*. Englewood Cliffs, NJ: Prentice Hall.

Montoro, C., & Hampel, R. (2011). Investigating language learning activity using a CALL task in the self-access centre. *Studies in Self-Access Learning Journal, 2*(3), 119-135.

Vygotsky, L. (1978). *Mind in society. The development of higher psychological processes*. Cambridge, MA: Harvard University Press.

Vygotsky, L. (1987). *The collected works of L. S. Vygotsky. Volume 1. Problems of general psychology: including the volume Thinking and speech*. New York, NY: Plenum Press.

The Euroversity Good Practice Framework (EGPF) and its application to minority languages and elder learners

Gary Motteram[1], Ton Koenraad[2], Hanna Outakoski[3], Kristi Jauregi[4], Judith Molka-Danielsen[5], and Christel Schneider[6]

Abstract. The Euroversity Network project (2011-2014) has built a Good Practice Framework (GPF) that functions as a heuristic for course and activity designers wishing to develop courses and other materials for use in a range of virtual worlds. This framework has been tested with a number of courses during the running of the project and the aim is that it will be useful for new designers as a starting point for their own ideas development. The GPF is still open for adjustment and negotiation and this paper shows how two new case studies that were not the direct focus of the project, minority languages and elder learners, help to expose some of the framework's weaknesses, but also many of its strengths. These case studies illustrate that a tool like the GPF can provide an effective mediating function for a variety of courses and other activity in virtual worlds.

Keywords: course development, good practice framework, virtual worlds, minority languages, teaching older learners.

---

1. University of Manchester; gary.motteram@manchester.ac.uk.
2. TELLConsult; ton.koenraad@gmail.com.
3. Umea University; hanna.outakoski@samiska.umu.se.
4. University of Utrecht; k.jauregi@uu.nl.
5. Molde University College; Judith.Molka-Danielsen@himolde.no.
6. CSiTrain; chris.schneider@web.de.

How to cite this article: Motteram, G., Koenraad, T., Outakoski, H., Jauregi, K., Molka-Danielsen, J., & Schneider, C. (2014). The Euroversity Good Practice Framework (EGPF) and its application to minority languages and elder learners. In S. Jager, L. Bradley, E. J. Meima, & S. Thouësny (Eds), *CALL Design: Principles and Practice*; Proceedings of the 2014 EUROCALL Conference, Groningen, The Netherlands (pp. 241-247). Dublin: Research-publishing.net. doi:10.14705/rpnet.2014.000225

1. Introduction

The Euroversity Network project (2011-2014) has aspirations to bring together practitioners of any discipline to develop and run educational courses and activities in virtual spaces, e.g. Open Sim, Second Life, Minecraft, etc. (Molka-Danielsen, Mundy, Hadjitassou, & Stefanelli, 2012). The project, however, does not exclude the use of non-3D tools like desktop video conferencing, or more conventional Virtual Learning Environments (VLEs). The expectation is that these tools will be used in combination to support each other; exploiting their particular affordances (Conole & Dyke, 2004). At the core of the project is an exploration of the process of course design and development. This network project builds on the outcomes of previous European language projects like NIFLAR and AVALON and reaches forward to other ones like CAMELOT and TILA.

In the initial stages, the Euroversity Network project used case studies from the earlier projects to build a draft GPF for course design in virtual worlds; this draft framework was then tested with the development of new courses which were then also trialled. The draft framework was finally adapted and updated following the evaluation received from running these new courses. Further case studies were then based on these newly tried courses. The case studies and the framework can be found on the Euroversity wiki[7].

1.1. Evaluation and feedback

The evaluation and feedback were based on data collected from running a number of courses developed taking the GPF as a reference across a range of disciplines, including languages, economics, sciences, anthropology and game design. Feedback was collected via questionnaires that were distributed both to the course instructors and the students. Interviews were also conducted with a number of instructors. A full analysis of the data is ongoing.

Following on from this initial trial period, we now offer two additional areas that have considered the use of the framework, since its initial drafting and revision. These are (1) minority languages and (2) the recognition of the affordances and constraints that virtual worlds offer for the teaching of such languages. The second area of application is that of age and disability. This initial paper will focus on a brief summary of the explorations of these course designers.

---

7. http://euroversity.pbworks.com/w/page/52279279/Euroversity

2. Two case studies

2.1. Indigenous and minority languages in virtual 3D learning spaces

Endangered indigenous languages, such as North Sámi, and minority languages such as Basque, are potential beneficiaries of online teaching (Outakoski, 2014). This is due to the fact that the teaching of these languages often involves smaller student groups, who can be widely distributed, low speaker density communities, and language stigma of various kinds. However, the presence of lesser-spoken language communities and their practitioners in virtual worlds is negligible.

In the context of Euroversity, an exploratory study was carried out in order to find out whether (and how) teachers of Basque do use virtual environments, particularly 3D virtual worlds, in their teaching and what their perceptions are about using virtual environments in education. A questionnaire was sent to Basque schools, Basque institutions, European universities where Basque is being taught, and Basque cultural institutions around the world. In the end, 38 teachers of Basque completed the survey. The results show that most teachers (85%) were not familiar with 3D virtual worlds at all; only two teachers reported to sometimes use Second Life in their teaching but they offered no further information about what they did and how they used Second Life. As for the use of other virtual environments, 36% of the teachers reported to use Moodle (very) frequently in their courses, and 30% use Facebook (very) frequently; however, the most popular digital application was YouTube: 41.7% of teachers reported to use it. A 5-point Likert scale was used to measure teachers' views on the relevance of integrating virtual environments in education. As can be seen in Table 1, teachers were positive about the integration of virtual environments in their teaching and would like to know more about the pedagogical affordances these virtual environments offer to enrich the teaching of Basque. The GPF together with (virtual) training sessions might be a very good start for these teachers to develop their pedagogical skills, yet the fact that the GPF is only available in English might constitute a big problem for most of them.

While the Euroversity GPF (EGPF) is of potential value in course design for indigenous and minority languages, one immediate barrier is the choice of English as the single common language of the framework. This is an infrastructural obstacle in the same way as would be the access to modern computers with updated graphic cards, fast Internet connection and adequate support (both pedagogical and technical). These problems cease to be an issue if human and financial resources are invested both in a multilingual framework and to local or regional support of the educational programs that require the use of virtual worlds in education. If the infrastructural problems are overcome, then the framework itself will be the engine for developing new pedagogical models and solutions for teaching and learning in virtual environments.

Table 1. Teachers of Basque ($N=36$) about the relevance of teaching in virtual worlds. 5 point Likert scale (1: strongly disagree / 5: strongly agree)

Items	Mean	SD
Teaching in virtual worlds is a hot topic.	4	0.8
I am interested and would like to know more about teaching in virtual worlds.	4.2	0.7
I think teaching in virtual worlds can enhance teaching different aspects of Basque.	4.1	0.8
I would like more information about the educational possibilities of the integration of virtual worlds in language teaching.	4.2	0.8
I would like to collaborate with others in developing a curriculum for the teaching of Basque in virtual worlds.	3.4	1.1
It is important to reach students who cannot attend regular classes. In this sense virtual worlds may facilitate access to education.	4.3	0.7
Virtual environments for teaching seem interesting but I think that integration is difficult because of the technical aspect.	3.3	1.2

If we now consider the Sámi and the Basque cases in particular, it seems unlikely that the infrastructural obstacles would be the only reason why these groups are so imperceptible in virtual educational environments in general. And indeed, in both cases some of the problems besides infrastructure have to do with users' lack of time (work overload), adequate technical skills or knowledge of the different 3D teaching environments, or with the rigidity of the teaching programs (course design and curriculum). Such structural challenges ask more from the educational system and are sometimes harder to tackle than the infrastructural challenges.

Indigenous contexts are also often bound to a certain 'place' (Kuokkanen, 2009, p. 95; McCarty, Nicholas, & Wyman, 2012), such as traditions, ideologies, identities and locations that determine where one belongs. Language and traditional knowledge are also often seen as collective heritage that are held sacred and are in need of protection. When we view the potential that the new, versatile and open virtual learning spaces offer to learners and teachers against the perception of accepted knowledge transfer within an indigenous community, then it seems that the openness and novelty of the learning space, although being its best assets, are also at the same time some of the main reasons why indigenous communities might remain reluctant to establish educational presence in virtual environments.

In the Basque case, virtual educational environments might rather be seen as offering yet another "expanded dimensio[n] for the creation and re-creation of ethnicity and carr[y] the potential to unite virtually what is impossible to unite physically" (Totoricaguena, 2003, p. 177). And although the educational sector and practitioners are still only learning about the potential of virtual learning spaces, the "community is expanding into virtual reality" (Totoricaguena, 2003, p. 178). For example, the Basque Cultural Institute has plans of creating a culture centre, Artean (EKE-ICB), in Second Life. It is therefore rather the structural than the epistemological reasons that are behind the invisibility of Basque educators and learners in virtual environments.

We find that the obstacles experienced by users of computer assisted learning models such as infrastructure or lack of information can, to some extent, be overcome and the EGPF has been helpful here. On the other hand, obstacles experienced by, for instance, an indigenous learning community may involve so many compounding factors independent from the educational context that providing a course design or examples of good practice is not enough to attract the community to the virtual learning environment.

2.2. Designing a social communicative space for learning for the elderly in virtual worlds

This case study explores the opportunities and challenges of designing a virtual social communicative space for (language) learning for the target group of elderly learners. Although in general, society identifies "elderly" as age 65 and older, there is a great range of abilities and (physical and cognitive) limitations within this age group (Merriam, 2001) that would make categorisation by age alone meaningless. Hence, to arrive at useful recommendations to make VLEs more accessible for elderly learners, the factors need to be identified that distinguish sub-groups in this population segment by types of impairments.

On the elderly use of ICT in general (PC, Internet, mobile devices), the authors report research showing that it has increased considerably over the last six years. The motivation for the use of virtual technologies for the elderly appears to be as diverse as for any group in society, as some of the findings show: reduction of loneliness (Sawyerr & Pinkwart, 2011), situated learning and gaining experiences in a safe place (Falconer, 2014), and compensation of limited mobility in the physical world (Eliot, Rost, & Singh, 2013).

To define design considerations particularly for the elderly population segment, data were collected through an interview with A. Krueger, founder of Virtual Ability Inc. and the Virtual Ability Island (VA) in Second Life was explored. The authors undertook two tours on VA. In one guided tour, Krueger (2013) pointed out specific (features of) builds, the related application of universal design principles, as suggested by Extension, America's Research-based Learning Network (2013), and the theory of andragogy. The second tour, of a more exploratory nature, led by Professor Waller, an expert in the field of Augmentative and Alternative Communication (AAC), was also recorded.

Relating the analysis of these experiences and observations to the Euroversity GPF, the authors present a number of questions that should be asked and answered by module designers to define considerations for a Target Group (TG) of elderly population. The GPF-related topics include aims/objectives, technical issues and support, interaction, risks and world related technical issues and post module evaluation.

Drawing from the suggested answers to these questions, several abilities and limitations factors are identified that can influence the preferred use of an interface (the interaction with the Second Life browser in this case). For example, for impaired vision ability, the availability of recorded sound clips and snap-to signboards that fill the screen are suggested.

3. Conclusions

This paper has shown that the Good Practice Framework has significant values for the design and development of various kinds of courses and activities in virtual worlds. The case studies discussed here show that there are still issues with the framework when it moves into new realms, but that in both cases there are positive attributes that make the EGPF of value to a broad community of materials developers. While the Euroversity Network project itself did not focus specifically on language learning, it can be seen that there are definite reasons to make use of it for the design of language courses and other related activities.

Acknowledgements. We would like to thank all of the teachers and students who have taken part in the design, development and use of the different courses that have been used to collect data on the framework. This project has been funded with support from the European Commission. This publication reflects the views only of the authors, and the Commission cannot be held responsible for any use which may be made of the information contained therein.

References

Conole, G., & Dyke, M. (2004). What are the affordances of information and communication technologies? *Association for Learning Technology Journal, 12*(2), 113-124. doi:10.1080/0968776042000216183

EKE - ICB (The Basque Cultural Institute). *Artean: Basque culture in Second Life*. Retrieved from http://www.eke.org/en/basque-cultural-institute/euskal_kulturgune_birtuala

Extension, America's Research-based Learning Network. (2013). *7 Principles of Universal Design*. Retrieved from http://www.extension.org/pages/24193/1:-principle-one:-equitable-use#.Uqduj-IQTIU

Eliot, L., Rost, S., & Singh S. (2013). The Drax Files: World Makers [Episode 13: Creations for Parkinson's], Published by Draxtor Despres and PBS, 1.11.2013. Retrieved from http://www.youtube.com/watch?v=nyiiWxNguGo&feature=youtu.be

Falconer, E. (2014). Learning in virtual environments: Dimensions of situated learning. *University of West England. Video recorded by Schneider, C., 14 April 20.14*. Retrieved from http://www.youtube.com/watch?v=v_1HT_VcA0k

Krueger, A. (2013). *Guided tour through virtual ability* [Second Life]. Virtual Ability Island in Second Life.

Kuokkanen, R. (2009). *Boaris dego eana: eamiálbmogiid diehtu, filosofiijat ja dutkan* [Old as the earth: indigenous peoples' knowledge, philosophies and research]. Kárášjohka: ČálliidLágádus.

McCarty, T. L., Nicholas, S. E., & Wyman, L. T. (2012). Re-emplacing place in the "global here and now" – Critical ethnographic case studies of Native American language planning and policy. *International Multilingual Research Journal, 6*(1), 50-63. doi:10.1080/19313152.2 012.639244

Merriam, S. B. (2001). *The new update on adult learning theory*. San Francisco: Jossey-Bass.

Molka-Danielsen, J., Mundy, D., Hadjitassou, S., & Stefanelli, C. (2012). Working towards good practice in virtual worlds teaching: Developing a framework through the Euroversity project. *Conference Proceedings, IRIS, 2012*.

Outakoski, H. (2014). Teaching an endangered language in virtual reality. In M. C. Jones & S. Ogilvie (Eds), *Keeping languages alive: documentation, pedagogy and revitalization* (pp. 128-139). Cambridge: Cambridge University Press.

Sawyerr, W. A., & Pinkwart, N. (2011). Extending the private and domestic spaces of the elderly. *CSCW, March 19-23, Hangzhou, China*.

Totoricaguena, G. P. (2003). *Identity, culture, and politics in the Basque diaspora* [Electronic resource]. University of Nevada Press.

university of groningen

Authentic oral language production and interaction in CALL: An evolving conceptual framework for the use of learning analytics within the SpeakApps project

Mairéad Nic Giolla Mhichíl[1], Jeroen van Engen[2], Colm Ó Ciardúbháin[3], Gearóid Ó Cléircín[4], and Christine Appel[5]

Abstract. This paper sets out to construct and present the evolving conceptual framework of the SpeakApps projects to consider the application of learning analytics to facilitate synchronous and asynchronous oral language skills within this CALL context. Drawing from both the CALL and wider theoretical and empirical literature of learner analytics, the framework sets to theorise and problematise one construct, such as the authenticity of language production and interaction during a CALL mediated session. It is considered within this paper that a CALL learning analytics approach is usefully conceptualised from a student-centred perspective as opposed to an interventionist perspective based on action-oriented approaches to language learning. The paper considers that structured data –usually represented by statistics from Virtual Learning Environments (VLEs) or Learning Management System (LMS)– and unstructured data (user generated content) can be harnessed to support the oral language learning process. The paper considers the implications of using this framework with the SpeakApps platform.

Keywords: SpeakApps, language learning analytics, conceptual framework, online oral language learning.

---

1. Dublin City University; mairead.nicgiollamhichil@dcu.ie.
2. University of Groningen; j.van.engen@rug.nl.
3. Dublin City University; colm.ociardubhain@dcu.ie.
4. Dublin City University; gearoid.ocleircin@dcu.ie.
5. Universitat Oberta de Catalunya; mappel@uoc.edu.

How to cite this article: Nic Giolla Mhichíl, M., van Engen, J., Ó Ciardúbháin, C., Ó Cléircín, G., & Appel, C. (2014). Authentic oral language production and interaction in CALL: An evolving conceptual framework for the use of learning analytics within the SpeakApps project. In S. Jager, L. Bradley, E. J. Meima, & S. Thouësny (Eds), *CALL Design: Principles and Practice*; Proceedings of the 2014 EUROCALL Conference, Groningen, The Netherlands (pp. 248-254). Dublin: Research-publishing.net. doi:10.14705/rpnet.2014.000226

1. Introduction

The SpeakApps project, funded by the Lifelong Learning Programme of the European Commission, was designed to engage with some of the challenges and issues faced by language learners by providing both technical and pedagogical solutions for teachers and learners in the project's target languages. The emphasis of many online language learning environments is usually to enhance three of the four language skills, such as writing, reading, and listening (Appel, Santanach, & Jager, 2012). The SpeakApps project's objective was to develop a bespoke online environment designed specifically to enhance the oral language competencies of its users and to support teachers by providing access to contextualised task-based activities and resources. The principle outcome of the project is the SpeakApps platform: www.speakapps.eu. The platform is Moodle based and combines virtual classrooms with the SpeakApps tools (Langblog, Tandem and VideoChat), with a Mahara space to support the SpeakApps community of teachers and an Open Educational Resource (OER) which houses the task-based language learning activities designed and categorised using the Common European Reference Framework for Languages (Council of Europe, 2001). Furthermore, info blogs, technical and pedagogical user-guides and tutorials are available on the platform. The SpeakApps tools can also be downloaded from the platform and have been designed using Learning Technology Interoperability standards, thus facilitating their integration across a wide variety of LMS and other virtual spaces.

The SpeakApps project is currently engaged in its second iteration and its objectives include the integration of five new languages into the SpeakApps platform, the engagement with new language education sectors, the enhancement and the design of a scalable digital language learning environment and the dissemination of SpeakApps methodologies and solutions to the wider community. The SpeakApps project partners are developing a research agenda based on their current work in the area of online oral language learning but have also expanded this to consider broader educational based questions such as the use and the application of learning analytics within this domain. This paper briefly sets out the SpeakApps conceptual framework and the means by which this framework is evolving to consider learning analytics in the context of the SpeakApps platform.

2. Method

The evolution of the conceptual framework underpinning the SpeakApps project can be considered as being aligned to Maxwell's (2013, p. 39) considerations of such frameworks to include the fundamental concepts, assumptions, theories and expectations which inform the research. This conceptualisation is guided not only by the theoretical literature but also expands to draw from the experiential knowledge of the researchers and the empirical findings from the research itself. The activities engaged in to evolve the framework include a review of the learning analytics and CALL literature, the completion of thought experiments by the researchers to consider, and the problematisation of the use of learning analytics to further authentic language production, interaction during a CALL mediated session, and the design and implementation of pilot studies to test and refine the framework. The following section outlines the overarching SpeakApps conceptual framework and the findings of the research conducted to evolve the framework with respect to learning analytics based on the literature review.

3. Conceptual framework discussion

A fundamental cornerstone of the original SpeakApps conceptual framework was based on the acknowledgment that developing oral language competencies is particularly challenging, independent of the learning environment. This assumption was further evidenced as part of a comprehensive need analysis of 815 learners within the SpeakApps project. A further belief based on the experiential knowledge of the project team was that providing sufficient opportunities and space for the learner to produce language and to receive feedback is a significant challenge which learners and language teachers navigate on an ongoing basis. Additionally, the literature emphasised that the ephemeral nature of speaking itself contrives to complicate the monitoring of progress by learners and teachers, as both must rely on the memory of what was said (Wells, 1999, p. 115). Furthermore, the range of opportunities available for learners to practice a language beyond the classroom can be quite restricted (Gardner, 2001). The status and context of use of some languages can impede students in their oral interaction of that language on a daily or indeed a regular basis, as in the case of some minority languages such as Irish.

The provision and use of authentic material in the learning process, which is used to underpin meaningful language interaction opportunities, was considered particularly important (Brandl, 2002) where access to formal and informal acquisition opportunities in the target languages are limited to learners. This understanding was of particular relevance in the design and contextualisation of tasks developed and made available in the SpeakApps OER. Designing context-driven tasks facilitates the learner to consolidate language meaning from context which in turn can lead to deeper understanding (Ellis, 1995). The SpeakApps task-based approach incorporates the use of these materials in the target language and guides learners to practice a language with respect to real life experiences and scenarios. The SpeakApps pedagogical framework is situated in action-oriented approaches to language learning where teacher and learner agency are viewed as critical and are at the centre of curriculum and task design (Engeström, 2006; Lipponen & Kumpulainen, 2011; van Lier, 2004).

Action-oriented approaches are drawn from sociocultural and cultural historical activity theoretical approaches to language teaching and learning (see for example Blin, 2010; Blin & Appel, 2011; Blin & Thorne, 2011). A review of the literature was undertaken to commence the initial expansion of the conceptual framework to consider the integration and use of learning analytics within the SpeakApps environment. The review revealed the following insights and challenges in considering developing learning analytics based on the SpeakApps platform.

3.1. Learner agency, data sources, oral language constructs and privacy

Fundamental to the action-oriented language learning approach is the notion of learner agency. Maintaining the agency of the learner was viewed as key in some areas of the analytics literature. Adopting a learner-centred approach to analytics is claimed to support inquiry-led and active learning, which implies that the learner reflects on the analytical data and actively determines a course of action. It was considered by the SpeakApps researchers that a learning analytics objective of being purely interventionist and prescriptive could potentially inhibit learner agency; the objective of learning analytics in SpeakApps should be to facilitate feedback and adaptation (Chatti, Dyckhoff, Schroeder, & Thüs, 2012). The SpeakApps LMS provides a wide variety of data based on user activity. The analytics literature advocated the use of both structured and unstructured data in the development of a comprehensive analytics approach (Dawson, 2010; Siemens & Long, 2011). The SpeakApps platform is, however, a closed environment and access to unstructured data from the platform is, therefore, limited to engagement in Mahara. Metrics are available from the LMS and could possibly be modelled in a variety of ways to establish possible correlations between behavioural data and language proficiency as benchmarked by the CEFR. The experiential knowledge of the SpeakApps researchers problematised that those who engage more with language activities correlated to enhanced proficiency. From this basis, measuring online behavioural characteristics using LMS metrics may provide correlations between online language activities and proficiency.

Conceptual limitations are well documented in the analytics literature related to such an approach and include (a) the contested notion of using (only) LMS metrics as an indicator of learning, (b) the corruption of these metrics, (c) the validity and reliability of models and the considerations of learner characteristics, and (d) the quality of feedback received by learners based on such approaches (see Gibson, Kitto, and Willis (2014) for further discussion). Developing the platform to encompass a personal learning environment may provide a greater opportunity to include data related to students' engagement with other online resources; this presents a further challenge with the integration and aggregation of multi-formatted data from a variety of sources (Chatti et al., 2012).

Challenging as integrating multi-sourced data may be, there is also a specific need to develop a privacy and ethical framework to protect learners and to ensure that they are active agents and collaborators within this process. SpeakApps researchers, whilst exploring if the authenticity of language interaction could be measured using a learning analytics framework, considered the following activities in oral production as potential areas where learning analytics could be applied to provide feedback to the learner:
- listening and responding to questions measured in the turns of interactions and transitions;
- new language forms and meaning, i.e. application in a variety of contexts;
- intonation and pronunciation.

4. Conclusions

The SpeakApps conceptual framework has at its centre the notion of action-oriented approaches to language learning. The platform in its current form gathers LMS behavioural data. Furthermore, the platform stores audio and video files created by both learners and teachers. The analysis of SpeakApps richer multimedia data is potentially targeted at a wider breadth of stakeholders including learners, teachers, institutions and researchers. The objective of learner analytics in SpeakApps is linked to the objective of facilitating learner agency in the language learning process. This paper, however, did not consider the means or techniques (i.e. statistics, data mining or visualisations) to analyse SpeakApps data. Initial considerations examine the use of pattern modelling and the use of statistics to underpin this analysis. SpeakApps researchers in the next phase are setting out to operationalise how the SpeakApps data can be collected, pre-processed and analysed whilst concurrently establishing and considering ethical and privacy issues of learners and the use of their data. Learners' expectations with respect to the use of data and the principle of informed consent is central to promoting active and collaborative student engagement. There are significant issues associated with the implementation of learning analytics within a learning environment, the breadth of which is beyond the scope of this paper. However, in the evolution of the SpeakApps conceptual framework, a consistent focus on learner agency is being maintained.

Acknowledgements. This project was funded by the Lifelong Learning Programme of the European Commission. The paper reflects the views of the authors, and the European Commission cannot be held responsible for any use which may be made of the information contained herein.

References

Appel, C., Santanach, F., & Jager, S. (2012). SpeakApps: New tools and activities for the development of speaking skills in a second language. *Paper presented at the EDULEARN12, Barcelona, Spain.*

Blin, F. (2010). Designing cybertasks for learner autonomy: Towards an activity theoretical pedagogical model. In M. J. Luzón, M. N. Ruiz-Madrid, & M. L. Villanueva (Eds), *Digital Genres, New Literacies, and Autonomy in Language Learning* (pp. 175-196). Newcastle Upon Tyne: Cambridge Scholars Publishing.

Blin, F., & Appel, C. (2011). Computer supported collaborative writing in practice: An activity theoretical study. *CALICO Journal, 28*(2), 473-497. doi:10.11139/cj.28.2.473-497

Blin, F., & Thorne, S. (2011). Mediation, expansion and remediation in digitally mediated language learning environments. *Paper presented at the CALICO 2011 Conference, University of Victoria, British Columbia Canada.*

Brandl, K. (2002). Integrating internet based reading materials into the foreign language into the foreign language curriculum: From teacher– to student centred approaches. *Language Learning & Technology, 6*(2), 87-107.

Chatti, M. A., Dyckhoff, A. L., Schroeder, U., & Thüs, H. (2012). A reference model for learning analytics. *International Journal of Technology Enhanced Learning Analytics, 4*(5/6), 318-331. doi:10.1504/IJTEL.2012.051815

Council of Europe. (2001). *Common European Framework of Reference for Languages: Learning, teaching, assessment.* Cambridge: Cambridge University Press.

Dawson, S. (2010). 'Seeing' the learning community: An exploration of the development of a resource for monitoring online student networking. *British Journal of Educational Technology, 41*(5), 736-752. doi:10.1111/j.1467-8535.2009.00970.x

Ellis, N. C. (1995). The psychology of foreign language vocabulary acquisition: Implications for CALL. *CALL, 8*(2-3), 103-128. doi:10.1080/0958822940080202

Engeström, Y. (2006). Development, movement and agency: Breaking away into mycorrhizae activities. *Building activity theory in practice: Toward the next generation, 1,* 1-43.

Gardner, R. C. (2001). Language learning motivation: The student, the teacher, and the researcher. *Texas Papers in Foreign Language Education, 6*(1), 1-18.

Gibson, A., Kitto, K., & Willis, J. (2014). A cognitive processing framework for learning analytics. *Paper presented at the LAK'14, Indianapolis, USA.*

Lipponen, L., & Kumpulainen, K. (2011). Acting as accountable authors: Creating interactional spaces for agency work in teacher education. *Teaching and teacher education, 27*(5), 812-819. doi:10.1016/j.tate.2011.01.001

Maxwell, J. A. (2013). *Qualitative research design: An interactive approach* (3rd ed.). Thousand Oaks: Sage.

Siemens, G., & Long, P. (2011). Penetrating the fog: Analytics in learning and education. *EDUCASE Review, 46*(5).

Van Lier, L. (2004). *The ecology and semiotics of language learning: A sociocultural perspective.* Boston, MA: Kluwer Academic. doi:10.1007/1-4020-7912-5

Wells, G. (1999). *Dialogic enquiry: Towards a sociocultural practice and theory of education.* Cambridge: Cambridge University Press. doi:10.1017/CBO9780511605895

Language learning in virtual worlds: Designing for languaging, the role of affordances

Susanna Nocchi[1]

Abstract. This article will utilise data collected during SLItaliano, an Italian language course run in the Virtual World (VW) of Second Life® (SL®) in 2012. The course was offered to third level students of Italian as a Foreign Language (FL) in an Irish college, the Dublin Institute of Technology (DIT). It was designed and coordinated by the researcher and is at the core of a research on FL teaching in VWs. The focus of the paper is on identifying affordances for language learning in VWs, particularly languaging as a communicative practice (Swain, 2006). The concept of affordance is approached from an Activity Theory (AT) standpoint (Kaptelinin & Nardi, 2012) as an "action possibility" present in the environment, which may or may not emerge. In the case of VWs as learning environments, such possibilities are not only provided by the characteristics of the hardware and of the software, but they are also shaped by the users and their history and by the context they find themselves in and may be "sequential and nested in time" (Hammond, 2010, p. 216). The possibility to engage in languaging was one of the affordances that emerged during SLItaliano. Languaging is defined as that practice when language is used in order to work at solving a problem or clarifying an issue (Swain & Lapkin, 2011). The data showed how certain tasks had a higher occurrence of *languaging episodes* and how particular situations prompted the recourse to languaging. The data will also show that when affordances which were expected to emerge failed to be noticed by the participants, the results were sometimes surprising and provided further insight into the potential of VWs for FL teaching.

Keywords: virtual worlds, language learning, affordances, languaging.

---

1. Dublin Institute of Technology, Ireland; susanna.nocchi@dit.ie.

How to cite this article: Nocchi, S. (2014). Language learning in virtual worlds: Designing for languaging, the role of affordances. In S. Jager, L. Bradley, E. J. Meima, & S. Thouësny (Eds), *CALL Design: Principles and Practice*; Proceedings of the 2014 EUROCALL Conference, Groningen, The Netherlands (pp. 255-260). Dublin: Research-publishing.net. doi:10.14705/rpnet.2014.000227

1. Introduction

In 2010, Hew and Cheung highlighted that the number of studies concerning FL learning in VWs was still low and stressed the need for more investigation into the affordances of these environments for language learning. The study mentioned in this article aims at delivering a contribution in this field through a detailed analysis of data collected during a course of Italian in SL® and an identification of emerging affordances during the language tasks.

VWs are seen here as heterotopias of our time, spaces comprising different (and sometimes incompatible) places at the same time, environments that are part of our physical space but can only be accessed via actual 'gateways' (Foucault, 1967). These spaces interact with our physical space, and such interaction affects their users, who act spatially (and chronologically) in the virtual and, at the same time, in the physical world they inhabit. Presence, time/space dimensions and affordances are three main concepts that can help us understand how VWs can best be used for learning (Blin, Fowley, & Nocchi, 2013), and this paper will discuss how certain VW characteristics and task design conditions resulted in the emergence of languaging, an affordance for language learning.

1.1. Theoretical framework

The study adopts an AT approach for data analysis. AT sees a collective activity as a complex historically evolving process, carried out through goal-directed actions that are composed of a number of automatic operations (Engeström, 1987). During the course of an activity, however, when changed conditions occur, there can be breakdowns or disturbances that bring about a shift in the focus of that activity, which may turn to what used to be automatic operations, in order to solve the occurring issue.

When looking at what happens in a computer-mediated environment, breakdowns and focus shifts can be good pointers for understanding how an application mediates (or does not mediate) an activity. Also, they may be evidence of important moments in the development of that activity.

1.2. Affordancesas possibilities for action

In the last decade, affordances have been adopted as a useful concept for the analysis of educational tasks (Blin et al., 2013; Dalgarno & Lee, 2010; Hammond, 2010; Hollins & Robbins, 2008). Affordances can indeed assist in clarifying aspects of the intricacies of teaching and learning in computer mediated learning environments and are a suitable tool for finding how best to incorporate media attributes into the design of learning tasks. Additionally, in the field of new media psychology (Riva, 2007), affordances have been recognised as one of the four conceptual tools that allow a psychological analysis of new media.

The definition of affordance, however, is still causing some debate. In this study, the concept of affordance is approached from an AT standpoint; its definition is re-grounded in a Vygotskian sociocultural approach, where technology is seen as a culturally developed tool mediating a human being's activity. Affordances are action possibilities (Kaptelinin & Nardi, 2012) offered by an environment where different elements relate to each other in different ways depending on the user, the time and the way they are used.

1.3. Languaging

The idea of languaging was first introduced by Swain in 2006 and sees language as a process, a tool used to mediate thinking. Languaging is a verbalisation used to mediate a cognitively demanding activity, it is a "talking-it-through" (Swain, 2006, p. 99) which people use to communicate with each other (or in a dialogue with the self) in order to solve problems or clarify issues. Languaging enables people to create and negotiate meanings and intentions and to transfer them across time and space, thus becoming a major source of L2 learning (Swain, 2006; Swain & Lapkin, 2011).

2. Method

SLItaliano, an Italian language course, was run in Second Life© in 2011/2012. The course was intended for a group of four International Business and Languages students at DIT (Ireland) who wanted to develop their FL intercultural and language competence. SLItaliano consisted of nine in-world sessions, each with a different theme and language tasks. The course took place in the Italian island of Imparafacile, and enlisted a group of Italian volunteers, who participated in the sessions, helped with the set-up, and took part in most of the language tasks.

3. Data collection and analysis

The nine sessions were recorded using a screen-capture software, Camtasia. Three sessions were then transcribed and analysed. Special attention was paid to the activities around the tasks, the issues arising during those activities, and the affordances that emerged (or failed to).

One of the educational affordances of VWs identified by the author is the possibility to connect, interact and engage in synchronous (and asynchronous) discourse, in written and oral form. During data analysis, languaging stood out as a language learning affordance.

4. Results

The instances of languaging recorded in the three sessions were 98 and the students were involved in 96 of them.

4.1. Technical characteristics of VWs and languaging

Voice Chat (VC) was the preferred medium; it was used in 39 cases, compared to 8 cases of languaging in local chat (LC) and 6 using Instant Messaging (IM). Also, in 44 cases the students used both VC and LC, switching the communication between the two. In 1 instance a student used IM to add to a VC languaging episode (see Figure 1).

Figure 1. Modes of languaging

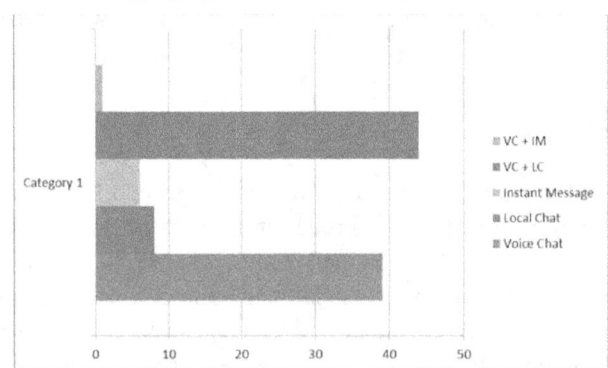

4.2. Task design and languaging

A 'trigger' for the use of languaging had been consciously designed in some of the language tasks. Role-plays, for instance, were organised so that the players needed to talk to resolve conflicting information. Indeed, the highest occurrence of languaging was noticed during collaborative tasks and role-plays. It was noticed, however, that languaging occurred mostly when 'un-designed' issues arose in the activity. Those issues were Language related (64%), Technical (25%) or Intercultural (11%).

4.3. Technical breakdowns and affordances

If, on the one hand, language and intercultural issues are common to language tasks, technical issues were specific to the environment mediating the activity. Sometimes, due to a technical breakdown or to the inability of the user to fully exploit the VW's characteristics, some affordances, such as the possibility for exploration and immersion, did not emerge. In these cases languaging became a way of finding a solution.

An example was the set-up of Session 6, a moment when participants would get together, get to know each other, and talk about the session. In this case two students had problems rezzing (i.e. showing their avatar). As a result, the initial activity was abandoned and everyone turned their attention to solving the issue through FL languaging (see Figure 2).

Figure 2. Focus shift in Session 6: solving the rezzing problem

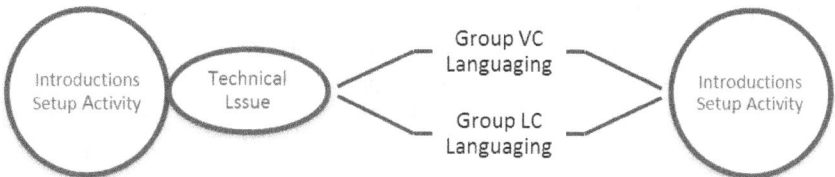

5. Conclusions

After a data analysis, it is clear that the possibility for languaging is an important language learning affordance of VWs. This affordance was sequential to the VW technical and social affordances provided by this environment. However, even in cases when technical breakdowns prevented some affordances to emerge, FL languaging was used to deal with the issues, creating substantial FL language interaction.

Acknowledgements. I would like to thank the owner and the volunteers of the Imparafacile Island in SL®, as their help was invaluable to this study. Also, I would like to thank DIT for funding my attendance to the 2014 EUROCALL conference.

References

Blin, F., Fowley, C., & Nocchi, S. (2013). Mondes virtuels et apprentissage des langues: Vers un cadre théorique émergent. *Recherches et applications, 54*, 94-107.

Dalgarno, B., & Lee, M. J. W. (2010). What are the learning affordances of 3-D virtual environments? *British Journal of Educational Technology, 41*(1), 10-32. doi:10.1111/j.1467-8535.2009.01038.x

Engeström, Y. (1987). *Learning by expanding: An activity-theoretical approach to developmental research*. Retrieved from http://lchc.ucsd.edu/mca/Paper/Engestrom/Learning-by-Expanding.pdf

Foucault, M. (1967). *Of other spaces: Utopia and heterotopias*. Retrieved from http://www.colorado.edu/envd/courses/ENVD4114-001/Spring%2006/Theory/Foucault.pdf

Hammond, M. (2010). What is an affordance and can it help us understand the use of ICT in education? *Education and Information Technologies, 15*(3), 205-217. doi:10.1007/s10639-009-9106-z

Hew, K. F., & Cheung, W. S. (2010). Use of three-dimensional (3-D) immersive virtual worlds in K-12 and higher education settings: A review of the research. *British Journal of Educational Technology, 41*(1), 33-55. doi:10.1111/j.1467-8535.2008.00900.x

Hollins, P., & Robbins, S. (2008). The educational affordances of multi user virtual environments (MUVE). *ReLIVE08, Researching Learning in Virtual Environments* (pp. 172-180). Milton Keynes: Open University.

Kaptelinin, V., & Nardi, B. (2012). Affordances in HCI: Toward a mediated action perspective. *Proceedings of CHI 2012, New York* (pp. 967-976).

Riva, G. (2007). Cyberpsicologia. Ambienti virtuali, emozioni reali. *Psicologia contemporanea, 201*(3), 18-23. Retrieved from http://www.giusepperiva.com/

Swain, M. (2006). Languaging, agency and collaboration in advanced language proficiency. In H. Byrnes (Ed.), *Advanced language learning: The contribution of Halliday and Vygotsky* (pp. 95-108). Continuum: London.

Swain, M., & Lapkin, S. (2011). Languaging as agent and constituent of cognitive change in an older adult: An example. *Canadian Journal of Applied Linguistics, 14*(1), 104-117.

university of groningen

Creating tasks in a less-commonly taught language for an open educational resource: Why the CEFR is important for Irish

Colm Ó Ciardúbháin[1] and Mairéad Nic Giolla Mhichíl[2]

Abstract. If teachers of Less-Commonly Taught Languages (LCTLs), such as Irish, are to make use of Open Educational Resources (OERs) and many other CALL tools, then there must be an appropriate adaptation of the Common European Framework of Reference (CEFR) in that LCTL. The need to be "Bologna-compliant" has seen language courses and syllabuses in Ireland being set out according to Common Reference Levels of the CEFR. Many CALL tools and resources which have been developed in a European context are underpinned by the Common Reference Levels of the CEFR. This symbiosis means that, in many cases, making use of one cannot be done properly without due regard to the other. In Ireland, however, the applications of the CEFR and integration of CALL have been engaged in separately for the most part. As the demand for CALL grows in Ireland, the lack of an Irish language adaptation of the CEFR becomes more problematic. This paper presents a case study on the Irish language partner on the SpeakApps project (http://www.speakapps.eu/). It will begin with a brief literature review on implementing CALL principles in LCTLs, and application of the CEFR to LCTLs. It then examines the experiences of the Irish partner in designing online oral production and interaction tasks according to the CEFR to be used on language courses that have not previously used CEFR learning goals or reference levels. In this paper we conclude that adaptations of the CEFR's Common Reference Levels with clear illustrative descriptors are needed before teachers of LCTLs can optimise OERs and other CALL tools.

Keywords: Irish language, CEFR adaptation, open educational resource.

---

1. Dublin City University, Ireland; colm.ociardubhain@dcu.ie.
2. Dublin City University, Ireland; mairead.nicgiollamhichil@dcu.ie.

How to cite this article: Ó Ciardúbháin, C., & Nic Giolla Mhichíl, M. (2014). Creating tasks in a less-commonly taught language for an open educational resource: Why the CEFR is important for Irish. In S. Jager, L. Bradley, E. J. Meima, & S. Thouësny (Eds), *CALL Design: Principles and Practice*; *Proceedings of the 2014 EUROCALL Conference, Groningen, The Netherlands* (pp. 261-266). Dublin: Research-publishing.net. doi:10.14705/rpnet.2014.000228

1. Introduction

The CEFR and the OERs present a number of opportunities for both the teaching and the learning of LCTLs. In spite of this, it is acknowledged that the application and implementation of the CEFR varies greatly across LCTLs (Lotti, 2007). The CEFR provides LCTLs (as it does with other languages) with a meta-framework to communicate competencies and proficiencies as well as providing a mechanism to benchmark linguistic outcomes (Council of Europe, 2001, p. 5). The proliferation of the CEFR within teaching and learning of the Irish language to date can be described as limited, although a number of initiatives are under way to integrate the CEFR at various levels across the Education System. It is argued in this paper, however, that the wider implementation of the CEFR for the Irish language should coincide with an adaptation of the CEFR to reflect the socio-linguistic context of the language.

The adaptation of the CEFR is important in the case of the Irish language, particularly if considered in the context of the proliferation of OERs as means by which learners and teachers have access to language specific resources underpinned or benchmarked to the CEFR. OERs are defined as resources released under open licences for the use and re-use by a number of stakeholders such as teachers, learners or researchers for both academic and non-academic learning, usually in a not-for-profit capacity (D'Antoni, 2009; Martinez, 2010; Smith & Casserly, 2006). OERs can be considered to embody the tradition of education of the sharing and dissemination of knowledge for the public good. OERs are viewed by Blyth (2013) as allowing stakeholders to create their own "knowledge ecology", which is of particular relevance to LCTLs, where economies of scale of learners and teachers may be potentially limited (p. 3). In such cases, investment in language resources are significantly more costly than would be the case where significant scale exists. OERs, thus, present an opportunity for languages such as Irish to develop open repositories of language resources. However, these resources should be cognisant and reflective of the socio-linguistic context of the language.

2. Method

2.1. CEFR, the Irish language education and OERs

In the last seven years, the CEFR has gained some traction in the Irish education system. In Higher Education, an initiative to design a core syllabus for the teaching of Irish at third level is benchmarked at learners achieving B2 on its completion (Walsh & Nic Eoin, 2010). *An Meitheal um Theagasc na Gaeilge ar an Tríú*

Leibhéal (the task force for teaching Irish at third level) designed a syllabus for each of the three years of Irish language university education. These syllabuses, as well as sample tasks and accompanying audio visual material, are available online. At second level, The Teaching Council of Ireland (2013) has stipulated that individuals applying to become post-primary language teachers must demonstrate B2.2 proficiency in the European language they wish to teach. The National Qualifications Authority of Ireland asserts that students who pass language subjects in the post-primary terminal examinations (The Leaving Certificate) will have achieved B1 (NQAI, 2007, p. 8). A further evaluation initiative, *Teastas Eorpach na Gaeilge* known as TEG (The European Certificate in Irish), has made significant use of the CEFR. Individuals who successfully complete the TEG exams can receive a general language proficiency certificate. TEG is identified as being "broadly based on the *Common European Framework of Reference for Languages*" (Teastas Eorpach na Gaeilge, 2006, para. 2). Resources are available and include syllabi based on the levels of the CEFR as well as the lessons plans, worksheets and accompanying audio visual material[3]. For instance, the *Clilstore* website (multidict.net), developed as part of the European project Tools for CLIL Teachers, allows teachers to create language learning units, categorised according to the CEFR, which facilitates content and language integrated learning. The website also contains a repository of these learning units (Gimeno, Ó Dónaill, & Zygmantaite, 2013).

Despite these initiatives and in comparison to other LCTLs, the integration and influence of the CEFR in Irish language teaching is unclear. Lotti's (2007) report into the take-up of the CEFR in LCTLs was that "it was not possible to gather enough information about the language education situation for Irish in Ireland" (p. 10). While the CEFR is a language-independent instrument, difficulties in using the CEFR for regional or minority languages are described by Lotti (2007) as firstly centering on the CEFR being designed primarily for foreign language learning, whereas minority languages are learnt as a first or second language (pp. 16-17). Secondly, language activities are not always as relevant at lower language levels. Thirdly, linguistic situations, such as touristic ones, are not necessarily relevant to the LCTL.

3. Discussion

The SpeakApps project is aimed at enhancing the oral language competencies of language learners and delivering support to teachers by providing access to

---
[3]. For further information see http://www.teg.ie.

contextualised task-based activities and resources via the SpeakApps OER. It can be accessed via the SpeakApps platform, and tasks have been developed in the project's target languages using the CEFR as a developmental framework. Tasks developed in the SpeakApps OER can be used with SpeakApps Tools, Langblog, Tandem and Videochat, but they have also been designed to be applied with other technological tools. The SpeakApps OER allows teachers to upload tasks to the repository. Meta-tags are added to the uploaded tasks which provide the following data: the name of the task, the language, the CEFR level, the tool with which the task can be accomplished, and the status of the task. The status of the tasks can be *work in progress*, *published*, *in pilots*, *evaluated*, and *revision requested*. Tasks can be developed individually or can make up components of larger activities or projects. The SpeakApps project is currently in its second iteration with the objective of further developing the tasks and the OERs, and to disseminate the project results through workshops and seminars. Whilst engaged in task development, workshops and discussing task creation with teachers of Irish, the following issues came to light in relation to using the OER and the CEFR.

3.1. Assessment and the CEFR

Teachers considered that the tasks in the SpeakApps OER could be used for assessment purposes, summative or formative or a combination of both. Increasingly, institutional stakeholders in Ireland require that language qualifications be equated to the CEFR, e.g. registration with The Teaching Council of Ireland or matriculation on postgraduate teaching-oriented courses. To ensure criterion-related validity of tasks, an inventory of the forms, morpho-syntactic elements, and phonetic and intonation skills needs to be prescribed to the various levels of the CEFR in Irish. This exercise would be of particular use to language teachers in their selection of tasks, but also as part of a valid and transparent assessment process.

3.2. Task-based language learning and task creation

Task-based learning should facilitate a learner's current and future communicative needs (Byram, 2004). The SpeakApps OER contains task-based activities and projects. It is difficult to create a varied range of tasks in the absence of a task-based needs analysis of the Irish language sector, and indeed to reflect the socio-linguistic circumstances of the language. An adaptation of the CEFR with illustrations of the type of language activities learners should be engaged in and the principal domains in which the language is used would underpin task creating and contribute to the integrity and viability of the OER.

4. Conclusions

It is acknowledged that the CEFR provides a comprehensive framework to develop, assess and benchmark language competency. This paper has not sought to engage with the limitations of the framework as identified in the existent literature; rather, it identifies the challenges faced by one LCTL in the application of the framework and the development of tasks for the SpeakApps OER during the project. The issues highlighted are not uniquely associated with the OER and CEFR, but can also be considered as relating to the socio-linguistic status of this particular LCTL. The issues relating to the application of the CEFR to the Irish context could be addressed with the adaptation of the CEFR's Common Reference Levels to take into account an LCTL's socio-linguistic context, with the provision of clear illustrative descriptors so that teachers of LCTLs can optimise OERs and other CALL tools more effectively for learners. This paper concludes that a national level project is needed to engage in such an endeavour.

Acknowledgements. The SpeakApps project was funded by the Lifelong Learning Programme of the European Commission. The paper reflects the views of the authors, and the European Commission cannot be held responsible for any use which may be made of the information contained herein.

References

Blyth, C. (2013). LCTLs and technology: The promise of open education. *Language Learning & Technology, 17*(1), 1-6.
Byram, M. (2004). *Routledge encyclopedia of language teaching and learning*. New York: Routledge.
Council of Europe. (2001). *Common European Framework of Reference for Languages: Learning, teaching, assessment*. Cambridge: Cambridge University Press.
D'antoni, S. (2009). Open educational resources: Reviewing initiatives and issues. *Open Learning: The Journal of Open, Distance and e-Learning, 24*(1), 3-10. doi:10.1080/02680510802625443
Gimeno, A., Ó Dónaill, C., & Zygmantaite, R. (Eds). (2013). *Clilstore Guidebook for Teachers*. Project: Tools for CLILTeachers. Retrieved from http://www.languages.dk/archive/tools/guides/ClilstoreGuidebook.pdf
Lotti, B. (2007). *Investigation into the use of the common European framework of reference for languages in regional and minority language education*. Mercator: European Research Centre on Multilingualism and Language Learning. Retrieved from http://goo.gl/Kr6oey
Martinez, M. (2010). How a new generation of teachers will change schools. *The Phi Delta Kappan, 91*(7), 74-75. doi: 10.1177/003172171009100716

NQAI. (2007, December). *Towards the establishment of a relationship between the common European framework of reference for languages and the national framework of qualifications.* National Qualifications Authority of Ireland. Retrieved from http://www.nqai.ie/documents/reltionshipbetweenCommonEuroF-W.doc

Teastas Eorpach na Gaeilge. (2006). *About TEG.* Retrieved from http://teg.ie/english/about_teg.htm

The Teaching Council of Ireland. (2013, October). *Curricular subject requirements (post-primary) - for persons applying for registration on and after 1 January 2017.* Retrieved from http://goo.gl/Q0kd7w

Smith, A. N. & Casserly, C. M. (2006). The promise of open educational resources. Change, 38(5), 8-17. doi:10.3200/CHNG.38.5.8-17

Walsh, J., & Nic Eoin, M. (2010). Siollabas nua Gaeilge don chéad bhliain ollscoile. *Teagasc na Gaeilge, 9,* 13-23.

university of groningen

Impact of a blended environment with m-learning on EFL skills

Hiroyuki Obari[1] and Stephen Lambacher[2]

Abstract. A longitudinal study conducted from April 2013 to January 2014 sought to ascertain whether a blended learning (BL) environment incorporating m-learning could help Japanese undergraduates improve their English language skills. In this paper, various emerging technologies (including Globalvoice English, ATR CALL Brix, the mobile learning-oriented TOEIC Practice Kit, Course Power), as well as online materials (MOOCs, TED Talks, top 10 most popular educational web tools) will be demonstrated. The study focuses on examining the use of emerging e-learning and m-learning technologies and activities, ranging from speech recognition to web-based learning both in and out of the classroom, in order to determine their effectiveness in improving the English proficiency of non-native learners. Pre- and post-training TOEIC scores revealed that the BL activities had a positive effect on the students' overall English proficiency.

Keywords: MOOCS, TED talks, ATR CALL Brix, Globalvoice English, blended learning, mobile technologies.

1. Introduction

Mobile learning technologies are rapidly gaining popularity around the world as an effective way to enhance foreign language education. Mobile learning (m-learning) is highly motivating to learners, as it offers a rich, informal, contextual, and ubiquitous learning environment in which it is possible for them to control their learning time, environment, and speed (Kukulska-Hulme, Sharples, Milrad, Arnedillo-Sánchez, & Vavoula, 2009). M-learning has other advantages over

---

1. Aoyama Gakuin University; obari119@gmail.com.
2. Aoyama Gakuin University; steve.lambacher@gmail.com.

How to cite this article: Obari, H., & Lambacher, S. (2014). Impact of a blended environment with m-learning on EFL skills. In S. Jager, L. Bradley, E. J. Meima, & S. Thouësny (Eds), *CALL Design: Principles and Practice*; Proceedings of the 2014 EUROCALL Conference, Groningen, The Netherlands (pp. 267-272). Dublin: Research-publishing.net. doi:10.14705/rpnet.2014.000229

conventional teaching and learning methods, including the almost limitless number of English news programs, language learning apps, podcasting, video-casting, etc., that can be easily accessible and downloadable for free or for little cost. Today, mobile devices are omnipresent. Recent innovations in technology that brought such social networking sites as Facebook and Twitter to such popularity can be handheld today. Voice over Internet Protocol (VOIP) technology is no longer tied to the desktop or laptop computer. Although not without drawbacks, credit card purchases and payments are possible from a mobile device. However, can what is being used so easily and by so many today in society be altered, borrowed, copied or transformed to serve as an effective tool in an educational setting? That is one question we address herein.

In the field of second language (L2) learning, and in CALL in particular, there has been an increasing body of research dedicated to the use of mobile devices in language learning over the past several years (Chen, 2012). Teachers and researchers use the term MALL (mobile-assisted language learning) as if it were familiar to everyone in the field. It is not our intention here to trace the roots of MALL and its place in language learning today (see Stockwell, 2012 for a detailed discussion).

Instead, our purpose as educators is to try to determine whether m-learning holds benefits for our students, to see how and why students come to use this technology, and how mobile learning compares with more traditional classroom approaches. TED Talks is also one of the most useful online learning resources available and is very conducive to m-learning, whereby learning takes place at any time and at any place due to the swift development of mobile technologies. According to Sherimon, Vinu, and Krishnon (2011), mobile technologies have succeeded in transforming learning methodologies.

One such methodology that has received great attention in recent years is BL (Sherimon et al., 2011). According to Graham (2006), there are three common definitions of BL mentioned in the literature: (a) combining instructional modalities; (b) combining instructional methods; and (c) combining online and face-to-face instruction. Also known as hybrid learning (Kaleta, Skibba, & Joosten, 2006), BL combines traditional face-to-face classroom methods with computer-mediated activities, resulting in a more integrated approach for both instructors and learners.

To date, few empirical studies have been carried out to examine the effectiveness of blended-learning environments compared with traditional classroom methods.

The goal of the present paper is to examine the effectiveness of BL activities using mobile devices for the purpose of improving the English language proficiency of native Japanese undergraduates, including their written, oral communication, and presentation skills.

The research questions were as follows:

a) Can online TED Talks, Newton e-Learning Practice Kit, and ATR CALL Brix help improve the TOEIC scores of native Japanese learners?

b) Can learning online TED Talks help improve students' oral communication and writing skills?

c) Are blended learning activities and flipped class lessons using mobile devices useful in improving learners' English skills?

2. Methods

A total of 100 undergraduates enrolled at Aoyama Gakuin University, all native speakers of Japanese, were the participants of this study. The study was conducted during a single academic year (April to January 2014). Students were administered TOEIC in April 2013 and again in January 2014, the purpose of which was to ascertain the effectiveness of the BL program. Students were required to spend roughly 50 hours to complete the on-line TOEIC course and flipped classroom learning materials using a PC and mobile phone for the purpose of improving their four English skills.

By the end of the semester (January 2014), the students had completed nearly 100% of the online course contents and wrote down about 20 summaries of TED Talks. Blended-learning activities included: (1) watching online Coursera lectures and TED Talks with PC and mobile devices; (2) presenting oral summaries of lectures to classmates both face to face and in front of the class; and (3) spending extensive time watching 20 TED Talks during commuting hours and writing a 300-word summary of each lecture for 20 weeks, while also spending extensive time using the Newton TOEIC practice kit and ATR CALL Brix. In the classroom, the students created several digital stories and gave oral presentations of the international heritage sites. Students were also required to write blogs based upon their presentations during the second semester. The activities as a whole were based upon the concept of flipped classroom lessons. Before their presentations, students also used Globalvoice English to practice English pronunciation and prosody. At the end of the course (January 2014), a questionnaire was administered to students for their feedback on their BL environment experience.

3. Results

For assessment purposes, we present a sampling of the data results, including the results from TOEIC, which revealed that the students' overall English had improved after their exposure to the BL activities. Also included are some results of the questionnaire.

3.1. TOEIC

TOEIC results revealed the mean scores significantly increased from 570 (SD=102) in the pretest to 687 (SD=108) in the posttest. The TOEIC pre- and post-test results were analyzed using a t-test, indicating a difference in scores at a significant level of 1%. This improvement in scores would seem to indicate that the utilization of a learning environment integrating m-learning and e-learning helped the students to improve their overall English proficiency.

3.2. Questionnaire results

The questionnaire was administered to students after their exposure to the blended-learning program, which included Ted Talks, ATR CALL Brix learning, e-Learning TOEIC Practice Kit, weblogs, and speech training with Globalvoice English. In response to the first question "Did you find writing TED Talks summary useful in improving your English proficiency?", 91% of students felt they were very useful. In the second question "Did you find ATR CALL Brix useful in learning English and in improving TOEIC scores?", 79% of students (N=90) felt that ATR CALL Brix were useful. In the third question, 81 % (N=90) felt that the Newton e-Learning TOEIC Practice Kit was very useful in improving their TOEIC scores. In the fourth question, 83% (N=36) of students felt that blog writing was useful in improving their English. Finally, in the fifth question, 82% (N=86) felt that Globalvoice English was useful in improving English prosody and segmental features.

3.3. Assessment of English writing and oral summaries

At the start of the semester in April 2013, students made numerous grammatical and structural mistakes in their summary writings. However, by the end of year, their writings had fewer grammatical errors, were better organized and longer in duration. In addition, by comparing the first and final oral summaries, many of the students demonstrated significant improvement in their oral skills, particularly in terms of segmental and prosodic features, including pitch, intonation, and vowel duration.

4. Discussion and conclusion

The pre- and post-training TOEIC scores revealed that the BL activities had a positive effect on the students' overall English skills. In addition, the students' listening and oral communication skills improved as a result of the online TED Talk learning activities, including 20 summaries. A questionnaire administered after their exposure to the BL activities indicated they were satisfied with the online TED Talks and blended learning activities and motivated by the BL environment incorporating m-learning. Overall, these results indicate that blended learning using mobile technologies can be effectively integrated into the language learning curriculum and can play a positive role in improving students' language proficiency. Additionally, instructor observations of the BL activities revealed that students were excited by using the variety of IT tools, which was greatly aided by accessing the materials from their mobile devices. M-learning helped to increase the amount of comprehensible English input and was highly motivating to students by offering them a rich, informal, contextual, and ubiquitous learning environment.

References

Chen, X. (2012). The MALL : Where language learning takes place anytime anywhere. *Proceedings of 2012 International Symposium—Educational Research and Educational Technology* (pp. 462-465).

Graham, C. R. (2006). Blended learning systems: Definition, current trends, future directions. In C. J. Bonk & C. R. Graham (Eds), *The handbook of blended learning: Global perspectives, local designs* (pp. 3-21). San Francisco, CA: Pfeiffer Publishing.

Kaleta, R., Skibba, K., & Joosten, T. (2006). Discovering, designing and delivering hybrid courses. In C. Picciano & C. Dzuiban (Eds), *Blended learning: Research perspectives* (pp. 111-143). Needham, MA: The Sloan Consortium.

Kukulska-Hulme, A., Sharples, M., Milrad, M., Arnedillo-Sánchez, I., & Vavoula, G. (2009). Innovation in mobile learning: A European perspective. *International Journal of Mobile and Blended Learning, 1*(1), 13-35. Retrieved from http://oro.open.ac.uk/12711/

Sherimon, P. C, Vinu, P. V., & Krishnan, R. (2011). Enhancing the learning experience in blended learning systems: a semantic approach. *Proceedings of the 2011 International Conference on Communication, Computing & Security, ICCCS 2011, Odisha, India* (pp. 449-452). ACM.

Stockwell, G. (2012). Mobile-assisted language learning. In M. Thomas, H. Reiders, & M. Warshauer (Eds), *Contemporary computer-assisted language learning* (pp. 201-216). London: Bloomsbury Publishing.

university of groningen

The LMS development for a blended EFL e-learning

Takeshi Okada[1], Yasunobu Sakamoto[2], and Kensuke Sugiura[3]

Abstract. This paper illustrates the general idea of an on-going project for the development of a new blended e-learning package for the English as a foreign language (EFL) reading instruction in Japanese universities. The authors want to draw the attention of the readers to the Learning Management System (LMS) of the package and focus on the role a new e-learning system plays in actual face-to-face classrooms. Through an e-learning system, an EFL teacher can browse particular words, phrases or sentences where his/her students have learning difficulty on a real-time basis on the tablet screen. Grasping graphically particular parts the students need to be instructed, the teacher can determine the level of teaching in response to the students' demands. The system is designed to generate word/phrase lists for individual learners' further self-learning. These word/phrase lists, accompanied by additional information about learning records such as date, passage ID, reading ease score, type/token ratio and lexical density, may function as eligible e-portfolios for both teachers and learners. Instead of getting involved in the discussion on the technical details of the e-learning system itself, the authors show how the actual EFL reading instruction and learning can dynamically be designed through a newly-proposed system that provides opportunities to share pedagogical issues with people working on similar project.

Keywords: e-learning, mobile device, LMS, blended learning, CALL technology, EFL reading instruction.

---

1. Tohoku University; t-okada@intcul.tohoku.ac.jp.
2. Tohoku Gakuin University; yasube@mail.tohoku-gakuin.ac.jp.
3. Tohoku University; sugiura@m.tohoku.ac.jp.

How to cite this article: Okada, T., Sakamoto, Y., & Sugiura, K. (2014). The LMS development for a blended EFL e-learning. In S. Jager, L. Bradley, E. J. Meima, & S. Thouësny (Eds), *CALL Design: Principles and Practice*; *Proceedings of the 2014 EUROCALL Conference, Groningen, The Netherlands* (pp. 273-277). Dublin: Research-publishing.net. doi:10.14705/rpnet.2014.000230

1. Background

Whereas Japanese students are often considered to be good at reading and writing but not at listening and speaking in EFL, recent surveys show that for a number of Japanese university students, reading is a greater problem than usually thought (Okada, forthcoming). Therefore, helping students have a sufficient level of EFL reading ability is a challenging task. In particular, in some leading Japanese universities for which the authors are working, a great majority of undergraduate students are required to obtain a certain level or score in standardised tests such as TOEFL® and TOEIC® in order to have opportunities to study at universities in English speaking countries. Although the students are intelligent and have learning skills and motivation, the English instruction classes are sometimes criticised for not producing satisfying results.

The authors pay attention to classrooms in which EFL reading instruction is given: computer-assisted language learning (CALL) classrooms, where e-learning systems or software play a central role on a number of stationary PC's; and ordinary classrooms, where reading instruction is given by human teachers in a common face-to-face mode. In genuine autonomous CALL classrooms, EFL teachers cannot intervene in students' learning activities, whereas in face-to-face mode classrooms, a teacher and students cannot utilise external resources that can be easily accessed via internet. Furthermore, what is more important and significant for our idea of a new blended EFL e-learning package is the fact that unexpected discrepancies exist between what teachers try to teach and what students want to learn regardless of the type of classrooms. The authors believe that many teachers tend to assume that they understand what their students need to be taught, but this is not always the case.

To overcome the discrepancy of understanding and fill the gaps between a teacher's assumption and the actual learners' needs, we emphasise the need for a mobile e-learning system that enables its users to highlight specific parts of a given reading material they have to pay attention to and work on together. The precise positions of any highlighted parts of a given passage are successfully managed through RDBMS (relational database management system) technology described in Okada and Sakamoto (2010), whose basic idea is an extended definition of the corpus annotation (Zinsmeister, Hinrichs, Kübler, & Witt, 2008).

The authors hope that the new blended e-learning package proposed here provides opportunities to share pedagogical issues with people working on similar projects. For example, the role played by human teachers and their teaching assistants must be reconsidered in actual face-to-face mode classrooms where e-learning systems on mobile devices are used to fill the gaps between, or even among, class participants.

2. Proposed system

As illustrated in Figure 1, the blended e-learning package consists of three major components to be developed: (1) teaching materials for in-class versus out-of class modes; (2) a robust e-learning system that operates on mobile devices and the LMS; and (3) a teaching program that efficiently combines in-class (face-to-face) with out-of-class (CALL) modes.

Figure 1. Components of the package

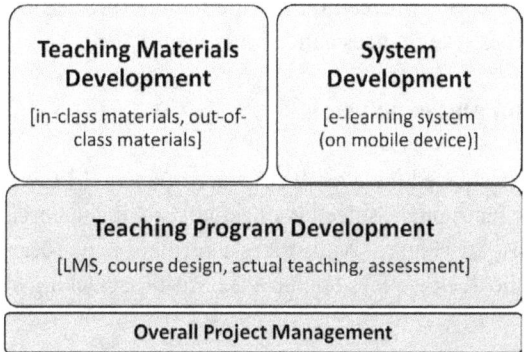

Of these three components, the authors would like to draw specific attention to the development of the teaching program including LMS, course design, teaching method and assessment. The role played by a newly-developed e-learning system in actual face-to-face classrooms can be defined clearly by concentrating on the LMS designing.

In a face-to-face teaching mode using mobile devices, a teacher can even browse particular words, phrases or sentences which his/her students have difficulty learning on a real-time basis. Hence, the teacher can decide where he/she should put heavier stress in reading instruction without overlooking students' needs. In this sense, our new e-learning system would successfully bridge the gap between the teacher and the students.

On the basis of graphical representations of parts in a given passage that the students need to be instructed on, the teacher can choose the 'granularity' of information the students are permitted to browse, e.g. the readability of the entire passage, word/phrase level, Japanese translation, etc. These functionalities are based on a corpus building/analysing technology presented in Okada and Sakamoto (2010) and Chang and Kuo (2011). In other words the teacher is allowed to determine the level of teaching in accordance with the students' capability, even if he/she uses the same teaching materials for different EFL classes. The teacher can even specify the reading speed if he/she wants the students to prepare for the reading section of standardised English tests such as TOEFL® or TOEIC®.

In addition to the management of the students' learning status, such as learning date/time, log-in places, and quiz scores, the LMS generates word/phrase lists for individual learners. The list is tabulated for further autonomous vocabulary training, which is indispensable for foreign language learning as mentioned in Nation (2001) and Biber (2006). The table consists of words or phrases a learner 'highlighted' on the tablet screen during the reading process together with their corresponding word level indices and Japanese equivalents.

3. Discussion and conclusion

The section above showed the overall structure of a new EFL e-learning package. The authors now focus on the selection of actual teaching materials, course design, teaching methods, etc. Figure 2 illustrates the role a new e-learning system that operates on mobile devices plays both in a face-to-face teaching mode and a CALL mode.

Figure 2. New blended e-learning package

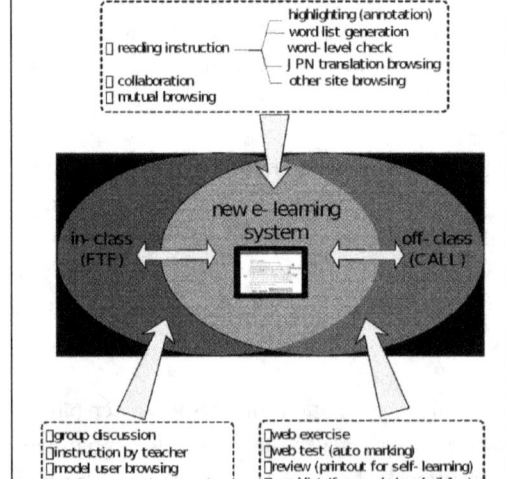

One of the most important effects of using an e-learning system that operates on mobile devices is that its users are allowed to interact with each other on a real-time basis, just like using convenient electronic textbooks with communication facilities. The teacher can select particular parts of a given material passage on which his/her students want to be instructed; and the students have the opportunities to notice the points which their teacher wants to put stress on. By receiving real-time feedback from students, a teacher can dynamically manage and design the class to meet the students' demands. In other words, a teacher can set a series of temporary sub-goals, each of which best suits the students' needs within a single class that is heading for a designated goal. In this sense our new e-learning system requires highly pedagogical expertise of the EFL teachers. Based on these preliminary reflections, the authors hypothesise that the use of the new e-learning system would encourage further pedagogical discussions, hoping EFL teachers and learners embrace the benefits of blending actual face-to-face classroom meetings with online CALL technologies. Further research is therefore required.

Acknowledgements. This research has been partially supported by the JSPS Grant-in-Aid for Scientific Research (B) (Research No. 26284075).

References

Biber, D. (2006). *University language: A corpus-based study of spoken and written registers*. Amsterdam: John Benjamins. doi:10.1075/scl.23

Chang, C.-F., & Kuo, C.-H. (2011). A corpus-based approach to online materials development for writing research articles. *English for Specific Purposes, 30*(3), 222-234. doi:10.1016/j.esp.2011.04.001

Nation, I. S. P. (2001). *Learning vocabulary in another language*. Cambridge: Cambridge University Press. doi:10.1017/CBO9781139524759

Okada, T., & Sakamoto, Y. (2010). A new RDBMS and flexible POS tagging for EFL learners and researchers: Designing a corpus analysis system based on the three-tier model. *CAHE Journal of Higher Education, Tohoku University, 5*, 43-52.

Okada, T. (forthcoming). Designing a new blended EFL e-learning package. *E-Learning Kyouiku Kenkyu, 9*.

Zinsmeister, H., Hinrichs, E., Kübler, S., & Witt, A. (2008). Linguistically annotated corpora: Quality assurance, reusability and sustainability. In A. Lüdeling & M. Kytö (Eds), *Corpus linguistics: An international handbook* (pp.759-776). New York: Walter de Gruyter.

Development of an automatic judging system for determining the difficulty levels of English audio materials

Hironobu Okazaki[1], Kanji Watanabe[2], Shinichi Hashimoto[3], Mitsuko Suzuki[4], Eri Fukuda[5], and Kazuhiko Kido[6]

Abstract. Okazaki and Nitta (2005) developed an e-learning program called PLIMA (your Personal LIstening Manager) which focuses on improving poor phonological analysis such as the inability to hear liaison or unstressed sounds. However, the fact remains that there are certain types of liaison sounds that learners do not catch, and some types they do. This means if we specify what type, in other words, what level of liaison sounds they cannot catch, that will help PLIMA offer more effective learning to learners who lack certain listening skills. To automatically determine the difficulty levels of the English audio materials, text evaluation techniques using lexical databases have been employed in many cases so far. However, automatic judging systems on the difficulty levels of the English audio materials themselves, not using lexical databases, are almost unseen. In this paper, we are going to propose a listening difficulty level determination system, to overcome such a challenging task. It applies a processing technique to extract the acoustic feature quantities that are employed in speech recognition engines.

Keywords: difficulty level determination, acoustic feature quantities, e-learning.

---

1. Akita Prefectural University; okazaki@akita-pu.ac.jp.
2. Akita Prefectural University; kwatanabe @akita-pu.ac.jp.
3. The University of Electro-Communications; heiwanian@gmail.com.
4. Soka High School; smitsuko1129@gmail.com.
5. Chugoku Junior College; efukuda@cjc.ac.jp.
6. International Pacific University; k.kido@ipu-japan.ac.jp.

How to cite this article: Okazaki, H., Watanabe, K., Hashimoto, S., Suzuki, M., Fukuda, E., & Kido, K. (2014). Development of an automatic judging system for determining the difficulty levels of English audio materials. In S. Jager, L. Bradley, E. J. Meima, & S. Thouësny (Eds), *CALL Design: Principles and Practice; Proceedings of the 2014 EUROCALL Conference, Groningen, The Netherlands* (pp. 278-283). Dublin: Research-publishing.net. doi:10.14705/rpnet.2014.000231

1. Introduction

One of the major weaknesses of Japanese EFL learners is the lack of ability to correctly comprehend the simple daily conversations by native English speakers. It seems that Japanese learners rely heavily on a top-down approach to understanding the natural conversation, trying to piece together meaning from the few words they are able to discern and the overall direction of the content, and often give inappropriate responses because of miscomprehension. In order to minimize such reliance on guessing, it is necessary to increase learners' ability to understand content bottom-up by building up their knowledge of the English language.

Our previous research project (Okazaki & Nitta, 2005) developed an effective e-learning program called PLIMA (your Personal LIstening MAnager) that personalizes tasks so that learners can intensively work on their weakest areas to increase their knowledge of English and to increase their percentage of using bottom-up approaches to understanding.

Figure 1 is the data of 270 students from three Japanese universities, showing their listening ability when native English speakers speak at normal rates. The column chart shows word recognition ratios, which indicate what percent of words that students already know are recognizable. At the time of testing, the students already knew more than 99% of the words the speaker used. The line chart shows the tendency of students who try to guess the meaning of what was said (Okazaki & Nitta, 2005).

Figure 1. Word recognition and meaning guessing

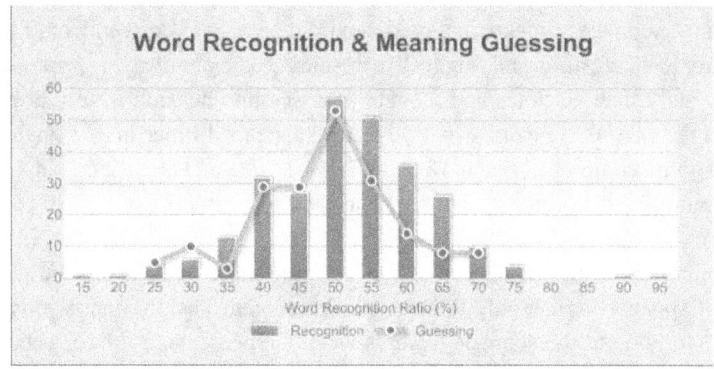

Figure 1 tells us that, when native speakers speak to Japanese EFL students in the same manner as they speak to other native speakers, average students cannot comprehend half of the words spoken in spite of having knowledge of the words. Instead, they try to guess the meaning of what was said based on the half they were able to comprehend. As the word recognition ratio improves, they can get enough information and the guessing line declines. The line also declines as the word recognition ratio drops lower than the average. That is probably because students might not be able to comprehend enough to even guess, and just give up trying to understand the speakers.

PLIMA clearly helped learners overcome problems of not being able to hear liaison sounds and unstressed syllables, as well as increased their ability to analyse phonemes (Okazaki, Nitta, & Kido, 2011). However, it is true that there are certain types of liaison sounds that learners do not catch, and some types they do. That means if we specify what type, or, what level of liaison sounds they cannot catch, this will help PLIMA offer more effective learning to learners who lack certain listening skills.

The next challenge is to develop an automatic system to determine the difficulty levels of the English audio materials.

2. Method

2.1. Making use of PLIMA data

In PLIMA, there is a large volume of stored data from monitoring hundreds of college students practicing on this listening system, including the results of assessment tests they were required to take when using the system for the first time (see Figure 2). First of all, we analyzed the results of the assessment test taken by 83 Japanese college students that consists of 30 sentences derived from films and found some interesting and suggestive results. For example, the pronoun 'you' appears more than 10 times and the rate of miscomprehension is very broad: 10–70%. In the case of the word 'what', the word appears 4 times in 30 sentences and the rate of miscomprehension is 18.2%, 27.3%, 29.1% and 69.1%; one in 4 'what's is apparently hard to comprehend for Japanese EFL learners.

These numbers demonstrate that it can be impossible to measure the difficulty levels of spoken English only through text-based analyses. In other words, if it is possible to find out the acoustic features when the percentages of correct answers are low, the priority to overcome will become more clear. Therefore, based on the result of analyses above, we started considering how to digitize the difficulty levels of spoken English by using the method of acoustic information processing.

Figure 2. An example of the results of the PLIMA assessment test

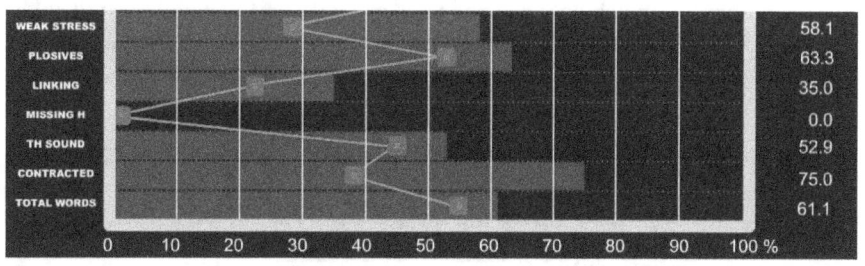

2.2. A model of an automatic judging system

Generally speaking, speech recognition systems use frequency analysis to process unknown sound signals by matching the features of that signal to known signal features which have been stored beforehand in a database. Matching is usually realized by comparing an aspect of the sound features, and then finding a counterpart which is "closest in distance" to that particular sample. Problems may arise when an input sound signal is difficult to recognize. The output from the database which is "closest in distance" may be using a very wide tolerance, or there may be a large number of candidates which are "closest in distance", making it difficult to make a clear determination of the match. Taking all these factors into consideration, however, it seemed plausible to configure software that would allow for determining the difficulty level of an English listening sample by comparing the acoustic sound features with items of known difficulty level.

Our goal is to design a practical automatic judging system to determine the difficulty of a listening passage by comparing distance measures of acoustic features inside a speech recognition engine. Figure 3 is a diagram of the model of that system. The portion enclosed by a dotted line represents existing speech recognition technology in the form of publicly available freeware. First, the acoustic features of the input are extracted using mel-frequency cepstral coefficients (MFCC), which is often used for speech recognition (Lee & Kawahara, 2009). This allows for the calculation of the power and first and second differences of the sound data. In general speech recognition processing, these features are compared to known items within a database and the match is output by pairing items that are closest in distance in a particular aspect of the acoustic feature. Our system then compares that item to items in a second database of items of known difficulty levels, and assigns a value to the output which indicates its difficulty level. As a technical detail, instead of using MFCC, a simple cepstrum (CEP) or other methods of extracting the acoustic features may be used in the final version of the software. For the purpose of matching items, the Hidden Markov Model will most likely be used. The second database for determining difficulty level is concurrently under development.

Figure 3. A model of an automatic judging system

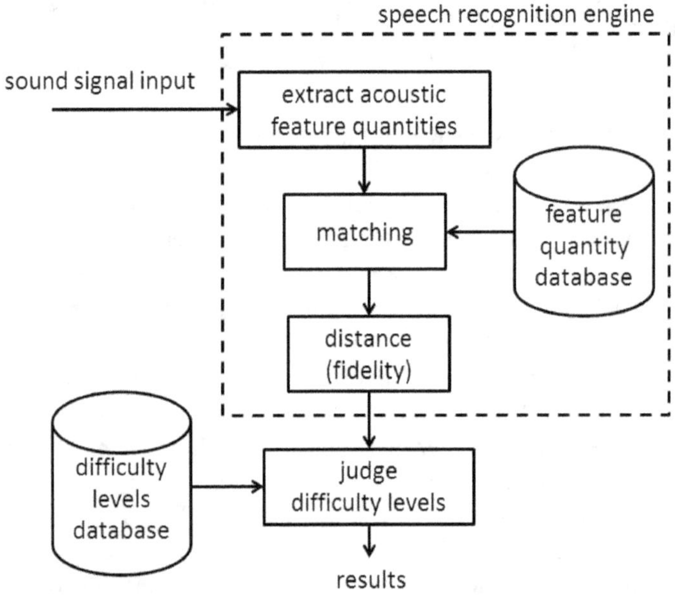

3. Our future system

In order to make use of a particular English listening material for class, such as listening from a broadly available news source, the instructor or the students themselves have to rely mainly on personal judgement to determine if that material is appropriate or not. Recently, the movement to incorporate corpus linguistics in the discussion for determining the difficulty level of language material is gaining popularity, but this discussion is strictly limited to text-based methods of analysis, and cannot be applied to analysing sound data. As this paper explains above, through this study, we hope to apply sound analysis engineering technology to the task of determining the difficulty level of listening material, which up to now has depended heavily on human judgement. If this technology can be successfully developed, it can be applied to e-learning programs. The automatic judging system that we are aiming to create will be part of a completely automatic e-learning program.

Acknowledgements. This research was partially supported by Grant-in-Aid for Scientific Research (C) (18520444) by Japan Society for the Promotion of Science (JSPS).

References

Lee, A., & Kawahara, T. (2009). Recent development of open-source speech recognition engine Julius. *The Proceedings of APSIPA ASC 2009* (pp. 131-137).

Okazaki, H., & Nitta, H. (2005). Internet-based personal listening program: A program for Japanese EFL learners to overcome individual weaknesses. In *FLEAT5 Proceedings* (pp. 92-99).

Okazaki, H., Nitta, H., & Kido, K. (2011). Practical use and validation of an original learning assistance program "Movie English Listening System". *ATEM Journal, 17*, 21-31.

university of groningen

Patterns and effectiveness of mobile device usage by Japanese undergraduates for L2 acquisition purposes

James W. Pagel[1] and Stephen G. Lambacher[2]

Abstract. Mobile technologies, such as smartphones and tablets, are rapidly gaining popularity as an effective means to enhance foreign language learning. However, does the incorporation of these mobile devices really benefit the learner or simply satisfy the instructor's need to be innovative and ahead of the learning curve? The present study seeks to answer this question, in part, by targeting a survey to English as a foreign language (EFL) learners at a private university in Tokyo, Japan. The survey was administered to Japanese undergraduates studying academic English in two separate departments during a three academic year period (2012 to 2014). The main purpose of the survey was to determine students' attitudes toward and patterns of usage of mobile learning technology, and how effective they felt it was compared with traditional methods of teaching English skills. The results revealed the students were satisfied with and motivated by their exposure to mobile learning, and that they had a preference for using mobile devices when learning English. At the same time, however, there were some students who did not feel comfortable using mobile devices for language learning. The results of the survey are discussed in light of emerging theories of autonomous learning and second language motivation.

Keywords: smartphone, tablet, mobile (m-)learning, mobile-assisted language learning, MALL, L2 acquisition, autonomous learning.

---

1. College of Science and Engineering, Aoyama Gakuin University, Tokyo, Japan; jwpagel@yahoo.com.

2. School of Social Informatics, Aoyama Gakuin University, Tokyo, Japan; steve.lambacher@gmail.com.

How to cite this article: Pagel, J. W., & Lambacher, S. G. (2014). Patterns and effectiveness of mobile device usage by Japanese undergraduates for L2 acquisition purposes. In S. Jager, L. Bradley, E. J. Meima, & S. Thouësny (Eds), *CALL Design: Principles and Practice; Proceedings of the 2014 EUROCALL Conference, Groningen, The Netherlands* (pp. 284-289). Dublin: Research-publishing.net. doi:10.14705/rpnet.2014.000232

1. Introduction

Mobile (m-)learning technologies are rapidly gaining popularity around the world as an effective way to enhance foreign and second language (L2) learning. M-learning is highly motivating, as it offers a rich, informal, contextual, and ubiquitous learning environment by which one can control his/her own learning time, environment, and speed. M-learning has other advantages over conventional teaching and learning methods, including the almost limitless number of English news programs, language learning apps, podcasts, videocasts, etc., that can be easily accessible and downloadable for free or for little cost.

Previous studies addressing m-learning and students' reactions to it are somewhat limited, as publications to date have tended to focus on describing the types of devices used, e.g. PDAs, cell phones, etc., and outcomes expected. See Kukulska-Hulme and Shields (2008) for an investigation into collaborative learning regarding listening and speaking activities and Stockwell (2008) for a study focusing on vocabulary. However, Fujimoto (2013) recently reported on Australian students' mobile device ownership and usage patterns, while Miangah and Nezarat (2012) reported on employing mobile devices in Iran as a means of cutting costs and ties to CALL.

The purpose of the present study was to determine whether m-learning holds benefits for native Japanese students, seeing how and why students have come to use this technology, including student mobile device usage in and out of the classroom and its effectiveness in improving English skills. It also attempts to ascertain whether m-learning has the positive impact in and out of the classroom that is being claimed by recent L2 acquisition and how it compares with more traditional classroom approaches. Another matter of concern was to determine whether students are willing participants in this transformation to use m-learning technologies. Do students gravitate to this new technology on their own, or is it necessary for instructors to urge or recommend them to reach out for new ways to learn?

2. Method

2.1. Participants

The survey was administered three times over a three academic year period (2012-14). All participants ($N=863$) were university undergraduates from two separate colleges at Aoyama Gakuin University, with an average of 144 students each year from both colleges, respectively). All participants were native speakers of Japanese from various parts of Japan, ranging in age from 19 to 23. The percentages of the other demographic variables within this population were as follows: female 34.6%, male 65.4%, Science and Engineering (SE) majors 50%, Social Informatics (SI) majors 50%, freshmen 49.6%, sophomores 16%, juniors 25.1%, and seniors 9.3%.

2.2. Materials

The survey (in Japanese) was posted on MonkeySurvey®, an online survey and software questionnaire tool. The survey consisted of four questions to provide demographical information, two questions to indicate owners of smart phones and tablets, and 31 questions comprised of Likert scale items that reported agreement with the affective items (1=strongly disagree to 6=strongly agree).

2.3. Procedure

The survey was administered each time on the final day of the semester (in January). The students were informed that the survey was for research purposes only, and since the responses were online, their privacy would be protected. The survey took approximately five to eight minutes for the participants to complete.

3. Results

Due to space limitations, we present just a sampling of the results, which have been categorized into three sections: 3.1) Student motivation for using mobile devices; 3.2) Smartphone usage characteristics (English Skills); and 3.3) Student attitudes toward m-learning. In addition, it should be noted that before the analysis we removed all responses from students who claimed to be 'non'-mobile device users.

3.1. Student motivation for using mobile devices

We were interested in assessing the motivation for students in their decision to start using a mobile device to improve their English. This information might be helpful for teachers to better understand the type of motivation (intrinsic or extrinsic) that influences students in their decision to use a mobile device, as well as potentially guide the future development of L2 pedagogy incorporating m-learning.

As shown in Table 1 below, the vast majority of students (98%) responded that they owned a smartphone in January of 2014, a 17% increase from their polling two years earlier. Conversely, the number of students owning a tablet was 24% in

2014, an 11% increase from the 2012 poll. Additionally, in response to Q3, "*I use a mobile device for learning or practicing English*", there was a slight increase during the three-year period in the number of students using their devices to study English (42% to 49%).

Table 1. How mobile device ownership among Japanese students changed over three years

	Smartphone	*Tablet*
2014	98%	24%
2013	91%	11%
2012	82%	13%

The next set of questions dealt with the motivation behind usage of mobile devices for studying English: Q8, "*I made my own decision to start using a mobile device for practicing English*" (**Self**); Q9, "*I started using a mobile device to study English because my teacher required me to use it*" (**Required**); and Q10, "*I started using a mobile device to study English because my teacher encouraged me to use it*" (**Encouraged**).

Overall, the results indicate that a higher percentage of SE students compared to SI students responded they were "required" (19% vs. 13%) and also "encouraged" (40% vs. 36%) to use a smartphone to learn English. However, there were a greater number of SI students (38%) who reported being "self" motivated in their gravitation toward m-learning in comparison to SE students (28%).

3.2. Smartphone usage characteristics (English skills)

This section presents the results of questions dealing with the types of English skills students practiced with their mobile devices. The responses were collapsed across the variables 'school' and 'year'.

A majority of students (80%) responded that they did not pay for mobile apps for language learning and used only free programs. The results also showed that students spent significantly more time practicing *listening* (69%) than *reading* (42%). Additionally, a majority of students (66.6%) responded that they used their mobile devices to improve their English *vocabulary*.

In examining dual-skill language practice, students preferred using their smartphones to study *listening & reading* (59.3%) over *reading & writing* (44.3%).

Finally, when asked 'where' they preferred to use their mobile devices to study English, a majority of students (60.4% vs. 54.7%) responded that they preferred studying English on the *train* compared to at *home*, respectively; however, we should mention that this difference was greater for students two years ago in 2012 (71.5% vs. 61%, respectively) than in 2014, when both locations were reported to be equally preferred.

3.3. Student attitudes toward m-learning

In this section, we were interested in gaining a better understanding of student satisfaction with m-learning for studying English, as it could help confirm the benefits and effectiveness of m-learning. As in Section 3.2, all responses were collapsed across the variables 'school' and 'year'.

In response to Q17, "*My English has improved using a mobile device*", 47.7% of students answered in the affirmative. The results also show that 59.2% of students reported that using a mobile device to study English was "fun and interesting". Furthermore, a significant number of students (37.9%) answered negatively when polled if MALL "was not helpful for learning English". In addition, 58.5% of respondents indicated m-learning "was more efficient" than other styles of learning.

4. Conclusion

The overall results revealed many students were satisfied with and motivated by their exposure to m-learning. Furthermore, a significant number had a preference for using mobile devices when learning English and found m-learning to be more efficient than traditional methods. It was also encouraging to find that many students had started to utilize their mobile devices to learn English on their own. At the same time, however, there were some students who did not feel comfortable using mobile devices for language learning. A lack of motivation and confidence can have a negative effect on students' attitudes and classroom behaviors, resulting in long-term and widespread negative learning outcomes. One of the main goals of any L2 learning program incorporating m-learning should thus be to motivate students by offering them a more integrated approach to learning English, including individualized guidance and support during the learning process.

References

Fujimoto, C. (2013). Perceptions of mobile learning in Australia: How ready are learners to study on the move? *JaltCALL Journal, 8*(3), 165-195.

Kukulska-Hulme, A., & Shield, L. (2008). An overview of mobile assisted language learning: Can mobile devices support collaborative practice in speaking and listening. *ReCALL, 20*(3), 271-289. doi:10.1017/S0958344008000335

Miangah, T. M., & Nezarat, A. (2012). Mobile-assisted language learning. *International Journal of Distributed and Parallel Systems, 3*(1), 310-319. doi:10.5121/ijdps.2012.3126

Stockwell, G. (2008). Investigating learner preparedness for and usage patterns of mobile learning. *ReCALL, 20*(3), 253-270. doi:10.1017/S0958344008000232

university of groningen

L2 immersion in 3D Virtual Worlds: The next thing to being there?

Edith Paillat[1]

Abstract. Second Life is one of the many three-dimensional virtual environments accessible through a computer and a fast broadband connection. Thousands of participants connect to this platform to interact virtually with the world, join international communities of practice and, for some, role play groups. Unlike online role play games however, Second Life is a user-generated social platform where users have the freedom to chat and learn, build, exhibit and sell their creations, and participate in immersive Role Play. This paper reports on findings and personal reflections on a project run over two and half years with students of three language programs at Victoria University of Wellington's School of Language and Cultures. The purpose of the project was to measure language students' willingness to use the L2 naturally and holistically when performing semi-authentic tasks while immersed in culturally themed 3d virtual environments.

Keywords: virtual environments, language learning, immersive education, situated learning, higher education.

1. Introduction

Following Lave and Wenger's (1991) beliefs in the value of situated learning and with the wealth of visual and interactive resources 3D Multi-User Virtual Environments afford, our university's School of Languages and Cultures initiated a pilot project in 2012 to explore the viability of Second Life for immersive language practice with selected students of French, Spanish and Italian.

---

1. Victoria University of Wellington, Wellington, New Zealand; edith.paillat@vuw.ac.nz.

How to cite this article: Paillat, E. (2014). L2 immersion in 3D Virtual Worlds: The next thing to being there? In S. Jager, L. Bradley, E. J. Meima, & S. Thouësny (Eds), *CALL Design: Principles and Practice; Proceedings of the 2014 EUROCALL Conference, Groningen, The Netherlands* (pp. 290-295). Dublin: Research-publishing.net. doi:10.14705/rpnet.2014.000233

The project intent was to find ways of bridging the language learnt in the classroom and authentic language used in real-life situations, thus contextualise and consolidate newly acquired knowledge (Brown, Collins, & Duguid, 1989; Lave & Wenger, 1991). The affordances of 3D Virtual environments can be such that they can provide opportunities for students to interact with a rich environment and native speakers, and therefore enhance their cultural and linguistic awareness. Following the research by Wehner, Gump, and Downey (2011), the second purpose of the project was to gauge students' level of engagement and motivation when interacting with a 3D synthetic environment through an avatar.

This paper reports on findings and observations collated over two and half years with varied groups and contexts of participation, and explores the logistics and design of sessions in light of the nine principles of situated learning compiled by Herrington (2006).

2. Method

2.1. Participants

The project started in 2012 with three volunteer students of French B1 who were able to connect from home with their personal laptops. In June 2012, a teaching grant allowed to extend the project to Spanish and Italian. Graphic cards were installed on five dedicated lab PCs. Groups' levels differed from A1 to B1 and each tutor prepared weekly hour and a half sessions with the author following their respective course outline. Both the French and Spanish groups were invited to present their Second Life experience in the final oral exam. Though not compulsory, 80% of the overall 25 participants did, with a dropout of 30% mid-trimester.

In 2014, supplementary funding allowed the purchase of 15 graphic cards for the lab to host a class of 14 students of Italian. The class level ranged from A2 to B1 and the sessions were held once a week for 50 minutes.

2.2. Data collection

2.2.1. Questionnaire

An online questionnaire was given at the end of the trimester to collect students' impressions. 15 out of 18 volunteer students responded. Seven students in the Italian class responded mid-trimester and 12 to the end of trimester (19 responses overall).

The generic questionnaire was set up to investigate:

- their personal use of social media and online games and L2 practice;
- their level of comfort with the software;
- their impressions of the environment and guest participation;
- their impression on tasks carried out versus language practice.

2.2.2. Author's observations

Personal observations were also collected throughout the whole project. They encompass the implementation phase, the preparation of the sessions, tutor and student training, student responses to the type of activities, and students' general impressions conveyed in their final oral exam. Language learning outcomes were not studied as part of this project but should be researched to extend the viability of such a project.

3. Design: building the bridge

3.1. Volunteers

We endeavoured to align our sessions with the course outline. With the Spanish A2 and the French B1, most sessions revolved around virtual tourism, often with (a) native speaker(s). We visited real-life replicas (Paris, Mexico, Venice) and other places focussing on arts, cultural events and shopping areas. Interviews were conducted with native in-world "professionals" following the topic of the lesson. We attempted to maximise students' participation during the sessions by letting them read signs aloud, describe what they saw and communicate with guests. Objectives were loose as the point was to allow for unpredicted events to occur, and thus engage students emotionally.

For the Italian A1-A2 program, we kept to a more rigid structure to limit cognitive overload. Native language teachers offered assistance and we strictly focussed on situations and simulations based on the course book (e.g. describing, buying, likes and dislikes). Seven participants out 25 dropped out early in the programme, mainly from the Italian group.

3.2. Phase 2: the Italian class

Students were grouped for better management and collaborative work. They were instructed to take photos in-world to complement a short written account of each session on their learning management system (LMS) wiki. This task was to assist them in preparing for their final oral exam: a group presentation. They interviewed native speakers about their Second Life occupations, explored three Italian islands and wrote a tale. They also changed their avatars to impersonate their tale's characters and complemented their writing with pictures illustrating the plot.

4. Selected findings

4.1. The actors and implementation

Tutors responded differently to the platform. Surprisingly, it did not correlate with their computer proficiency. Their respective mind-set and the systematic use of L2 during class had a strong impact on the students' linguistic performance and engagement with the environment, (instructions, technical assistance and software interface).

It took two training sessions before students started to feel comfortable in-world and an average of five sessions for them to apprehend the world and other avatars unless they had experience with 3D games. Most students tended to participate with text chat rather than using voice with guest speakers. The most confident B1, however, often took the opportunity to speak up for the group when questions arose in the lab.

4.2. The real-life location and level of immersion for L2 practice

The level of linguistic immersion was blatant with the group who connected from home. They relied on what they saw on their screen. Their only means of contact for assistance and meaning was in-world so production in L2 was maximum.

While in the lab, volunteer students were keen to maximise their practice but were at time distracted by communication in Real-Life so the level of immersion was limited. They nevertheless responded very positively to meta-linguistic challenges (instructions, software interface and assistance given in L2). The "class", however, tended to speak L1 while in-world and mostly focussed on L2 for their wiki task. The latter commented that they would have liked more opportunities to speak L2. We also noticed that the class dynamics were very similar to traditional class participation after the session. A mixture of peer-pressure, lack of preparation to express spontaneous emotional engagement in L2, and lack of confidence probably influenced their level of participation during round-table discussions.

4.3. Technical considerations

Bandwidth and firewall settings on campus at times limited the level of interaction to text chat only. While all students enjoyed meeting native speakers, voice was prime to their experience.

Students connecting from home had difficulties with their hardware which also hindered maximum exposure and immersion.

Training on the interface and functionalities demanded at least two sessions to be included in the programme. Video tutorials in L2 were uploaded on the LMS for consultation. Students reported feeling fairly comfortable after five sessions.

5. Conclusions

New Zealand students of European languages have very few opportunities to experience authentic synchronous communication with native speakers. Therefore, it is imperative to find ways to simulate authenticity in student learning experience. It is often challenging for both learners and teachers to bridge learned content to semi-authentic communication skills if the learning environment is not modelling realistic situations. 3D virtual worlds may not model reality per se but an environment such as Second Life with its many international communities and landscapes comes close to what we can afford to broaden students' cognitive engagement in the practice of the L2. This said, it is important to ensure that students understand why they are involved in such an environment and what is expected of them so that they can commit to the environment and its parameters. Herrington (2006) argues that

> "[d]esigning a learning environment to exhibit cognitive realism is one step towards creating an immersive and engaging online learning environment. However, the fact that a learning context has been well-designed is of insufficient. Students must commit to the environment and its parameters [… and if they don't, they] need to be *persuaded* that they are participating in an authentic learning environment" (section "suspension of disbelief").

Overall, participants enjoyed the experience but did not always comprehend the use of a 3D environment as opposed to other learning material. The "class" expected more structured sessions with the controlled tasks that they were accustomed to. Some also tended to dissociate having fun with actual learning, hence the use of L1. However, the students who were mentally ready to take the plunge and maximise their learning opportunities during the sessions showed constant progress and a gain in confidence to participate in class. The triangulation between language input/output, immersive environments and student motivation is a valuable research to validate the critical importance of situated cognition and authenticity in second language acquisition.

References

Brown, J. S., Collins, A., & Duguid, P. (1989). Situated cognition and the culture of learning. *Educational Researcher, 18*(1), 32-42. doi:10.3102/0013189X018001032

Herrington, J. (2006). Authentic e-learning in higher education: Design principles for authentic learning environments and tasks. In *World Conference on E-Learning in Corporate, Government, Healthcare, and Higher Education (ELEARN) 2006, 13-17 October 2006, Honolulu, Hawaii, USA.*

Lave, J., & Wenger, E. (1991). *Situated learning: Legitimate peripheral participation.* Cambridge, UK: Cambridge University Press. doi:10.1017/CBO9780511815355

Wehner A. K., Gump, A. W., & Downey, S. (2011). The effects of Second Life on the motivation of undergraduate students learning a foreign language. *Computer Assisted Language Learning, 24*(3), 277-289. doi:10.1080/09588221.2010.551757

ICT in EFL: The global effect of new technologies in the language classroom

Salomi Papadima-Sophocleous[1], Christina Nicole Giannikas[2], and Elis Kakoulli-Constantinou[3]

Abstract. Research studies conducted around the globe have shown that Information and Communication Technologies (ICT) can lead to increased student learning and improved teaching methods. ICT's growth has brought about numerous changes to the education world, making the technological revolution that is happening around us impossible to disregard. Although the revolution in language education is here to stay, language professionals seem reluctant to embrace ICT in their classrooms. The purpose of this paper is 1) to present the field with an overview of how far the integration of ICT in language education and the development of language teacher education regarding the use of ICT have come, and 2) to contribute suggestions on how the situation can improve. The overview in question entails literature from around the globe.

Keywords: new technologies, EFL, professional development, language classrooms.

1. Introduction

The evolution of new technologies witnessed during the last two decades has prompted a great deal of debate in education. More specifically, technology has added new dimensions to the nature of English as a Foreign Language (EFL). However, the issue of its integration in the language classroom is still a topic of great discussion in the field of language education. The development of ICT has

---

1. Cyprus University of Technology; salomi.papadima@cut.ac.cy.
2. Cyprus University of Technology; christina.giannikas@cut.ac.cy.
3. Cyprus University of Technology; elis.constantinou@cut.ac.cy.

How to cite this article: Papadima-Sophocleous, S., Giannikas, C. N., & Kakoulli-Constantinou, E. (2014). ICT in EFL: The global effect of new technologies in the language classroom. In S. Jager, L. Bradley, E. J. Meima, & S. Thouësny (Eds), *CALL Design: Principles and Practice*; Proceedings of the 2014 EUROCALL Conference, Groningen, The Netherlands (pp. 296-300). Dublin: Research-publishing.net. doi:10.14705/rpnet.2014.000234

brought a number of changes to the modern world and their education systems, which have made it impossible to ignore the change that is occurring around us. Students of all ages have become frequent technology users, starting from a very early age, which makes the integration of new technologies in language education all the more crucial and thought provoking.

Though professional evolution seems to be near, many language practitioners around the globe are reluctant to apply ICT in their classes (Albirini, 2006; Goldstein, 1997; Stylianou, 2012). This fact intrigued the researchers to look into a global scope of the situation. Therefore, the purpose of this paper is to present 1) an overview of how far the integration of new technologies has come in language education, and 2) to contribute suggestions on how the situation can improve.

2. Method

The aim of this study was to carry out a literature review, in a 2001-2013 timeframe, of similar studies conducted in various parts of the world in order to explore what the situation is globally. A first small scale examination of a global body of literature included a review of recent publications of *CALL*, *ReCALL*, *CALL-EJ*, *Computers & Education* and *CALICO*, among others, with a focus on ICT in the language classroom, the integration of new technologies, language teachers' attitudes towards the integration of ICT and professional development. This literature review gave the researchers the opportunity to evaluate the situation in a broader capacity, and suggest ways for improvement.

3. Results and discussion

In recent years, education systems around the world have gradually been raising their interest towards new technologies and their use in language classrooms. The potential of ICT has become an important and debated issue, since even though the value of ICT is not questioned, complexities occur among practitioners when applying these technologies (Balanskat, Blamire, & Kefala, 2006).

Current governmental policies from around the world aim to inspire educators of all subject areas to implement ICT in their practice. Ramanair and Uyu Sagat (2007) have stated that the Malaysian Ministry of Education has invested in a number of programs in order to provide schools with new technologies in the hope to facilitate the development of language learning skills. EACEA (2009) reports that even though the impact of new technologies continues to develop within the continent of Europe, the informants question whether this possibility has been acknowledged and understood by teachers.

Albeit Ministries of Education worldwide are spending immense amounts of capital to support and encourage new technologies in education, for instance, the US spent $5.7 billion in the year 2000 alone (Doherty & Orlofsky, 2001), practitioners are hesitant to incorporate new technologies in their language classes (Buabeng-Andoh, 2012; Eugene, 2006). Substantial research has been conducted on teachers' attitudes towards technology in education in general. However, this review revealed that only some research has been specifically conducted on language teachers' attitudes towards the use of ICT in language teaching and learning. According to studies conducted during 2001-2013 and published in *CALL*, *ReCALL*, *CALL-EJ*, *Computers & Education* and *CALICO* journals, language practitioners are hesitant to integrate new technologies in their teaching.

Mueller, Wood, Willoughby, Ross, and Specht's (2008) have argued that Canadian primary and secondary school teachers' views towards technology can be seen as a barrier and encourage researchers to focus on teachers' attitudes and perceptions as important influences in order to raise awareness and help improve the situation. Şahin-Kizil's (2011) findings suggest "that EFL teachers hold positive attitudes towards the use of ICT for educational purposes [..., h]owever, the responses indicate that insufficient class time and inadequate training opportunities are the major obstacles in the process of ICT integration" (p. 1). Aydin's (2013) study "indicated that Turkish EFL teachers have little knowledge about certain software and experience difficulties using the software programs and that they suffer from a lack of technical and instructional support, although they have positive perceptions of computer integration and attitudes toward computer use" (p. 218).

Research was also carried out in the teacher Computer Assisted Language Learning (CALL) preparation. Kessler (2007) findings suggest that "there is a general lack of CALL preparation in teacher preparation programmes and that there is evidence that teachers obtain a majority of their CALL knowledge from informal sources and personal experience rather than through formalized preparation" (p. 173). He further points out that there is a need for more insight into the role of CALL within teacher preparation (Kessler, 2007). Kessler and Plakans (2008) also claim that "CALL teacher preparation may benefit from a focus on developing contextualized confidence within certain teaching domains or types of technology rather than expecting teachers to develop a high level of confidence with technology across domains" (p. 269). The study in general revealed the need for more research in that area.

4. Conclusions

The purpose of this paper was 1) to present the field with an overview of how far the integration of ICT in language education and the development of language teacher education regarding the use of ICT have come, and 2) to contribute suggestions on how the situation can be improved. The overview in question entails literature from around the globe, including that of the research project conducted in Cyprus by the authors of this paper.

The first finding was that more research is required in examining the effect of new technologies in the language classroom, and particularly the extent to which new technologies are accepted and embraced by language teachers. The present literature review indicates that there is an interest on behalf of policy-makers, and an effort to train language teachers has been made in many countries. Nonetheless, teachers have been recorded to still be hesitant to apply ICT in their classes, a situation which should be modified so that language practitioners can appreciate the benefits of technology, progress within their occupation, and offer their learners language classes equal to that of the technological era they are in. This cannot transpire if conscious efforts are not made to review the training situation and the process of ICT implementation.

The second finding suggests that in order for the situation to change, the approach of introducing and integrating ICT has to be modified. Teachers must be suitably exposed to new technologies, which would be the initial stage of regaining their self-assurance; therefore, language teachers must undertake in- and pre-service training that will include the use of new technologies for language educational purposes. If language teachers' training needs are not met, funds amounting to millions will be wasted, since practitioners will not make the optimum use of the equipment and resources available to them.

References

Albirini, A. (2006). Teachers' attitudes toward information and communication technologies: The case of Syrian EFL teachers. *Computers & Education, 47*(4), 373-398.

Aydin, S. (2013). Teachers' perceptions about the use of computers in EFL teaching and learning: the case of Turkey. *Computer Assisted Language Learning, 26*(3), 214-233. doi:10.1080/09588221.2012.654495

Buabeng-Andoh, C. (2012). An exploration of teaching skills, perceptions and practices of ICT in teaching and learning in the Ghanaian second-cycle schools. *Contemporary Educational Technology, 3*(1), 36-49.

Balanskat, A., Blamire, R., & Kefala, S. (2006). *A review of studies of ICT impact on schools in Europe*. European Schoolnet.

Doherty, K. M., & Orlofsky, G. F. (2001). Student survey says: Schools are not using educational technologies as wisely or effectively as they could. *Education Week: Technology Counts 2001, 20*(35), 45-48.

Eugene, J. (2006). How teachers integrate technology and their beliefs about learning: Is there a connection? *Journal of Technology and Teacher Education, 14*(3), 581-597.

EACEA. (2009). *Study on the impact of information and communications technology (ICT) and new media on language learning, final report*. European Commission.

Goldstein, S. (1997). *OFSTED Report on IT use in secondary schools, 1995-97*. HMSO, London.

Kessler, G. (2007). Formal and informal CALL preparation and teacher attitude toward technology. *CALL, 20*(2), 173-178. doi:10.1080/09588220701331394

Kessler, G., & Plakans, L. (2008). Does teachers' confidence with CALL equal innovative and integrated use? *Computer Assisted Language Learning, 21*(3), 269-282. doi:10.1080/09588220802090303

Mueller, J., Wood, E., Willoughby, T., Ross, C., & Specht, J. (2008). Identifying discriminating variables between teachers who fully integrate computers and teachers with limited integration. *Computers and Education, 5*(4), 1523-1537. doi:10.1016/j.compedu.2008.02.003

Ramanair, J., & Uyu Segat, G. (2007). Multimedia technology: Teachers' knowledge and attitudes. CALL-EJ Online, 8(2).

Şahin-Kizil, A. (2011). EFL teachers attitudes towards information and communication technologies (ICT). *Proceedings of the 5th International Computer & Instructional Technologies Symposium, Firat University, Laziğ Turkey*.

Stylianou, A. (2012). The attitudes of the teachers in Cyprus concerning the adjustment of the ELT curriculum to the technological advancements. In D. Tsagari (Ed.), *Research on English as a foreign language in Cyprus, Volume II* (pp. 33-52). University of Nicosia Press.

university of groningen

Are we there yet? Normalising CALL in the context of primary languages in England

Monika Pazio[1]

Abstract. The presence of technology in foreign education dates back to the 1960's. After over 50 years of research and practice, we are now moving towards discussion of identifying the end goal of integration that became known as normalisation (Bax, 2003). The majority of Computer-Assisted Language Learning (CALL) approaches and normalisation research is conducted within the English as a Foreign Language (EFL) context. CALL, however, is not restricted to EFL and there is a lot of good practice observed in the mainstream language classroom. This paper explores the concept of normalisation of CALL, applying it to a new context of primary Modern Languages (ML). The research identifies factors that impede successful CALL, with a special focus on pedagogical practice and examines it closely in relation to specialist and non-specialist teachers.

Keywords: CALL, normalisation, primary languages, MFL.

1. Introduction

The abundance of CALL research relates mostly to an EFL context. As Egbert (2008) points out, there is a need to extend the inquiry to other settings as contextual differences are currently not represented well. Primary ML settings in England offer an interesting insight in relation to CALL. While with an EFL context there is no need for discussion about the importance of the subject, the place of ML in the primary curriculum has been unstable due to its non mandatory status which is only to change from September 2014. This lack of stability impacts provision, i.e. variety of languages taught, how often and who delivers them –specialist or

---

1. University of Bedfordshire; monika.pazio@beds.ac.uk.

How to cite this article: Pazio, M. (2014). Are we there yet? Normalising CALL in the context of primary languages in England. In S. Jager, L. Bradley, E. J. Meima, & S. Thouësny (Eds), *CALL Design: Principles and Practice*; *Proceedings of the 2014 EUROCALL Conference, Groningen, The Netherlands* (pp. 301-306). Dublin: Research-publishing.net. doi:10.14705/rpnet.2014.000235

non-specialist (generalist) teachers[2]. On the other hand, the Whiteboard Expansion Project was the catalyst for technology integration (Lewin, Somekh, & Steadman, 2008). The cross-curricular nature of information and communications technology (ICT) made that integration present and embedded it within teachers' everyday practice, also in ML education (Wade, Marshall, & O'Donnell, 2009). However, the common problem of focusing on technology rather than pedagogy also applies here (O'Hara, 2008). According to Macrory, Chretine, and Martin (2009), this is especially true within primary ML being a relatively new field for teachers who feel uneasy about their new roles.

With the growing importance of ICT in language education, the term normalisation (Bax, 2003) started to appear in the CALL literature. Normalisation has been defined by Bax (2003, 2011) as a stage when technology is so integrated into teaching practice that it becomes unnoticed and its use enhances learning. The current project researches the concept of normalisation of CALL, applying it to a new context of primary languages. It aims to identify broader factors which impede normalisation in primary CALL, with special focus on pedagogy and redefine the concept to fit the given context. The research draws largely on previous normalisation studies (Chambers & Bax 2006; Ward, 2007) as well as wider research on primary language learning and ICT integration.

2. Method

The researcher's philosophical position placed the study within the interpretive paradigm. Ethnography was chosen as the most suitable approach, allowing greater immersion and understanding of the researched context, and aligning the design with the sociocultural theory behind normalisation (Bax, 2011). Since true ethnography is difficult to achieve in educational research, the study adopted Holliday's (1997) perspective and was ethnographic in nature.

The methods used included participant and non-participant observations, interviews with the pupils, staff and stakeholders, a diary and audio recording of chosen lessons. Both specialist and non-specialist teachers participated. Non-specialists were also observed while teaching other subjects to allow for comparisons of pedagogy.

---

2. In the present work, a specialist is defined as an MFL trained teacher (be it primary or secondary) who has a very good knowledge of the language and/or language teaching pedagogy and who is hired by the head to deliver MFL lessons on a weekly basis; a non-specialist is defined as a primary trained teacher with very limited language knowledge and skills and no language teaching training.

3. Discussion

Analysis of the data revealed that the factors impeding normalisation revolve around issues related to technology, but also general problems surrounding primary language provision. Hence the discussion below focuses on both, as both need to be addressed for normalisation to take place.

3.1. Attitudes

In the researched school, the management's attitudes and beliefs about the role of technology in education, the place of Early Language Learning (ELL) in the curriculum as well as beliefs about successful provision were the driving force behind ICT integration and the form in which language teaching was conducted. They determined the type and the quality of equipment that was available as well as the type of provision adopted; the latter refers to who taught languages, how often and which languages were delivered.

Teachers' attitudes towards language learning in general and ELL in particular as well as the role of ICT influenced the actions in relation to the degree of integration of both language and technology and actual pedagogical changes. Teachers' actions were also influenced by children's attitudes since if the reaction to ML lessons or particular integration of equipment was negative, they were likely to either diminish (or completely eliminate) language learning time and/or eliminate that particular type of equipment.

3.2. Training, support and skills

Formal and informal training both play an important role. When it comes to ML, the non-specialist teachers would quite often comment on their informal exposure to the language through family members and holiday trips as the source of contact with and knowledge of the language rather than formal qualifications obtained at secondary level. The generalists feel they do not have sufficient linguistic skills to confidently and effectively deliver the lessons. Hence, there is a general feeling of not being the right person for the job and over reliance on the specialists' expertise and assistance. With the funding for primary language training reduced, secondary school support proves to be an important factor here, as in order to ensure continuity, there needs to be closer collaboration between the subject leaders and other teachers.

When it comes to ICT, official training is no longer provided in the researched school as the generalist teachers feel fairly confident and proficient with the technical aspects of the equipment. Any support offered relates to pedagogical aspects. The teachers admit that when it comes to ICT, "training on the job" is the best way of acquiring skills. This is why specialists feel less capable as they do not have the same amount of exposure as generalists for whom ICT –especially interactive whiteboards (IWBs)– is a part of their daily practice.

3.3. Logistics

Successful implementation of CALL relied on good logistical arrangements. Those referred to how teaching was organised around ICT, i.e. availability, placement and quality of available equipment and the arrangements around language provision in relation to both specialist and non-specialist teachers.

3.4. Pedagogy

A close comparison of specialist and non-specialist teachers' lessons allowed to comment on the strengths and weaknesses of each type of CALL provision. While specialist teachers have a clear linguistic advantage, they do not always have an understanding of primary teaching and primary context, especially in relation to overall curriculum knowledge, knowledge of subject specific methods, children's individual needs and to some extent ICT skills. Lack of knowledge of children as individuals was quite transparent in the researched school and led to lack of differentiation at all stages as well as problems with behaviour.

Both specialists and non-specialists in the researched school used technology in a similar way which centred around plenary IWB use. The specialist admitted that she used the IWB because she felt most comfortable with it considering the limited amount of time she had to deliver a lesson, while non-specialists used the IWB as it made use of readily available resources with audio files which compensated for their limited language skills and lack of confidence and was simply considered a "job done". Generalists quite often felt insecure moving away from the resource which resulted in "constrained" pedagogical CALL practice.

However, when observing non-specialists using technology in other subjects (those they were trained to teach), integration was much more varied and creative, incorporating group work, pair work as well as different technology types. This mix of tasks and variety of equipment was valued by the pupils who enjoyed plenary IWB use, but expressed a preference for autonomy rather than individual and pair interaction, which the equipment gave them. In the researched school, this usually took place in the ICT suite or when using mobile equipment. This three-dimensional application was not widely utilised for ML, which in some instances led to pupils' dissatisfaction with CALL and ML lessons in general, especially when delivered by a specialist.

4. Conclusions

The study identified broader factors which impede normalisation in primary contexts. Those main themes related to attitudes, logistical solutions, training and support and pedagogy, and touched upon the problematic nature of primary language provision and general technological issues. Normalisation, then, needs to be redefined to accommodate the complexities of primary language context. While with EFL the language provision was taken for granted, the situation is not that clear in the primary ML. The subject will be mandatory from September 2014, this, however, does not eliminate the problems related to the quality of teaching that have only been partially addressed. Hence, before we speak of normalisation of primary CALL, we need to consider normalisation of technology and language provision separately.

The discussion of pedagogy centred around the type of knowledge (and what follows skills) that primary CALL practitioners should possess. Those include subject knowledge, subject specific methods of teaching, children's individual needs, practical and pedagogical ICT knowledge, curriculum knowledge and knowledge of age specific teaching methods. All these affect application of CALL and both specialist and non-specialist teachers at the researched school did not possess a full set of those skills. A primary trained teacher with ML subject specialism would be most likely to master all of them; however, with the dropping numbers of language entries, finding this type of teacher has become a sort of "quest for the holy grail". It is necessary to develop these skills in whomever undertakes language provision through enabling connectivist skills and knowledge exchange to fill in the current gap and allow for better technology use in language education. More practical work resulting from this research will attempt to achieve just that.

References

Bax, S. (2003). CALL – past, present and future. *System, 31*(1), 13-28. doi:10.1016/S0346-251X(02)00071-4

Bax, S. (2011). Normalisation revisited: The effective use of technology in language education. *International Journal of Computer-Assisted Language Learning and Teaching (IJCALLT), 1*(2), 1-15. doi:10.4018/ijcallt.2011040101

Chambers, A., & Bax, S. (2006). Making CALL work: Towards normalisation. *System, 34*(4), 465-479. doi:10.1016/j.system.2006.08.001

Egbert, J. (2008). Conducting research on CALL. In J. Egbert & G. M. Petrie (Eds), *CALL research perspectives* (pp. 3-8). Mahwah, New Jersey: Lawrence Erlbaum Associates.

Holliday, A. (1997). Six lessons: Cultural continuity in communicative language teaching. *Language Teaching Research, 1*(3), 212-238. doi:10.1177/136216889700100303

Lewin, C., Somekh, B., & Steadman, S. (2008). Embedding interactive whiteboards in teaching and learning: The process of change in pedagogic practice. *Education and Information Technologies, 13*(4), 291-303. doi:10.1007/s10639-008-9070-z

Macrory, G., Chretine, L., & Martin, J. L. (2009). *Technology-enhanced language learning pedagogy* (TELLP). Project number: 134244-2007-UK-COMENIUS-CMP. Final report to EU (2009).

O'Hara, M. (2008). Young children, learning and ICT: A case study in the UK maintained sector. *Technology, Pedagogy and Education, 17*(1), 29-40. doi:10.1080/14759390701847443

Wade, P., Marshall, H., & O'Donnell, S. (2009). *Primary modern foreign languages: Longitudinal survey of implementation of national entitlement to language learning at key stage 2*. Final Report (DCSF Research Report 127). London: DCSF.

Ward, M. (2007). Normalising CALL in the primary school context - an example. *IATEFL Conference, Ulster, 5-8 September 2007*.

Peer assessment in the classroom using mobile devices

William Pellowe[1], Trevor Holster[2], and J. Lake[3]

Abstract. Peer feedback can engage the learning process, but collecting the survey data into a usable format can be time-consuming, which can deter classroom teachers from undertaking the kind of in-depth analysis for classroom research. To overcome this detriment, and in order to research the effects of learning by assessing, we created a peer feedback module ("add-on") to a free, open-source student response system (SRS). Using this SRS, teachers create a survey for peer feedback. Students can access this survey through any web browser on any kind of device, from computers to smartphones, to rate their classmates' performances. The survey is reused for each feedback session. This module can output data files compatible with MFRM (many-faceted Rasch measurement) software, which allows teachers to analyse the collected data in a very short amount of time.

Keywords: peer assessment, learning by assessing, mobile devices.

1. Introduction

Teachers often use peer feedback surveys to help students focus on their classmates' speeches, writing samples, poster sessions, and other types of student performance. This process can actually engage students so that they learn while assessing. However, collecting, collating and inputting this data into a digital format for in-depth analysis is a very time-consuming endeavor, discouraging for teachers who are hard-pressed for time. The Peer Assessment (PA) module of MOARS (MObile Audience Response System) (Pellowe, 2010) was designed to overcome many of

---

1. Kinki University, Fukuoka Campus, Japan; pellowe@fuk.kindai.ac.jp.
2. Fukuoka Women's University, Japan; trevholster@gmail.com.
3. Fukuoka Jo Gakuin University, Japan; jlake@temple.edu.

How to cite this article: Pellowe, W., Holster, T., & Lake, J. (2014). Peer assessment in the classroom using mobile devices. In S. Jager, L. Bradley, E. J. Meima, & S. Thouësny (Eds), *CALL Design: Principles and Practice*; *Proceedings of the 2014 EUROCALL Conference, Groningen, The Netherlands* (pp. 307-311). Dublin: Research-publishing.net. doi:10.14705/rpnet.2014.000236

the time-consuming hurdles facing teachers and researchers who are interested in peer assessment.

Typically, when engaging in peer feedback, students receive a rubric that lists several areas to be assessed, with scales and descriptions for each level of the scale. Each student will review several other students' work, choosing the most accurate descriptor within each area of assessment. Each student's data is collated and later made available to him or her.

One way to collect a large amount of data is through scan sheets. Students mark the scan sheets, which are later fed through scan machines that can read the scores off of each sheet, collect the data from all of the students, and make it available in the form of an Excel spreadsheet. Even though this method represents a huge improvement over the days when one had to enter all of the data by hand into a computer, it is still time-consuming.

Using online survey tools also becomes problematic. For students to give individual feedback to each other, one would need to create a survey for each student, which is an unrealistic requirement with large classes, not to mention combined classes. Furthermore, coordinating and distributing the web URLs for each student would be quite a challenge.

2. Method

2.1. Overview of the peer assessment module design

The PA module for MOARS addresses these problems. MOARS is an open-source SRS designed to be used even with the most primitive browsers of old mobile phones, though it is optimized for smarter devices, such as the iPod Touch. The framework of MOARS allows for the devolvement of specialized modules. With the peer feedback module, teachers create a survey for peer feedback. This survey will be recycled by the system so that each student can be assessed using a new version of the same survey, relieving teachers of the need to create multiple digital versions for each student. Students are able to access these surveys with even the most basic of web browsers; they could, for example, do their evaluations on their own smartphones.

When MOARS is first installed, teachers are added to the system, course titles are added and assigned to teachers, and finally, students are added and assigned to classes. Students receive their individual usernames and passwords from their teacher, and then they can use MOARS for quiz-type and survey (questionnaire) activities through the web browsers of their mobile devices.

2.2. Using the peer assessment module

Using the PA module is very straightforward. The teacher first creates a survey, with questions and responses matching the rubric that the teacher wishes to use for the PA activity. Then, the teacher opens the PA module on her MOARS system. She selects the survey, then selects which class(es) are to be assessed. Various options exist for the title of each survey (for example, should the surname be first, followed by the given name?). When the teacher is ready, the system will create an individual shortcut for each student's peer assessment survey. So, there is no need for the teacher to make more than one "master" survey. Even after the shortcuts have been assigned, the survey questions and options can be edited, should a typo or mistake be discovered.

The list of student names and corresponding shortcuts can be exported into an Excel sheet. If desired, this allows students to include their shortcut on their work. For example, a piece of writing to be assessed could contain the shortcut on its pages. A poster could include the shortcut on the poster itself. Presentations could include the shortcut in the corner of each PowerPoint slide.

The teacher has two options available concerning student access to the data, and both are controlled by "yes/no" toggle switches. One, should students be able to see the results of peer assessment after they submitted their scores? Two, should students be able to see their own peer assessment results? Some teachers may select to withhold all results until after the peer assessment session has ended. When this option is enabled, students can see their own peer assessment feedback as a series of bar charts.

From the teacher side of the Peer Assessment module, the results are available in two formats, "classroom results" and "research data". In the classroom results section, teachers see bar charts for each student, showing the distribution of ratings on each question. This data can be exported as a CSV file (which can be opened in Excel or other spreadsheet programs). Student rankings are also available.

In the research data section, the teacher can create and export data files that are compatible with MFRM software such as FACETS (Linacre, 2010). The "Facets_Rating_Specification" file and the "Facets_data" files should both be saved to the same folder. The "Facets_Rating_Specification" file contains the instructions (specifications) telling the FACETS software how to read the data file, and the "Facets_data" file contains the data. This allows teachers and researchers to perform in-depth analysis on the data that was collected.

3. Discussion

The feasibility of the PA module was demonstrated in a pilot study (Holster & Pellowe, 2011), and it is being used in ongoing research by the authors on peer assessment and learning by assessing (Holster, Lake, & Pellowe, 2014; Holster, Pellowe, Lake, & Hahn, 2013). Also, its use as a classroom tool by teachers simply interested in the teacher data, rather than research data, has been explored (see for example Brown, 2013). On the negative side, the underlying MOARS itself is not easy for non-technical people to install. The system requires an Apache web server running PHP and MySQL. Also, every rater using the system has to have a username and password, making this system impractical for ad hoc use.

4. Conclusions

The Peer Assessment module for MOARS can be used by both teachers and researchers interested in using peer assessment in the classroom. A single survey can be created and then reused for each member of even very large groups of students, each with a personalized title for the survey. Teachers have fast access to classroom data, and researchers can quickly produce files for analysis by MFRM software. MOARS and the PA module are both open source software available for free download (Pellowe, 2010).

Acknowledgements. We would like to thank Robert Chartrand at Kurume University for providing an iPod Touch classroom for early versions of MOARS to be trialled, as well as the students and faculties of our respective universities where this system has been used. We would like to thank the early users of MOARS for their comments and suggestions.

References

Brown, I. (2013). Teaching languages with mobile devices. *Paper presented at the JALT 2013 International Conference, Kobe, Japan.*

Holster, T. A., Lake, J., & Pellowe, W. (2014). Many-faceted Rasch analysis of peer-assessment as a diagnostic tool. *Paper presented at the 36th Language Testing Research Colloquium, Amsterdam, The Netherlands.*

Holster, T. A., & Pellowe, W. (2011). Using a mobile audience response system for classroom peer assessment. *Paper presented at the JALT CALL 2011 Conference, Kurume, Japan.*

Holster, T. A., Pellowe, W., Lake, J., & Hahn, A. (2013). Learning by assessing in an EFL writing class. In Q. Zhang & H. Yang (Eds), *Pacific Rim Objective Measurement Symposium (PROMS) 2012 Conference Proceedings* (pp. 93-108). Germany: Springer.

Linacre, J. M. (2010). *Facets* (Version 3.67.0) [software]. Retrieved from http://www.winsteps.com/facets.htm

Pellowe, W. (2010). *MOARS* (Version 0.8.3) [software]. Retrieved from http://moars.com

Innovative training
of oral communication: Berlin Kompass

Laura Pihkala-Posti[1]

Abstract. In a classical instructed language classroom setting, the practicing of communication situations is too often limited to producing isolated phrases and sentences without actually testing their relevance for the intended action. An example is describing and finding a route. In this paper, results of the early pilots with a collaborative virtual language learning environment, especially intended for learner-centered training of oral communication skills, called *Berlin Kompass*, are presented. It is a new kind of a holistic and gamelike approach. A multimodal, interactive communication and action environment consisting of authentic Berlin-panoramas enables experiential learning. The communication happens in an immersive context, in which acting, problem solving and description of visual surroundings are trained collaboratively and combined with embodied interaction. The pilots, with around 200 language learners in upper secondary school and at university level, have shown that the authentic situation and the inbuilt multimodal scaffolding of the *Berlin Kompass* system motivates and enables for language learners on different levels to successfully exercise their oral communication skills in the target language. Interesting examples for the remarkable variation in the ways and strategies are given of what the users made use of in order to fulfill the task to reach a tourist attraction.

Keywords: virtual panorama world, embodied interaction, holistic training of oral communication, pair collaboration.

---

1. University of Tampere, School of Language, Translation and Literary Studies; laura.pihkala-posti@uta.fi.

How to cite this article: Pihkala-Posti, L. (2014). Innovative training of oral communication: Berlin Kompass. In S. Jager, L. Bradley, E. J. Meima, & S. Thouësny (Eds), *CALL Design: Principles and Practice; Proceedings of the 2014 EUROCALL Conference, Groningen, The Netherlands* (pp. 312-317). Dublin: Research-publishing.net. doi:10.14705/rpnet.2014.000237

1. Introduction

The continual challenge in formal education is to find various ways to support different types of learners in an appropriate way in order to keep their learning motivation alive. This is very essential also in foreign language education. During my PhD project, I have been searching for new ways of applying interactive computer technology to create new kind of learning possibilities, especially for oral communication skills (cf. Pihkala-Posti, 2012; Pihkala-Posti & Uusi-Mäkelä, 2014). Describing and finding a route is a situation in which a traditionally instructed classroom approach with a map often used for pair conversations does not give an equal learning experience, as moving in a real visual environment according to the given instructions would offer. This means often isolated phrases and sentences are produced with the pair without experiencing their relevance and adequateness in action. In contrast to actual real life situations, there are no consequences even if the advice given is incorrect or misunderstood (cf. Pihkala-Posti et al., 2014). In order to see whether an interactive virtual authentic-like environment could create a new way to enhance learning, I started developing and researching this. With computer scientists of University of Tampere in an interdisciplinary research project, it was possible to further develop this idea of a virtual, authentic-like approach for training orientation in a target language environment.

In this paper, our collaborative virtual language learning environment, called *Berlin Kompass*, and interesting findings of the series of pilot studies in autumn 2013 will be presented. In the environment, two remotely located users communicate using a foreign language in the context of a wayfinding task, one providing guidance to the other. They negotiate through this virtual environment until the goal is reached. The interaction in the system is done via gestures (Kinect steering) and the physical setup of the environment consists of two separate locations, which are connected via audio and network connection to enable spoken communication. The system offers a realistic 360 degree panorama picture environment to communicate and move around in, as well as scaffolding (to the description of the system cf. Pihkala-Posti et al., 2014, Kallioniemi et al., 2014). This means that lexical and phrasal help is offered on user's request with hints in the panoramas (see Figure 1). By pointing at the hotspots (i.e. objects of interest), the user receives related supporting phrases and words both as text and as voice, produced by speech synthesis. The guide also has a map to help navigate around the city (see Figure 2). The guided users move forward by walking towards the direction in the panorama they were instructed to head for. If there are problems in the communication, they end up in a dead end and need to solve the problem in order to come further on the route. The use of different modalities aims to strengthen the learning effect and support different types of learners, especially those who learn most effectively by doing things themselves and by moving during the learning (cf. also Kallioniemi et al., 2013, 2014; Pihkala-Posti et al., 2014).

Figure 1. Interface for the guided user with an activated hotspot

Figure 2. A guide view with map

2. Research material and method

A round of evaluation studies took place in October-December 2013. 156 school pupils (from ninth graders to upper secondary students) and 36 university language center students (in total around 200 persons) took part. Both German and English versions of the application were used. The intention with piloting with different user groups was to find out in which language skill level it is meaningful and possible to use the application. The setup was as follows: two learners used the application at a time. This normally took around 15-20 minutes. The research materials from the evaluation sessions consist of audio and video recordings, observation notes, log data and feedback questionnaires (to the description of the pilots and questionnaires, cf. Pihkala-Posti et al., 2014).

After using the application, the students answered a questionnaire about the application. The survey included answers from 156 students. Over 84 % of them chose the three highest possibilities of seven on the Likert-scale regarding their satisfaction with the application. Especially interesting is that almost a half of the students (48 %) found that the use of gestures and embodied interaction improved their concentration on language use and learning. These might be the kind of learners that prefer action-oriented learning or the so called kinesthetic learning style. In the open-ended student feedback of the questionnaire, clear indications could be found with the qualitative content analysis for a successful realization of our pedagogical framework (Pihkala-Posti et al., 2014).

According to my participants' observations and the student feedback, *Berlin Kompass* system enables high freedom for the language learners on different levels to exercise their oral communication skills in the target language (see also Pihkala-Posti et al., 2014). My next step was to research this closer. In this context, interaction and conversation analytical approaches were used. I chose to make so called illustrative transcripts (*Anschauungstranskripte*, Imo, 2013, pp. 152-153) of the recorded products of the communication pairs in order to be able to show differences and equalities between the interaction and language use of different pairs.

3. Discussion of the results

Remarkable variation was found in the ways and strategies that the users made use of in carrying out the task. Some concrete examples of our research data show how different level communicators can manage the task successfully and how the interaction between these communicators varies. Interestingly, different pairs used different route and visual environment description strategies, as well as solved the dead end situations in different ways. In several cases, their problem solving reflections are made available through thinking aloud. According to my judgement, the examples give evidence for the assumption that the *Berlin Kompass* application creates an authentic-like situation and an environment that enables training of free oral communication in a new adequate way.

The embodiment realized with the Kinect-steering seems to bring added value into the situation. This means, the experience of moving according to the instructions either further along the route or ending up in a dead end strengthen the feeling of immersion and authenticity, in addition to the Berlin-panoramas. The motivation to fulfill the task kept the target language production alive regardless of the language skill level of the participants: instead of focusing on mistakes, the focus was shifted to concentrating on finding relevant ways of communication to reach the goal (cf. Pihkala-Posti et al., 2014).

4. Conclusions

In this approach, the technology is used to create a communication and an action environment as realistic as possible which creates learning situations where what is said and done matters (cf. Pihkala-Posti et al., 2014). Compared with earlier approaches, our purpose to offer a new kind of holistic, autonomous and authentic approach to learning oral communication seems to become true.

My next steps in the research project are among others to deepen the analysis of the transcriptions in order to find new interesting factors in how the users of Berlin Kompass communicate and collaborate while acting in this virtual environment. Also the video recordings and the log data that among others reveal the different strategies to use the hotspots are of interest.

Acknowledgements. I would like to thank the rest of our *Berlin Kompass* development team, the professors Markku Turunen and Roope Raisamo from *Tampere Unit for Computer Human Interaction* with the researchers Pekka Kallioniemi, Jaakko Hakulinen, Pentti Hietala, Sanna Kangas, Jussi Okkonen, Tuuli Keskinen as well as Mikael Uusi-Mäkelä from *Tampere Research Center for Information and Media*.

Thanks also go to Tekes for financing our project *Active Learning Spaces*, and finally to PhD Olli Salminen from our *School of Language, Translation and Literary Studies* for all of his support, e.g. concerning the language editing.

References

Imo, W. (2013). Sprache in Interaktion. Analysemethoden und Untersuchungsfelder. In S. Günthner, K.-P. Konerding, W.-A. Liebert, & T. Roelcke (Eds), *Linguistik – Impulse & Tendenzen* (Band 49). Berlin/ Boston: De Gruyter Mouton. doi:10.1515/9783110306323.59

Kallioniemi P., Hakulinen J., Keskinen T., Turunen, M., Heimonen, T., Pihkala-Posti L., Uusi-Mäkelä, M., Hietala, P., Okkonen, J., & Raisamo, R. (2013). Evaluating landmark attraction model in collaborative wayfinding in virtual learning environments. *MUM '13 Proceedings of the 12th International Conference on Mobile and Ubiquitous Multimedia* (Article No. 33). doi:10.1145/2541831.2541849

Kallioniemi, P., Pihkala-Posti, L., Hakulinen, J., Uusi-Mäkelä, M., Turunen, M., Hietala, P., Okkonen, J., Kangas, S., & Raisamo, R. (2014). The Berlin Kompass language learning environment. In *Proceedings of World Conference on Educational Multimedia, Hypermedia and Telecommunications 2014* (pp. 1240-1245). Chesapeake, VA: AACE.

Pihkala-Posti, L. (2012). Mit Internet und sozialen Medien Deutsch lernen. Motivationssteigerung durch "diginative" Lernwege. *GFL 2-3*/2012 (Themenschwerpunkt: Innovative Wege des Deutschlernens) (pp. 114-137). Retrieved from http://www.gfl-journal.de/2-2012/Pihkala-Posti.pdf

Pihkala-Posti, L., & Uusi-Mäkelä, M. (2014). Kielenopetuksen tilat muutoksessa [Language teaching spaces in transition]. In E. Yli-Panula, H. Silfverberg, & E. Kouki (Eds), *Ainedidaktisia tutkimuksia 7. Opettaminen valinkauhassa. Ainedidaktinen symposiumi Turussa 15.3.2013*. Turku: Suomen ainedidaktinen tutkimusseura. Retrieved from https://helda.helsinki.fi/handle/10138/42530

Pihkala-Posti, L., Kallioniemi, P., Uusi-Mäkelä, M., Hietala, P., Hakulinen, J., Turunen, M., Okkonen, J., Kangas, S., Raisamo, R., & Keskinen, T. (2014). Collaborative learner autonomy and immersion in embodied virtual language learning environment. In *Proceedings of World Conference on Educational Multimedia, Hypermedia and Telecommunications 2014* (pp. 1313-1322). Chesapeake, VA: AACE.

Getting off the straight and narrow: Exploiting non-linear, interactive narrative structures in digital stories for language teaching

Andrew Prosser[1]

Abstract. Digital storytelling is already used extensively in language education. Web documentaries, particularly in terms of design and narrative structure, provide an extension of the digital storytelling concept, specifically in terms of increased interactivity. Using a model of interactive, non-linear storytelling, originally derived from computer game design, this presentation aims to illustrate how digital stories may be developed into more interactive experiences for learners. This paper will show an example of teacher-created digital story, which allows learners to choose and follow their own individualized paths through the story. Interactivity often means a more engaging, personalized experience for the user, but in terms of educational, instructional design, it also means such stories may become more adaptable to the specific needs, interests and abilities of the individual language learner. Ultimately, interactive narrative models can be used to create, it could be argued, more constructivist, active learning environments. Alongside, the potential benefits of such narrative designs in educational contexts, however, possible drawbacks in their use need to be addressed. Specifically, to what degree interactivity is actually exploited by a user, and to what degree interactive stories may actually increase the cognitive load a learner experiences, ultimately having a negative impact on their learning.

Keywords: web documentaries, interactive narratives, digital stories.

---

1. Hankuk University of Foreign Studies, Seoul, South Korea; prosserandrew@hotmail.com.

How to cite this article: Prosser, A. (2014). Getting off the straight and narrow: Exploiting non-linear, interactive narrative structures in digital stories for language teaching. In S. Jager, L. Bradley, E. J. Meima, & S. Thouësny (Eds), *CALL Design: Principles and Practice*; Proceedings of the 2014 EUROCALL Conference, Groningen, The Netherlands (pp. 318-323). Dublin: Research-publishing.net. doi:10.14705/rpnet.2014.000238

1. Introduction

The growth and development of the web documentary is perhaps a result of the greater levels of interactivity it affords compared to more traditional forms of the genre. Such interactivity is in part achieved through the application of a variety of multimedia tools, such as video, audio, animation, graphics, and infographics, in the creation of these media. However, the interactive heart of the web documentary is most fully located in the distinctive, non-linear forms of narrative design that such documentaries often employ. Web documentaries may, for example, allow a user to choose particular routes through the story's architecture, or allow them to step to one side at particular moments in an otherwise linear narrative to investigate or learn more about a particular theme in the story, for example.

The link between the kinds of interactivity that multimedia can afford and effective pedagogy has been noted by Kennedy and McNaught (1997). Instructional design models for creating materials for learning which are sourced in a more constructivist model of knowledge development would situate the learner, their existing knowledge and mental models at the centre of their learning. The requirement of the multimedia courseware designer, from this pedagogical viewpoint, is in designing an adaptive, individualized learning environment which seeks to engage the student at their level of comprehension, and in which they may develop a personal perspective on content, while generating their own representations and hypotheses about content and language on their own terms (Kennedy & McNaught, 1997). The clear role that non-linear, interactive narrative design, in the form of digital stories or web documentaries, may play in delivering such an individualized, non-linear learning environment is immediately clear.

2. Interactive narrative design

2.1. Interactive narratives

The debt that web documentary narrative design owes to online gaming is noted by Maurin (2011). In an online course on game design, Schreiber (2009) provides a useful summary of available interactive narrative structures (Appendix 1), which, as Maurin (2011) shows, are also used extensively by web documentary makers. Each narrative type has its advantages and disadvantages, related, for example, to potential information overload, or design time and costs. However, each structure displays a relative level of interactivity, in which the user can, to different extents, shape content and decide the next stage in the development of the narrative.

2.2. A trip to Kyoto

This paper demonstrates an example of a 15- minute interactive digital story called 'A Trip to Kyoto'. The central story is on the theme of the value of travelling to a tourist destination out of season. The story is designed for use by advanced learners of English, largely because of lexical and grammatical complexity. As an interactive narrative model, the story uses a 'Fishbone' structure (Appendix 1). This structure was chosen because it tends to avoid issues of potential loss of storyline coherence, which is a possibility with more complex interactive narrative forms. There are losses, however, relatively speaking, in terms of the level of interactivity the story can offer. The software used to make the basic digital story was 'iMovie', while the software used to create the interactive story as a whole was 'Klynt', which has been created specifically for developing interactive digital stories.

2.3. A trip to Kyoto: specific features

The story is divided into six 'chapters' which are linear when played from start to finish; however, via the index feature of the software, the learner can listen to the chapters out of order. There is also information on the index informing the user which chapters they have already seen. Each chapter gives the learner the choice, via on-screen interactive buttons, to access help in understanding the voiceover, should they require it. Specifically, the learner can open a glossary of potential problem words contained in the voiceover of that chapter, and also read the script of the voiceover. Moreover, the learner can access a listening quiz for each chapter in the form of a 'Hot Potatoes' activity in order to check their comprehension of the voiceover. Each chapter also offers the user the chance to access a 'language tip', isolating an element of the voiceover for grammatical analysis and explication. This is done not only to help the learner understand that element of the voiceover, but these features are also designed to encourage the learner to reconsider their existing understanding of particular grammar points, as well as think about and develop their own productive language use. Thus, for example, a learner's attention is drawn to slightly more complex examples of conditional structures featured in the voiceover. In addition, the user is able at the end of each 'chapter' to open sequences containing further cultural content which may address conceptual difficulties related to intercultural difference, or else give background information on cultural themes in the voiceover. Help features are offered in two different ways, textually, but also with video. Each interactive button is colour-coded in terms of the kind of information or activity (e.g. grammatical information, quiz, etc.) it offers, with a 'key' tutorial provided at the start of the story.

2.4. A trip to Kyoto: interactive narratives and pedagogical effectiveness

By employing an interactive narrative design, the digital story, 'A Trip to Kyoto', potentially offers, then, a learning environment in which the user/learner may move through the material in a relatively autonomous manner, based on the choices they make about what extra material or support to access. This structure also makes the content adaptable to the level of comprehension of the language learner: glossaries can be consulted, a script can be opened, and information on language and culture can be viewed, if the user requires it.

Furthermore, such a narrative design affords the user the ability to pause within the flow of the story, in order to investigate grammatical points or cultural themes contained therein, accessing material which may be designed to challenge existing conceptual models the learner may have. As Maurin (2011) shows, however, in a brief summary of the disadvantages of the various interactive narrative models, a story based on the 'Fishbone' design, which this digital story employs, faces the question of how much the extra material provided is either useful, or actually viewed by the user.

Moreover, a concern with interactive digital stories generally is whether additional material can contribute to cognitive overload, which may negatively affect the immersive quality of the experience, affecting the users' concentration and even their willingness to complete the story.

Two research questions are suggested: 1) to what degree do users access material or complete activities while viewing the interactive digital story used in this project, and 2) does such material actually negatively affect the user in terms of cognitive load, and thus their ability to comprehend the story?

3. Method

Having identified these two research questions, at the time of writing, small scale research is being carried out to provide relevant data. In a small series of studies, a language student is provided with access to the story via a website[2] to which the digital story had been uploaded. While the learner views the story, their on-screen behavior is recorded using screen capture software. The video is then viewed by the researcher, and the number of times additional information is accessed, what

---

2. http://clockworkstar.com/kyoto/index.html#Home

kind of information, whether activities are opened and completed, is recorded. Moreover, a post-task questionnaire is administered to the user to gather their subjective opinions on the usefulness of the additional material, its potential for distraction, and whether they feel the interactivity of the story lead to a greater sense of control and autonomy in the user.

4. Discussion

Data so far suggests that learners may need more than one view of a story in order to more fully avail themselves of help features and extra informational content. Indeed, a user may access these features as much as five times as often on a second viewing, compared to a first viewing. Moreover, support for listening, according to results so far, tends to be called upon a great deal more than either grammatical or cultural information. Finally, data gathered from the post-task questionnaire to date suggests a learner does not feel cognitively over-burdened with information, and this may be linked to positive views, again as reported in the questionnaire, on how far the user feels in control of their navigation of the story/program, linked to its interactive design.

5. Conclusions

Interactive digital stories are still relatively new, and just as interactive narrative design is still in the process of definition, as Maurin (2012) points out, so are the habits of the user. Introducing such media into language learning brings its own particular benefits, but also concerns. While interactive media may afford more student-centered, autonomous and even constructive learning environments, continued research needs to be done as to how much a learner/user does or is even able to afford themselves of these opportunities. With an interactive digital story, one cannot assume all users are at the same level of interactive literacy, or able to deal with the additional cognitive load it can bring.

References

Kennedy, D., & McNaught, C. (1997). Design elements in interactive multimedia. *Australian Journal of Educational Technology, 13*(1), 1-22. Retrieved from http://ascilite.org.au/ajet/ajet13/kennedy.html
Maurin, F. (2011). Freedom and engagement in interactive narratives. *The Pixel Hunt*. Retrieved from: http://florentmaurin.com/?p=174
Maurin, F. (2012). How to help your audience go with the flow. *The Pixel Hunt*. Retrieved from http://florentmaurin.com/?p=316

Schreiber, I. (2009). *Game design concepts: An experiment in game design concepts* [web blog]. Retrieved from: http://gamedesignconcepts.wordpress.com

Appendix 1. Interactive narrative structures (Schreiber, 2009[3])

Concentric Narrative: The user is given a central 'hub', such as a menu or map, and moves out to different parts of the story, often returning to the 'hub' after each 'turn'. Larger elements may be sub-divided.	
Fishbone Narrative: A linear story is provided, but at certain points a digression is offered the user, such as a sub-story or bonus material. The user returns to the main storyline once they have viewed the extra material.	
Branching Narrative: At certain points of the story, the user is offered a choice about what to do or see next. Multiple possible story endings are possible.	
Parallel Narrative: A simplified version of a branching narrative. Users have a number of possible paths, but all users must visit certain 'nodes', retaining the coherence of the central story.	
Dynamic Object-Orientated Narrative: A series of mini-stories, with multiple exit and entry points. 'Chapters' need not be read in strict order, but can be ordered by the user.	

---

3. Published under a CC-BY licence, retrieved from http://gamedesignconcepts.wordpress.com/2009/07/

The *7 Keys of the Dragon*: An e-learning game-like environment for Albanian and Russian

Anthi Revithiadou[1], Vasilia Kourtis-Kazoullis[2],
Maria Soukalopoulou[3], Konstantinos Konstantoudakis[4],
Christos Zarras[5], and Nestoras Pelesoglou[6]

Abstract. In this article we report on the development of an interactive open source extensible software, dubbed *The 7 Keys of the Dragon*, for the teaching/learning of Albanian and Russian to students (9-12 years old) with the respective languages as their heritage languages. Based on the assumption that games in language learning are associated with intrinsic motivation and meaningful exposure to the target language, the environment is set on the basis of a fictional storyline in which the wizard of a village is captured by a dragon. The user needs to go through certain learning tasks in order to collect enough points that would allow him/her to set the wizard free. A variety of scaffolding materials (synchronized audio texts, translations, glossaries), quiz types and in-class or at home activities accompany each of the ten texts that comprise the current version of the environment. The software is designed to provide real-time correction of all quizzes. A separate application for teachers facilitates essay correction and commenting on the students' language learning progress and achievements. The e-learning environment builds on *constructivist* and *transformative pedagogy*.

Keywords: online language learning, heritage languages, Russian, Albanian.

---

1. Aristotle University of Thessaloniki/AUTh; revith@lit.auth.gr.
2. University of the Aegean; kazoullis@rhodes.aegean.gr.
3. Aristotle University of Thessaloniki/AUTh; mariasoukalopoulou@hotmail.com.
4. Aristotle University of Thessaloniki/AUTh; kkonstant@ee.auth.gr.
5. Aristotle University of Thessaloniki/AUTh; chzarras@auth.gr.
6. No affiliation; nightbreedcreative@gmail.com.

How to cite this article: Revithiadou, A., Kourtis-Kazoullis, V., Soukalopoulou, M., Konstantoudakis, K., Zarras, C., & Pelesoglou, N. (2014). The 7 Keys of the Dragon: An e-learning game-like environment for Albanian and Russian. In S. Jager, L. Bradley, E. J. Meima, & S. Thouësny (Eds), *CALL Design: Principles and Practice; Proceedings of the 2014 EUROCALL Conference, Groningen, The Netherlands* (pp. 324-328). Dublin: Research-publishing.net. doi: 10.14705/rpnet.2014.000239

1. Introduction

The program 'Education of immigrant and repatriate students', funded by the National Strategic Reference Framework (NSRF) 2007-2014 and Greek national resources, is directed to improve the education of students of immigrant or repatriate background and to lower school failure/dropout rates by giving them equal learning opportunities.

A particular action, Action 5, aims at the reinforcement of the mother tongues (or heritage languages) of such students. Therefore, mother tongue language classes for Albanian and Russian were organized in several schools as part of a pilot program (2011-2013). For this purpose, a team of linguists, education and bilingualism specialists and Albanian/Russian-speaking writers-editors of educational materials designed and constructed language learning materials in the form of textbooks and grammars while also producing a game-like e-learning environment, dubbed the *7 Keys of the Dragon* (henceforth 7Keys), to supplement the materials created for the language classes.

2. Method

2.1. Pedagogical orientation and language proficiency

Web-based language learning environments today are based on a combination of pedagogical orientations (e.g. Skourtou, Kourtis-Kazoullis, & Cummins, 2006), but mainly focus on socio-cognitive (Spantidakis, 2012) and social-constructivist orientations, in contrast to environments in the past that focused mainly on behaviorist pedagogy. The 7Keys is mainly based on *constructivist pedagogy*, as ICT is used to encourage students to actively construct meanings and become cognitively engaged in challenging activities. However, *transformative pedagogy* is also employed in this ICT environment, as collaborative critical inquiry is used to motivate students to analyze and understand the social realities of their own lives and communities (Cummins, 2000; Cummins, Brown, & Sayers, 2007). Scaffolding is provided in order to support students in learning the target language. Motivation is central in both the design of the activities and the setting of the environment.

The 7Keys mostly focuses on academic language proficiency (e.g. knowledge of less frequent vocabulary, ability to interpret/produce complex written language) since in immigrant situations, conversational fluency is often more developed due to the use of language at home or in the community.

2.2. Language learning methodology

Since the focus is on academic language proficiency, the design of the 7Keys is mainly based on Cummins's (2000) framework for the development of academic expertise. According to this framework, the environment creates an interpersonal space for maximum cognitive engagement and identity investment and has three foci: focus on language, focus on meaning and focus on use. Activities that focus on language are designed to cultivate an awareness and critical analysis of language forms and uses. Activities of this sort help students understand the similarities/differences between Greek and Albanian/Russian. Activities that focus on meaning are geared to making input comprehensible and to developing critical literacy. Activities that focus on use are designed so as to allow students to use language in creative ways.

3. Discussion

Users of the 7Keys are divided into three distinct tiers: student, teacher, and administrator. Following the class/school structure that the 7Keys was designed to supplement, each student is assigned to a teacher, and all teachers of the same language are supervised by the administrator in a pyramid-like structure.

The educational material is also organized in a pyramid-like structure; after login, students can select a text. They may then read the text, read the Greek translation, browse a dictionary of selected words or listen to a native speaker read the text out loud, with an option of highlighting the text in sync with the narration or hide it entirely. The student may also have the narration move to a specific point in the text by clicking on it.

The next step is to move on to the quizzes. There are ten types of quizzes, each consisting of a variable number of questions: true or false, fill in the blanks, fill in the table, multiple choice, sorting, pairing, listening, essays, and crosswords, plus the non-graded activity type. Each quiz is assigned to one of three difficulty levels and to one of three different foci: language, meaning, or use of language. Quizzes are laid out dynamically, with an option to view the quiz on either half or full screen. Full screen provides a more comfortable view, while half screen view enables the student to see the text, translation or dictionary in the other half.

All gradable quizzes except essays are graded automatically by the program upon submission. Essay grading requires the teacher, and upon submission, a notification is sent to the teacher's account, flagging the essay as ungraded.

The 7Keys is set up as a game-like environment on the basis of a fantasy storyline: the dragon has captured the wizard, and the students can only help free him if they earn enough points by completing quizzes. The program's graphics are designed to match the fantasy premise and are supplemented by music, sound effects, two animated videos and two cartoon-like characters that provide help to the student. The dragon provides help with navigation through the program and the wizard's young apprentice helps the students with the quizzes, pointing to specific chapters of the accompanying grammar theory document.

Completing the game-like atmosphere and providing extra motivation, the students can earn badges for specific achievements (e.g. scoring perfect in a multiple choice quiz) and can track their own performance through their profile.

The 7Keys e-learning environment consists of five distinct units: (1) the student, (2) the teacher, (3) the administrator clients, each providing appropriate functionality to each user type, (4) the database, in which all data is stored, including user data and educational data, and (5) the server, which facilitates communication between the clients and the database.

New texts and quizzes can be added over time using the administrator application which also provides an environment for user management. All data, including user information, learning material and user answers to quizzes, is stored in and retrieved from an online database. An embedded updater automatically downloads the latest version of the application, ensuring all users are always up to date.

The clients and server were developed using JavaFX 2, with the server being deployed using Glassfish, while the database was built with MySQL.

4. Conclusions

Given that all data is drawn from the database, the most welcome feature of the 7Keys is its open-ended expandability: new quizzes, texts, and narrations can be easily added and modified using the administrator application, and the inclusion of more languages will require only very little programming work.

Acknowledgements. We would like to thank Amalia Rodou-Gorou and Tania Zouravliova for constructing the language material, and Giannis Spantidakis for his guidance in the pedagogical design of the e-learning environment. This research was supported by the program 'Education of immigrant and repatriate students' (Scientific Director: Prof.dr. A. Anastassiadis, http://www.diapolis.

auth.gr/), funded by the European Social Fund, National Strategic Reference Framework (NSRF) 2007-2014, the Ministry of Education, and Lifelong Learning and Religious Affairs of the Hellenic Republic. The usual disclaimers apply.

References

Cummins, J. (2000). *Language, power and pedagogy: Bilingual children in the crossfire*. Clevedon: Multilingual Matters.

Cummins, J., Brown, K., & Sayers, D. (2007). *Literacy, technology and diversity: Teaching for success in changing times*. New York: Pearson.

Skourtou, E., Kourtis-Kazoullis, V., & Cummins, J. (2006). Designing virtual learning environments for academic language development. In J. Weiss, J. Nolan, J. Hunsinger, & P. Trifonas (Eds), *International handbook of virtual learning environments* (pp. 441-468). Dordrecht, The Netherlands: Springer. doi:10.1007/978-1-4020-3803-7_18

Spantidakis, G. (2012). *Socio-cognitive multimedia environments for learning and production of written language* [in Greek]. Athens: Gutenberg.

Mobile purposive-extensive-podcast-listening versus mobile self-regulated-podcast-development: A critical framework for designing foreign language listening

Serkan Şendağ[1], Mustafa Caner[2], and Hüseyin Kafes[3]

Abstract. Nowadays mobile technologies are widely employed in almost all fields of education for varying reasons. The present study intends to explore the role of mobile technologies in the development of students' listening skills in a higher education context. The aim of the present study is twofold; while it seeks for the feasibility of mobile technologies in listening activities of higher education students, it will also try to propose solutions to a rather neglected side of teaching listening within the frame of foreign/second language education. Although there are several studies on listening skills in foreign/second language teaching, almost none of them clearly or scientifically deal with the elaboration of the listening activities (i.e. conditions describing listening skills). Thus, using mobile technologies, the present study will also try to find an evidence-based answer to this issue. However, since this presentation is part of an ongoing study, supported by The Scientific and Technological Research Council of Turkey (TUBITAK), we will just propose two critical frameworks for its methodology, introduce the proposed framework for integration of the mobile technology and welcome the contributions of the scholars about its function in the field of language education.

Keywords: second language learning, higher education, mobile assisted language learning, call design, emerging technologies.

---

1. Akdeniz University, Department of Computer Education & Instructional Technologies; serkansendag@akdeniz.edu.tr.
2. Akdeniz University, Department of Foreign Language Education; mcaner@akdeniz.edu.tr.
3. Akdeniz University, Department of Foreign Language Education; hkafes@ akdeniz.edu.tr.

How to cite this article: Şendağ, S., Caner, M., & Kafes, H. (2014). Mobile purposive-extensive-podcast-listening versus mobile self-regulated-podcast-development: A critical framework for designing foreign language listening. In S. Jager, L. Bradley, E. J. Meima, & S. Thouësny (Eds), *CALL Design: Principles and Practice*; Proceedings of the 2014 EUROCALL Conference, Groningen, The Netherlands (pp. 329-333). Dublin: Research-publishing.net. doi:10.14705/rpnet.2014.000240

1. Introduction

Today, there are several factors that urge learners to engage in mobile learning activities in any ways, such as learning at the work place, need for lifelong learning, ease of use, and accessibility. As in many fields, suitability of mobile devices for foreign language learning attracts researchers' attention to explore new venues for both design and practice. Thus, we developed two methodological frameworks to deliver mobile assisted foreign language learning.

2. Method

2.1. Design

Critical frameworks offered in this study are a result of a comprehensive literature review on foreign language learning approaches/methods and on learning with podcasting and mobile environments. Afterwards, we will briefly provide the theory and rationale behind the proposed frameworks.

2.2. Mobile-purposive-extensive-podcast-listening

There is a good deal of evidence in the literature that reveals the positive contribution of intensive listening activities both on listening comprehension and speaking skills of the language learners (Gradman & Hanania, 1991). Nevertheless, almost none of the studies in the available literature highlight the relationship between listening comprehension and attentive and controlled listening activities that focus on learning outcomes. In this respect, Tolman's (1932) purposive learning concept is worth mentioning here; purposive learning requires learners to set up the learning process by being familiar with the learning outcomes that will be gained at the end of the learning process (Senemoğlu, 2012). If the learners know that they will have a purpose throughout the narrowed, context-driven, and repetitive listening activities, they may focus on the learning content, and thus, as Schunk (2012) states, have a higher motivation towards learning and fostering their eagerness to learn. In turn, this will cause a shortening in the listening duration of narrowed, context-driven, and repetitive listening activities and lead to a better comprehension in listening, as Krashen (1996) suggested in "narrow listening"; that is, if the listeners listen to a specific passage several times, they might gain a more comprehensible language input.

During the mobile-purposive-extensive-podcast-listening process proposed in this study, the participants' attention to the listening text they were listening to necessitates an active employment of metacognition (Fernandez-Duque, Baird, & Posner, 2000). This enables an active use of attention and will result in better quality listening activities that ensure second/foreign language input processing.

Another concept related to mobile-purposive-extensive-podcast-listening is the learning environment. The learning environment consists of the media that deliver learning materials and items that support the actual learning content. Therefore, it has been concluded that the integration of mobile-purposive-extensive-podcast-listening method should be facilitated with an appropriate medium and learning environment. With this in mind, provision of technology enhanced learning environments have been suggested (TELEs) (Wang & Hannafin, 2005). Concisely, the purpose of the proposed method is provision of a more mobile and individualized learning support.

2.3. Mobile-self-regulated-podcast-development

This method is set up concerning three basic approaches; a) free listening, b) intensive listening, and c) design-based learning environments.

Although Dupuy (1999) assumes that listening to audio records performed by high proficient speakers in leisure times is effective in the development of skills in second language learning, she did not define the qualification of leisure time. For example, the time while driving a car, reading a book or even the time spent while sleeping can be considered as a leisure time, and listening can be performed in such times as well. However, different from mobile-purposive-extensive-podcast-listening, i.e. highlighting the initiative of the listener, this method basically offers a listening technique which allows the listeners to listen to the passage as much as possible at any time and anywhere without focusing on the accompanying listening material. Thus, the proposed listening method puts forward a perspective which goes hand in hand with constructivist learning theory and hypothesizes that learning occurs as a result of individualized experiences, autonomous learning and self-regulated learning that emphasizes individualized experiences in learning (Zimmerman, 1990).

In the process of creating design-based learning environments followed by extensive listening processes, learners are expected to make some linguistic productions. In this context, students are required to publish and evaluate their own podcasts which are developed in the target language. As this approach provides an authentic application where both learners and teachers interact with each other, it enables learners to learn through experience (such as creating their own original podcasts). This can be considered as the reflection of a constructivist theory and interactionist language learning approach. There are various forms of interaction in learning processes. As Cook (1981) claims, interaction is the obvious point about any form of learning in that it consists of an interaction between the learner and the environment. Similarly, according to Krashen's (1985) input hypothesis, language acquisition takes place during human interaction in the target language environment. The learner is then exposed to rich comprehensible input in the target language. The interactionists believe that language emerges from the interplay between learners' linguistic and cognitive capacities and their social language environment. In this approach, meaning and correctness are negotiated by the learner through interactions. According to this approach, if a learner spends a limited amount of time in the language environment, acquisition will be limited. Very briefly, it is claimed that interaction can enhance second language acquisition and fluency.

3. Discussion and conclusions

The focus of the present study is to contribute to the development of the learners' second/foreign language learning skills in higher education through organizing their listening activities. Two complementary methodological frameworks that were based on the use of mobile technologies are offered in the present study.

Of these methodological frameworks, while mobile-purposive–extensive-podcast-listening requires participants to focus on listening material and do narrowed and learning-guide-supported extensive listening, mobile-self-regulated-podcast-development method proposed a framework which requires participants to produce podcasts in the target language immediately after doing extensive listening activities without focusing on any point in their free time. It is supposed that the two proposed frameworks might have an effect on the individualization of mobile based second/foreign language learning processes. However, more empirical studies need to be conducted in order to examine the level of the effectiveness and feasibility of the proposed frameworks. Additionally, it is anticipated that the proposed methods that keep track of listeners digitally (electronically) will help us a) model listening behaviors with an ontological approach and b) contribute to the development of adaptive hypermedia for foreign language learning as well as expert systems that will individualize language learning. In particular, it is supposed that the mobile-self-regulated-podcast-development method, which can be used in studies examining such purposes, might have a specific structure that will help figure out learner models with reference to their leisure time listening habits and skills on production in the target language.

Mobile based second/foreign language learning alternatives will empower the individualization of the learning process and contribute to the spread of the autonomous learning strategies and systems. Therefore, it is assumed that there will be a tendency towards conducting similar studies in the field. Especially, it is supposed that the approaches that we proposed within the scope of the present study will be effectively used in the adaptation of the teaching and learning strategies.

Acknowledgements. The study reported in this article is based on a project being funded by the Scientific and Technological Research Council of Turkey (TUBITAK).

References

Cook, V. (1981). Second language acquisition from an interactionist perspective. *International Studies Bulletin, 6*(1), 93-111.

Dupuy, B. C. (1999). Narrow listening: An alternative way to develop and enhance listening comprehension in students of French as a foreign language. *System, 27*(3), 351-361. doi:10.1016/S0346-251X(99)00030-5

Fernandez-Duque, D., Baird, J. A., & Posner, M. I. (2000). Executive attention and metacognitive regulation. *Consciousness and Cognition, 9*(2), 288-307. doi:10.1006/ccog.2000.0447

Gradman, H. L., Hanania, E. (1991). Language learning background factors and ESL proficiency. *The Modern Language Journal, 75*(1), 39-51. doi:10.1111/j.1540-4781.1991.tb01081.x

Krashen, S. D. (1985). *The input hypothesis: Issues and implications*. London: Longman.

Krashen, S. D. (1996). The case for narrow listening. *System, 24*(1), 97-100. doi:10.1016/0346-251X(95)00054-N

Schunk, D. H. (2012). *Learning theories an educational perspective* (6th ed.). Boston, MA: Pearson.

Senemoğlu, N. (2012). *Gelişim Öğrenme ve Öğretim* [Development Learning and Instruction]. Ankara: Pegem Akademi.

Tolman, E. C. (1932). Purposive behavior in animals and men. London: Cambridge University Press.

Wang, F., & Hannafin, M. J. (2005). Design-based research and technology-enhanced learning environments. *Educational Technology Research and Development, 53*(4), 5-23. doi:10.1007/BF02504682

Zimmerman, B. J. (1990). Self-regulated learning and academic achievement: An overview. *Educational Psychologist, 25*(1), 3-17. doi:10.1207/s15326985ep2501_2

Learning by doing: A city trip combining TBLLT, blended learning and social media

Leen Stevens[1] and Viviane Grisez[2]

Abstract. For several years, the University of MONS (UMONS) has been organising a trip to a Flemish city, either Leuven, Ghent, or Antwerp, for the students on the Masters programmes at the Faculty of Engineering who attend Dutch courses. This project has been combining blended learning and task-based learning for several years, but for the most recent edition (March 2014), a new aspect was added, namely the incorporation of mobile web devices and social media. This new approach was warmly welcomed by the students. The trip became a more personal, more lively and more authentic experience. Moving away from the traditional pen and paper based learning reduced the "school experience" and raised the students' awareness of social presence (Kehrwald, 2008). This led to much more spontaneous language production during face-to-face interactions with locals and real-time computer-mediated conversations. It also encouraged some competition and led to spontaneous input from the students, and created a new kind of supervision for the teachers. In this paper, the principles which were taken into account to develop the project, as well as the different phases of the project, are presented. This first experience with social media was a successful experiment that should now be integrated in a broader context so it can be used for other language programmes or projects.

Keywords: TBLLT, blended learning, social media, language learning.

---

1. Centre for Modern Languages, UMONS; Leen.Stevens@umons.ac.be.
2. Centre for Modern Languages, UMONS; Viviane.Grisez@umons.ac.be.

How to cite this article: Stevens, L., & Grisez, V. (2014). Learning by doing: A city trip combining TBLLT, blended learning and social media. In S. Jager, L. Bradley, E. J. Meima, & S. Thouësny (Eds), *CALL Design: Principles and Practice*; Proceedings of the 2014 EUROCALL Conference, Groningen, The Netherlands (pp. 334-339). Dublin: Research-publishing.net. doi:10.14705/rpnet.2014.000241

1. Introduction

UMONS, a Francophone Belgian university, organises a yearly trip to a Flemish city, which is considered to be a learning-by-doing activity in the framework of the Dutch Master's classes for students from the Faculty of Engineering.

For several years the trip has been based on two modern language learning approaches, namely the task-based language learning and teaching (TBLLT) (Ellis, 2005) and blended learning approaches. TBLLT enables students to learn by undertaking concrete action.

In the language activity, which has been carried out over the past ten years, students have to organise the city trip themselves. In order to organise this trip, they took the six task types formulated by Edwards and Willis (2005) and Willis and Willis (2006) to a higher level as their trip to Leuven was not a simulation. It is a very concrete, authentic project in which each individual participant plays a role. The tasks given are as follows: listing and brainstorming, ordering and sorting, matching, comparing, thinking and problem solving, stimulating more interaction, and the most complex task, sharing personal experiences and story-telling. The teacher acts only as a supervisor. The students have to find solutions themselves by looking up information and expressing their opinions (Prabhu, 1987). The project also makes use of blended learning: it combines individual e-learning exercises with face-to-face classroom conversational activities and computer-mediated instruction in the language lab.

The most recent edition of the city trip (Leuven, March 2014) added a new component: the use of social media and the opportunity to have an online exchange of information in real-time. Social media is very present in our lives, young people's lives in particular, and this offers a great opportunity for language teachers as they can move away from pen and paper to create more lively and more authentic tasks which can lead to more involved and more enthusiastic students (Kern & Warschauer, 2000).

This paper shows the impact of social media on the students who participated in their self-organised city trip.

2. Method

The project consisted of three stages: the pre-task, the task and the review (Ellis, 2005; Willis, 1996).

2.1. The pre-task

The project was launched in the classroom by solving the unit "visiting a city" on the online learning platform www.franel.eu. FRANEL is the outcome of a collaboration between three academic partners in neighbouring regions: UMONS in Wallonia, KULAK, KU Leuven in Flanders, and Université Charles de Gaulle Lille 3 in Lille, France. The website consists of several themes for learners of French or Dutch at A2-level (CEFR). Each of these themes offers the learner a series of exercises based on video clips. During this pre-task, the students revised the lexicon concerning "giving and asking directions" and "taking public transport". They also discovered the city and they formulated their expectations and opinions.

2.2. The task

The task consisted of two parts: the preparation of the trip at the home university and the city trip itself.

2.2.1. Preparation

In this preparatory stage, the students worked in small groups in the language lab. Each group had to gather as much information as possible on Dutch websites on the following topics: city history and architecture, tourism, transport, lunch, meetings at the city's university, and day schedule and programme, to name but a few. Afterwards, they had to present their findings to each other, find compromises and make their preparations, i.e. send the necessary e-mails, make reservations and order tickets.

2.2.2. City trip

The most important objective of the city trip was face-to-face communication with locals. In order to motivate the students to speak Dutch, they had to gather information at the market. They worked together in small groups. In 2013, it was noted that the students were not really competitive and that the groups collaborated by exchanging their answers. To avoid this, the teachers created three different routes through the city for the most recent trip that took place in March 2014. Each group could meet the other groups but exchanging information would have been absolutely useless. Moreover, each group was provided with online tasks and had access to a blog on which there were ten common questions. These questions were not included in their search but it was an extra challenge based on current events in the city (Leuven). The students could only solve these extra questions by talking to locals and to students. A page was also created on Facebook on which the students had to share their experiences by posting pictures (selfies and others) and self-made clips, and where they could react to each other's written comments. To make sure they would be active on Facebook, this activity was part of their task. The students were learning Dutch the whole day, applying blended learning and learning-by-doing principles without even being aware of the learning process.

2.3. Review

The week following the trip, the students had to tell each other how they had found Leuven. Each group had different things to share as they had had different questions to answer in Leuven. The students also had to correct each other's writing on Facebook, which gave them another opportunity to revise their Dutch grammar.

3. Evaluation of the city trip in combination with real-time computer-mediated communication

On the whole, it must be said that Facebook had an added value to the trip to Leuven. The intention was to make the passive students more active and more interactive. This goal was certainly achieved: all of the students were surprised by the innovating aspect that Facebook created and they were immediately drawn into the project. The online activity made the trip more authentic for them because they did not associate this modern networking tool with their studies, only with their friends.

The impact of the awareness of social presence was also seen, online as well as offline. The different groups felt connected because of the page on Facebook. They had contact with each other and also with their friends who were not even part of the Dutch class. This was extra stimulation for them to post photos and comments on Facebook, even if it was not a part of their project. They even made jokes in Dutch and posted photos of their "new Flemish friends".

Furthermore, this new medium allowed the teachers to supervise their students constantly from a distance, in such a way that the students were not aware of it. They felt as if they had the freedom to discover the city, without any supervision. In reality, they provided real time evidence of how they were organising themselves and how they were interacting with the local population.

When asked how this trip could be improved, they suggested to turn this one day-trip into a weekend as it takes some time to answer all the questions. One group completed the task, but they had not had enough time to meet the locals. The groups that had taken time to interact with the locals had not been able to finish their search. All the groups were involved in the project and they had even forgotten about the extra blog with the ten questions.

The combination of face-to-face conversations and real-time online activity was warmly welcomed by the students. Now, the next step is to implement the use of the new social media in a larger context. For this approach to be more than a one-off experience it must be extended and turned into a full mixed pedagogy. That way it can be adapted easily for other language courses or for other projects. Facebook was chosen for this project because of the students' familiarity with the network, but other social networks (Twitter, Instagram, etc.) also offer new possibilities.

4. Conclusion

This paper has shown how a trip in the context of a language course, based on task-based learning and blended learning, turned into an authentic, interactive city trip by incorporating new social media. The city trip demonstrated how the awareness of a social presence and online interactivity reduced the "school experience" so that the passive students became really enthusiastic about doing the required tasks. This positive first experience with real-time online communication must inspire the modernisation of traditional language courses and help teachers to turn away from "simulations" within the confines of the classroom. New media (tablets, phones, computers, etc.), in combination with the internet and the students' familiarity with social networks, provides the means to interact with the world and apply even more authentic learning-by-doing and blended learning principles. The next challenge is to develop standard exercises, based on real computer-mediated communication, that can be easily applied for any language course and for several types of projects. A further challenge is to systemise the use of social media in language courses.

References

Edwards, C., & Willis, J. (2005). *Teachers exploring tasks in English language teaching*. Basingstoke: Palgrave Macmillan.
Ellis, R. (2005). Instructed language learning and task-based teaching. In E. Hinkel (Ed.), *Handbook of research in second language teaching and learning* (pp. 713–728). Mahwah, NJ: Erlbaum.

Kehrwald, B. (2008). Understanding social presence in text-based online learning environments. *Distance Education, 29*(1), 89-106. doi:10.1080/01587910802004860

Kern, R., & Warschauer, M. (2000). Theory and practice of network-based language teaching. In M. Warschauer & R. Kern (Eds), *Network-based language teaching: Concepts and practice* (pp. 1-19). New York: Cambridge University Press. doi:10.1017/CBO9781139524735.003

Prabhu, N. S. (1987). *Second language pedagogy*. Oxford: Oxford University Press.

Willis, J. (1996). *A framework for task-based learning*. London: Longman.

Willis, D., Jr., & Willis, J. (2006). *Doing task-based teaching*. Oxford: Oxford University Press.

Student engagement in learning vocabulary with CALL

Robert Stroud[1]

Abstract. Ensuring that students are *engaged* in learning is a key concern for instructors across many fields. With regards to vocabulary in language learning, teachers should provide students with tasks which promote high levels of motivation and resultant engagement. The recent trend of online systems which have dynamic, collaborative, and even competitive style approaches can potentially take students to new levels of physical and psychological engagement in and out of the classroom. Despite newfound enthusiasm for such systems, there is currently little data regarding student engagement in using such systems when compared to textbooks or other more traditional paper-version approaches. Recent survey data from 131 Japanese university students on the use of a vocabulary learning system (Quizlet, http://quizlet.com) was collected. Findings unsurprisingly showed a clear improvement in the overall engagement of students through using an online system to learn vocabulary. However, a great deal more research is needed to ensure that such engagement amongst students actually leads to better learning and acquisition of words compared to traditional paper-based learning methods.

Keywords: engagement, motivation, flow, CALL, vocabulary.

1. Introduction

Teachers can often confuse the word *engagement* in learning with others such as *motivation* and *participation*, which are often judged based upon observable actions of students. Engagement however, also considers the factors in learning which can remain hidden from the view of a teacher. According to Fredericks, Blumenfeld, and Paris (2004), the three elements which make up engagement

---

1. Kwansei Gakuin University, Japan; robertstroud@kwansei.ac.jp.

How to cite this article: Stroud, R. (2014). Student engagement in learning vocabulary with CALL. In S. Jager, L. Bradley, E. J. Meima, & S. Thouësny (Eds), *CALL Design: Principles and Practice; Proceedings of the 2014 EUROCALL Conference, Groningen, The Netherlands* (pp. 340-344). Dublin: Research-publishing.net. doi:10.14705/rpnet.2014.000242

are (1) *behavioral* (the actions they undertake), (2) *emotional* (their enjoyment and feeling towards doing work) and (3) *cognitive* (how much effort they invest to learn and retain material). It is important for students to experience all levels of such engagement, for example during the learning of new vocabulary, so as to best improve their chances of noticing and retention. With the use of modern technology, the recent creation and incorporation of online vocabulary learning systems into academic settings has been a positive step towards enhancing student engagement to motivate students to focus more deeply upon their learning.

Research on the improvement and maintenance of student engagement in class has often had similar findings in factors which are crucial for students to become focused upon tasks at hand. These have included students having a sense of control (Egbert, 2003) and elements which grab the attention and interests of the student (Keller, 2000), ultimately resulting in an undisturbed state of focus called *flow* (Csikszentmihalyi, 1997). Stroud (2013) recently developed the CARCS model to improve the motivational design of classroom tasks for students with the ultimate goal of increasing and maintaining student engagement across time. He focused on improving student engagement in classroom tasks by offering Control (C), grabbing Attention (A), matching Relevant task content (R), building Confidence (C), and giving a Satisfying outcome (S) to learners. The same theory can apply to vocabulary learning with the aid of modern technology (in comparison to self-learning of vocabulary, with textbooks for example).

One recent website in widespread use in language learning is Quizlet. The system offers learners the chance to build their own card sets online and learn them through playing games. Online systems such as Quizlet offer students more chances for control (with the words they study, games they play, as well as place and method of access to their cards), attention (with graphics and scores to grab their focus), relevance (with system feedback telling students their weak points and needs for study focus from game scores for example), confidence (with measurable progress being made through scores), and satisfaction (with competitions and game rankings between different class members). However, little research has been done on examining the details of the behavioral, emotional and cognitive engagement which may result from the implementation of such a system. A recent study which focuses upon these three elements will now be discussed.

2. Method

70 first year and 61 second year non-English major students studying in English writing courses in a Japanese university took part in the study. All the students were

Japanese nationals with English as a second language and were of mixed gender. All of the students used Quizlet instead of textbooks, which was the primary method for all of the students up until that time, as the tool for vocabulary study across a 14 week semester. At the end of each class, the students were given 10 minutes to enter new words from the class content and then another 20 minutes to play games of their choice on Quizlet to study their word sets. At the end of the course a survey was administered to the students regarding feelings towards study using Quizlet.

3. Results and discussion

3.1. Emotional engagement

Table 1. Using Quizlet to study vocabulary was more fun than using my textbooks…

Strongly disagree	Disagree	Somewhat disagree	Somewhat agree	Agree	Strongly agree
2%	3%	4%	17%	34%	40%

Students answered the above question post-course and it was clear that most students felt using Quizlet to study vocabulary was a more enjoyable method than using a textbook. This suggests that the majority of students were more emotionally engaged in learning due to the incorporation of the system into the course.

3.2. Cognitive engagement

Table 2. Using Quizlet made me try harder to remember vocabulary than with my textbooks…

Strongly disagree	Disagree	Somewhat disagree	Somewhat agree	Agree	Strongly agree
1%	4%	8%	50%	23%	14%

An additional question answered by the students post-course also makes clear that using Quizlet made the majority of the students try to remember the vocabulary sets they had made and practiced more than with a textbook they had previously used.

This suggests that students were paying more attention to their learning, perhaps making a larger effort to remember words in order to get higher scores in the games they played, and were thus more cognitively engaged when using the online learning system compared to previous learning with textbooks.

3.3. Behavioral engagement

Table 3. During the weekly 20 minutes of game time with Quizlet, how often did you usually play the following games?

Quizlet game	Practice type	Average usage score (0 = Never, 6 = very often)
Flashcards	Reading (receptive)	1.77
Scatter	Reading (receptive)	3.76
Space Race	Writing (productive)	2.63
Learn	Writing (productive)	2.10
Speller (without headset)	Reading into Writing (productive)	1.26
Speller (with headset)	Listening into Writing (productive)	2.12
Test	Reading / Writing (receptive / productive)	1.89

During the 20 minutes of post-class Quizlet game time allocated by the teacher, students were free to choose any of the available system games to study their card sets. Table 3 above shows an overview of the differences between student preferences with this freedom of choice and the differences of focuses on language skills practiced (receptive versus productive). Although student behavioral engagement was often very high during practice time (due to the freedom of study choices of fun games which Quizlet offers), allowing students to practice their cards sets without any guidance from the teacher or system might have slightly limited students' progress. Students may have perhaps focused on games they enjoyed playing or specific vocabulary they were good at getting high scores with, rather than focusing on improving their weaker language skills, or vocabulary for example.

4. Conclusions

It is not surprising from the results that switching learners to using online vocabulary learning systems such as Quizlet can increase the behavioral, emotional, and cognitive engagement of classes compared to more traditional methods such as textbooks. This clearly has the potential to improve learners' learning, with higher acquisition and potential retention of vocabulary. However, it should not be assumed by teachers that high levels of observable participation of their students during class will result in *efficient* learning of vocabulary (where time spent studying vocabulary is resulting in better learning and acquisition of those words than with other approaches). Although the introduction of engaging task elements such as choice, competition and autonomy may result in higher motivation and resultant engagement of students, teachers still need to consider guiding students on the structure of practice they are undertaking to learn vocabulary (with regards to the skills being used, recycling of difficult words and spacing of repetition for example). This way, the obviously engaging elements that systems such as Quizlet offer can be utilized to create focused and effective vocabulary learning environments for language learning classrooms.

References

Csikszentmihalyi, M. (1997). Flow and creativity. *NAMTA Journal, 22*(2), 61-97.

Egbert, J. (2003). A study of flow theory in the language classroom. *The Modern Language Journal, 87*(4), 499-518. doi:10.1111/1540-4781.00204

Fredericks, J., Blumenfeld, P., & Paris, A. (2004). School engagement: Potential of the concept, state of the evidence. *Review of Educational Research, 74*(1), 59-109. doi:10.3102/00346543074001059

Keller, J. (2000). How to integrate learner motivation planning into lesson planning: The ARCS model approach. *Paper presented at VII Semanario, Santiago, Cuba.*

Stroud, R. (2013). Increasing and maintaining student engagement during TBL. *Asian EFL Journal. Professional Teaching Articles, 59*(April), 28-57.

university of groningen

A quantitative and qualitative evaluation of student participants' contribution to carrying out an online international collaborative project on education

Chizuko Suzuki[1], Kenichi Ishida[2], Shota Yoshihara[3], Klaudia Schultheis[4], and Barbara Riedhammer[5]

Abstract. This study evaluates an international collaborative project developed and practiced on the internet, as a form of SNS, focusing on how much university students from six countries worldwide participated in the project, from the viewpoint of the participants' contribution to the forum discussion of their own group's topic on education. The 66 participating students' communication data posted in the eight group forums were compiled and analyzed by quantitative and qualitative methods. As for the quantitative method, the corpus data comprising 48,990 running words was analyzed by topics and countries to obtain profiles of the characteristics of the participants' English language use in terms of message volume as well as vocabulary density, sentence length, and key words. As to the qualitative method, the data were analyzed by KBDeX software focusing on some key words such as 'agree/disagree' and 'opinion' to investigate the interactive discourse of discussion, negotiation, or mediation in each group. The results from both quantitative and qualitative analyses revealed the students of each country had their own distinguishing features in language use and communication patterns.

Keywords: online intercultural exchange, knowledge building, negotiation, mediation.

---

1. Nagasaki Junshin Catholic University; Suzuki@n-junshin.ac.jp.
2. Nagasaki Junshin Catholic University; ishida@n-junshin.ac.jp.
3. Nagasaki Junshin Catholic University; shota@n-junshin.ac.jp.
4. Catholic University of Eichstaett-Ingolstadt; klaudia.schultheis@ku.de.
5. Catholic University of Eichstaett-Ingolstadt; riedhammer@gmail.com.

How to cite this article: Suzuki, C., Ishida, K., Yoshihara, S., Schultheis, K., & Riedhammer, B. (2014). A quantitative and qualitative evaluation of student participants' contribution to carrying out an online international collaborative project on education. In S. Jager, L. Bradley, E. J. Meima, & S. Thouësny (Eds), *CALL Design: Principles and Practice*; *Proceedings of the 2014 EUROCALL Conference, Groningen, The Netherlands* (pp. 345-351). Dublin: Research-publishing.net. doi:10.14705/rpnet.2014.000243

1. Introduction

A German university in 2004 initiated the project called "International Project (IPC)" (http://www.internationalproject-ipc.com/) for the purpose of nurturing teacher-training course students' competence in carrying out an international project in the English language. Since then, it has been continually expanded yearly to include eight universities in North America and Asia beyond Europe.

The IPC international project carried out in 2012, working on nine group topics under the main theme of "Children's Perspective on School, Teaching and Learning" was already evaluated to show the overall effectiveness of the project (Suzuki, Ishida, Yoshihara, Schultheis, & Riedhammer, 2013).

In terms of the extent to which the educational goal had actually been achieved, it was mainly based on the participants' response data to an end-survey of the project and pre- and post- English proficiency test results. This previous study, eventually, indicated that there remained room for improvement in the project's administration. This study has aimed at exploring in more detail the content and process of the participants' communication developed in the eight-group discussion forums of the IPC 2012, as the research project's final goal to determine effective ways to facilitate the students to participate more comfortably and collaboratively.

2. Method

2.1. Data

The total of 1076 messages posted into the general discussion forum and in the nine group forums by 99 student participants were compiled as the IPC 2012 Learner Corpus of 76,500 words. For the present minute examination, from this corpus, a smaller corpus specified for group activity was prepared as the Group Activity (GrpA) Corpus by excluding the general discussion forum data, one virtually inactive group's data and participants who existed in name only contributing few messages to their group discussions. This sub-corpus was comprised of 471 messages by 66 students with 48,990 running words. The GrpA corpus was analyzed both in quantitative and qualitative ways by individual students, countries, and group topics to obtain profiles of the characteristics of the participants' English language use in terms of message volume, sentence length, and key words. Specifically for the current paper, six sub-corpora were designed, divided by country (in alphabetical order): Bulgaria, Germany, Japan, Poland, Spain, and the USA.

2.2. Analyses

2.2.1. Quantitative analysis

WordSmith 6.0 (Scott, 2012) was utilized for corpus profiling. Furthermore, in order to identify words/phrases that are prominent in each sub-corpus divided by country, these were submitted to a keyword analysis using AntConc. 3.2.4w (Anthony, n.d.); in each sub-corpus analysis, the other five sub-corpora files were used as a reference corpus option. The following kinds of results were obtained: 1) Corpus profiles by countries, which included the type token ratio, the mean length of sentences, and the mean length of messages of each country, besides the overall volume, and 2) each country's list of the top twenty keywords which were used more frequently by the country's participant students compared with the other countries. Taking an example from the case of Japan, the list gave 'teaching', 'Japanese', 'Hi', 'Kaori', and so on, including some proper names such as Japanese and Kaori.

2.2.2. Qualitative analysis

The occurrence of certain words contributing to consensus building such as 'agree/disagree', 'opinion', and 'propose' in each group was examined using the word search tool of KBDeX (Knowledge Building Discourse Explorer) –software developed by Oshima, Oshima, and Matsuzawa (2012)–, and the ratios by country were manually counted to observe which country's member(s) uttered or posted the keywords proportionally more than the other countries' members. Furthermore, the discourse in which the selected words were used by the members interactively to develop their discussion was analyzed using the network creation tools of KBDeX to obtain animated visualizations of the context and process of the three kinds of discussion networks: the students/participants' network, the discourse unit network, and the selected word network.

3. Results and discussion

3.1. Quantitative reflection

As can be seen in Table 1 below, there was a considerably wide diversification among the participating countries, particularly in the message volume represented by the token per student as well as the sentence total posted by the country. Except for the few Polish students who joined the project for the first time in the year 2012 in a later stage, German students posted sentences the most, with each student having uttered the most, while Japanese students posted the fewest sentences with each student uttering the least. A more noticeable diversification was observed among the countries in terms of the top twenty keywords, which were statistically calculated as prominent words for each country, first ranked by numerical order from the highest and then categorized by seven functions from 'greetings' to 'topic-related words'.

Table 1. Profile of group discussion corpus by participating country

Text file	Overall	Bulgaria	Germany	Japan	Poland	Spain	USA
file size	274,463	38,018	107,515	23,786	1,478	35,697	67,969
tokens (running words) in text	48,990	6,915	19,345	4,128	248	6,547	11,807
tokens used for word list	47,896	6,763	18,981	4,011	240	6,421	11,480
sum of entries	0	0	0	0	0	0	0
types (distinct words)	3,304	1,006	1,753	825	84	1,023	1,665
type/token ratio (TTR)	6.9	14.88	9.24	20.57	35	15.93	14.5
standardised TTR	33.07	31.68	32.21	34.5		33.63	34.47
standardised TTR std.dev.	65.05	57.8	62.69	51.45		55.14	58.57
standardised TTR basis	1,000	1,000	1,000	1,000	1,000	1,000	1,000
mean word length (in characters)	4.31	4.26	4.3	4.4	4.63	4.2	4.37
word length std.dev.	2.42	2.38	2.37	2.44	2.86	2.32	2.54
sentences	51,478	486	1,258	372	24	463	1,003
mean (in words)	13.97	13.92	15.09	10.78	10	13.87	11.45
std.dev.	3.18	11.81	13.24	9.7	5.36	13.24	10.09
no. of students	66	8	13	11	5	14	15
token/student ratio	272.27	864.38	1488.08	375.27	49.6	467.64	787.13

N.B.: This table shows how many words (tokens), how many kinds of words (types) and how often each word type (TTR) were used in group discussions by participant students' country.

Table 2 shows most countries except for Germany used limited types/functions of keywords. For example, the keywords of Bulgaria, Poland and the USA were categorized into three types, and those of Spain were two, besides 'greetings'. On the other hand, the keywords of only Germany indicated a variety including 'inclusive we' and 'IPC specific' words, showing that the German students were taking on the leadership of the project consciously.

These results support a finding from the previous study of the students' project-end survey that the students did not participate quantitatively in an equally active way (Suzuki et al., 2013) and further suggest that the participants of each country played their own role in the group's entire activity, depending on their ability, concerns or peculiar characteristics.

Table 2. Keywords list by participant students' country categorized by type/function

Rank	Bulgaria	Germany	Japan	Poland	Spain	USA
1	from	anna	teaching	questionnaire	spain	rules
2	presentation	greetings	japanese	audience	granada	class
3	ve	we	thank	century	Ive	classroom
4	denica	sophia	kaori	embrace	greeting	everyone
5	research	maybe	hi	extracurricular	pass	grade
6	results	ipc	draft	gathered	draws	student
7	bulgaria	everybody	q	relate	think	does
8	dear	lt	however	target	yolanda	follow
9	bulgarian	our	japan	childhood	is	happens
10	make	story	group	documents	gymkhana	your
11	oppinion	gdo	m	holiday	ls	these
12	questionairre	german	sorry	hi	first	savannah
13	katrin	com	questionsin	appear	rules	states
14	put	networks	contents	attached	in	assignments
15	educational	researches	elementary	available	gadgets	united
16	one	mixxt	yuki	recess	spend	dr
17	publish	it	ask	compare	convivence	internet
18	summarize	folder	questionnaire	download	eassier	how
19	m	drawing	chika	times	image	following
20	luck	http	margarethe	favorite	imageshack	powerpoint

Category Legend
Addressing/greeting words
Inclusive 'we'
Epistemic expressions

Category Legend
IPC-specific terms
Project-specific words
Method-specific words
Topic-related words

3.2. Qualitative reflection

An interesting phenomenon relevant to the role-sharing observed above was revealed by closely looking into the use of a selected consensus-building word, such as 'agree', comparatively with the rest of the words within a country. The word was used more proportionally by the Japanese students compared with the ratio of all their messages in most groups as seen in Table 3. Hence, it may demonstrate that the Japanese students attempted to make the project proceed by responding to an opinion proposed by another country's member with a positive word.

Furthermore, the process of how the word 'agree' was used by a Japanese member interactively with the other countries' members within the group could be visually illustrated by the network results of KBDeX seen in Figure 1 below.

Table 3. Comparison of the consensus-building word use ratios among countries

	Bulgaria		Germany		Japan		Poland		Spain		USA	
	agree(%)	msge(%)	agree(%)	msge(%)	agree(%)	msge(%)	agree(%)	msge(%)	agree(%)	msge(%)	agree(%)	msge(%)
Group 1			75.0 > 63.0		12.5 > 6.3		12.5 > 11.3					
Group 3	11.1 < 24.4		61.1 > 54.9		11.1 > 2.4				16.7 < 18.3			
Group 4	27.3 < 30.1		27.3 < 54.8		9.1 > 2.7						36.4 > 12.3	
Group 5					11.1 < 17.4				44.4 > 10.1		44.4 < 72.5	
Group 6	33.3 > 20.0				33.3 > 8.0						33.3 < 56.0	
Group 7	50.0 > 5.6				25.0 > 13.9				25.0 < 47.2			
Group 8			33.3 < 88.2		66.6 > 11.8							
Group 9	37.5 > 27.8		37.5 > 27.8		12.5 > 2.8				12.5 < 41.7			

4. Conclusions

The facts discussed in the preceding sections based on some of the results of this study indicate that a disparity in the amount of the students' activity existed between the participating countries and that the students of each country might have endeavoured to contribute to advancing the project by playing their roles. Both of these facts can be taken into consideration when administering a further project. At least, the participating students and teachers should be informed of imbalanced jobs in quantity but shared ones in quality in order that they can exert their own characteristic potentials while trying to overcome weaknesses respectively for their common final goal of accomplishing the project more collaboratively and comfortably.

Figure 1. Animated visualizations of discussion networks when 'agree' was used in a group

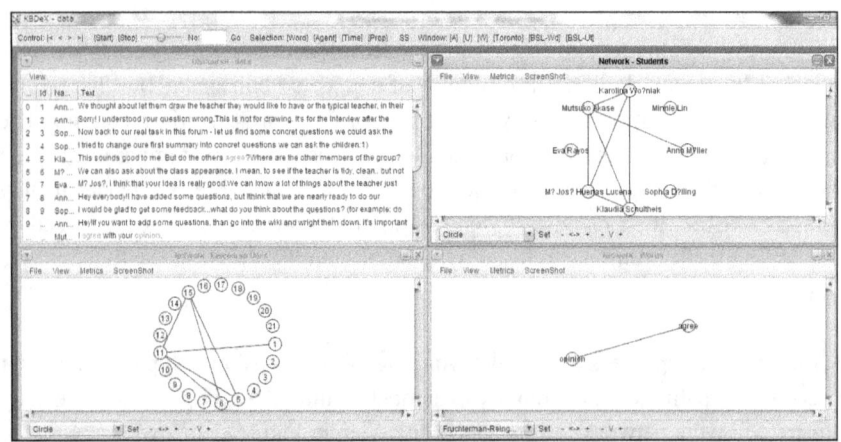

Acknowledgements. This study has been supported by JSPS (Japan Society for Promotion of Science) KAKENHI Grant No. 24520685. We also extend our gratitude to all of the participating students and teachers.

References

Anthony, L. (n.d.). AntConc. 3.2.4w. *Laurence Anthony's website*. Retrieved from http://www.laurenceanthony.net/software.html

Oshima, J., Oshima, R., & Matsuzawa, Y. (2012). Knowledge building discourse explorer: A social network analysis application for knowledge building discourse. *Educational technology research and development, 60*(5), 903-921. doi:10.1007/s11423-012-9265-2

Scott, M. (2012). *WordSmith tools version 6*. Liverpool: Lexical Analysis Software.

Suzuki, C., Ishida, K., Yoshihara, S, Schultheis, K., & Riedhammer, B. (2013). An international project developed on an SNS mixxt system making use of Web 2.0 technology to increase the students' core competence as future teachers. *World CALL 2013 conference proceedings, University of Ulster* (pp. 334-336).

Bring your own device to language class – applying handheld devices in classroom learning

Tord Talmo[1], Even Einum[2], and Robin Støckert[3]

Abstract. Language students often struggle to understand the logic in foreign language grammar, reducing their ability to reproduce and create texts on their own. There are several reasons for this; everything from the methodology to lack of motivation might influence the situation. Since the 1980's, Computer Assisted Language Learning (CALL) has become one of the fastest-growing areas of development in language learning and teaching. Several point to new technology as a great possibility in the area of language learning. Can new technology available to practically all students enable them to improve their understanding of the logic behind languages? An alternative to the traditional ways of teaching grammar could be to focus "on the advantages provided by technology already available, [... and] on how the teacher should utilize the fact that more and more students [...] are bringing their own devices to class. There are certain advantages provided by usage of mobile technology in class that are difficult to achieve in other ways, like anonymity, engagement by all of the students, peer learning effects" and several others (Talmo & Einum, 2013, para. 3). This paper will provide methods, introduce a new software designed especially for the purpose and try to explain why and how this could improve grammar teaching in foreign languages.

Keywords: BYOD, EFL, logic, web application.

---

1. Sør-Trøndelag University College; Tord.Talmo@hist.no.
2. Sør-Trøndelag University College; Even.Einum@hist.no.
3. Sør-Trøndelag University College; Robin.Stockert@hist.no.

How to cite this article: Talmo, T., Einum, E., & Støckert, R. (2014). Bring your own device to language class – applying handheld devices in classroom learning. In S. Jager, L. Bradley, E. J. Meima, & S. Thouësny (Eds), *CALL Design: Principles and Practice; Proceedings of the 2014 EUROCALL Conference, Groningen, The Netherlands* (pp. 352-357). Dublin: Research-publishing.net. doi:10.14705/rpnet.2014.000244

1. Introduction

When it comes to foreign language teaching (FLT), innovations in technology have not yet been sufficiently researched, although the use of multimedia computing, the internet, language laboratories and other technology has become common in classrooms all over the world (Chapelle, 2001). This is mainly due to the assumption that new possibilities of language learning through the internet and other computer interfaces are just a new form for already established approaches and methods. It seems that the most popular method of CALL in FLT is to let traditional exercises and activities (albeit communicative, grammar-based, etc.) be copied/pasted into a digital format, with the advantage of distance learning, faster distribution to students and the possibility of students working faster through the materials. CALL now handles a wide range of activities that exceeds these traditional activities, including listening, reading and writing skills.

One of the most modern innovations in CALL is the introduction of handheld devices like smartphones, which in many ways transform the learning and teaching processes, among others, through enhancing learners' autonomy by enabling students to acquire skills at their own pace (Kukulska-Hulme, 2010). According to Chapelle (2001) it has been suggested that the extended research of technology and its role in FLT methodology could provide understanding in the debate on the role of classic grammar-based education. Could it, however, also be possible to help students understand the logic of how language works by utilizing modern technology and a new approach towards language training? This is what the LLP Comenius project, named *"Identifying the Logical structure of languages by use of new Interactive mobile services, new diagnostic training methods for development of Key competences, and new Evaluation methods introducing assessment for learning practices"* (iLike) (Stav & Talmo, 2014), aims at investigating.

The activities in iLike will allow the students to construct their own knowledge of language through collective, creative peer learning problem-solving processes. iLike targets English as a foreign language (EFL) and specifically looks at English verbs. This highly important and consequential area of grammar is already being grappled within EFL education, and iLike seeks to provide a tool which is easy to apply to this process within the existing methodological framework of the subject. However, the project also provides an alternative software and method which makes the students actively analyse their initial assumptions about language and, mobile devices in hand, be instrumental in the construction of their own understanding of language and language structures.

2. Method

iLike consists of two parts; a new methodology and a software designed especially for the purpose of grammar learning. The software includes a teacher and a student interface, running as a web-application (Figure 1). The teacher runs the system from a laptop and the students use some kind of handheld device in order to submit their answers.

Figure 1. The components of the software in iLike

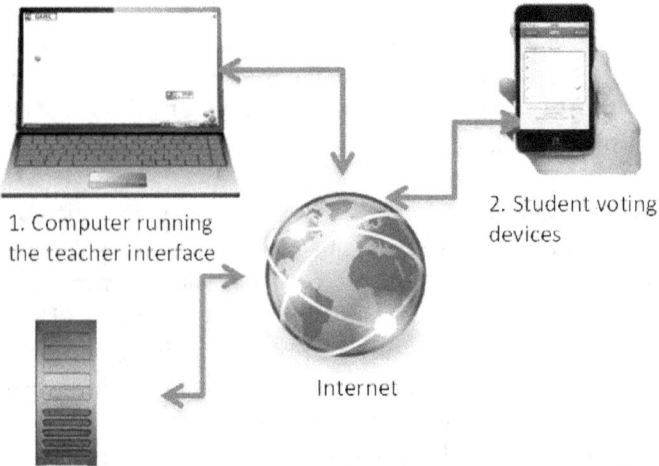

Utilizing the student's own handheld devices allows for a seamless and cost effective way of bringing interactive technology into class. With the software developed through iLike, the students will be able to do three things: 1) move words around on the screen to create new meanings and build correct sentences, 2) look into different possibilities according to the choice of verbs in the sentence (i.e. synonyms, negations and compound verbs), and 3) choose the correct conjugation, both according to tense and numbers.

iLike focuses on involving the students in the learning process, and reversing the way students learn rules of grammar. Instead of providing students with a rule, giving them tasks to drill that rule and correcting them afterwards, the consortium presents a case in which the students work, manipulate, discuss and self-assess their solutions before the teacher corrects and/or provides them with the correct answer. In addition to teaching the rules, this raises cognitive awareness within the students about the way we create language, and makes sure that the students are more capable of producing and reproducing meaningful, fluent and correct sentences/texts in the future.

3. Discussion

The big advantage of utilizing handheld devices in the classroom is the opportunity to get more voices heard on the same question. iLike aims at finding and developing good ways to involve all the students and the teacher in the same process. The most obvious advantage with the methodology is the possibility to let all students feel responsible, by commenting on the results and easily use the submitted answers in new tasks.

Another advantage is the anonymity handheld devices provide. In bigger groups, students are often hesitant to ask questions, answer or indicate in other ways if they have understood what the teacher is talking about. With iLike, all students can participate without fear.

A critical element of learning is collaboration, both in a teacher-student relations but also between peers. According to Vygotsky (1978), social conversation and interaction is the basis for learning in a socio-cultural perspective. Danaher, Gururajan, and Hafeez-Baig (2009) propose an m-learning framework based on three key principles: engagement, presence and flexibility. In this framework, in-class activities are ideal and promote collaborative work. However, this is often difficult to pursue when it comes to grammar learning. With iLike, the students will have immediate access to what the group as a whole has answered, thus preparing the ground for an actual discussion about different solutions to the tasks. This will create a metalanguage about grammar which can help students in their understanding of the logic in languages. More and more, researchers acknowledge mobile tools like social networks, instant message apps and mobile voting systems, like the software built in iLike, as efficient in classroom language training (Dudeney, Hockly, & Pegrum, 2013).

The software in iLike is designed in a dynamic and flexible way, making sure that it can be easily integrated and used for more or less all the tasks a teacher could want. This ensures a possibility to precisely target every group, no matter their level of competence.

Using the iLike methodology, the students will get a sense of being involved and heard in the learning process/environment. Previous studies performed at Sør-Trøndelag University College (HiST), Trondheim, Norway confirm the effects of collaboration and use of handheld devices in classroom activities (Talmo, Sivertsen Korpås, Mellingsæter, & Einum, 2012).

4. Conclusions

It is too early to conclude anything from the results obtained so far. It seems like iLike can function as a positive and engaging alternative or supplement to the more traditional grammar teaching in EFL. There are still some issues which need to be solved; the most important one being how to make it possible to differentiate the tasks given to the students. In the target group, the students are on very different levels, and the most talented students have a tendency to get bored when the task takes too long and they have already solved it. This is something that forces the teachers to direct these students to the textbook to solve extra tasks. The consortium is currently working on a way to stack and save tasks inside the software to make it easily accessible for the teacher, creating a more dynamic way to differentiate when using iLike.

iLike is considered as a first in the field of language education. In this project, the focus is on grammar, and more specifically, verbs. It is foreseen that the project could evolve and that the software could include possibilities for targeting more areas in FLT; more word classes, listening exercises and extended writing possibilities.

More and more students own some handheld smartphone, iPod, iPad or similar. Teachers and the educational system should be ahead of the development and utilize this technology. Digital literacy includes creativity and innovation not only towards new technology and systems, but also towards new methodology that actually takes into account the possibilities the new technology brings with it. It is easy to see ways of using technology in order to learn languages, but until now, this technology is mainly created with the idea that the individual can use it on their own, not in a creative process with others. The available systems for language learning to date were mainly produced to digitalize tasks and cases the students could just as easily have done with pen and paper. iLike focuses on creating variations to this way of thinking about language training, and aims to overcome the barrier that many students sense when it comes to understanding the logic behind languages. iLike is also an innovation when it comes to student response systems, opening for text response questions and answers which are easy to utilize in a training session.

iLike starts with EFL, drawing on already existing open source databases, but the software will be created as a language neutral service, meaning that it should be possible to look into both different languages as well as different word groups like nouns and adjectives in the future.

Acknowledgements. These results have been obtained with support from the European Commission. This publication reflects the views only of the authors, and the Commission cannot be held responsible for any use which may be made of the information contained therein.

References

Chapelle, C. (2001). *Computer applications in second language acquisition*. Cambridge: Cambridge University Press. doi:10.1017/CBO9781139524681

Danaher, P. A., Gururajan, R., & Hafeez-Baig, A. (2009). Transforming the practice of mobile learning: Promoting pedagogical innovation through educational principles and strategies that work. In H. Ryu & D. P. Parsons (Eds), *Innovative mobile learning: Techniques and technologies* (pp. 21-46). Hershey, PA and New York: Information Science Reference/IGI Global.

Dudeney, G., Hockly, N., & Pegrum, M. (2013). *Digital Literacies: Research and Resources in Language Learning*. London: Routledge.

Kukulska-Hulme, A. (2010). *Mobile learning for quality education and social inclusion*. Moscow:UNESCO IITI.

Stav, J. B., Talmo, T. (2014). *The iLike project* (2012-2014), contract 527585-LLP-1-2012-1-NO-COMENIUS-CMP. Retrieved from http://www.histproject.no/node/725

Talmo, T., & Einum, E. (2013). Smartphones as didactical possibility and technological advantage in language learning. In *Proceedings from the International Conference on Education and New Learning Technologies (EduLearn13), 1-3 July 2013, Barcelona, Spain* (pp. 4467-4473). International Association of Technology, Education and Development (IATED).

Talmo, T., Sivertsen Korpås, G., Mellingsæter, M., & Einum, E. (2012). Experiences with use of new digital learning environments to increase academic and social competence. In *Proceedings of the 5th International Conference of Education, Research and Innovation* (pp. 4540-4545). Madrid, Spain.

Vygotsky, L. (1978). *Mind in society: The Development of Higher Psychological Processes*. Cambridge, MA: Harvard University Press.

Online Estonian language learning

Maarika Teral[1] and Sirje Rammo[2]

Abstract. This presentation focuses on computer-assisted learning of Estonian, one of the lesser taught European languages belonging to the Finno-Ugric language family. Impulses for this paper came from Estonian courses that started in the University of Tartu in 2010, 2011 and 2012. In all the courses the students gain introductory knowledge of Estonian and develop active skills in Estonian. E-courses include asynchronous learning activities available in Moodle and the synchronous computer mediated communication via Skype. This provides the learners with the flexibility of performing drill and practice tasks at one's own pace as well as communicating extensively through the computer. This presentation addresses the linguistic challenges that the students face. The special linguistic characteristics of Estonian that make its learning and teaching via the Internet different from learning other languages will be discussed. The short overview also discusses the attitudes of the students towards the computer-assisted Estonian courses and considers both the positive and negative aspects of Internet-based language learning. Data was collected via a questionnaire survey.

Keywords: Estonian, e-learning, Estonian e-learning courses for beginners, computer-assisted learning of Estonian for grown-up learners, teaching Estonian online.

1. Introduction

This short overview is based on the course "Estonian Course for Beginners", which was created and taught at the University of Tartu in 2010, and on the course "Video-based Estonian Course for Beginners" which was opened in the spring of 2011 (both courses were created and taught by Maarika Teral and Sirje Rammo).

---

1. University of Tartu, the Department of Estonian as a Foreign Language; maarika.teral@ut.ee.
2. University of Tartu, the Department of Estonian as a Foreign Language; sirje.rammo@ut.ee.

How to cite this article: Teral, M., & Rammo, S. (2014). Online Estonian language learning. In S. Jager, L. Bradley, E. J. Meima, & S. Thouësny (Eds), *CALL Design: Principles and Practice; Proceedings of the 2014 EUROCALL Conference, Groningen, The Netherlands* (pp. 358-362). Dublin: Research-publishing.net. doi:10.14705/rpnet.2014.000245

In 2012, the same authors also constructed a new e-course, "The Basic Course of Estonian Vocabulary", which focuses on introducing vocabulary to learners on the A1 level. The one year teacher-assisted courses are intended for adult learners at the beginner level (A1 according to the CEFR) and are based on English. Next, we will not only focus on the aforementioned courses but will also expand upon Internet-based language learning, concentrating on the positive and negative aspects of this type of learning as well as discuss the special linguistic characteristics of Estonian that make its learning via Internet different from learning other languages.

2. Short introduction of the Estonian language e-courses

People who participate in the Estonian e-courses come from many countries. The learners have previously studied other foreign languages but are doing so online for the first time. All the courses are available in the University of Tartu Moodle study environment.

2.1. Estonian course for beginners

The course offers a chance to study Estonian by using authentic study materials which help improve different constituent skills: reading, listening, writing and speaking. The course is entirely web-based, to support the learning of Estonian of the growing number of people outside Estonia who are interested in studying Estonian, but are not able to do so in their home area (see also Teral, 2013). The ten lessons of the course cover different areas of life.

Grammar references and pedagogical suggestions assist the student with the exercises. The vocabulary and grammar exercises include tasks with multiple choice answers, matching, and filling in the blanks. The Moodle environment gives feedback to the student during the tasks and it gives the teacher a chance to observe the process of solving the tasks and comment the work.

Meanwhile, students can also get help from various additional online materials: the webpage ONENESS (http://www.oneness.vu.lt/) which is intended for independent learners (created by the authors), online dictionaries, links to websites that introduce Estonian culture and life, etc.

The online learning environments cannot check creative writing exercises so these were assessed by the teachers. The students are given feedback on their work in Moodle (in the forums and private messages that are sent to the students) as well as via e-mail. One of the drawbacks of Internet-based language learning is little spoken communication. One of the possibilities to develop direct communication in the foreign language is to use Skype. We used Skype successfully in video as well as in audio communication.

2.2. Video-based Estonian course for beginners

The video-based Estonian course for beginners was planned to be somewhat methodically different from other language courses. The material of a lesson is based on a video clip. It is especially suitable for students who prefer web-based learning materials with plenty of illustrations. The use of video clips in teaching is also appropriate for introductory courses (Berk, 2009).

As Berk (2009) points out, it is recommended to use short video clips, not longer than one or two minutes, to keep the students from watching the videos passively. Thus, short two minute clips were chosen as the bases of the course materials. Video players allow the students to view the clip several times and work thoroughly with the materials.

2.3. The basic course of Estonian vocabulary

After a year, the two aforementioned courses were accompanied by a vocabulary course, which was created by taking into account the previous experience of composing courses and the wishes and recommendations of the students. The lessons of the course are put together so that they cover topics that introduce everyday life and the Estonian way of living: *nations and countries, institutions, services, appearance and clothing, holidays, climate, nature, travelling,* etc. The course is first and foremost about developing the students' vocabulary on these topics at the beginner level (A1-A2).

The course introduces inter-word relations of meaning (synonyms, antonyms), and deals to some extent with words from the aspect of word-formation properties. In addition to traditional formation tasks, it also includes exercises which help understand the meanings of words and use them in the correct context. The course uses a lot of illustrative materials, such as photos, drawings, and schemes.

3. The positive and negative aspects of e-learning

Carrying out the studies, analysing the students' work, and communicating with them orally as well as in writing raised the need to find out the students' attitudes towards the current courses. A questionnaire was conducted which was answered by 17 participants.

One of the questions was: what differentiates Internet-based language learning from learning languages in the classroom? Bring out the positive and negative aspects of e-learning.

The following were brought out as the positive aspects of e-learning:
- the chance to study at a suitable pace and at the time and place of own choice;
- not depending on other students or the teacher;
- the chance to study from afar, without attending the classroom;
- a user-friendly study environment, easily accessible information;
- the chance to study a foreign language which is not taught in regular courses in the student's home country;
- it is possible to study grammar systematically and at a pace suitable for the student;
- e-learning improves self-discipline.

The following were brought out as the negative aspects of e-learning:
- e-learning is more time consuming than the students had planned. The students think that work in the classroom would take less time because then the questions could be answered immediately;
- problems with planning the time and motivation;
- lack of competitiveness and little chance to compare one's language skills to other students;
- not a lot of speaking opportunities;
- technical problems.

Several of the positive and negative aspects of e-learning that were mentioned have also been pointed out by previous researchers of Internet-based language learning.

In addition to the general problems of online language learning, the language specific aspects also need to be taken into account when creating the courses. During international projects, study materials are created simultaneously for studying several European languages. Usually, the technical and methodical framework of the materials is based on teaching Indo-European languages, and Finno-Ugric languages have to be forced into the same framework. In addition to the general principles of foreign language didactics, the grammatical structure of the particular language should also be taken into account when devising study materials and e-courses.

Estonian is rich in morphological forms. In addition to word endings, inflection and conjugation may also change the medial sounds. When introducing vocabulary, the students' attention should therefore also be drawn to morphological word formation.

4. The key issues of computer based learning

Although computer software offers more and more opportunities, it is difficult for teachers to grasp all of them because language teachers often lack the computer-related knowledge needed to create/use language learning programmes with a complicated structure.

Computer-assisted language learning should not be seen as separate from other language learning and studying forms (e-learning should definitely take into consideration the general pedagogical developments and tendencies).

Limited chances to improve pronunciation and speaking skills have always been considered the biggest shortcomings of computer-assisted language learning. In recent years, more attention has been given to improving speaking skills by using a computer.

5. Conclusion

Computer-assisted teaching of Estonian brought out the same positive and negative aspects that were highlighted in international studies. Based on initial experience, it can be said that using the computer to teach Estonian at the beginner level is practical and efficient. The development of new web-based study materials must consider the special features of the grammatical structure of the language.

References

Berk, R. A. (2009). Multimedia teaching with video clips: TV, movies, YouTube, and mtvU in the college classroom. *International Journal of Technology in Teaching and Learning, 5*(1), 1-21. Retrieved from http://www.sicet.org/journals/ijttl/issue0901/1_Berk.pdf

Teral, M. (2013). Computer assisted Estonian language learning. *Proceedings of the International Conference ICT for Language Learning, 6th Edition* (pp. 166-169). Italy: liberariauniversitaria.it edizioni.

Discovering English with the Sketch Engine

James Thomas[1]

Abstract. *Discovering English with the Sketch Engine* is the title of a new book (Thomas, 2014) which introduces the use of corpora in language study, teaching, writing and translating. It focuses on using the Sketch Engine to identify patterns of normal usage in many aspects of English ranging from morphology to discourse and pragmatics. This paper discusses the findings from the most recent semester when corpora were used by three different groups of university students studying English for different ends. It was found that learners who are capable of drawing conclusions from data are quick to recognize the potential of corpora. Through training in the relevant aspects of linguistics and the software, all 60 students were able to create and exploit corpora. Although the book itself was still under development, its approach was piloted on these students using extended excerpts and was demonstrated to be of value in fulfilling quite different needs.

Keywords: Sketch Engine, guided discovery, corpus creation, corpus exploitation, learning language from language, patterns of normal usage.

1. Introduction

Discovering English with the Sketch Engine is the name of a new book (Thomas, 2014) which aims to inculcate descriptive and neo-Firthian views of English through teaching the Sketch Engine, a multi-faceted, web-based corpus tool that generates concordances, word sketches and various lists, has many pre-loaded corpora and facilitates corpus building (Kilgarriff, Rychlý, Smrz, & Tugwell, 2004). The book is aimed at teachers and trainees, advanced students and translators.

---

1. thomas@phil.muni.cz.

How to cite this article: Thomas, J. (2014). Discovering English with the Sketch Engine. In S. Jager, L. Bradley, E. J. Meima, & S. Thouësny (Eds), *CALL Design: Principles and Practice; Proceedings of the 2014 EUROCALL Conference, Groningen, The Netherlands* (pp. 363-367). Dublin: Research-publishing.net. doi:10.14705/rpnet.2014.000246

The *discovering* of the title is manifested in the hundreds of questions whose answers the reader discover through learning how to form queries, how to use the Sketch Engine tools to process the data, and then to interpret it. I refer to this as *task-based linguistics*.

It is no exaggeration to say in 2014 that corpus linguistics has fundamentally changed our view of how language works. It is enough to open a mono-lingual learner dictionary (MLD), such as the ground-breaking COBUILD (1987) and a corpus-informed grammar such as Longman Grammar of Spoken and Written English (Biber, Johansson, Leech, Conrad, & Finegan, 1999) to see that the dictionary contains a vast amount of grammatical information and the grammar contains just as much lexical information. The interdependence of these two strands of language is empirically demonstrated on almost every page of these books and others of their ilk, through the use of corpora. Publishers such as Macmillan, Oxford University Press, Cambridge University Press, and HarperCollins all use the Sketch Engine in the preparation of dictionaries which makes it a resource worth putting in the hands of foreign language users.

Neo-Firthian linguists, such as Sinclair, Hoey, Hunston and Hanks were among many involved in the COBUILD project and at the core of their work, then and now, lies collocation and colligation. These underpin the work in multi-word units, grammar patterns, word templates and discourse studies whose linguistic significance is measured in terms of frequency: patterns of normal usage are invaluable to language pedagogy.

Discovering English with the Sketch Engine is particularly keen that language learners et al. understand the importance of patterns of normal usage so that they acquire them and a sense for them. This further empowers them to recognize language users' use of metaphors and other kinds of creative language, which Hanks (2013) refers to as *exploitations*. It is important that both norms and exploitations are recognized in all language input and output.

2. Method

2.1. Differing groups of students

Task-based linguistics has been evolving over a number of years and involves work with various groups of students. In two-year masters program training secondary school English teachers, we work with both in-service and pre-service teachers whose common European framework level is C2. In our bachelor program, whose students are hovering around C1, a new course called Collocation Plus was opened to experiment with corpus-based approaches to introducing neo-Firthian linguistics practically. At the Faculty of Informatics, doctoral students of academic writing, whose English ranges from A2 to C1, have long been trained in using the Sketch Engine to discover and use patterns of normal usage. None of this semester's 'informaticians' had ever heard of corpora, which made their wholesale acceptance of its value quite significant. Interestingly, they had not heard of the Sketch Engine, which was born at their faculty, and its international user base is managed from there as is its on-going development.

2.2. Student use of the Sketch Engine

The Sketch Engine is introduced via the BNC so that the concept of "core English" is well-established: it then serves as a standard against which their specialized corpus work is undertaken.

In the spring semester of 2014, all groups were taught to use the Sketch Engine tools that are relevant to their areas of study, and were required to produce work relevant to their future studies and careers. The students of *Collocation Plus* used the Sketch Engine's *Corpus Builder* to make a corpus of one novel that they downloaded from the Gutenberg Project. They explored the corpus looking for words and phrases they considered interesting. This assignment was partly inspired by an interview with David Crystal (2014) at IATEFL (online) in which he describes creating a glossary for a single book, something which he considers surprisingly innovative. The students published their glossary on a dedicated website and in addition, described the process in a five-minute video using JING.

The teacher trainees worked on graded readers. In pairs, they chose one graded reader, scanned it, uploaded it to our Graded Reader Corpus (GRC) and explored it to find examples of language features that we studied in the course, *Linguistic for Language Teachers* that ran in parallel to their methodology course, *Syllabus, Lesson and Material Design for ELT*. They produced draft teaching material that they presented using Moodle tools, some of which linked to the GRC using the Sketch Engine's permalinks, while other material they produced was related to the literary and cultural aspects of their chosen reader. They will use these resources next semester in their internal practice teaching.

The academic writing students are required to add ten personally relevant texts to the Informatics Reading Corpus (IRC) which I launched ten years ago and now contains almost eight million words. When uploading, the students add XML tags to generate metadata that includes the sections of papers and the field of Informatics in which they work. This permits targeted searches, e.g. the four word bundles that start sentences in the Future Work sections of papers in the field of natural language processing. The main assignment for their course is an academic paper they are currently working on.

3. Conclusions

From a self-assessment questionnaire of 90 linguistic, language acquisition and teaching constructs given to the masters students (25 pre-service and 11 in-service teacher trainees), it emerges that they acknowledge various levels of improvement in almost all areas, including the use of corpora. More objectively, the assignments of the bachelor and masters students evidence their grasp of many new linguistic concepts. It could also be seen in computer-equipped classrooms throughout the semester that the students gained a wide range of corpus skills as they interpreted data and added it to the course wiki under such headings as phrasal verb particles, bound and free prepositions and the word templates of specific nouns and verbs. As this was the first time that these assignments were set, future work will include a stronger focus on the relationships between discrete linguistic items and the discourse in which they appear. This manifests a top-down, bottom-up dichotomy that was introduced at the beginning of the courses, but needs reinforcing at later stages.

Accounting for the progress made by the informaticians is complicated by their various levels of English, as this dictates different uses of corpora. The students were able to derive information about collocation and colligation in general English from the BNC, whereas from the IRC, they were able to study terms and phrases related to their fields. They observed the use of parentheses, the use of first person, sexist language, writing numbers, the ubiquitous *the Noun of Noun* pattern. Some were able to observe hedging and tease out word templates.

As *Discovering English with the Sketch Engine* was under development during the semester described, the students in all courses piloted sections of it as it evolved, and were given chapters that pertained to the assignments as the semester drew to a close. Through learning new linguistic concepts, many of which are manifestations of corpus studies, and exploring them in corpora, students develop a new view of language itself. Such discoveries make concordancing a subversive activity (Thomas, 2009) as it displaces such notions as sentence grammar as the primary organizing unit for language study and teaching.

References

Biber, D., Johansson, S., Leech, G., Conrad, S., & Finegan, E. (1999). *Longman grammar of spoken and written English*. London: Longman.

COBUILD. (1987). *Collins COBUILD English Dictionary*. Michigan: Collins.

Crystal, D. (2014). I*nterview with David Crystal - David talks about two projects he has recently been working on...* [video]. Harrogate Online. Retrieved from http://iatefl.britishcouncil.org/2014/sessions/2014-04-02/interview-david-crystal-david-talks-about-two-projects-he-has-recently-been-work

Hanks, P. (2013). *Lexical analysis: Norms and exploitations*. Cambridge MA: MIT Press. doi:10.7551/mitpress/9780262018579.001.0001

Kilgarriff, A., Rychlý, P., Smrz, P., & Tugwell, D. (2004). The Sketch Engine. In G. Williams & S. Vessier (Eds), *Proceedings of the 11th Euralex Congress* (pp. 105-116). Lorient: Université de Bretagne Sud.

Thomas, J. (2009). Concordancing as a subversive activity. *Presentation at the PALC Conference* (unpublished).

Thomas, J. (2014). *Discovering English with the Sketch Engine*. Brno: Laptop Languages.

university of groningen

Applying dynamic assessment principles to online peer revisions in written English for specific purposes

Sylvie Thouësny[1] and Linda Bradley[2]

Abstract. The aim of this paper is to explore the extent of the applicability of dynamic assessment with respect to peer written student online revisions. More specifically, it observes how groups of Swedish computer engineering students learning English for Specific Purposes engage in cooperative interactions and negotiations with their peers as they work together towards the revision of a written report. Using Google Drive as a means to engage in their report writing assignment in groups of three, students also discussed their text with another group in a peer response activity through comment insertions. Following a discussion of the progressive scale used to provide assistance, learners' turns during corrections and revisions of linguistic, structural, and content features are analysed. Finally, implications for peer revisions and provision of feedback according to learners' developmental level are discussed in relation to the outcomes of the study.

Keywords: online peer revision, dynamic assessment, interaction, negotiation, text revision.

1. Introduction

Lundstrom and Baker (2009) maintain that students who review other students' texts gain as much from peer response activities as students who merely receive comments from their teachers. As such, student feedback under dynamic assessment principles should provide a practical framework for offering learners the appropriate amount of explanations they need as well as assisting them in peer reviewing on all text levels: language, content and structure. Corrective feedback

---

1. Independent researcher, Dublin, Ireland; sylvie.thouesny@icall-research.net.
2. Chalmers University of Technology, Gothenburg, Sweden; linda.bradley@chalmers.se.

How to cite this article: Thouësny, S., & Bradley, L. (2014). Applying dynamic assessment principles to online peer revisions in written English for specific purposes. In S. Jager, L. Bradley, E. J. Meima, & S. Thouësny (Eds), *CALL Design: Principles and Practice*; Proceedings of the 2014 EUROCALL Conference, Groningen, The Netherlands (pp. 368-373). Dublin: Research-publishing.net. doi:10.14705/rpnet.2014.000247

in an interactionist, as opposed to interventionist, approach to dynamic assessment is generally provided on a scale ranging from implicit to explicit guidance, the aim being to co-construct knowledge through cooperative interactions and negotiations between learners and correctors (Lantolf & Poehner, 2004). Dynamic assessment, in that case, reveals both the actual and emerging development of the learners, in other words, their zone of proximal development, as well as helps promote their ongoing progress through tailored mediated assistance. Although Villamil and De Guerrero (2006) pointed out that mediation is not only limited to that of teachers but also applies to that of peers (p. 25), little research has as of yet studied peer revisions under dynamic assessment principles.

2. Methodology

2.1. Educational settings

The students in this study took part in an English for Specific Purposes course where one of the main tasks was writing a technical report on a chosen topic in groups. This study focuses on one of the course elements, a peer response activity where students participate in improving the argumentation of their group reports, producing clear and logic structures in English. All in all, there were 29 groups of students with two to three persons in each group.

With a view of improving learners' writing, text owners were asked to invite a peer group on Google Drive to discuss the form and content of their document by means of text highlighting and comment insertion. Peers were given a set of guidelines to help them provide gradual corrective feedback ranging from implicit to explicit (taken from Thouësny, 2011, pp. 90-91, adapted from Aljaafreh & Lantolf, 1994, p. 471).

Concerning ethical considerations, data was only gathered from persons over the age of 18. The participants gave their informed consent outlining their rights and obligations. Further, they were informed about the project goals and how the data will be used. In addition, their names and usernames will be protected at all times.

2.2. Data collection

The peer response activities took place within a brief period of time of less than two weeks. The existing 29 groups were first searched for (a) peer in-text editing by manually scanning the revision history of the document and (b) peer interventions and interactions by considering all inserted comments. Comment blocs, representing an entire discussion on one specific item from either text owners and/or peers occurring in the document, were codified so as to identify the ones containing interactions and interventions from both text owners and peers. Out of the 29 existing groups, 22 participated in the peer response activity; 3 peer groups were investigated in-depth since they were particularly active with 129 inserted comments by the text owners and 36 peer group comments all in all. The comments were investigated from the perspective of the interaction in the 36 comments between text owners and responding peer group.

2.3. Data analysis

Through a sociocultural lens, and more specifically, a microgenetic approach, we explored the students' language revisions to determine the extent to which text owners' and peers' turns appeared to be in line with dynamic assessment principles. The microgenetic approach is characterised by three key properties: (a) observation of the entire period of a change from beginning to end, (b) high density of observation during that change, and (c) analysis of both quantitative and qualitative aspects of the change in question (Siegler & Crowley, 1991, p. 606).

The data was analysed from two angles. Firstly, we observed learners' turns and categorised them in accordance with Liu and Sadler's (2003) grid of distribution, in which feedback is classified with respect to (1) area, i.e. global and local, (2) nature, i.e. revision-oriented and non-revision-oriented, and (3) type, i.e. evaluation, clarification, suggestion, and alteration (p. 202). Additionally, all peers' interactions were labelled from L1 to L4 depending on the amount of assistance that was provided, where a level 1 indicates a 'very implicit' move and a level 4 denotes a 'very explicit' comment.

Secondly, we performed a text analysis of peers' comments, investigating the content of the comments more in-depth from the perspective of how the peer recommendations were picked up by the text owners.

3. Results and discussion

3.1. Progressive scale of assistance

Results show that peers never intervened at the most implicit level of assistance (L1). In other words, they did not highlight words in text without providing any further information. Findings also indicate that peers rarely provided assistance on a progressive scale: 33 over 36 interactions were never followed by the next step of support as defined in the regulatory scale. Most of these interactions (85%) started at L3 or L4, where peers either provided explanations on how to improve the identified issue or gave the correct answer directly, respectively. The remaining 15% were offered at L2, which designates that peers provided the error type the most. Within all these instances of corrective feedback, 3 of them were followed by the next step of mediated assistance (L2->L3, L2->L3, and L3->L4). Figure 1 illustrates a mediated progression of assistance ranging from L2 to L3.

Figure 1. Mediated assistance ranging from L2 (providing peers with error type) to L3 (providing explanation for improvement)

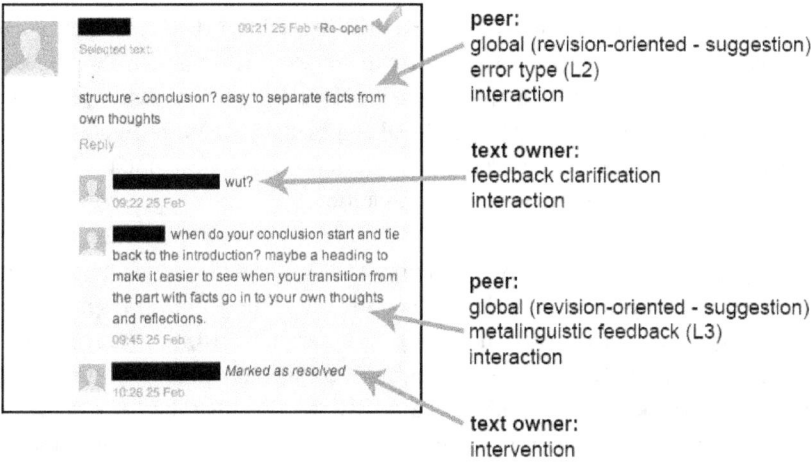

The above discussion took place between peers and text owners during a period of one day. After providing a comment (L2) that was not properly grasped by the text owners, the peer group expanded their explanations (L3). From the screen capture, the thread was marked as resolved by the text owners. However, the analysis of the revision history demonstrated that text owners also intervened and modified their text accordingly.

The students (a) mostly gave metalinguistic feedback and direct correct answers and (b) did not comply with the principles of dynamic assessment when dispensing feedback to their fellow students. One of the reasons for the former might be related to the difficulty of identifying and stating error types. While some of them are easily noticeable, others, such as misplaced modifiers or coordination errors might be considered more difficult to classify. One explanation for the latter might be related to the fact that students had neither expertise nor experience in dynamic assessment.

Yet, the students did collaborate on the revision of their texts. All peer interactions triggered at least one response from text owners, and we counted 66% of them with a minimum of 2 responses.

3.2. Text analysis of peers' comments

When analysing the content of the comment turns, adapting Liu and Sadler's (2003) framework, the comments were mainly of revision-oriented nature and only three comments were non-revision oriented. In other words, the comments were geared at concrete text improvement.

Out of the 36 peer comment turns, a majority were local (Liu & Sadler, 2003). However, even if pointing at a specific item in the text, such comments were geared at improving the text, for example: "consider removing to increase flow", when pointing at a comma in the text. The global comments were more comprehensive, for example: "The subtitle does not directly refer to anything in the text". Such a comment requires quite extensive text elaboration.

From a peer response perspective, certain aspects of the text were commented, but far from everything in the text. This connects to the purpose of peer response work for writing development. Even if not all errors are covered, it is suggested that feedback that is timely and relevant can motivate learners (Nix & Wyllie, 2011). Peer work was taking place, since it was possible to see that the peers addressed themselves as "we" even if only one of the peer persons posted a specific comment; it was still a joint endeavour to comment the other text.

4. Conclusions

Our preliminary study shows that peer reviewing in a web-based environment such as Google Drive supports text development. Thus, there are implications that peer revision related to providing and receiving feedback is an enriching activity. This type of collaborative writing with technology offers a way of achieving an insight into text from different perspectives, both from the partners engaged in the writing process and from the joint construction of meaning (Warschauer & Grimes, 2007).

This study leads to the idea that applying principles of dynamic assessment in peer review is not as straightforward as it might appear. Peers did not offer corrective feedback ranging from implicit to explicit. They rather provided metalinguistic feedback or correct answers as one standalone interaction. Their interactions, in any case, generated interventions and interactions from their student counterparts, all directed to the improvement of their writing.

References

Aljaafreh, A., & Lantolf, J. P. (1994). Negative feedback as regulation and second language learning in the zone of proximal development. *The Modern Language Journal, 78*(4), 465-483. doi:10.2307/328585

Lantolf, J. P., & Poehner, M. E. (2004). Dynamic assessment of L2 development: Bringing the past into the future. *Journal of Applied Linguistics, 1*(1), 49-72. doi:10.1558/japl.1.1.49.55872

Liu, J., & Sadler, R. W. (2003). The effect and affect of peer review in electronic versus traditional modes on L2 writing. *Journal of English for Academic Purposes, 2*(3), 193-227. doi:10.1016/S1475-1585(03)00025-0

Lundstrom, K., & Baker, W. (2009). To give is better than to receive: The benefits of peer review to the reviewer's own writing. *Journal of Second Language Writing, 18*(1), 30-43. doi:10.1016/j.jslw.2008.06.002

Nix, I., & Wyllie, A. (2011). Exploring design features to enhance computer-based assessment: Learners' views on using a confidence-indicator tool and computer-based feedback. *British Journal of Educational Technology, 42*(1), 101-112. doi:10.1111/j.1467-8535.2009.00992.x

Siegler, R. S., & Crowley, K. (1991). The microgenetic method: A direct means for studying cognitive development. *American Psychologist, 46*(6), 606-620. doi:10.1037/0003-066X.46.6.606

Thouësny, S. (2011). *Modeling second language learners' interlanguage and its variability: A computer-based dynamic assessment approach to distinguishing between errors and mistakes.* Unpublished PhD dissertation. Dublin City University, Dublin.

Villamil, O. S., & De Guerrero, M. C. M. (2006). Sociocultural theory: A framework for understanding the social-cognitive dimensions of peer feedback. In K. Hyland & F. Hyland (Eds), *Feedback in second language writing: Contexts and issues* (pp. 23-41). Cambridge: Cambridge University Press. doi:10.1017/CBO9781139524742.004

Warschauer, M., & Grimes, D. (2007). Audience, authorship, and artefact: The emergent semiotics of Web 2.0. *Annual Review of Applied Linguistics, 27*, 1-23. doi:10.1017/S0267190508070013

university of groningen

Mobile voting tools for creating collaboration environment and a new educational design of the university lecture

Svetlana Titova[1]

Abstract. Mobile devices can enhance learning experience in many ways: provide instant feedback and better diagnosis of learning problems; enhance learner autonomy; create mobile networking collaboration; help design enquiry-based activities based on augmented reality, geo-location awareness and video-capture. One of the main objectives of the international research *Enhancing Technology Awareness and Usage of m-Learning in Russia and Norway* was to evaluate the pedagogical impact of mobile voting system (Student Response System) integration on re-designing a traditional university lecture course, creating a high level collaboration environment and changing student learning and academic performance. The framework of university lectures discussed in the paper enables lecturers to transform the way of material presentation and turn the traditional lecturing into interactive Student Response System (SRS) supported lectures, then into a flipped classroom, and then, in the long run, into a MOOC lecture. The analysis based on qualitative and quantitative data collected from two student groups (56 undergraduate students) in the 2012-2013 academic year showed that SRS supported lectures encouraged foreign language learners to produce more output in the target language, improve their intercultural competence and language skills and enhance their motivation.

Keywords: mobile learning, mobile voting tools, collaboration environment, immediate feedback.

---

1. Lomonosov Moscow State University; stitova3@gmail.com.

How to cite this article: Titova, S. (2014). Mobile voting tools for creating collaboration environment and a new educational design of the university lecture. In S. Jager, L. Bradley, E. J. Meima, & S. Thouësny (Eds), *CALL Design: Principles and Practice; Proceedings of the 2014 EUROCALL Conference, Groningen, The Netherlands* (pp. 374-378). Dublin: Research-publishing.net. doi:10.14705/rpnet.2014.000248

1. Introduction

Mobile networking enables instructors to create a collaboration environment based on an enquiry-based learning approach which inspires students to learn for themselves, bringing a genuinely research-like approach to the subject. This interactive, dialogic model of learning is similar to the processes of participation in research. The particular emphasis in this case is placed on fostering the development of collaborative, informal communities in which students learn by seeing and engaging with other people's approaches. Ubiquitous access to information mediated by mobile devices potentially enables a paradigmatic shift in education, since it changes the way classes are managed and the instructor's role (Beatty, 2004). This approach implies a fundamental change in the philosophy of teaching and learning. Mobile devices and tools are particularly applicable for achieving this as they effectively act as accelerators of the social interaction in the classroom.

2. Method

2.1. Research objectives

Mobile voting systems or clickers which have been used successfully within the context of the classroom for the last decade are very challenging, since they require instructors to rethink their instruction to leverage their potential advantages (Laurillard, 2007). Teachers may start with just minor changes, but major pedagogical changes may also be introduced. SRS is a polling mobile system that was developed at Sør-Trøndelag University College (HiST). The major advantages of SRS "compared to traditional clickers are independence of software and flexibility in use of voting devices" (Arnesen, Sivertsen Korpås, Hennissen, & Birger Stav, 2013, p. 169). It also provides instructors with an opportunity for quickly determining the level of class understanding at any given point in time, without the extra burden of grading.

SRS implementation allows for significant feedback pattern changes and material assessment re-design. The task/enquiry-based learning approach and SRS implementation are central to transformation of the lecture design as well as assessment and feedback patterns. SRS-supported lecture design presents a challenge for a lecturer because, first, the content material under discussion has to be re-arranged into chunks of 5-6 slides which are followed by a short SRS-supported test that consists of 4-5 statements; second, at least three SRS-supported tests should be created to provide better diagnosis of learning problems and to highlight weak points of content presentation on the part of a lecturer; and third, a lecturer has to be ready with some enquiry-based activities to initiate post-test group discussion or brainstorming.

The main objective of the international research *Enhancing Technology Awareness of m-Learning in Russia and Norway* was to investigate the pedagogical impact of SRS integration on developing learner language and social skills. The participants of the research were 56 second-year undergraduate Russian students enrolled at Lomonosov Moscow State University who took part in SRS piloting as volunteers during the 2012-2013 academic year in a CLIL course *Introduction to American Studies*.

2.2. Data collection

Data collection was done in three cycles: pre-study evaluation of ICT (mobile) competence of experimental group students and their attitude to mobile learning before SRS implementation; intervention of SRS-supported tests as formative assessment tools and re-design of the traditional lecture pattern; post-study evaluation of learner attitude to SRS-supported lectures.

2.3. Reports of findings and data analysis

Data analysis of the pre-study cycle demonstrated that students had advanced levels of mobile competence; technologically and psychologically they were ready to use their own mobile devices in the classroom. At cycle 2, students of both control and experimental groups were supposed to fulfil practically the same in-class and out-of-class activities: pass summative tests; do weekly reading to participate in three course colloquiums (for control group) and in weekly SRS-supported tests and post-test discussions (for experimental group); and write an essay. For the experimental group, formative assessment was provided in the form of SRS tests –usually three tests per lecture. The learners of the two groups were given the same midterm and final tests. Average scores were included to compare overall performance of the control and experimental groups after the implementation of SRS. The data collected on the overall scores of three summative tests suggested that introduction of the SRS-supported approach helped improve academic performance of the experimental group in overall results of midterm 2 and final test whereas the control group demonstrated a decrease in overall scores.

The intervention data were supplemented by student feedback gained from a post-study paper-based questionnaire and some interviews conducted after the final test. Student answers indicated that they had an overall positive outlook regarding the SRS approach to university lecture courses. Some participants noted initial difficulties in dealing with the SRS-supported approach. They commented on the challenging nature of weekly tests and post-test activities. However, they claimed that this approach improved their overall satisfaction with the program of study because of an innovative way of interaction in large lecture formats. There was general agreement that smart phones and tablets were the most handy and suitable devices to use in large auditoriums. Some of them commented that they now understood what the active learning approach meant in practice.

3. Discussion

The likely interpretation of the improvement in academic performance of the experimental group is that the results of regular formative SRS-supported tests based on the lecture and required reading materials helped the instructor determine what difficulties students had. It was also helpful in designing better quality questions and feedback to improve their understanding of the subject. The increase in the overall test results was encouraging, but not conclusive to show that only SRS tests were beneficial. One more reason for better academic performance is that students of the experimental group were involved in post-test activities.

Although the SRS-supported approach enabled instructors to create a collaboration environment and according to our survey results influenced our learners' academic attainment and motivation, there is still much room for improvement. First, it is necessary to introduce new formats of interactive in-class activities based on instant messaging tools because SRS provides teachers only with a one-way but instant kind of feedback support. Second, we are planning to pilot a more advanced mobile assessment system –PeLe with SRS installed as an assessment tool both for summative and formative purposes as this tool enables instructors to save test results of individuals and group dynamics, to give students opportunity to go through as many attempts as they want and to provide more test formats. Third, for creating a collaboration environment it is recommendable to analyse the impact of more common mobile social apps and instant message services for learners on their motivation and class performance and output. Fourth, another direction of further research consists in crafting questions that help students to engage more meaningfully with course content and to foster critical thinking skills.

4. Conclusions

The SRS-supported approach influenced not only lecture design –time management, the mode of material presentation, activity switch patterns– but also learner-teacher interaction and formats of activities; from the test results data and the post-study questionnaires, it is known that they encouraged foreign language learners to produce more output in the target language, improve their intercultural competence and language skills and enhance their motivation. SRS is likely to become a supportive mobile tool for lecturers who would like to implement flipped classrooms because it enables them to transform the way of material presentation and turn a traditional lecture into an interactive lecture, then into flipped classrooms, and then, in the long run, into MOOCs.

References

Arnesen, K., Sivertsen Korpås, G. S., Hennissen J. E., & Birger Stav, J. (2013). Experiences with use of various pedagogical methods utilizing a student response system – motivation and learning outcome. *The Electronic Journal of e-Learning, 11*(3), 169-181.

Beatty, I. (2004). Transforming student learning with classroom communication systems. *EDUCAUSE Research Bulletin, 3*. Colorado: ECAR.

Laurillard, D. (2007). Pedagogical forms of mobile learning: Framing research questions. In N. Pachler (Ed.), *Mobile learning: Towards a research agenda* (pp. 153-176). London: WLE Centre, Institute of Education.

Investigating EFL teachers' technological pedagogical content knowledge: Students' perceptions

Jun-Jie Tseng[1]

Abstract. Technological pedagogical content knowledge (TPACK) has received much attention recently, serving as a lens to examine the ways in which teachers integrate technology into teaching. Questionnaire instruments have been developed to examine teachers' TPACK. However, teacher-perceived TPACK may not fully reflect their real practices in classrooms. To address this problem, students' perspectives could be incorporated to achieve a balanced assessment of TPACK. Thus, the present study was to assess English as a foreign language (EFL) students' perceptions of their teachers' TPACK through a validated student-based TPACK instrument. Two hundred and fifty-seven EFL students of junior high school in Taiwan participated in this study. The results of the survey showed that the teachers were thought to be more proficient in the three individual domains of core knowledge than in the intersections between them. In particular, the students perceived that their teachers demonstrated content knowledge more adequately than their integrated TPACK. The resulting perceptions of the students could be used to help teachers enhance their teaching practices associated with technology.

Keywords: technological pedagogical content knowledge, teacher knowledge, EFL students' perceptions, TPACK instrument.

1. Introduction

Teacher knowledge of integrating technology into teaching is taking on a greater prominence in the field of educational technology; it is known as TPACK, which is proposed by Mishra and Koehler (2006) to expand Shulman's (1987) framework of pedagogical content knowledge (PCK). The TPACK model serves as

---

1. Department of English at National Taiwan Normal University; jjtseng@ntnu.edu.tw.

How to cite this article: Tseng, J.-J. (2014). Investigating EFL teachers' technological pedagogical content knowledge: Students' perceptions. In S. Jager, L. Bradley, E. J. Meima, & S. Thouësny (Eds), *CALL Design: Principles and Practice*; *Proceedings of the 2014 EUROCALL Conference, Groningen, The Netherlands* (pp. 379-384). Dublin: Research-publishing.net. doi:10.14705/rpnet.2014.000249

a theoretical underpinning, which can guide teachers to examine how technology is incorporated into teaching.

TPACK encompasses three bodies of core knowledge (technology, pedagogy, and content) and the intersections between them, as illustrated Figure 1 that follows: technological knowledge (TK), which refers to the teachers' ability to operate a variety of technologies for instructional purposes; pedagogical knowledge (PK), which deals with their competency of utilizing particular teaching strategies to improve student learning; content knowledge (CK), which is associated with their knowledge and skills of subject matter; technological pedagogical knowledge (TPK), which involves their ability to employ teaching strategies supported by technologies; technological content knowledge (TCK), which is concerned with their knowledge of using technologies to improve student learning of subject matter; PCK, which is known as their knowledge of employing various teaching strategies to represent subject matter; and TPACK, which requires the teachers to help their students acquire content using particular teaching strategies via the use of specific technologies.

Figure 1. The framework of technological pedagogical content knowledge[2]

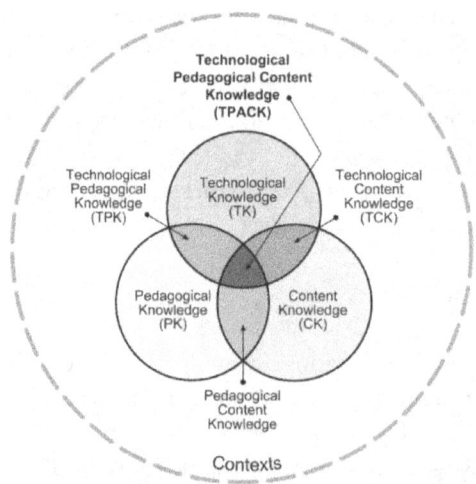

The TPACK framework is utilized to explain the complexity involved in the integration of technology into classroom teaching. Questionnaire instruments have been developed to assess teachers' perceptions of their TPACK (Archambault & Crippen, 2009; Chai, Chin, Koh, & Tan, 2013; Xiang & Ning, 2014). Archambault

---

2. Reproduced by permission of the publisher, © 2012 by tpack.org, source: http://tpack.org/

and Crippen (2009) measured 596 K-12 online teachers' TPACK and found that the teachers gave higher ratings to the domains of PK, CK, and PCK. This suggested that they were aware of how to teach content using appropriate pedagogical strategies, but not of how to teach content using technology. Similarly, Chai et al. (2013) found that Chinese language teachers in Singapore perceived themselves to be most proficient in the domain of content knowledge but felt less competent in TPACK.

However, teacher-perceived TPACK may not reflect their real practices in classrooms. There is a need to examine teachers' TPACK from other perspectives. The present study intended to present a balanced assessment of TPACK by investigating students' perceptions of their teachers' TPACK. One research question was addressed: What were EFL students' perceptions of their teachers' TPACK?

2. Method

2.1. TPACK instrument

A student-based TPACK instrument developed by Tseng (forthcoming) was adopted in the present study due to the fact that it was contextualized in an EFL setting; its validity and reliability ensured.

There are 30 items in the questionnaire. Example items selected from each of the seven sub-scales are listed below for the convenience of reference.

- TK: My teacher knows about basic computer software (e.g. media players, word processing programs, and web browsers).

- PK: My teacher adjusts the ways he/she teaches according to student performance and feedback.

- CK: My teacher has sufficient knowledge of English rammar.

- TPK: My teacher uses technologies to interact more with us.

- TCK: My teacher uses digitalized teaching materials with which I can learn vocabulary better.

- PCK: My teacher conducts group activities in which I can use English more.

- TPACK: My teacher represents content using appropriate strategies via the use of various technologies.

2.2. Data collection and analysis

The questionnaire was administered to 257 students from the classes of three junior high English teachers in northern Taiwan. The three teachers often integrated technology into their teaching, so their students were thought to be qualified to take the survey which used a 5-point Likert-type scale (1=strongly disagree, 2=disagree, 3=not sure, 4=agree, 5=strongly agree). The students responded to each item by indicating the degree to which they agreed with it.

Descriptive measures were used to assess the degree the students perceived their teachers' TPACK illustrated in the items of the survey. The results included mean score and standard deviation for each item. These descriptive statistical measures were also tabulated for each subscale.

3. Results and discussion

Table 1 presents the descriptive statistics of the students' responses to the questionnaire. Overall, the mean scores of all sub-domains were over 4.00. The students generally agreed that their teachers exhibited good knowledge in all aspects of TPACK as described in the questionnaire. In particular, the teachers were thought to be more confident in the three individual domains of core knowledge, as compared to the intersections between them. This result suggested that the teachers were perceived to be less proficient in the ways in which the three bodies of knowledge are tactfully combined to enhance student learning.

Table 1. Descriptive statistics of sub-domains of the TPACK scale

Sub-domains	Items	N	Mean	SD
TK	5	257	4.22	.835
PK	3	257	4.23	.839
CK	4	257	4.38	.718
TPK	5	257	4.15	.864
TCK	5	257	4.08	.862
PCK	3	257	4.11	.925
TPACK	5	257	4.07	.853

More specifically, while the highest mean score went to the CK (M=4.38, SD=.718), the lowest mean score was obtained by the TPACK (M=4.07, .853). This meant that the students perceived their teachers' CK a little more strongly than their TPACK. This result corroborates Chai et al.'s (2013) study that the teachers rated themselves highest in CK but lowest in TPACK.

In order to provide a picture of the students' responses to individual items, the items with higher and lower scores are presented as well. While the top five items are listed in Table 2, the items with mean scores lower than 4.00 are shown in Table 3. The teachers were perceived to be particularly proficient in content such as pronunciation and grammar; however, the students did not give equal rating to the way the content was enhanced with the computer. These results help readers gain a detailed understanding of what is strong and what is weak in the perceptions of teachers' TPACK.

Table 2. Top 5 items

Items	Sub-domains	M	SD
My teacher has good pronunciation.	CK	4.53	.781
My teacher keeps up with important new technologies (e.g. e-books, Facebook, and white board).	TK	4.45	.936
My teacher has sufficient knowledge of English grammar.	CK	4.37	.810
My teacher solves students' questions about English.	CK	4.33	.908
My teacher knows how to manage his/her class (e.g. drawing up clear class rules, creating a friendly atmosphere in class, and developing a good relationship between students and the teacher).	PK	4.32	.890

Table 3. Items with mean scores lower than 4.00

Items	Sub-domains	M	SD
The way my teacher teaches English with the computer is engaging.	TPACK	3.92	1.101
My teacher knows how to solve technical problems associated with hardware (e.g. setting up printers, using webcams, and changing hard drives).	TK	3.90	1.125

4. Conclusions

It can be concluded that what students perceived about their teachers' TPACK was consistent with what teachers perceived about their TPACK. Effective integration of technology into teaching requires teachers not only to know about technology, pedagogy, and content, but also to master the interplay between the three domains of core knowledge. Future studies could be conducted on pre- and post-surveys of TPACK of pre-service and in-service language teachers for their TPACK development.

References

Archambault, L., & Crippen, K. (2009). Examining TPACK among K-12 online distance educators in the United States. *Contemporary Issues in Technology and Teacher Education, 9*(1). Retrieved from http://www.citejournal.org/vol9/iss1/general/article2.cfm

Chai, C. S., Chin, C. K., Koh, J. H. L., & Tan, C. L. (2013). Exploring Singaporean Chinese language teachers' technological pedagogical content knowledge and its relationship to the teachers' pedagogical beliefs. *The Asia-Pacific Education Researcher, 22*(4), 657-666. doi:10.1007/s40299-013-0071-3

Mishra, P., & Koehler, M. J. (2006). Technological pedagogical content knowledge: A framework for teacher knowledge. *Teachers College Record, 108*(6), 1017-1054.

Shulman, L. S. (1987). Knowledge and teaching: Foundations of the new reform. *Harvard Educational Review, 57*, 1-22.

Tseng, J.-J. (forthcoming). Developing an instrument for assessing technological pedagogical content knowledge as perceived by EFL students. *Computer Assisted Language Learning*.

Xiang, K., & Ning, L. (2014). Evaluating Chinese pre-service mathematics teachers' knowledge of integrating technology in teaching. *Journal of Mathematics Education, 7*(1), 48-58.

university of groningen

Using iPads to help teens design their own activities

Joshua Underwood[1]

Abstract. This paper reports on action research aimed at helping teenage English language learners become more aware of ways they might use technology to support their learning. Over nine-months we used iPads to support a wide variety of teacher-designed learning activities and then used design thinking to help students co-design their own activities. Students' design ideas were iteratively refined in collaboration with the teacher over several weeks. Finally, groups tried out each other's activities. Evidence suggests students did reflect on their English learning practices and ways technology could support these. However, there is no indication that students adopted new practices outside class. Nevertheless, students did produce useful designs for classroom activities. This paper describes the activities we developed and indicates how the co-design process will be modified in future iterations in ways that might better promote uptake of technology-enhanced learning practices outside class.

Keywords: learner-centred approaches, learning design, MALL, iPads.

1. Introduction

iPads can alter the dynamics of classrooms: enabling routine engagement in a wider range of learning activities; encouraging exploration of alternative forms of homework, assessment and feedback; and increasing opportunities for collaboration and creative expression (Burden, Hopkins, Male, Martin, & Trala, 2012). However, while students often feel iPads enhance the learning experience, using iPads does not necessarily lead to better learning outcomes (Nguyen, Barton, & Nguyen, 2014). Indeed, one similar study for mobile devices suggests students felt having iPhones had been detrimental to their educational goals (Tossell, Kortum, Shepard, Rahmati, & Zhong, 2014). Nevertheless, there is widespread belief that iPads do

---

1. British Council, Bilbao; josh.underwood@gmail.com.

How to cite this article: Underwood, J. (2014). Using iPads to help teens design their own activities. In S. Jager, L. Bradley, E. J. Meima, & S. Thouësny (Eds), *CALL Design: Principles and Practice; Proceedings of the 2014 EUROCALL Conference, Groningen, The Netherlands* (pp. 385-390). Dublin: Research-publishing.net. doi:10.14705/rpnet.2014.000250

have potential, particularly when teachers and learners are given time and support to develop effective practices (Kaganer, Giordano, Brion, & Tortoriello, 2013). This paper is about developing such practices.

A key challenge in our teaching centre, particularly with teenagers, is to engage and sustain student interest. We also aim to help learners become more self-regulated. Many of our students find using new technology motivating. Yet, despite being digital natives, they rarely use technology to effectively support their own learning. We recently acquired a class set of iPads. As well as enabling a wider variety of classroom activities, iPads offer opportunities to help students better understand how they might use their own devices to support their learning. One way to help students become more reflective about how they learn is to involve them in designing learning activities. The objectives of this action research were:

- To develop engaging and effective activities through co-designing with students.
- To prompt learners to reflect on their learning practices and how they use technology.

2. Method

2.1. Educational settings

A class of thirteen teenage Spanish and Basque speaking English language learners (2 boys, 11 girls, aged 13 to 14) participated in the research. All had mobile phones, mainly low-end Androids. All had access to computers and/or tablets and the Internet at home. At the beginning of the course none had iPads.

As Cuban (cited in Hu, 2011) notes: "iPads are marvellous tools to engage kids, but then the novelty wears off and you get into hard-core issues of teaching and learning" (para 9). To counteract this effect, we followed our centre's normal B2 CEFR level course but integrated activities using iPads throughout. The class ran for seventy-five minutes twice a week after school over nine-months. On average, we used iPads in approximately one session per week. We had access to a class set of fifteen, 4th generation iPads and intermittent Internet access. Most often pairs or groups of three students shared one or two iPads. Occasionally, students worked individually. Students did not take the iPads home.

Following Chen (2013), we first aimed to give students some experience in ways they might use iPads to support learning. To this end we used iPads and a range of apps in various teacher-designed activities for over five months before initiating the co-design process. For example:

- Reading and listening to an interactive story, noticing, noting down, and researching new words and phrases, and then recording their own versions.
- Creating and recording animated dialogues.
- Making a digital class magazine.
- Collaborative writing and dictation using voice recognition.
- Online research for projects.
- Video and audio-recording paper slide presentations, role-plays, and assessed tasks.
- Preparing presentations.

After activities, students discussed whether they enjoyed the activities, whether activities were useful, and how they might be improved.

2.2. Design phase

For the design phase, we adapted design thinking, "a structured approach to generating and developing ideas" (IDEO, 2012, p. 14). We set the challenge: *Design a learning activity that you will enjoy.* Groups of three or four students shared their initial ideas in class. Then, for written homework, students used the class blog to review what we had done throughout the course and identify two activities they had enjoyed and two they had found particularly useful. They shared their thoughts in class. Some weeks later, following warm-up exercises (see IDEO, 2012, pp. 50-53), small groups brainstormed ideas for their own learning activities and presented these to the rest of the class. Then, for homework, students answered questions derived from the Ecology of Resources Design Framework (Luckin, 2010):

- What is your activity going to help people learn? Why?
- Why will people want to do your activity?
- What materials and technology will people use?
- Who will people work with? Who will help them?
- Where and when will people do your activity?
- How will your activity work? What will the sequence of events be?

They then wrote narrative descriptions of their activity ideas. In a subsequent session, groups discussed these ideas and decided which activity they would like to try. From their ideas, we then developed activities based on their ideas. In the final session, each group tried and discussed all activities.

3. Designs and discussion

At first, students had ideas that were impractical to implement (e.g. a worldwide poetry writing competition using social-media). A universal theme was that activities should be 'fun' or 'not boring'. More than half the students suggested using songs. Gradually, ideas evolved into four activities.

3.1. Learners' learning designs

- Play Ludo. Take turns answering a question correctly from a Quizlet[2] keyword transformation set, displayed on an iPad. If you can't and someone else can, it's his or her turn.

- Pairs play Clash of Clans[3] in English for a set time. On another iPad look up and note down new vocabulary or expressions. After playing for a set time present what you have learnt.

- Use Lyrics Training[4] to get the lyrics to a song you like. Note words or phrases you don't know and look them up. Sketch ideas for a 'lyrics video'[5] or write an alternative verse.

- Find three or four 'Use of English' questions your group can't answer. Find out the answers. Create an amusing dialogue using vocabulary or structures from those questions. Make a photo-story of your dialogue. Present your photo-story.

3.2. Learners' reflections on the activities

Students noted that fifteen minutes was not long enough to complete any of the activities satisfactorily. However, they enjoyed all the activities and felt they were potentially useful. The song was the most popular activity. Students were very enthusiastic to produce a lyrics video, though there was only time to exchange

---

2. http://quizlet.com/
3. http://www.supercell.net/games/view/clash-of-clans
4. http://lyricstraining.com/
5. http://en.wikipedia.org/wiki/Lyric_video#Lyric_videos

ideas for this. Students noted that, apart from the initial tutorial, exposure to new language in Clash of Clans was slow. Making a photo-story was felt to be creative and even students who did not initially want to appear in photos were happy with the comic like images produced by ComicBook Camera[6].

3.3. Teacher's reflections on the activities

All activities were satisfactory in that students appeared happily engaged in using English, practising language at an appropriate level, and sometimes starting to acquire new language. Both game activities felt like somewhat inefficient uses of class time but, as discussed later, they inspired other ideas that may be more productive. The song idea and the photo-story seemed particularly productive but would require much more time to enact and produce outputs students would be happy with. The photo-story idea was later used with another class in a two and a half hour session. These students worked enthusiastically in English throughout the session to produce amusing photo-stories with text and spoken dialogues, which they were proud of, using language they felt was new to them.

4. Conclusion

In summary, students produced ideas for promising activities. One of these has been used very effectively with another class. There was no apparent change in enthusiasm for using iPads over the nine months; in the end of year feedback, most students mentioned using iPads positively (e.g. "I love the iPads", "I love use of Internet and the iPads"). In designing activities, students' main concern was that they should be fun. However, students also showed awareness of the need for their activities to stretch their language. In class, students began to use iPads naturally to support their learning, sometimes suggesting appropriate uses that had not occurred to the teacher. Students also showed evidence of thinking about how they learnt (e.g. "Before, I thought the best way to improve […] was to just do my homework and study. But [now] I know more ways to improve and learn […]"). However, very few students installed apps used in class on their own devices (despite most apps being available for free for both iOS and Android) or reported using these out of class. Getting students of this age to be more pro-active about their English learning outside of class is a challenge. As one student noted, "The first thing is you have to want […]. If you want [to do something] then you can start doing things for it". In future iterations of the design thinking process, we intend to prompt learners to think specifically about the things they enjoy doing outside class

---

6. https://itunes.apple.com/us/app/comic-book-camera-free/id593817786?mt=8

and then consider how they could learn English through these. We will also try a homework idea inspired by the Clash of Clans activity; play one of your favourite games, make notes about it, and produce a presentation for class.

Acknowledgements. I would like to thank all participants and the British Council, Bilbao for supporting this work.

References

Burden, K., Hopkins, P., Male, T., Martin, S., & Trala, C. (2012). *iPad Scotland evaluation final report*. University of Hull. Retrieved from https://xmascotland.wufoo.eu/forms/scottish-mobile-personal-device-evaluation-2012/

Chen, X. (2013). Tablets for informal language learning: Student usage and attitudes. *Language Learning & Technology, 17*(1), 20-36. Retrieved from http://llt.msu.edu/issues/february2013/chenxb.pdf

Hu, W. (2011, January 4). Math that moves: Schools embrace the iPad. *NYTimes*. Retrieved from http://www.nytimes.com/2011/01/05/education/05tablets.html

IDEO. (2012). *Design thinking for educators toolkit*. Retrieved from http://designthinkingforeducators.com/

Kaganer, E., Giordano, G. A., Brion, S., & Tortoriello, M. (2013). Media tablets for mobile learning. *Communications of the ACM, 56*(11), 68-75. doi:10.1145/2500494

Luckin, R. (2010). *Re-designing learning contexts*. London: Routledge.

Nguyen, L., Barton, S. M., & Nguyen, L. T. (2014). iPads in higher education-hype and hope. *British Journal of Educational Technology* [early view]. doi:10.1111/bjet.12137

Tossell, C. C., Kortum, P., Shepard, C., Rahmati, A., & Zhong, L. (2014). You can lead a horse to water but you cannot make him learn: Smartphone use in higher education. *British Journal of Educational Technology* [early view]. doi:10.1111/bjet.12176

MALL in the wild: Learners' designs for scaffolding vocabulary learning trajectories

Joshua Underwood[1], Rosemary Luckin[2], and Niall Winters[3]

Abstract. This study aims to inform the design of mobile apps for vocabulary learning. Learning vocabulary involves developing, connecting, and sustaining various types of knowledge and skills. Learners do not typically acquire these all at once, but rather over the course of distinct episodes of activity. Yet, little is known about learning experience designs that help learners connect these episodes, which often make use of different socio-technical resources, and are distributed over time, and across settings. We use participatory design to explore how mobile apps might help learners enact episodes of learning activity and connect these in effective vocabulary learning trajectories. In order to stimulate design thinking, six adult language learners used an app for self-directed vocabulary learning in authentic conditions for from six weeks to six months. Then, in a post-study workshop, participants developed new designs for scaffolding self-directed vocabulary learning trajectories, grounded in reflection on their own experiences.

Keywords: vocabulary, MALL, learning design, seamless learning, self-directed learning.

1. Introduction

This study aims to inform the design of apps for vocabulary learning. Learning vocabulary involves developing, connecting and sustaining various kinds of knowledge (e.g. knowledge about meanings, form, usage, collocations, etc.) and

---

1. British Council, Bilbao; josh.underwood@gmail.com.
2. LKL, Institute of Education, London, UK; r.luckin@ioe.ac.uk.
3. LKL, Institute of Education, London, UK; n.winters@ioe.ac.uk.

How to cite this article: Underwood, J., Luckin, R., & Winters, N. (2014). MALL in the wild: Learners' designs for scaffolding vocabulary learning trajectories. In S. Jager, L. Bradley, E. J. Meima, & S. Thouësny (Eds), *CALL Design: Principles and Practice; Proceedings of the 2014 EUROCALL Conference, Groningen, The Netherlands* (pp. 391-397). Dublin: Research-publishing.net. doi:10.14705/rpnet.2014.000251

productive and receptive skills (Nation, 2001). Learners typically acquire this knowledge and these skills by engaging in various activities distributed over distinct episodes.

Yet, despite much interest in promoting distributed practice, particularly through flashcard type apps, little is known about how designs for learning help learners to enact and connect a wider variety of activities that typically, and perhaps critically for durability and transfer, are distributed over time and across varied physical and social settings. Hence, the question we aim to address through design research is: How might mobile apps help learners to enact and connect incidental and deliberate learning activities in sustained and effective vocabulary learning trajectories?

We use the concept of trajectories to focus designers' attention on: 1) the challenges of designing engaging learning experiences that "draw together multiple technologies, interfaces, physical artifacts and people into complex structures that extend across space and time" (Benford, Giannachi, Koleva, & Rodden, 2009, p. 709); and 2) theory-based conjecture about "how learning in a specific context and for a specific concept will develop over time under the influence of instruction" (Reimann, 2013, p. 45). That is to say, designs should act on what is known about how people learn at micro and macro timescales and attend to the complexities of delivering engaging coherent experiences, employing varied activities and resources, across episodes and settings.

Technology can facilitate many activities that contribute to vocabulary learning. For example:

- Tasks and vocabulary can be made more meaningful by adapting to individual learners' interests, competences, current activity, and physical and social settings.

- Exposure can be increased by embedding target language in learners' day-to-day L1 interactions.

- Noticing and processing can be encouraged, for example, through automated highlighting, glossing, and inserting questions about target vocabulary in texts.

- Spaced review, look-up, retrieval, testing, generative use, etc. can be prompted through SMS/messaging, system notifications, and flashcards.

- Games and social media can provide motivation and opportunities for practice.

- Formation of rich associations can be promoted through reception and production of multimedia.

- Learners can look up vocabulary, capture, share, and access help, anywhere, anytime.

For examples of the activities above, see Underwood (2014).

Because mobile devices are very often to hand, they provide opportunities to help learners connect such activities across episodes and settings. Yet, most apps do not make it easy to integrate activities. Designs also often fail to exploit connections between life, "what learners happen to come across", and learning (Kukulska-Hulme, 2013, p. 2). There are only a few studies that describe designs for seamless vocabulary learning (Wong, 2013) and features that may help learners connect incidental and deliberate learning activities (Gaved et al., 2013). However, individuals interpret designs in their own ways and often do not exploit opportunities as designers envisage (Stockwell & Hubbard, 2013).

How can we accommodate diverse interpretations of learning designs? At design time, we address this by involving learners in design and by using a learner-centred model of context (Luckin, 2010). This model suggests learners' enact learning trajectories under the influence of their changing motivations and access to knowledge, skills, social, technological, and physical resources. Designs and collaborators can influence learners' motivations and change access to resources. At use time, we aim to support meta-design (Fischer, 2013) by enabling learners to reconfigure designs to support their own goals and make use of their preferred resources. Previously, we developed miLexicon, an app that aims to prompt learners to collect, investigate, and share observations of new vocabulary and provides easy access to a learner's preferred social and technology resources (Underwood, Luckin, & Winters, 2012).

2. Method

We used miLexicon as a technology probe (Balaam, 2013) in order to give participants a vocabulary of authentic experiences to draw on in a subsequent design workshop (see Figure 1). This paper focuses on the design workshop outcomes. However, we briefly summarise participants' prior use of miLexicon.

Figure 1. miLexicon Android app/technology probe

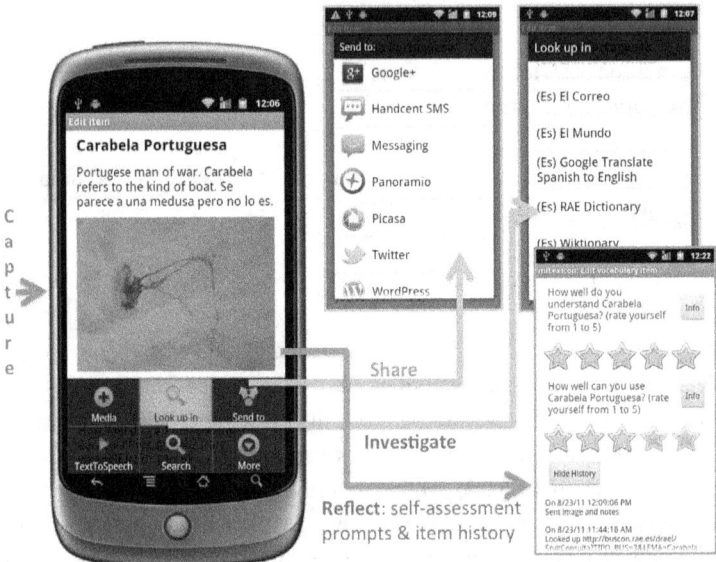

Six adult language learners, with expertise in technology-enhanced learning, used miLexicon to support self-directed vocabulary learning on borrowed phones. Usage varied greatly (see Table 1), likely reflecting: competence (e.g. CEFR B2, C2); exposure (e.g. living in target language culture, or not); motivations (e.g. for work, as a hobby); changing circumstances (e.g. on holiday, working); and whether the phone was used with a personal SIM card. The length of the study gave ample opportunity to initiate and pursue (or not) a number of genuinely motivated vocabulary learning trajectories. However, log and interview data suggest that although most participants occasionally reviewed the words they added, they rarely used miLexicon to help develop knowledge beyond initial capture and inquiries into meaning.

Table 1. Overview of participants' usage of miLexicon prior to design workshop

Participant ID	SIM card	Approx. target language/s competence	Located in target language culture	Weeks with phone (approx.)	Days miLexicon used (approx.)	Number of items added	Number of items added per day used (approx.)
A	Own	A2 | C1	No | For 1 week	9	19	83	4
B	Own	B2	For 3 weeks	16	37	82	2
C	Lent	C2	Yes	15	15	19	1
D	Lent	C2	Yes	6	9	9	1
E	Own	C1	Yes	20	135	1520	11
F	Lent	C1	Yes	6	12	53	4

In the design workshop, participants shared their experiences and then worked in pairs or individually to sketch ideas. Facilitators prompted for explanation of sketches. Audio recordings and sketches (see examples in Figure 2) were analysed to identify design ideas. These were labelled in terms of activities supported and then sorted into categories.

3. Designs and discussion

Figure 2. Sketches of designs for: 1) suggesting things to do with vocabulary items; 2) helping learners see what they have done, or not done, with any item; and 3) prioritising items to work on

Three categories encompass design ideas generated at the workshop:

- Ways to help learners capture new language easily (e.g. for speech, always on audio recording; for text, OCR capture and contextual 'send to vocab app' menu items).

- Ways to help learners manage learning (e.g. word frequency information; visualisation of what has been done; enhanced filtering, search, and prioritisation of vocabulary lists).

- Ways to help learners learn (e.g. prompts with suggested activities, and for spaced practice; automated adaptive testing and hints; motivators through gamification and social interaction, for example, shared word challenges and word collection leaderboards).

There was also a persistent theme; the occasional need to push learners to act, in particular to follow up initiated vocabulary-learning trajectories. One suggestion was to use temporally and spatially distributed reminders. However, such persuasive messaging should be: 1) adaptive - nudging learners to act only when behaviour is not meeting objectives; and 2) adaptable - allowing learners to easily set objectives and the ways they are nudged to match their changing goals, preferences, and circumstances.

4. Conclusions

Evidently, initial design ideas generated in a workshop are not complete. Rather, we use them as stimuli for further design work. One idea in particular, coupled with the concept of designing for end-user re-design (Fischer, 2013), offers an interesting way to help learners design and enact their own vocabulary learning trajectories:

- Provide a checklist of activities that can help learners practice and develop vocabulary knowledge.

- Allow learners and teachers to customise and share this list and the activities.

- For each vocabulary item track and visualise which activities have been completed.

- Use adaptive spaced prompting to push learners to follow up initiated vocabulary-learning trajectories and suggest activities.

Acknowledgements. We would like to thank all participants. This work was supported by EPSRC grant EP/E051847/1.

References

Balaam, M. (2013). Using technology probes to understand the educational design space. In R. Luckin, S. Puntambekar, P. Goodyear, B. Grabowski, J. Underwood, & N. Winters (Eds), *Handbook of design in educational technology* (pp. 71-79). New York: Routledge.

Benford, S., Giannachi, G., Koleva, B., & Rodden, T. (2009). From interaction to trajectories. *In Proceedings of CHI 09* (pp. 709-718). New York: ACM Press. doi:10.1145/1518701.1518812

Fischer, G. (2013). Meta-design: Empowering all stakeholders as co-designers. In R. Luckin, S. Puntambekar, P. Goodyear, B. Grabowski, J. Underwood, & N. Winters (Eds), *Handbook of design in educational technology* (pp. 135-145). New York: Routledge.

Gaved, M., Kukulska-Hulme, A., Jones, A., Scanlon, E., Dunwell, I., Lameras, P., & Akiki, O. (2013). Creating coherent incidental learning journeys on mobile devices through feedback and progress indicators. In *QScience Proceedings mLearn2013* (pp. 13-16). doi:10.5339/qproc.2013.mlearn.13

Kukulska-Hulme, A. (2013). *Re-skilling language learners for a mobile world*. Retrieved from http://www.tirfonline.org/wp-content/uploads/2013/11/TIRF_MALL_Papers_Kukulska-Hulme.pdf

Luckin, R. (2010). *Re-designing learning contexts*. London: Routledge.

Nation, I. S. P. (2001). *Learning vocabulary in another language*. Cambridge: Cambridge University Press. doi:10.1017/CBO9781139524759

Reimann, P. (2013). Design-based research – Designing as research. In R. Luckin, S. Puntambekar, P. Goodyear, B. Grabowski, J. Underwood, & N. Winters (Eds), *Handbook of design in educational technology* (pp. 135-145). New York: Routledge

Stockwell, G., & Hubbard, P. (2013). *Some emerging principles for mobile-assisted language learning*. Retrieved from http://www.tirfonline.org/wp-content/uploads/2013/11/TIRF_MALL_Papers_StockwellHubbard.pdf

Underwood, J. (2014). Seven challenges for open mobile vocabulary learning. In *Proceedings Ikasnabar 2014*. Retrieved from http://www.researchgate.net/publication/263239027

Underwood, J., Luckin, R., Winters, N. (2012). Managing resource ecologies for mobile, personal and collaborative self-directed language learning. *Procedia - Social and Behavioral Sciences, 34*, 226-229. doi:10.1016/j.sbspro.2012.02.045

Wong, L. (2013). Analysis of students' after-school mobile-assisted artifact creation processes in a seamless language learning environment. *Educational Technology & Society, 16*(2), 198-211.

Social networking: Developing intercultural competence and fostering autonomous learning

Ruby Vurdien[1]

Abstract. With the emergence of Web 2.0, the incorporation of internet-based social networking tools is becoming increasingly popular in the foreign language classes of today. This form of social interaction provides students with the opportunity to express and share their views with their peers, and to create profiles as well as online communities of common interests. Furthermore, through their engagement in online social networking, students develop relationships, build friendships and collaborate with others (Lomicka & Lord, 2009). Online social networking sites have enhanced the environment for language learning and have become a potential platform for internet-based cultural tasks in L2 classes. As a form of telecollaboration, social networking fosters online intercultural interaction between students of different countries with a view to developing intercultural competence. With this in mind, the present study aims to explore how students from two countries, namely, Spain and Mauritius, can develop intercultural competence through the use of the social networking platform Elgg as a telecollaborative learning context. It also discusses whether online social interaction can foster student learning autonomy.

Keywords: social networking, autonomous learning, telecollaboration, online interaction, critical thinking.

1. Introduction

The incorporation of internet-based social networking tools has been gaining popularity nowadays among foreign language learners since they are provided with the opportunity to interact in authentic ways so as to share their views with their peers, create profiles and develop relationships online (Thorne,

---

1. whiterose_va@yahoo.es.

How to cite this article: Vurdien, R. (2014). Social networking: Developing intercultural competence and fostering autonomous learning. In S. Jager, L. Bradley, E. J. Meima, & S. Thouësny (Eds), *CALL Design: Principles and Practice*; Proceedings of the 2014 EUROCALL Conference, Groningen, The Netherlands (pp. 398-402). Dublin: Research-publishing.net. doi:10.14705/rpnet.2014.000252

2010). Furthermore, through their engagement online, they build friendships and collaborate with others (Lomicka & Lord, 2009). The use of Web 2.0 tasks that encourage interactivity can stimulate students' interest and increase their motivation in language learning.

The primary objective of L2 culture learning is that students should gain an in-depth understanding of cultural traits, and not simply learn about culture at a surface level. As Bennett (1993) posits, for learners to become interculturally competent, they need to be unbiased towards other people's cultures so that they can appreciate cross-cultural perspectives with this open-minded attitude. As a result, learners are encouraged to reflect on their own similarities and differences as well as on those of their counterparts to better their understanding of each other's culture. Since the classroom situation has been deemed insufficient for the learning of culture, social networking sites are bridging the gap by affording learners the opportunity to interact with their counterparts in distant locations.

Nevertheless, there is currently a lack of research into the application of Web 2.0 for intercultural exchange (Lomicka & Lord, 2009), and the target of the present study is to make a contribution in this area. Consequently, the study aims, firstly, to explore how students of two countries, Spain and Mauritius, can develop intercultural competence through their interaction on the social network platform Elgg, and, secondly, to discuss whether social online interaction can foster autonomous learning. The following questions guided the study:

- What can students learn about each other's culture online?
- Can social interaction foster learning autonomy?

2. Method

2.1. The project

The project, which was designed for the present study, was task-based and lasted for four months, from March to June 2013. Twenty-four students, of whom fourteen were Spanish and ten were Mauritian, were involved in the study. The Spanish participants were preparing for Cambridge ESOL examinations at levels C1 and C2 (on the Common European Framework of Reference), whereas the Mauritian participants were studying a degree in Computer Science. All the participants were non-native speakers of English, although English was the Mauritian students' medium of instruction. The participants were expected to interact asynchronously by completing weekly tasks geared towards building a mutual intercultural understanding and thereby leading to intercultural competence. The tasks comprised introducing themselves, talking about their university education, traditions, lifestyle, hobbies, gastronomy, interviewing each other about a cultural trait and making a video.

2.2. Data collection and analysis

The study adopted a qualitative approach and data were gathered from various sources, namely, online blogs, two questionnaires administered at the beginning and end of the project, and interviews conducted individually on its conclusion. Finally, a survey in the form of a questionnaire consisting of ten statements was completed by the participants to collate more data. A five-point Likert scale ranging from 1 (strongly disagree) to 5 (strongly agree) was used to gauge the students' reactions to the project.

3. Results

Interestingly, almost all the participants claimed in the final questionnaire and interview that their learning experience had been positive and that they had enhanced their knowledge of their counterparts' university education, traditions, lifestyle, hobbies, food, religion and music. Due to the asynchronous nature of social networking, they were able to reflect upon their own views on the aforementioned items before understanding their peers' comments on their respective cultural features. As certain participants reported, the tasks they had to perform online aroused their curiosity, which increased their motivation to discover and discuss pertinent information about each other's culture.

Whilst the Spanish participants stated that their reflecting upon their peers' comments enabled them to understand certain cultural traits that were different from theirs, some of their Mauritian counterparts said that although the responses they read were informative, they occasionally found it difficult to follow the thread of the discussion; this was due either to their lack of knowledge of, or simply disinterest in, the subject. Others also mentioned that they were not acquainted with the idea of reflecting upon their peers' responses, which resulted in their unsuccessful completion of the task.

Most participants mentioned that they had benefited from sharing information with their peers, which assisted them in developing collaborative and independent learning skills. As several indicated, as a result of the amount of information they had exchanged, there was enough scope for critical reflection to take place;

meanwhile, those who did not perform their tasks effectively thought differently, attributing this failure either to a lack of time or the unavailability of internet access.

4. Discussion

Judging from the participants' reaction to their engagement in the tasks they performed, internet-based activities may be considered meaningful in the learning process and can increase students' motivation (Thorne, 2003; Ware, 2005). The findings suggest that such online collaborative tasks can aid students to gain cross-cultural awareness and develop intercultural communicative skills, which, as a result, might be useful to enrich their learning experience. Furthermore, a rich learning environment may be conducive for learners to become interculturally competent (Pollak, 2010). However, due to the participants' lack of experience in performing some of the tasks, clear instructions should be provided and the subject of discussion carefully chosen so that students may benefit from their thought-provoking nature during their interaction; in this way, they may be encouraged to be critical, an aspect deemed essential in intercultural competence.

The fact that the participants reported a high degree of motivation in social interaction online indicates that they were able to manage their learning autonomously (Ushioda, 2006). Therefore, in order for learning goals to be achieved, it is of the utmost importance that teachers should encourage their students to perform their tasks successfully. Another important aspect in fostering learner autonomy is critical reflection through collaborative tasks online (Swienhorst, 2008). In the case of those participants who engaged in critical reflection, it suggests that they exhibited the capacity to take the initiative and manage their learning more effectively than others, as pointed out by Lee (2011).

Arguably, it can be inferred from the findings that students should seek the help of their peers when interacting online in order to achieve their goals as independent learners. Social networking can provide the opportunity for learners to develop such skills if they are afforded proper guidance by their instructor.

5. Conclusions

This study has shed some light on how social networking can foster intercultural competence and autonomous learning. Students are able to discover aspects relating to each other's culture in a virtual environment which is conducive for learning to take place. The learning tasks provided them with the opportunity to ponder both their own and their peers' thoughts to achieve that aim. Social networking seems to be an appropriate platform for students to negotiate meaning and construct knowledge together, since they can plan their own learning approach at their own pace. They feel less intimidated when expressing their views as there is no peer pressure similar to that which tends to prevail in face-to-face classes. As a result, the outcome is meaningful learning. However, because of the small-scale nature of this study, the findings cannot be generalized. Hopefully further research in this field will contribute to benefiting the learning process.

Acknowledgements. I would like to thank all the participants who provided the data for this study as well as my colleagues, Sameerchand Pudaruth and David Rixham, for their support and feedback.

References

Bennett, M. (1993). Towards ethnorelativism: A development model of intercultural sensitivity. In M. Paige (Ed.). *Education for the intercultural experience* (pp. 21-77). Yarmouth, ME: Intercultural Press.

Lee, L. (2011). Blogging: Promoting learner autonomy and intercultural competence through study abroad. *Language Learning and Technology, 15*(3), 87-109.

Lomicka, L., & Lord, G. (2009). Introduction to social networking, collaboration and Web 2.0 tools. In L. Lomicka & G. Lord (Eds), *The next generations: Social networking and online collaboration in FL learning* (pp. 1-11). San Marcos TX: CALICO Consortium.

Pollak, C. (2010). *Online communication and its potential of promoting the foreign language learners' intercultural competence* [Online]. Retrieved from http://othes.univie.ac.at/9902/1/2010-04-29_0403328.pdf

Swienhorst, K. (2008). *Learner autonomy and CALL environments*. New York: Routledge.

Thorne, S. (2003). Artifacts and cultures-of-use in intercultural communication. *Language Learning and Technology, 7*(2), 38-67.

Thorne, S. (2010). The 'intercultural turn' and language learning in the crucible of new media. In F. Helm & S. Guth (Eds), *Telecollaboration 2.0 for language and intercultural learning*. Bern: Peter Lang.

Ushioda, E. (2006). Motivation, autonomy and sociocultural theory. In P. Benson, (Ed.), *Learner autonomy 8: Insider perspectives on autonomy in language teaching and learning* (pp. 5-24). Dublin: Authentik.

Ware, P. (2005). "Missed communication" in online communication: Tensions in fostering successful online interactions. *Language Learning and Technology, 9*(2), 64-89.

university of groningen

Context-aware writing support for SNS: Connecting formal and informal learning

Ikumi Waragai[1], Shuichi Kurabayashi[2], Tatsuya Ohta[3], Marco Raindl[4], Yasushi Kiyoki[5], and Hideyuki Tokuda[6]

Abstract. This paper presents another stage in a series of research efforts by the authors to develop an experience-connected mobile language learning environment, bridging formal and informal learning. Building on a study in which the authors tried to connect classroom learning (of German in Japan) with learners' real life experiences abroad by having smartphones detect the learners' location and supply them with multimedia content matching their real-time communicative situation, the authors developed a hybrid language learning environment supporting different types of learning. Based on observations that learners tended to use resources rather for preparatory or retrospective learning, and on considerations about the potential of social media as a space for informal language learning, the authors added a feature that supports learners when writing a social networking service (SNS) post about their everyday experiences abroad. Help is offered based on the analysis of the learners' geolocational position –hinting to what situation they might want to write about– and on the text they already entered. Based on these data, they are provided with help in the form of vocabulary and/or model texts.

Keywords: informal learning, smartphone, social network, situated learning, context awareness.

---

1. Keio University, Japan; ikumi@sfc.keio.ac.jp.
2. Keio University, Japan; kurabaya@sfc.keio.ac.jp.
3. Nanzan University, Japan; FZE00305@nifty.ne.jp.
4. Dokkyo University, Japan; raindl@dokkyo.ac.jp.
5. Keio University, Japan; kiyoki@sfc.keio.ac.jp.
6. Keio University, Japan; hxt@sfc.keio.ac.jp.

How to cite this article: Waragai, I., Kurabayashi, S., Ohta, T., Raindl, M., Kiyoki, Y., & Tokuda, H. (2014). Context-aware writing support for SNS: Connecting formal and informal learning. In S. Jager, L. Bradley, E. J. Meima, & S. Thouësny (Eds), *CALL Design: Principles and Practice*; *Proceedings of the 2014 EUROCALL Conference, Groningen, The Netherlands* (pp. 403-407). Dublin: Research-publishing.net. doi:10.14705/rpnet.2014.000253

1. Introduction

Recent discussion of learning design has emphasized the importance of informal learning, the need to build bridges between this type of situated learning happening in our learners' everyday interactions on the one hand, and formal learning in educational institutions on the other hand –and the potential of mobile devices in addressing this challenge. In her overview of the evolution of learning cultures in the 21st century, Kukulska-Hulme (2010) comes to the conclusion that learning will become increasingly learner-centered and more and more context-aware. Using their mobile devices, learners would look out for learning opportunities in their every-day experiences, examining them for learning partners ("who is nearby"), learning contents ("what's interesting here?") and possibilities for output ("what can I contribute?") (Kukulska-Hulme, 2010, p. 11).

Aiming to support this type of instantaneous learning in every-day life, the authors have been developing language learning environments that try to connect classroom learning of German in Japan with learners' real-life experiences when first going to a German speaking country. The basic idea of these language learning environments is that learners taking part in a summer course or embarking on an exchange year abroad are confronted with a great number of situations that are a challenge for their language skills, but at the same time constitute opportunities for situated learning. In order to facilitate that learning, we try to support learners with help based on courseware material already familiar to them, but tailored to the situation they are in. Thus, we assume, learners can match things they learnt in the classroom to their communicational needs in every-day life, exploring how they can use what they learnt in school, and, reversely, experiencing what situations they can already master with what they know.

2. Design of the learning environment

2.1. Context-aware learning support: two components

This learning environment was designed for learners of German (on CEFR[7] level A2-B1) at Keio University (Japan), who either take part in a four-week language course in a German speaking country or study there in the first months of an exchange year. Both components of the learning environment offer context-aware learning support via the learners' mobile devices, based on the analysis of the

---

7. Common European Framework of Reference for Languages

situation that they are about to interact in, or that they want to communicate about. Both components draw on courseware developed at the university.

2.1.1. Support for oral interaction

The component developed previously (Waragai, Ohta, Raindl, & Kurabayashi, 2013) offers learners support in an actual communicative situation. The mobile device detects the learners' geolocational position, infers what situation the learners might be in and then supplies them with learning materials from the courseware where interaction in a similar situation is represented: video, audios or texts. If, for example, learners wait at a bus stop, their mobile device would offer the video clip "Asking for directions at a bus stop". Thus, classroom content would be linked to a real social context. One of the findings of a trial operation and evaluation was, though, that many learners tended to use these learning resources for preparatory or retrospective learning, rather than as support for on-the-spot interaction (Waragai et al., 2013, p. 187).

2.1.2. Support for writing an SNS post

Based on these observations, we introduced a second component to our learning environment: a smart blog editor, offering help when writing about every-day experiences in an SNS. This new component aims at providing learners with input to support situated learning of writing. Our system recommends context-dependent courseware-based input in the form of vocabulary, sentences and paragraphs, or blog entries written by peers for assisting learners when writing about their experiences.

The selection of the material is based on two functions. The first function is content-aware vocabulary/sentences/paragraphs/blog entries recommendation. An important characteristic of this system is that it provides learning materials by analyzing text contents that a learner is writing. Concretely, the system captures three types of metadata from the contents that a learner is writing. The first metadata is the *last word*, referring to the word that the user entered last. The second metadata is the *current word*, referring to the as yet incomplete word that the user is just typing. The third metadata is a *word histogram* that summarizes the blog entry into a histogram structure. Each bin of this histogram corresponds to a keyword (except a number of so-called stop-words, like articles, prepositions, some pronouns, and conjunctions). Each bin represents word occurrence frequency in a single blog entry. So, by comparing two histograms, the system can detect entire similarity of two blog entries. The system uses the *last word* for executing keyword-based recommendation. The system obtains sentences and paragraphs that contain the *last word*. The *current word* is used for assistance to enter a word.

The second function is geolocation-aware keyword recommendation, through mapping of lecture materials onto actual life space. This system is equipped with a database that contains keyword metadata for several locations in German cities. This database is used for detecting the possible situational context of the current location of the user. Concretely, the system converts the GPS location value, such as "latitude: 35.64840502016192, longitude: 139.74251877904112", into a keyword readable by humans such as "University". By executing this conversion, the system can measure the relationship of the learner's current location and the learning materials. In addition, this system implements a function by which learners can share their experiences with other learners through the SNS on the basis of their current location.

The decision to shift from speaking support to writing support was backed by results of a survey amongst the target group, which showed that writing on SNS was an activity that our students engaged in very regularly, and that a number of advanced learners also used German in their postings on SNS. Thus, we could assume that this learning environment would connect well with our learners' habits and needs.

3. Evaluation of a first test run

A first trial run of the new component of our language learning environment in spring 2014 involved three students that were studying in Germany at that time. As they were already familiar with their University town, they were asked to travel to a different town and write posts about their experience there.

The students were interviewed about their experiences and observations. A general tendency was that students appreciated having an opportunity to write about everyday experience in German. It was stated that, compared to their opportunities to use the target language in spoken interaction while staying in Germany, their opportunities to write were rather limited. All three informants stated that they enjoyed writing on a social network in German.

On the other hand, some utterances pointed to students being dissatisfied too: students experienced their writing skills as inadequate to what they wanted to express, and noted that the learning environment often did not provide them with the help that they were looking for. Some stated that they had the impression that the contents of the database was too restricted. All three informants used other websites simultaneously to get help that they did not get within the learning environment.

It was observed that the database was slow when used on mobile phones. Thus, the informants accessed the system from their homes.

4. Conclusions

In order to be a viable support for learners when interacting in real-life situations or when writing about every-day experiences, a learning environment has to be accurately tailored to the needs of its users. Connecting learning to learners' experiences can only work if the learning environment allows learners to express what matters to them. One of the problems in the test run was that –for practical reasons– all of the informants had a German proficiency of about B2 CEFR, while the learning environment targets learners of A2 to B1. Thus, after having adjusted some details concerning the selection and display of data, we will run another trial implementation with a larger number of informants of levels A2 and B1. The positive response about the learning environment offering students the rare opportunity to write about personal experiences in the target language might allow the conclusion though that our learning environment has the potential to suit our exchange students' needs.

Acknowledgements. This research is being supported by the Japanese Ministry of Education and Culture by "MEXT KAKENHI Grant Number 24320107".

References

Kukulska-Hulme, A. (2010). Learning cultures on the move: Where are we heading? *Journal of Educational Technology and Society, 13*(4), 4-14.

Waragai, I., Ohta, T., Raindl, M., & Kurabayashi, S. (2013). An experience-oriented language learning environment supporting informal learning abroad. *Educational Technology Research, Japan Society for Educational Technology, 36*(1-2), 179-189.

university of groningen

'Sizing up' the online course: Adapting learning designs to meet growing participant numbers

Julie Watson[1]

Abstract. Online course design has experienced an upheaval recently with the arrival of Massive Open Online Courses (MOOCs), turning the model which underpins many online courses on its head. In contrast to MOOCs, conventional online courses have usually been designed for small private groups of participants, giving access to closed content and online tutors able to cater for individual needs and provide personalised feedback on tasks. What principles and practical considerations underlie these different design approaches? The development of a pre-arrival online distance learning course for international students offered by an elearning unit in Modern Languages between 2005 and 2014 illustrates interesting aspects of this evolution. This course, focusing on English language development and transitions to UK academic culture, reflects an historical design shift from accommodating small tutored groups of 25 to an open student-driven course for over 2500 participants which exhibits features of emerging MOOCs. This paper will describe the evolution of this course design to allow a flexible response to needs in a changing learning context. Specific features of the learning design which have changed or remained constant will be identified and adaptations made to 'size up' the course and cater for growing numbers of participants will be highlighted.

Keywords: online course, MOOC, learning design, international students, course evolution.

---

1. University of Southampton; J.Watson@soton.ac.uk.

How to cite this article: Watson, J. (2014). 'Sizing up' the online course: Adapting learning designs to meet growing participant numbers. In S. Jager, L. Bradley, E. J. Meima, & S. Thouësny (Eds), *CALL Design: Principles and Practice*; Proceedings of the 2014 EUROCALL Conference, Groningen, The Netherlands (pp. 408-412). Dublin: Research-publishing.net. doi:10.14705/rpnet.2014.000254

'Sizing up' the online course: Adapting learning designs to meet growing participant numbers

1. Introduction

The arrival of MOOCs is starting to create waves of impact across teaching and learning in higher education. Conventional online courses, designed for small private groups of participants, are also feeling the effect as designers consider how they might be scaled up to serve increasing numbers of students online. In offering an overview of the current MOOC landscape, Bayne and Ross (2013) acknowledge both the disruptive force that MOOCs represent and their capacity to act as a catalyst for innovation and change in the UK higher education sector. From their review of the MOOC literature, they identify several emerging themes:

- the troubling of the cMOOC/xMOOC binary;
- the teacher role;
- tensions around learner participation;
- the meanings and implications of 'massive';
- tracing the boundaries between openness and control (Bayne & Ross, 2013, p. 7).

The issues underlying all but one of these could be said to have equal relevance for the design of any online course. The use of the cMOOC or xMOOC label essentially differentiates the type of pedagogic approach (usually connectivist vs. didactic) reflected by the online learning environment, but as Bayne and Ross (2013) point out, in recent MOOCs surveyed, this distinction has been found to no longer be quite so clear-cut. Equally, this may be said to apply to the pedagogic design of other online courses, which can reflect mixed features.

This paper charts the changes in design of online courses produced by an elearning unit in Modern Languages at the University of Southampton, which have ranged from Small Private Online Courses (SPOCs) catering for closed groups of 25 students to a 'sized up' online course designed for, and open to, several thousand participants. It will highlight the impact that Web 2.0, innovations in online teaching and learning, and MOOCs have had on the evolution of this online course design.

2. The evolution of an online course

Since 2005, eLanguages, an elearning research and development team, has been running short courses online for international students. These focus on students' pre-arrival concerns and needs, introduce practical aspects of British life and culture, and familiarise participants with effective study skills and aspects of UK academic culture which may present challenges as well as offering opportunities for language development (eLanguages, 2014).

2.1. Small private online courses

Our first online course, named *POPC* (Preparatory Online Pre-sessional Course) and subsequently renamed *Arrive UK*, was delivered intensively in fixed five-week time slots over the summer of 2005 to groups of students who had been accepted for study on a taught pre-sessional course but were still based in their home countries. They were tutored in groups of circa 25, learning from content designed as interactive learning objects and tutor-led discussions in forums. These virtual learning environment-hosted courses were optional and included no formal or self assessment. They contained text-based interactive activities but made little use of other media (audio or visual).

A few years later, the podcast revolution and new approaches to their integration in different teaching contexts, spearheaded by Salmon, Nie, and Edirisingha (2007), led us to experiment with short informal podcasts made by teachers and students, adding both listening content and more in-course tutor 'presence' and 'scaffolding' to the online course. The podcasts were well-received by students; however, their engagement in formal tutor-led discussion tasks, even if they were still using the course content (learning objects) independently, highlighted 'tensions around student participation' and the 'teacher role'. Was a formal tutor and guided discussion really needed on this type of course? The addition of weekly tutor-led (synchronous and text-based) chat sessions indicated that for some students, contact with the tutor and peers was important in order to ask specific questions and alleviate their pre-arrival anxiety. This all raised interesting questions about what students really wanted, content and/or contact and interaction, and brings to mind the 'connectivist vs. didactic model' and the more recent 'cMOOC/xMOOC binary' debate identified by Bayne and Ross (2013).

2.2. Sizing up the course and letting go of the tutor

Phase 2 of the evolution of our online course really began with Web 2.0. Concurrent with growth in open content, institutions, including our own, were making student-created content available through their own websites and via social media, such as *YouTube*, in order to reach prospective students. Such videos provided a taste of campus life and offered a far more effective insight for international students than the traditional welcome document. Open student blogs also captured the experience of study abroad. Whereas previously we had needed to make all our own content, now we could curate these freely available resources for learning purposes and enhance our course with links to them. As well as extending the online course invitation to all incoming international students (circa 4000), sizing it up considerably, we also wanted to enhance the role of socialisation alongside academic acculturation.

We added a shared 'Social Wall', a Web 2.0 free application (e.g. *Linoit*; *Padlet*) as an ice-breaker, hosting students' short customised introductions and photos. We retained the discussion forum solely for student-driven extended conversations. Students created their own user community, started their own threads, answered each others' questions and shared contact details to meet and socialise 'off-course'. This adjustment in the 'boundaries of openness and control' took away the need for tutoring in this particular course, and so the course became untutored. It also became self-paced for the students, running from mid-April to early October and accommodating the international student community growing within it. In 2014, 3000 participants are expected to take part, suggesting it has reached MOOC-like proportions and raising Bayne and Ross' (2013) query over the 'meaning and implications of the word massive'.

3. Conclusions

The charting of this evolution illustrates how a 'conventional' online course in an educational context has benefited both from Web 2.0 innovation and openness, and from the impact of MOOCs to make itself more responsive to changing needs. Since 2005, modifications to the course tools, technologies and designs have, importantly, been driven by a desire to continually improve the student experience of the course. This has resulted in a rather hybridised approach to course design, retaining a core of provided course content (learning objects) and blending this with the connectivist possibilities produced by 'sizing up' to MOOC-like proportions. This paper has aimed to show how the evolutionary process of this online course has, interestingly, echoed the emerging issues of MOOCs identified by Bayne and Ross (2013).

Acknowledgements. I would like to thank my colleagues in the eLanguages team and department of Modern Languages at the University of Southampton who help deliver and tutor our online courses, and all international students, past and present, who have contributed to our online course design and development through their participation and valuable feedback.

References

Bayne, S., & Ross, J. (2013). *The pedagogy of the massive open online course: The UK view*. The Higher Education Academy. Retrieved from https://www.heacademy.ac.uk/sites/default/files/HEA_Edinburgh_MOOC_WEB_240314_1.pdf

eLanguages. (2014). *Get ready for Southampton*. Retrieved from http://www.elanguages.ac.uk/get_ready_for_southampton.php

Salmon, G. K., Nie, M., & Edirisingha, P. (2007). Podcasting for learning. *ALISS Quarterly, 2*(4), 11-17.

university of groningen

Instructional interaction development and its effects in online foreign language learning

Rong Zhao[1]

Abstract. This paper introduced the features of scaffolding to the development of instructional interaction in online foreign language learning, and testified their effects on learners' perceived usefulness, perceived ease of use, sense of community, and continuance intention by the integration of the Technology-Acceptance Model and the Organizational Framework of Online Learning Community. An instrument was developed, data were collected from 299 students, and the relationships among the variables of scaffolding features, learners' perceived ease of use, perceived usefulness, sense of community, continuance intention, etc., were examined by path analysis. The results showed that although instructional interaction developed in accordance with the scaffolding features cannot affect learners' continuance intention directly, it plays a partially mediating role by significantly affecting learners' perceived usefulness, perceived ease of use, and sense of community.

Keywords: instructional interaction, scaffolding, continuance intention.

1. Introduction

Instructional interaction refers to an event that takes place between a learner and the learner's environment inclusive of the instructor, other learners and course content (Wagner, 1994). Given that foreign language learning is greatly different from second language acquisition in learning context and learners' psychological process (Vroman, 1990), this study attempts at introducing scaffolding features to the development of instructional interaction in online foreign language learning.

---

1. Shanghai International Studies University, Shanghai, China; zrelino@gmail.com.

How to cite this article: Zhao, R. (2014). Instructional interaction development and its effects in online foreign language learning. In S. Jager, L. Bradley, E. J. Meima, & S. Thouësny (Eds), *CALL Design: Principles and Practice; Proceedings of the 2014 EUROCALL Conference, Groningen, The Netherlands* (pp. 413-421). Dublin: Research-publishing.net. doi:10.14705/rpnet.2014.000255

Scaffolding features have been applied widely in general education, such as direction maintenance, marking of critical features, demonstration (Wood, Bruner, & Ross, 1976), step-by-step directions, sortation of information (McKenzie, 2000), alignment, experiential value, collaboration, multiplicity (McLoughlin, 2002), channeling and focusing, modeling (Pea, 2004), occurrences in a collaborative context (Tuckman, 2007), and heuristic modelling (Radford, Bosanquet, Webster, Blatchford, & Rubie-Davies, 2014). With a view to pinpointing features which facilitate developing instructional interaction, this paper highlights the features of *continuity* (see McKenzie, 2000; McLoughlin, 2002), *contextual support* (see McLoughlin, 2002), *collaboration* (see McLoughlin, 2002; Tuckman, 2007), *modeling* (see Wood et al., 1976; Pea, 2004), *channeling and focusing* (see Pea, 2004), and *multiplicity* (see McLoughlin, 2002).

Continuity refers to alignment between the steps of instruction; *contextual support* to the provision of different means to expose learners to authentic experiences; *collaboration* to collaborative work with the instructor, other learners or online content for the perception of encouragement, confidence, or advance in study; *modeling* to the demonstration of an idealized form of the act to be performed to pinpoint discrepancies between the produced and the ideal solution; *channeling and focusing* to the indication of relevant sources to simplify the task and focus learners' attention; and *multiplicity* to the provision of multiple learning strategies, both direct and indirect (Zhao & Chen, 2014).

The Organizational Framework of Online Learning Community, which has been used to study the maintenance of online learning community, indicates that task, technological and social dimensions serve learners' requirements respectively on learning task fulfillment, technological convenience and social satisfaction (Carabajal, LaPointe, & Gunawarden, 2003). Thus, the scaffolding features listed above are examined in terms of task fulfillment, technological convenience and social satisfaction.

The Technology-Acceptance Model (TAM) has been applied to describe the impact of external variables on learners' intention towards e-learning. In the TAM, "perceived usefulness (PU) refers to the degree to which a person believes that using a particular system would enhance his job performance; perceived ease of use (PEOU) [to] the degree to which a person believes that using a particular system would be free of physical and mental effort" (Davis, 1989, cited in Chitungo & Munongo, 2013, p. 54). TAM is employed to test whether the suggested scaffolding features affect learners' PU in learning task fulfillment and PEOU in technological convenience.

A sense of community (SOC) underlines the feelings of connectedness, trust, etc., that community members have to each other and to their learning community (Rovai, 2002). In this paper, SOC is employed to study whether the scaffolding features can affect learners' social satisfaction.

Continuance Intention (CI) is a construct in the Expectation-Confirmation Model (ECM) (see Bhattacherjee, 2001), which has been widely applied to the studies of online education (see Lee, 2010; Limayem & Cheung, 2008). CI is defined as the "intention to continue using the information system" (Bhattacherjee, 2001, p. 351), and in this study, CI is applied to narrow down the behavioral intention in TAM, and to test foreign language learners' continuance intention towards online learning.

2. Method

2.1. Research model and hypotheses

Following TAM, this study hypothesizes that instructional interaction developed on the basis of scaffolding features can directly and indirectly affect foreign language learners' behavioral intention, that is, their continuance intention towards online learning. The scaffolding features, that is, continuity, contextual support, collaboration, modeling, channeling and focusing, and multiplicity work as the first-order constructs of instructional interaction.

On the basis of TAM, this study argues that (1) learners' PU and PEOU will affect positively learners' CI; (2) learners' PEOU will affect positively learners' PU; and (3) instructional interaction developed on the basis of scaffolding features will affect positively learners' PU, PEOU, and CI. This study, as seen in Figure 1, posits:

- H1. Learners' PU in online foreign language learning is positively related to their CI.
- H2. Learners' PEOU is positively related to their CI.
- H3. Learners' PU is positively influenced by their PEOU.
- H4. Instructional interaction is positively related to learners' PU in online foreign language learning.
- H5. Instructional interaction is positively related to learners' PEOU.
- H6. Instructional interaction is positively related to learners' CI.

According to the Organizational Framework of Online Learning Community, this study argues that instructional interaction will also affect positively learners' social satisfaction which is represented by the SOC in this study, and the SOC will affect positively learners' continuance intention. Thus, this study further posits:

- H7. Instructional interaction is positively related to learners' SOC.
- H8. Learners' SOC is positively related to their CI.

Figure 1. Research model

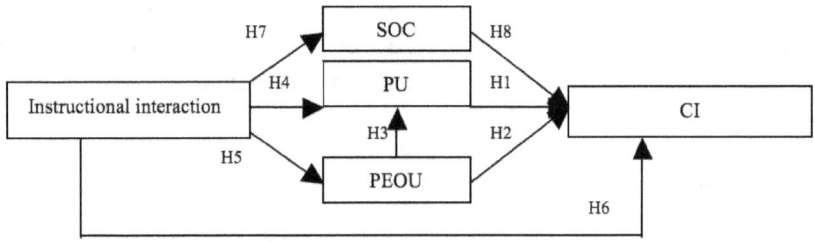

2.2. Participants and procedure

This study picked adult learners at the age of 19/20 from three universities. Of 356 questionnaires sent out, 299 questionnaires were collected as available. Among the 299 questionnaires, 102 learners were of the Web Supplemented Mode where participation online is optional for students, 99 learners were of the Web Dependent Mode where some traditional on-campus component is retained but there is a compulsory online component, and 98 learners were of the Fully Online Mode where there is no on-campus direct contact component in this mode. For the convenience of instrument development, all the participants were freshmen and sophomores of an approximate English proficiency level, who intended to pass ECT-Band4 or 6. They were of different majors and were picked randomly within each of the three above modes.

In data collection, this study sent out and collected the questionnaires in the second semester of 2011 to ensure that the participants had already used the language learning information system for a substantial period.

2.3. Survey Instrument

The constructs of continuance intention, perceived usefulness, perceived ease of use, and sense of community were reflective latent variables; while the construct of instructional interaction was a formative composite variable. The online language learning communities (OLLC) in this study were provided for the adult learners to master language points, including vocabulary and grammar. In the online language learning, the learners were instructed to learn written, visual or audial materials, and to complete various exercises and language tasks.

CI was measured with the items adapted from Bhattacherjee (2001):
- I will use the OLLC on a regular basis in the future.
- I will frequently use the OLLC in the future.
- I will strongly recommend others to use the OLLC.

PU was measured with the items adapted from Davis (1989):
- I feel that online study can improve my learning performance better than offline.
- The OLLC is effective and my educational needs are met.
- I find the OLLC is useful and promotes my desire to learn.

PEOU was measured with the items adapted from Davis (1989):
- Learning to operate the OLLC is easy for me.
- It is easy for me to become skillful at using the OLLC.
- Overall, the OLLC is easy to use.

SOC was measured with the items adapted from Rovai (2002):
- I feel learners of the OLLC care about each other.
- I feel, instead of alone, connected to others in the OLLC.
- I feel that this OLLC is like a family.
- I do not feel isolated in this OLLC.
- I trust others in this OLLC.
- I feel that I can rely on others in this OLLC.
- I feel that members of OLLC depend on me.
- I feel confident that others will support me in online language education.

Instructional interaction was conceptualized as a second-order factor consisting of six first-order constructs: continuity, contextualization, modeling, focusing and outlining, collaboration, and multiplicity. Each of the first-order constructs is important, but not individually sufficient, for reflecting the latent construct. With no established measures for the constructs, they were developed from the constructs' definitions.

The measurement items were proved and adjusted through interviews respectively with 6 adult learners, 3 university English teachers and an online language education system designer, a group discussion of 6 learners and an evaluation of a 3-person expert panel (see Appendix 1).

3. Analysis and results

Since the research model contains both reflective and formative components, SmartPLS version 2.0 was chosen for data analysis. In data analysis, availability is usually assessed by AVE, which should be more than 0.50. Reliability is usually assessed by two indicators –Cronbach's alpha and composite reliability. Both are supposed to be more than 0.70. In this study, of all the components, the lowest composite reliability (ρc) was 0.87, the lowest Cronbach's Alpha (α) was 0.77 and the lowest AVE score was 0.68. An R^2 value of .606 indicates that the model explains a substantial amount of variance in continuance intention. All hypotheses are supported except H6 (Table 1).

As the test of hypotheses indicates, foreign language learners' continuance intention is positively dependent on their PU, PEOU and SOC; learners' PEOU is proved to influence PU; instructional interaction, which is developed on the basis of the scaffolding features listed above, plays a significantly positive role in influencing learners' PU, PEOU and SOC.

Table 1. Test of hypotheses

No.	Hypothesis	T Statistics	P
H1	PU → CI	6.035915	***
H2	PEOU → CI	3.373664	***
H3	PEOU → PU	3.055354	**
H4	instructional interaction → PU	6.517316	***
H5	instructional interaction → PEOU	19.520094	***
H6	instructional interaction → CI	1.28048	Not supported
H7	instructional interaction → SOC	7.122064	***
H8	SOC → CI	4.041249	***

4. Discussion and conclusion

The results showed that although instructional interaction developed in accordance with the scaffolding features cannot affect learners' continuance intention directly, it plays a partially mediating role by significantly affecting learners' PU, PEOU and SOC. Thus, this paper suggests that with the conditions of foreign language learning greatly different from those of second language acquisition, more emphasis should be laid on scaffolding features in developing online instructional interaction.

Acknowledgements. I would like to thank Shanghai First Class University Discipline (B), Pedagogy in Shanghai International Studies University, and the National Significant Education Research Project (ZDA125-21).

References

Bhattacherjee, A. (2001). Understanding information systems continuance. An expectation–confirmation model. *MIS Quarterly, 25*(3), 351-370. doi:10.2307/3250921

Carabajal, K., LaPointe, D., & Gunawardena, C. N. (2003). Group development in online learning communities. In M. G. Moore & W. G. Anderson (Eds), *Handbook of distance education* (pp. 217-234). London: Lawrence Erlbaum Associates.

Chitungo, S. K., & Munongo, S. (2013). Extending the technology acceptance model to mobile banking adoption in rural Zimbabwe. *Journal of Business Administration and Education, 3*(1), 51.79.

Davis, F. (1989). Perceived usefulness, perceived ease of use, and user acceptance of information technology. *MIS Quarterly, 13*(3), 319-340. doi:10.2307/249008

Lee, M.-C. (2010). Explaining and predicting users' continuance intention toward e-learning: An extension of the expectation–confirmation model. *Computers & Education, 54*, 506-516. doi:10.1016/j.compedu.2009.09.002

Limayem, M., & Cheung, C. M. K. (2008). Understanding information systems continuance: The case of Internet-based learning technologies. *Information & Management, 45*, 227-232. doi:10.1016/j.im.2008.02.005

McKenzie, J. (2000). Scaffolding for Success. [Electronic version] *Beyond Technology, Questioning, Research and the Information Literate School Community*. Retrieved from http://fno.org/dec99/scaffold.html

McLoughlin, C. (2002). Learner support in distance and networked learning environments: Ten dimensions for successful design. *Distance Education, 23*(2), 149-162. doi:10.1080/0158791022000009178

Pea, R. D. (2004). The social and technological dimensions of scaffolding and related theoretical concepts for learning, education, and human activity. *The Journal of the learning sciences, 13*(3), 423-451. doi:10.1207/s15327809jls1303_6

Radford, J., Bosanquet, P., Webster, R., Blatchford, P., & Rubie-Davies, C. (2014). Fostering learner independence through heuristic scaffolding: A valuable role for teaching assistants. *International Journal of Educational Research, 63*, 116-126. doi:10.1016/j.ijer.2013.02.010

Rovai, A. P. (2002). Development of an instrument to measure classroom community. *Internet and Higher Education, 5*,197-211. doi:10.1016/S1096-7516(02)00102-1

Tuckman, B. W. (2007). The effect of motivational scaffolding on procrastinators' distance learning outcomes. *Computers & Education, 49*(2), 414-422. doi:10.1016/j.compedu.2005.10.002

Vroman, R. B. (1990). The logical problem of foreign language learning. *Linguistic Analysis, 20*(1-2), 1-49.

Wagner, E. D. (1994). In support of a functional definition of interaction. *American Journal of Distance Education, 8*(2), 6-29. doi:10.1080/08923649409526852

Wood, D., Bruner, J. S., & Ross, G. (1976). The role of tutoring in problem Solving. *Journal of Child Psychology and Psychiatry, 17*, 89-100. doi:10.1111/j.1469-7610.1976.tb00381.x

Zhao, R., & Chen, J. L. (2014). Scaffolding, perceived usefulness, satisfaction and continuance intention toward online foreign language learning. In F. Li (Ed.), *Language, Medias and Culture III; International Proceedings of Economics Development and Research Vol.77* (pp. 5-9). Singapore: IACSIT Press.

Appendix 1.

Continuity:
- Online learning provides a series of related materials for learning relevant specific language points.
- I can get acquainted with a language point, after learning a series of related articles.
- It is easy for me to master a systematically repeated language point.

Contextualization:
- In the authentic context in online learning, my language knowledge is activated.
- The pictures, films or other authentic sensory contexts in the online language learning make the foreign language accessible and engaging.
- The online learning brings language points closer to the authentic world experience by interesting articles, pictures or other means.

Modeling:
- In learning a new language point (a new word, or some grammar), I am given clear examples as to how to use it.
- When I am introduced a new language point, I know what is requested of me to imitate.
- With modeling help, I know how to accomplish a particular language task.

Focusing and outlining:
- I am given a brief introduction of the topic and organization of the foreign language articles.

- The online learning highlights the important points of the learning materials.
- The highlighted outlines help me have a systematic idea of the related article.

Collaboration:
- In online learning, I am encouraged to work with other learners to fulfill a learning task.
- In online learning, I am encouraged in time to communicate and play a role in team work.
- In collaboration with other learners, I am encouraged to perform at my best.

Multiplicity:
- The online learning helps me to find and adopt proper learning strategies.
- The online learning teaches me methods to improve my foreign language learning.
- The online learning enables me to plan with learning strategies according to my learning performance.

Author Index

A
Ajiki, Yuri 172
Akita, Yuya 230
Alghasab, Maha 1
Alsabaan, Majed 6
Alvarez, Claudia Patricia 52
Andersen, Kent 107
Appel, Christine 12, 248
Asztalos, Réka 18
Attridge, Ann 191

B
Bárcena, Elena 40
Barge, Martin 88
Benini, Silvia 23
Bradley, Linda 368
Buendgens-Kosten, Judith 29

C
Cameran, Christel-Joy 140
Caner, Mustafa 329
Carpi, Tiziana 35
Castrillo, María Dolores 40
Chen, Julian ChengChiang 47
Clayton, John 172
Cuesta Medina, Liliana 52

D
Davey, Ronnie 72
Dias, Joseph V. 59
Doshi, Natasha 185

E
Einum, Even 352
Elshoff, Joost 65

F
Farshad Nia, Sara 72, 77

Fatahipour, Majid 83
Fitzgerald, Alannah 88
Fredholm, Kent 96
Fukuda, Eri 102, 278

G
Ghaseminajm, Mahnaz 83
Giannikas, Christina Nicole 296
Gimeno-Sanz, Ana 107
Goda, Yoshiko 113
Grisez, Viviane 334
Guo, Sijia 119

H
Hamada, Mayumi 127
Hampel, Regine 237
Handley, Zöe 134
Harbusch, Karin 140
Härtel, Johannes 140
Hashimoto, Shinichi 102, 278
Hoffstaedter, Petra 146
Holster, Trevor 307
Huang, Chung-Kai 151, 158

I
Ino, Atsushi 165
Ishida, Kenichi 345
Iwata, Jun 172

J
Jager, Sake viii, 12
Jauregi, Kristi 241

K
Kafes, Hüseyin 329
Kakoulli-Constantinou, Elis 296
Kato, Hiroshi 113
Kawahara, Tatsuya 230

Kharrufa, Ahmed 202
Kido, Kazuhiko 278
Kiyoki, Yasushi 403
Koenraad, Ton 241
Kohn, Kurt 146
Kong, Zhuoran 202
Konstantoudakis, Konstantinos 324
Kosek, Michał 179
Kotikoski, Tuula-Harriet 185
Kourtis-Kazoullis, Vasilia 324
Kurabayashi, Shuichi 403

L
Lake, J. 307
Lambacher, Stephen G. 267, 284
Lapok, Paul 191
Lawson, Alistair 191
Lee, John 196
Lin, Chun-Yu 151, 158
Lin, Mei 202
Lison, Pierre 179
Lopes, António 209
Luckin, Rosemary 391
Lu, Zhihong 214

M
Marandi, Susan 77
Marsden, Emma 134
Martin, Véronique 220
Matsuda, Takeshi 113
Meima, Estelle J. viii
Mercurio, Marco 225
Mirzaei, Maryam Sadat 230
Miyagawa, Hiroyuki 113
Molka-Danielsen, Judith 241
Montoro, Carlos 237
Motteram, Gary 241

N
Nic Giolla Mhichíl, Mairéad 12, 248, 261
Nocchi, Susanna 255

O
Obari, Hiroyuki 267
Ó Ciardúbháin, Colm 248, 261
Ó Cléircín, Gearóid 248
Ó Dónaill, Caoimhín 107
Ohta, Tatsuya 403
Okada, Takeshi 273
Okazaki, Hironobu 102, 278
Outakoski, Hanna 241

P
Pagel, James W. 284
Paillat, Edith 290
Papadima-Sophocleous, Salomi 296
Pareja-Lora, Antonio 40
Pazio, Monika 301
Pelesoglou, Nestoras 324
Pellowe, William 307
Pihkala-Posti, Laura 312
Preston, Anne 202
Prizel-Kania, Adriana 12
Prosser, Andrew 318

R
Raindl, Marco 403
Rammo, Sirje 358
Ramsay, Allan 6
Revithiadou, Anthi 324
Riedhammer, Barbara 345

S
Saito, Yutaka 113
Sakamoto, Yasunobu 273
Schneider, Christel 241
Schultheis, Klaudia 345
Şendağ, Serkan 329
Shudong, Wang 172
Soukalopoulou, Maria 324
Stevens, Leen 334
Stickler, Ursula 237
Støckert, Robin 352

Stroud, Robert 340
Sugiura, Kensuke 273
Suzuki, Chizuko 345
Suzuki, Mitsuko 102, 278

T
Talmo, Tord 352
Tamaki, Yuko 172
Telloyan, John 172
Teral, Maarika 358
Thomas, James 363
Thouësny, Sylvie 368
Titova, Svetlana 374
Tokuda, Hideyuki 403
Torre, Ilaria 225
Torsani, Simone 225
Tseng, Jun-Jie 379

U
Underwood, Joshua 385, 391

V
Van Engen, Jeroen 248
Verspoor, Marjolijn viii
Villarreal, Daniel Steve 151, 158
Vurdien, Ruby 398

W
Wang, Yanfei 214
Waragai, Ikumi 403
Watanabe, Kanji 278
Watson, Julie 408
Winters, Niall 391
Wong, Tak-sum 196
Wu, Shaoqun 88

Y
Yamada, Masanori 113
Yoshihara, Shota 345

Z
Zarras, Christos 324
Zhao, Rong 413

www.ingramcontent.com/pod-product-compliance
Lightning Source LLC
Chambersburg PA
CBHW071225290426
44108CB00013B/1298